MC

T0259641

Windows Server
Virtualization Configuration
Study Guide

MCTS
Windows Server®
Virtualization Configuration
Study Guide

William Panek

WILEY

Wiley Publishing, Inc.

Acquisitions Editor: Jeff Kellum
Development Editor: Tom Cirtin
Technical Editors: Robert Shimonski and Randy Muller
Production Editor: Eric Charbonneau
Copy Editor: Liz Welch
Production Manager: Tim Tate
Vice President and Executive Group Publisher: Richard Swadley
Vice President and Publisher: Neil Edde
Media Development Project Supervisor: Laura Moss-Hollister
Media Development Specialist: Angie Denny
Media Quality Assurance: Josh Frank
Book Designers: Judy Fung and Bill Gibson
Compositor: Craig Woods, Happenstance Type-O-Rama
Proofreader: Jen Larsen, Word One
Indexer: Ted Laux
Project Coordinator, Cover: Lynsey Stanford
Cover Designer: Ryan Sneed

Library of Congress Cataloging-in-Publication Data.
Panek, William, 1970-
  MCTS : Windows server virtualization configuration study guide (exam 70-652) / William Panek. — 1st ed.
    p. cm.
  ISBN 978-0-470-44930-1 (paper/cd-rom)
  1. Electronic data processing personnel—Certification. 2. Virtual computer systems—Examinations—Study guides. 3. Microsoft Windows server. I. Title.
  QA76.3.P355 2009
  005.4'476—dc22
                              2009010844

Dear Reader,

Thank you for choosing *MCTS: Windows Server Virtualization Configuration Study Guide (70-652)*. This book is part of a family of premium-quality Sybex books, all of which are written by outstanding authors who combine practical experience with a gift for teaching.

Sybex was founded in 1976. More than thirty years later, we're still committed to producing consistently exceptional books. With each of our titles we're working hard to set a new standard for the industry. From the paper we print on to the authors we work with, our goal is to bring you the best books available.

I hope you see all that reflected in these pages. I'd be very interested to hear your comments and get your feedback on how we're doing. Feel free to let me know what you think about this or any other Sybex book by sending me an email at nedde@wiley.com, or if you think you've found a technical error in this book, please visit http://sybex.custhelp.com. Customer feedback is critical to our efforts at Sybex.

Best regards,

Neil Edde
Vice President and Publisher
Sybex, an Imprint of Wiley

To my wife Crystal and my daughters Alexandria and Paige

Acknowledgments

First, as with all my books, I would like to thank my wife, Crystal, and my two daughters, Alexandria and Paige. They put up with me missing many events while working on this project. Without their support and patience, none of this would be possible.

Thanks to all my friends and family who worked around my schedule to allow me to work on this book.

Thanks to Jeremy Hodgson, who works with me on most of my on-site trainings, for his dedication and friendship. His sense of humor always helps me through many long days.

Thanks to Jeff Kellum for helping me through this process and always being there when I needed guidance. Thanks to Thomas Cirtin for the endless hours of editing. It was a pleasure to work with him on this project.

Thanks to Rob Shimonski (another computer geek like me) who was my technical editor and thanks to Eric Charbonneau for guiding me through the finish line. Also, I would like to thank all the other editors and staff at Wiley who helped make this book better. I continue to always feel fortunate to have been able to work with all of you.

About the Author

After many successful years in the computer industry and a degree in computer programming, William Panek decided that he could better use his talents and his personality as an instructor. He started teaching for The Associates, instructing at such schools as Boston University, Clark University, and Globalnet Training Center, just to name a few. In 1998 William Panek started Stellacon Corporation. Stellacon Corporation has become one of New England's leading computer training companies. William brings years of real world expertise to the classroom and strives to ensure that each and every student has an understanding of the course material. William has helped thousands of students get certified over his many years of teaching experience. His certifications include MCP®, MCP+I®, MCSA®, MCSA® W/SECURITY & MESSAGING, MCSE—NT (3.51 & 4.0)®, MCSE—2000 & 2003®, MCSE W/SECURITY & MESSAGING, MCDBA®, MCT®, MCTS®, MCITP: Enterprise Admin®, CCNA®, and CHFI®.

William currently lives in NH with his wife and two daughters. In his spare time he is a commercially rated helicopter pilot and volunteer fire fighter.

Contents at a Glance

Introduction   xxi

Assessment Exam   xxxiii

Chapter 1   Hyper-V Overview   1

Chapter 2   Installing Hyper-V   29

Chapter 3   Configuring Hyper-V   67

Chapter 4   Creating Virtual Machines   115

Chapter 5   Migrating and Converting Virtual Machines   161

Chapter 6   Managing Virtual Machines   203

Chapter 7   Configuring Hyper-V for High Availability   247

Chapter 8   Backing Up and Restoring VMs   285

Appendix A   Extra Labs and Exam Questions   327

Appendix B   About the Companion CD   359

Glossary   **363**

Index   369

Contents

Introduction			*xxi*
Assessment Exam			*xxxiii*

Chapter	**1**	**Hyper-V Overview**	**1**

Introducing Hyper-V   2
    Hyper-V Benefits   3
    Hyper-V Features   4
Microsoft Networking Models   5
    Windows Peer-to-Peer Network   5
    Windows Server 2008 Active Directory Network   7
    Microsoft Networking Terms and Roles   9
Understanding Windows Server 2008   11
    New Features of Windows Server 2008   11
    Requirements for Windows Server 2008 Installation   15
    Activating and Installing Windows Server 2008   16
Summary   21
Exam Essentials   21
Review Questions   23
Answers to Review Questions   27

Chapter	**2**	**Installing Hyper-V**	**29**

Evaluating Your Network   30
    Microsoft Assessment and Planning Tool   31
Installing Hyper-V   41
    Hyper-V Hardware Requirements   42
    Installing Hyper-V on a Windows Server 2008
        Full Installation   43
    Installing Hyper-V on a Windows Server 2008 Server Core   49
Hyper-V with Virtual Machine Manager   56
Summary   57
Exam Essentials   58
Review Questions   59
Answers to Review Questions   64

Chapter	**3**	**Configuring Hyper-V**	**67**

Understanding the Configuration Tools and Techniques   68
    Understanding Virtual Hard Disks   69
    Using Pass-Through Disk Access   72
    Configuring Virtual Machine Snapshots   73

Configuring Hyper-V Server Settings 76
Using Authorization Manager 82
Introducing System Center Virtual Machine Manager 89
Configuring Virtual Networking 98
Configuring Remote Administration 102
Summary 105
Exam Essentials 106
Review Questions 108
Answers to Review Questions 113

Chapter   4   Creating Virtual Machines   115

Creating Virtual Disks 116
Creating Virtual Machines 123
System Preparation (Sysprep) Tool 129
Windows Deployment Service (WDS) 132
Configuring the System Center Virtual Machine
Manager (SCVMM) 2008 136
Summary 151
Exam Essentials 152
Review Questions 153
Answers to Review Questions 158

Chapter   5   Migrating and Converting Virtual Machines   161

Using Physical-to-Virtual (P2V) Conversion 162
P2V Conversions Using SCVMM 163
Using Virtual-to-Virtual (V2V) Conversion 171
Converting Virtual Machines from Virtual Server
and Virtual PC 177
Understanding Integration Services 178
Understanding Virtual PC 187
Migrating Microsoft Virtual Server 190
Microsoft Assessment and Planning Toolkit 193
Summary 194
Exam Essentials 194
Review Questions 196
Answers to Review Questions 201

Chapter   6   Managing Virtual Machines   203

Managing Virtual Machine Settings 204
Configuring Virtual Machines with SCVMM 205
Configuring Virtual Machine Properties 207
Configuring Hyper-V Host Properties 220
HyperCall Adapter 227

Managing Templates, Profiles, and the Image Library   227
    Creating and Managing Templates   228
    Creating Image Libraries   231
Summary   237
Exam Essentials   238
Review Questions   239
Answers to Review Questions   244

Chapter   7   Configuring Hyper-V for High Availability   247

Configuring Hyper-V to Be Highly Available   248
Understanding RAID   250
    Disk Storage Types   251
    Understanding the Disk Management MMC   253
Configuring Failover Clustering   260
    Failover Cluster Management   261
    Configuring Quorums   269
Understanding Quick Migration   273
Summary   276
Exam Essentials   277
Review Questions   278
Answers to Review Questions   283

Chapter   8   Backing Up and Restoring VMs   285

Monitoring and Optimizing Virtual Machines   286
    Reliability and Performance Monitor   286
Understanding Backups and Recoverability   296
    Configuring Backup Types   297
    Using Windows Server 2008 Backup   301
    Understanding the Data Protection Manager   312
Summary   318
Exam Essentials   319
Review Questions   320
Answers to Review Questions   325

Appendix   A   Extra Labs and Exam Questions   327

Setting Up a Virtual Network   328
Extra Review Questions   354
Answers to Extra Review Questions   357

Appendix   B   About the Companion CD   359

What You'll Find on the CD   360
    Sybex Test Engine   360
    PDF of Glossary of Terms   360

Adobe Reader   360
Electronic Flashcards   361
System Requirements   361
Using the CD   361
Troubleshooting   361
Customer Care   362

Glossary   **363**

Index   *369*

Table of Exercises

Exercise **1.1** Installing Windows Server 2008 17

Exercise **2.1** Downloading and Installing the Microsoft Assessment and
Planning Tool 33

Exercise **2.2** Configuring the Microsoft Assessment and Planning Tool 36

Exercise **2.3** Using MAP to Migrate Roles and Services to Windows Server 2008 . . . 37

Exercise **2.4** Installing Hyper-V on a Windows Server 2008 Full Installation 46

Exercise **2.5** Verifying the Installation of Hyper-V 48

Exercise **2.6** Installing Windows Server 2008 Server Core 51

Exercise **2.7** Installing Hyper-V on a Windows Server 2008 Server
Core Installation 55

Exercise **3.1** Setting the Default Storage Location for VHDs 72

Exercise **3.2** Setting the Default Snapshot Locations 75

Exercise **3.3** Installing Authorization Manager 84

Exercise **3.4** Configuring Authorization Manager 87

Exercise **3.5** Installing the .NET Framework 90

Exercise **3.6** Downloading and Installing SCVMM 2008 92

Exercise **3.7** Creating a Virtual Network Connection 100

Exercise **3.8** Configuring the Windows Firewall 104

Exercise **4.1** Creating a Virtual Hard Disk 118

Exercise **4.2** Converting a Fixed Disk to a Dynamic Disk 120

Exercise **4.3** Creating a Differencing Disk 121

Exercise **4.4** Creating a New Virtual Machine 124

Exercise **4.5** Exporting a Virtual Machine 128

Exercise **4.6** Importing a Virtual Machine into Hyper-V 129

Exercise **4.7** Installing Windows Deployment Services (WDS) 133

Exercise **4.8** Configuring the WDS Server 134

Exercise **4.9** Installing the SCVMM Administrator Console 138

Exercise **4.10** Configuring SCVMM Hosts 143

Exercise **4.11** Adding a New Virtual Machine Using SCVMM 146

Exercise **4.12** Adding a VMware VirtualCenter Server 148

Exercise **4.13** Installing the IIS Components 149

Exercise **4.14** Installing the VMM Self-Service Portal 150

Exercise **5.1** Converting a Physical Machine to a Virtual Machine 164

Exercise **5.2** Sharing the VMware Files 172

Exercise **5.3** Converting a VMware Machine to Hyper-V (V2V) 173

Exercise **5.4** Downloading and Installing Virtual Server 179

Exercise **5.5** Creating Virtual Machines in Virtual Server 183

Exercise **5.6** Installing an Operating System into a Virtual Server
Virtual Machine 185

Exercise **5.7** Downloading and Configuring Virtual PC 188

Exercise **5.8** Migrating a Virtual Server VM to a Hyper-V VM 191

Exercise **6.1** Configuring Virtual Machine Properties 218

Exercise **6.2** Creating a Master Template 230

Exercise **6.3** Adding a Library Server 232

Exercise **6.4** Adding a Share to the Library 233

Exercise **6.5** Creating Hardware Profiles 234

Exercise **7.1** Configuring Dynamic Hard Disks 254

Exercise **7.2** Configuring RAID 1 Mirroring 256

Exercise **7.3** Installing a Failover Cluster 263

Exercise **7.4** Creating a Cluster 265

Exercise **7.5** Changing the Quorum Mode 271

Exercise **7.6** Making a Virtual Machine Highly Available 274

Exercise **7.7** Manually Migrating a Virtual Machine 275

Exercise **8.1** Adding Counters to Performance Monitor 291

Exercise **8.2** Installing the Windows Backup Feature 299

Exercise **8.3** Completing a Full Backup 303

Exercise **8.4** Recovering Data Using the Windows Backup 308

Exercise **8.5** Installing Features Needed for DPM 314

Exercise **8.6** Installing DPM 315

Exercise **A1** Installing Hyper-V 328

Exercise **A2** Creating a Virtual Machine 330

Exercise **A3** Installing DNS 334

Exercise **A4** Installing Active Directory 336

Exercise **A5** Installing DHCP 340

Exercise **A6** Creating the Exchange Virtual Machine 341

Exercise **A7** Joining the MailServer VM to the Domain 342

Exercise **A8** Installing the PowerShell Feature and IIS Role 345

Exercise **A9** Installing Microsoft Exchange Server 2007 347

Exercise **A10** Joining a Windows XP Machine to the Domain 353

Introduction

Microsoft has recently changed its certification program to contain three primary series: Technology, Professional, and Architect. The Technology Series of certifications are intended to allow candidates to target specific technologies and are the basis for obtaining the Professional Series and Architect Series of certifications. The certifications contained within the Technology Series consist of one to three exams, focus on a specific technology, and do not include job-role skills. By contrast, the Professional Series of certifications focus on a job role and are not necessarily focused on a single technology, but rather a comprehensive set of skills for performing the job role being tested. The Architect Series of certifications offered by Microsoft are premier certifications that consist of passing a review board consisting of previously certified architects. To apply for the Architect Series of certifications, you must have a minimum of 10 years of industry experience.

When obtaining a Technology Series certification, you are recognized as a Microsoft Certified Technology Specialist (MCTS) on the specific technology or technologies that you have been tested on. The Professional Series certifications include Microsoft Certified IT Professional (MCITP) and Microsoft Certified Professional Developer (MCPD). Passing the review board for an Architect Series certification will allow you to become a Microsoft Certified Architect (MCA).

This book has been developed to give you the critical skills and knowledge you need to prepare for the MCTS: Windows Server Virtualization, Configuration (70-652) exam.

The Microsoft Certified Professional Program

Since the inception of its certification program, Microsoft has certified more than 2 million people. As the computer network industry continues to increase in both size and complexity, this number is sure to grow—and the need for *proven* ability will also increase. Certifications can help companies verify the skills of prospective employees and contractors.

Microsoft has developed its Microsoft Certified Professional (MCP) program to give you credentials that verify your ability to work with Microsoft products effectively and professionally. Several levels of certification are available based on specific suites of exams. Microsoft has recently created a new generation of certification programs:

Microsoft Certified Technology Specialist (MCTS)   The MCTS can be considered the entry-level certification for the new generation of Microsoft certifications. The MCTS certification program targets specific technologies instead of specific job roles. You must take and pass one to three exams.

Microsoft Certified IT Professional (MCITP)   The MCITP certification is a Professional Series certification that tests network and systems administrators on job roles, rather than only on a specific technology. The MCITP generally consists of passing one to three exams, in addition to obtaining an MCTS-level certification.

Microsoft Certified Professional Developer (MCPD)   The MCPD certification is a Professional Series certification for application developers. Similar to the MCITP, the MCPD is focused on a job role rather than on a single technology. The MCPD generally consists of passing one to three exams, in addition to obtaining an MCTS-level certification.

Microsoft Certified Architect (MCA)   The MCA is Microsoft's premier certification series. Obtaining the MCA requires a minimum of 10 years of experience and requires the candidate to pass a review board consisting of peer architects.

How Do You Become Certified on Windows Server Virtualization?

Attaining a Microsoft certification has always been a challenge. In the past, students have been able to acquire detailed exam information—even most of the exam questions—from online "brain dumps" and third-party "cram" books or software products. For the new generation of exams, this is simply not the case.

Microsoft has taken strong steps to protect the security and integrity of its new certification tracks. Now prospective candidates must complete a course of study that develops detailed knowledge about a wide range of topics. It supplies them with the true skills needed, derived from working with the technology being tested.

The new generations of Microsoft certification programs are heavily weighted toward hands-on skills and experience. It is recommended that candidates have troubleshooting skills acquired through hands-on experience and working knowledge.

Fortunately, if you are willing to dedicate the time and effort to learn Windows Virtualization, you can prepare yourself well for the exam by using the proper tools. By working through this book, you can successfully meet the exam requirements to pass the Windows Server, Configuring exam.

This book is part of a complete series of Microsoft certification Study Guides, published by Sybex Inc., that together cover the new MCTS, MCITP, MCPD exams, as well as the core MCSA and MCSE operating system requirements. Please visit the Sybex website at www.sybex.com for complete program and product details.

MCTS Exam Requirements

Candidates for Microsoft Certified Technology Specialist (MCTS): Windows Server Virtualization, Configuration must pass one exam: Windows Server, Configuring (70-652). Many Other MCTS certifications may require up to three exams. For a more detailed description of the Microsoft certification programs, including a list of all the exams, visit the Microsoft Learning Web site at www.microsoft.com/learning/mcp.

The Windows Server Virtualization, Configuration Exam

The Windows Server 2008 Virtualization, Configuration exam covers concepts and skills related to installing, configuring, and managing Windows Server 2008 Hyper-V. It emphasizes Hyper-V support and administration.

This exam is quite specific regarding Windows Server 2008 Hyper-V requirements and operational settings, and it can be particular about how administrative tasks are performed within Hyper-V and the System Center Virtual Machine Manager.

> Microsoft provides exam objectives to give you a general overview of possible areas of coverage on the Microsoft exams. Keep in mind, however, that exam objectives are subject to change at any time without prior notice and at Microsoft's sole discretion. Please visit the Microsoft Learning Web site (www.microsoft.com/learning/mcp) for the most current listing of exam objectives.

Types of Exam Questions

In an effort to both refine the testing process and protect the quality of its certifications, Microsoft has focused its newer certification exams on real experience and hands-on proficiency. There is a greater emphasis on your past working environments and responsibilities and less emphasis on how well you can memorize. In fact, Microsoft says that certification candidates should have hands-on experience before attempting to pass any certification exams.

> Microsoft will accomplish its goal of protecting the exams' integrity by regularly adding and removing exam questions, limiting the number of questions that any individual sees in a beta exam, limiting the number of questions delivered to an individual by using adaptive testing, and adding new exam elements.

Exam questions may be in a variety of formats: Depending on which exam you take, you'll see multiple-choice questions, as well as select-and-place and prioritize-a-list questions. Simulations and case study–based formats are included as well. You may also find yourself taking what's called an *adaptive format exam*. Let's take a look at the types of exam questions and examine the adaptive testing technique, so you'll be prepared for all of the possibilities.

> With the release of Windows 2000, Microsoft stopped providing a detailed score breakdown. This is mostly because of the various and complex question formats. Previously, each question focused on one objective. Recent exams, such as the Windows Server 2008 Active Directory exam, however, contain questions that may be tied to one or more objectives from one or more objective sets. Therefore, grading by objective is almost impossible. Also, Microsoft no longer offers a score. Now you will only be told if you pass or fail.

Multiple-Choice Questions

Multiple-choice questions come in two main forms. One is a straightforward question followed by several possible answers, of which one or more is correct. The other type of multiple-choice question is more complex and based on a specific scenario. The scenario may focus on several areas or objectives.

Select-and-Place Questions

Select-and-place exam questions involve graphical elements that you must manipulate to successfully answer the question. For example, you might see a diagram of a computer network, as shown in the following graphic taken from the select-and-place demo downloaded from Microsoft's website.

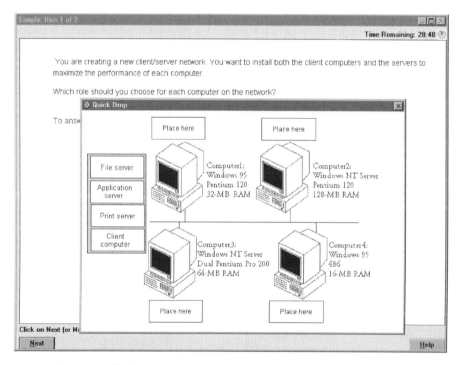

A typical diagram will show computers and other components next to boxes that contain the text "Place here." The labels for the boxes represent various computer roles on a network, such as a print server and a file server. Based on information given for each computer, you are asked to select each label and place it in the correct box. You need to place *all* of the labels correctly. No credit is given for the question if you correctly label only some of the boxes.

In another select-and-place problem you might be asked to put a series of steps in order, by dragging items from boxes on the left to boxes on the right, and placing them in the correct order. One other type requires that you drag an item from the left and place it under an item in a column on the right.

For more information on the various exam question types, go to
www.microsoft.com/learning/mcpexams/policies/innovations.asp.

Simulations

Simulations are the kinds of questions that most closely represent actual situations and test
the skills you use while working with Microsoft software interfaces. These exam questions
include a mock interface on which you are asked to perform certain actions according to a
given scenario. The simulated interfaces look nearly identical to what you see in the actual
product, as shown in this example:

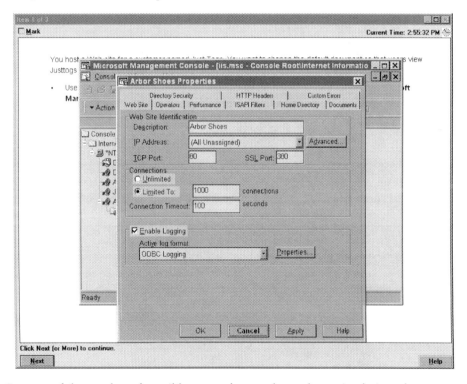

Because of the number of possible errors that can be made on simulations, be sure to
consider the following recommendations from Microsoft:

- Do not change any simulation settings that don't pertain to the solution directly.

- When related information has not been provided, assume that the default settings
  are used.

- Make sure that your entries are spelled correctly.

- Close all the simulation application windows after completing the set of tasks in the
  simulation.

The best way to prepare for simulation questions is to spend time working with the graphical interface of the product on which you will be tested.

Case Study–Based Questions

Case study–based questions first appeared in the MCSD program. These questions present a scenario with a range of requirements. Based on the information provided, you answer a series of multiple-choice and select-and-place questions. The interface for case study–based questions has a number of tabs, each of which contains information about the scenario. At present, this type of question appears only in most of the Design exams.

> Microsoft will regularly add and remove questions from the exams. This is called *item seeding*. It is part of the effort to make it more difficult for individuals to merely memorize exam questions that were passed along by previous test-takers.

Tips for Taking the MCTS: Windows Server Virtualization, Configuration Exam

Here are some general tips for achieving success on your certification exam:

- Arrive early at the exam center so that you can relax and review your study materials. During this final review, you can look over tables and lists of exam-related information.

- Read the questions carefully. Don't be tempted to jump to an early conclusion. Make sure you know *exactly* what the question is asking.

- Answer all questions. If you are unsure about a question, then mark the question for review and come back to the question at a later time.

- On simulations, do not change settings that are not directly related to the question. Also, assume default settings if the question does not specify or imply which settings are used.

- For questions you're not sure about, use a process of elimination to get rid of the obviously incorrect answers first. This improves your odds of selecting the correct answer when you need to make an educated guess.

Exam Registration

You may take the Microsoft exams at any of more than 1,000 Authorized Prometric Testing Centers (APTCs) around the world. For the location of a testing center near you, call Prometric at 800-755-EXAM (755-3926). Outside the United States and Canada, contact your local Prometric registration center.

Find out the number of the exam you want to take, and then register with the Prometric registration center nearest to you. At this point, you will be asked for advance payment for the exam. The exams are $125 each and you must take them within one year of payment.

for the exam. We have also included the complete contents of the Study Guide in electronic form. The CD's resources are described here:

The Sybex E-book for the Windows Server Virtualization, Configuration Exam Many people like the convenience of being able to carry their whole Study Guide on a CD. They also like being able to search the text via computer to find specific information quickly and easily. For these reasons, the entire contents of this Study Guide are supplied on the CD, in PDF. We've also included Adobe Acrobat Reader, which provides the interface for the PDF contents as well as the search capabilities.

The Sybex Test Engine This is a collection of multiple-choice questions that will help you prepare for your exam. There are four sets of questions:

- Two bonus exams designed to simulate the actual live exam.
- All the questions from the Study Guide, presented in a test engine for your review. You can review questions by chapter or by objective, or you can take a random test.
- The Assessment Test.

Here is a sample screen from the Sybex Test Engine:

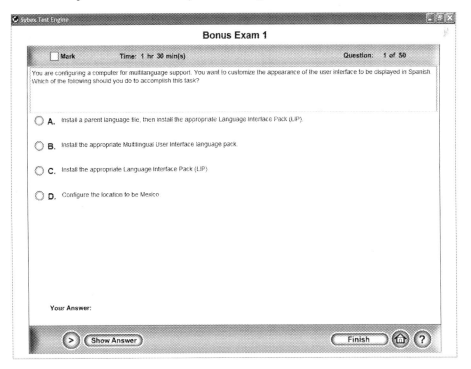

Sybex Flashcards for PCs and Handheld Devices The "flashcard" style of question offers an effective way to quickly and efficiently test your understanding of the fundamental concepts covered in the exam. The Sybex Flashcards set consists of 100 questions presented in a special engine developed specifically for this Study Guide series. Here's what the Sybex Flashcards interface looks like:

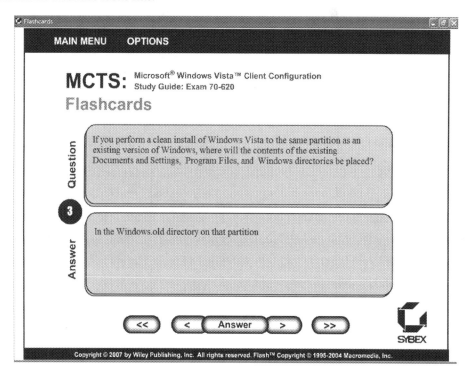

Because of the high demand for a product that will run on handheld devices, we have also developed, in conjunction with Land-J Technologies, a version of the flashcard questions that you can take with you on your Palm OS PDA (including the PalmPilot and Handspring's Visor).

Hardware and Software Requirements

You should verify that your computer meets the minimum requirements for installing Windows Server 2008 (for current Windows Server 2008 requirements, check out Microsoft's web site). We suggest that your computer meets or exceeds the recommended requirements for a more enjoyable experience.

The exercises in this book assume that your computer is configured in a specific manner. Your computer should have at least a 20GB drive that is configured with the minimum space requirements and partitions. Other exercises in this book assume that your computer is configured as follows:

- 20GB C: partition with the NTFS filesystem
- Optional D: partition with the NTFS filesystem
- 15GB or more of free space

Of course, you can allocate more space to your partitions if it is available.

The first exercise in the book assumes that you have installed Windows Server 2008 and that your partitions have already been created and formatted as previously specified.

Contacts and Resources

To find out more about Microsoft Education and Certification materials and programs, to register with Prometric, or to obtain other useful certification information and additional study resources, check the following resources:

Microsoft Learning Home Page

www.microsoft.com/learning

This website provides information about the MCP program and exams. You can also order the latest Microsoft Roadmap to Education and Certification.

Microsoft TechNet Technical Information Network

www.microsoft.com/technet

800-344-2121

Use this website or phone number to contact support professionals and system administrators. Outside the United States and Canada, contact your local Microsoft subsidiary for information.

Prometric

www.prometric.com

800-755-3936

Contact Prometric to register to take an exam at any of more than 800 Prometric Testing Centers around the world.

MCP Magazine Online

www.mcpmag.com

Microsoft Certified Professional Magazine is a well-respected publication that focuses on Windows certification. This site hosts chats and discussion forums and tracks news related to the MCTS and MCITP programs. Some of the services cost a fee, but they are well worth it.

WindowsITPro Magazine

www.windowsITPro.com

You can subscribe to this magazine or read free articles at the website. The study resource provides general information on Windows Vista, Server, and .NET Server.

How to Contact the Author

I welcome feedback from you about this book or about books you'd like to see from me in the future. For more information about my work, please visit my website at www.willpanek .com. To attend a class that I teach, feel free to visit www.stellacon.com.

Sybex strives to keep you supplied with the latest tools and information you need for your work. Please check their website at www.sybex.com, where we'll post additional content and updates that supplement this book if the need arises. Enter **MCTS Panek** in the Search box (or type the book's ISBN—**9780470449301**), and click Go to get to the book's update page.

Assessment Exam

1. What new Windows Server 2008 utility allows an administrator to install, configure, and manage roles on a server?

   A. Add/Remove Programs

   B. Server Manager

   C. Configure This Server

   D. Control Panel

2. What gives a network user the ability to determine the access level (open, read, modify, etc.) they would like to assign to other users in an organization?

   A. Active Directory Domain Services (AD DS)

   B. Active Directory Federation Services (AD FS)

   C. Active Directory Rights Management Service (AD RMS)

   D. Active Directory Lightweight Directory Services (AD LDS)

3. What gives administrators the ability to allow network access based on compliancy with corporate governance policies?

   A. Network Access Protection (NAP)

   B. Group Policy Object (GPO)

   C. Server Manager

   D. Remote Access Policy

4. What is an implementation of an operating system that runs in its own virtualization window called?

   A. Virtual window

   B. Virtual process

   C. Virtual machine

   D. Virtual host

5. What Microsoft utility will locate computers on a network and then perform a thorough inventory of these computers?

   A. Network Access Protection (NAP)

   B. Group Policy Object (GPO)

   C. Server Manager

   D. Microsoft Assessment and Planning Solution Accelerator (MAP)

6. What is the name of the thin Hyper-V layer of software that sits between the hardware and the Windows Server 2008 operating system?

    A. Windows hypervisor

    B. Windows driver

    C. Hyper-V driver

    D. HyperCall adapter

7. What is the unique identifier used on a Small Computer System Interface (SCSI) bus to differentiate up to eight separate devices?

    A. HyperCall adapter

    B. Logical unit number (LUN)

    C. Windows hypervisor

    D. BusAdapter

8. What type of installation gives an organization the ability to have a minimal environment for running specific server roles, which, in turn, reduces the attack surface for those server roles?

    A. Windows Server 2008 Full installation

    B. Windows Server 2008 Minimum installation

    C. Windows Server 2008 Server Core installation

    D. Windows Server 2008 Non-GUI installation

9. What are the minimum requirements for the CPU/BIOS to install Hyper-V properly? (Choose all that apply.)

    A. 32-bit processor

    B. 64-bit processor

    C. Hardware-assisted virtualization

    D. Hardware-enabled Data Execution Prevention (DEP)

10. You have very limited hard disk space for your Hyper-V virtual machines. How should you create the VHDs?

    A. Use fixed-size VHDs.

    B. Use dynamic VHDs.

    C. Use VHD differencing.

    D. Use Virtual Server 2005, fixed size.

11. When setting up the virtual machines, you need to support nonvirtualized and virtualized systems to access the virtual machines. How would you configure the virtual machines?

    A. Fixed-size VHD

    B. Dynamic VHD

    C. Differencing

    D. Pass-through disk access

12. What Hyper-V feature will take a copy of your virtual machine and place that copy in a specified location?

   A. Virtual Machine VHD Backup tool

   B. Virtual machine snapshots

   C. Virtual Machine Recovery tool

   D. VHDMount utility

13. What application can you use to give role-based access to users for ASP.NET web applications?

   A. Application Manager

   B. Virtual Machine Manager

   C. Authorization Manager

   D. Hyper-V Manager

14. What are the two utilities to manage your Hyper-V virtual machines?

   A. Hyper-V Manager

   B. System Center Virtualization Manager

   C. System Center Virtualization MMC

   D. System Center Virtual Machine Manager

15. When choosing which type of virtual hard disk you want to use, performance is the main issue. Which type of virtual disk would you use?

   A. Fixed-size

   B. Dynamic

   C. Pass-through

   D. Differencing

16. When choosing which type of virtual hard disk you want to use, you need to be able to roll back virtual machines to a previous state without the use of backups. How do you set up Hyper-V?

   A. Use fixed-size VHD.

   B. Use dynamic VHD.

   C. Use differencing disks.

   D. Use pass-through disks.

17. You decide to set up a Windows Vista machine and then make an image of the machine for mass duplication. Which Microsoft utility will allow you to create an image for mass duplication?

   A. Windows Deployment Service (WDS)

   B. System Preparation (Sysprep)

   C. Vista Preparation (Vprep)

   D. Windows Server 2008 Image Maker

18. Which Microsoft utility can you use to deploy your Sysprep image?

   A. ActiveX

   B. ImageX

   C. Image Maker

   D. Image Activate

19. In Windows Server 2008, what is new version of RIS that you use to do remote installations?

   A. Remote Installation Service v2

   B. Windows Deployment Service (WDS)

   C. Windows Installation Service (WIS)

   D. Remote Deployment Service (RDS)

20. You need to set up two virtual machines the same as the two servers that you have set up. What is the best way to create two virtual machines with the same settings as the two already created servers?

   A. P2V conversion

   B. V2V conversion

   C. V2P conversion

   D. P2P conversion

21. Which utility allows you to migrate a VMware ESX Server to Hyper-V virtual machines?

   A. P2V conversion

   B. V2V conversion

   C. V2P conversion

   D. P2P conversion

22. What is the Hyper-V equivalent to the Virtual Server Virtual Machine Additions?

   A. Virtual Machine Additions

   B. Integration Services

   C. Virtual Integration

   D. Integrated Machine Additions

23. What is the easiest procedure in Hyper-V to ensure that you can recover the virtual machine in the event of any errors occurring during the install?

   A. Create a new backup.

   B. Save the virtual machine to another Hyper-V server.

   C. Create a new checkpoint.

   D. No need to do anything. Virtual machines can automatically revert back to the previous state.

24. You need to move one of the virtual machines from one Hyper-V server to another. What command do you use to move the virtual machine?

    A. Move

    B. Migrate

    C. Copy

    D. Xcopy

25. What can your organization implement to allow your users to create and manage their own virtual machines through the use of Hyper-V?

    A. Microsoft Virtual Server

    B. Microsoft Virtual PC

    C. Self-service role

    D. User creation role

26. You want to preset the hardware configuration in advance for all of your virtual machines. What can you set up to preset hardware configurations in advance?

    A. Hardware profiles

    B. Configuration profiles

    C. Machine profiles

    D. Virtual machine profiles

27. You need to set up a quorum for failover clustering. You have decided that in the quorum, only the nodes will get to vote on the quorum. Which type of quorum would you configure?

    A. Node Majority Quorum mode

    B. Node and Disk Majority Quorum mode

    C. Node and File Share Majority Quorum mode

    D. No Majority: Disk Only Quorum mode

28. You need to change the basic disk to a dynamic. What are the two ways to convert a basic disk to a dynamic disk?

    A. `convert.exe`

    B. Active Directory Domains and Trusts

    C. Disk Management Utility

    D. Computer Configuration utility

29. What is the maximum number of nodes that you can have in a Windows Server 2008 cluster?

    A. 16

    B. 8

    C. 4

    D. 32

30. You are using the Reliability and Performance Monitor and you want to capture the data in bar format and also catch a point-in-time capture. What type of view would you use?

A. Graph view

B. Histogram view

C. Report view

D. Output view

Answers to Assessment Exam

1. B. Server Manager is a new Windows Server 2008 utility that allows you to install, configure, and manage all your services (DNS, DHCP, Hyper-V, etc.). See Chapter 1 for more information.

2. C. The advantage to AD RMS is that any user can secure confidential or critical company information. By using Microsoft Office 2003 Professional or Microsoft Office 2007, users have the ability to secure email messages, internal websites, and documents. See Chapter 1 for more information.

3. A. Administrators can now define network access, based on client requirements, using NAP. The advantage of using NAP is that administrators can define this access at the granular level. See Chapter 1 for more information.

4. C. A virtual machine (VM) is an implementation of an operating system that runs in its own virtualization window. See Chapter 1 for more information.

5. D. One utility that you can use to help design your network is the Microsoft Assessment and Planning Solution Accelerator (MAP). See Chapter 2 for more information.

6. A. The hypervisor is the mechanism that is responsible for maintaining isolation between the different Hyper-V partitions. See Chapter 2 for more information.

7. B. A logical unit number is a logical reference to a particular section of a storage subsystem. See Chapter 2 for more information.

8. C. A new feature in Windows Server 2008 is Server Core, which allows you to have a minimal environment for running specific server roles. See Chapter 2 for more information.

9. B, C, D. Hyper-V has to be installed on a 64-bit processor and the system has to support virtualization and enabled DEP. The processor also needs to be 1.4GHz at minimum but it should be 2GHz or faster. See Chapter 2 for more information.

10. B. Dynamic VHDs only use the amount of space that is currently being used for the VHD. This is the way you want to set up your VHD if hard drive space is limited on your server. See Chapter 3 for more information.

11. D. Virtual machines can access a file system directly through the use of pass-through disk access, thus eliminating the need for VHDs. See Chapter 3 for more information.

12. B. Setting up virtual machine snapshots involves taking a copy of your virtual machine and place that copy in a specified location. See Chapter 3 for more information.

13. C. Authorization Manager allows administrators to integrate role-based access control to applications. This gives administrators the flexibility to assign application access to users based on their job functions. See Chapter 3 for more information.

14. A, D. Hyper-V Manager and the System Center Virtual Machine Manager are responsible for managing virtual networks. See Chapter 3 for more information.

15. A. Fixed-size disks work well in a production environment. The advantage to this type of virtual disk is performance. See Chapter 4 for more information.

16. C. Differencing disks use a child-parent relationship. Differencing disks allow you to make changes to the virtual machine and these changes do not affect the base image. See Chapter 4 for more information.

17. B. The System Preparation (Sysprep) tool is a Microsoft utility that allows you to get an image ready for transfer. See Chapter 4 for more information.

18. B. To load an image onto a client machine you need to use a third-party utility or Microsoft ImageX to deploy the image that is created from Sysprep. See Chapter 4 for more information.

19. B. For Windows Vista and Windows Server 2008 a new version of RIS has been developed called Windows Deployment Services (WDS). See Chapter 4 for more information.

20. A. Creating the two servers by converting the physical machines to virtual machines is easiest through a process known as physical-to-virtual (P2V) conversion. See Chapter 5 for more information.

21. B. A virtual-to-virtual (V2V) conversion allows you to convert a VMware ESX server virtual machine to a Microsoft Hyper-V or Virtual Server virtual machine. See Chapter 5 for more information.

22. B. Integration Services are services that you want to offer to the Hyper-V virtual machine. See Chapter 5 for more information.

23. C. Checkpoints are a way to temporarily save your virtual machine. See Chapter 6 for more information.

24. B. The Migrate link is the way to move a virtual machine from one Hyper-V server to another. See Chapter 6 for more information.

25. C. The self-service role allows an administrator to give users the right to create and manage their own virtual machines. Users can create and manage their own virtual machines by using the self-service web portal. See Chapter 6 for more information.

26. A. Hardware profiles can be used for a new virtual machine or a virtual machine template. See Chapter 6 for more information.

27. A. In this quorum mode, just like many of the other quorums, the majority of votes (more than half) constitute the quorum. See Chapter 6 for more information.

28. C. There are two ways to convert a basic disk to a dynamic disk. First, you can use the `convert` command at a command prompt, or you can convert the disk in the Disk Management utility. See Chapter 7 for more information.

29. A. You can have up to 16 nodes in a failover cluster running on a 64-bit version of Enterprise or Datacenter edition of Windows Server 2008. See Chapter 7 for more information.

30. B. The Histogram view represents the percentage of usage by using colored bar graphs. See Chapter 8 for more information.

MCTS
Windows Server®
Virtualization Configuration
Study Guide

Chapter

1

Hyper-V Overview

One of the revolutionary developments that is sweeping through our rapidly changing field is the emergence of virtualization.

If you have been in this industry long enough, you realize one thing: technology is always changing. There are many advantages and disadvantages to this trend. The biggest disadvantage of changing technology is that we all need to stay on top of it. Doing so can feel like a full-time job in itself.

The greatest advantage of changing technology is that the industry has moved forward in leaps and bounds over the past 10 years. Less than 15 years ago, most people did not know what an email address was. The industry changes every day and we are the IT professionals who make it happen.

Virtualization is one of those changes that has started taking over the computer world. Many networks now use virtualization instead of paying thousands of dollars for server equipment.

Let's begin by looking at the basics of Microsoft's Windows Server 2008 and Hyper-V.

Introducing Hyper-V

One of the fastest-growing and hottest technologies to hit the market in the past few years is server virtualization. Server virtualization is making an impact due to the many economic advantages it brings. It allows an organization to run multiple operating systems, called virtual machines, on a single machine or group of machines called a *cluster*. The ability to run multiple operating systems on a single machine or cluster helps an organization reduce many of its hardware and software costs and allows it to reduce its IT department staffing overhead.

A *virtual machine (VM)* is an implementation of an operating system that runs in its own virtualization window. The advantage to using virtual machines is that you can have multiple VMs on the same Windows Server 2008 machine. Each VM can have its own unique resources running on its operating system. An administrator can run multiple operating systems (including non-Windows-based systems) or run multiple server roles in their own virtual machines, thus allowing an organization more flexibility without the need for more servers. One of the greatest advantages of Hyper-V technology is that you have the ability to run both 32-bit and 64-bit applications within the virtual environment.

Virtualization is not new, nor is this Microsoft's first attempt at providing virtualization services. Microsoft has been doing virtualization for years and has already released products currently in use today. The two Microsoft virtualization products that you may have used before are Microsoft Virtual PC and Microsoft Virtual Server 2005.

Microsoft Hyper-V, the company's latest version of server virtualization services, was officially released with Windows Server 2008. Formerly known under codename Viridian and as Windows Server Virtualization, Hyper-V is a hypervisor-based virtualization system for x64 systems that allows for the virtualization of guest operating systems. A hypervisor, also called virtual machine monitor, is a virtualization platform that allows multiple operating systems to run on a host computer at the same time.

Let's imagine an IT department for any size organization. You come in one morning before everyone else (a common practice in our field) and see that one of your servers has crashed. The first thing that's going to happen is your heart will drop into your stomach. After that, you will start trying to fix the error; you may find that you need to rebuild the machine. Now your heart is racing and your blood pressure is going through the roof because you have to get this server up and running before anyone else comes into work. We have all been there.

Now let's imagine the same situation but all of your servers are running Hyper-V. When you come in and see your crash, you know you can relax. All you need to do is move the Hyper-V virtual machine to another machine running Hyper-V and you are back up and running. This is what Hyper-V can do for you. Hyper-V is a role-based feature that enables an organization to have multiple virtual machines (using multiple operating systems) on a single Windows Server 2008 machine. Let's take a look at some of the key benefits of using Hyper-V technology.

Hyper-V Benefits

Hyper-V is a virtualization platform that gives you the ability to manage all of your physical and virtual resources from a single set of integrated management utilities. Here are some of the benefits of using Hyper-V:

Server Consolidation   This is one of the major benefits that Hyper-V offers. Server consolidation allows you to run many versions of server-based software and operating systems (even non-Microsoft versions) on a single box. Each one of these versions is isolated from the other versions running on the same machine through the virtual architecture. This arrangement allows an organization to have a lower total cost of ownership (TCO) while maintaining all the services and servers that are required to make the network operate properly.

Downtime and Recoverability   Two major concerns that all organizations face are downtime and recoverability. Downtime includes not only unscheduled events (such as machine errors or hardware failure) but also scheduled events like backups and maintenance. Hyper-V has many features, such as live backup, that help reduce the server downtime for an organization.

Recoverability is also something that all IT staff members should be concerned about. Most organizations could not afford to lose their data and still stay in business. Disaster recoverability is supported by Hyper-V through clustering and backups, thus reducing downtime and saving the organization money.

Testing and Development   One of the nice benefits of using Hyper-V is the ability to test or develop software in a safe virtual machine operating system. If you have been in this industry long enough, you have run into the situation of loading a service pack or utility and watching your system crash because of that install. By testing your service packs or software updates in Hyper-V, an administrator can reduce the chances of network downtime on a live server.

Dynamic Datacenter   Hyper-V virtualization lets you design and create a dynamic network environment that will not only address network problems, but also anticipate higher demands for network resources.

Now that you have seen some of the benefits of Hyper-V, let's take a look at some of its new features.

Hyper-V Features

Microsoft has built many new features into Hyper-V compared to its previous virtualization environments (Virtual Server and Virtual PC). Taking into account the progression of hardware over the past several years, Microsoft has included these features to allow an organization to take full advantage of the improved hardware environments:

Symmetric Multiprocessor (SMP) Support   Hyper-V allows a virtual machine environment to use up to four processors, allowing for SMP support.

New Architecture Design   Hyper-V was designed to run on a 64-bit processor only, which lets you use several types of devices. This 64-bit architecture also results in better system performance. Keep in mind that 32-bit guest systems can run as VMs on the host, but the host must be a 64-bit system.

Operating System Support   Hyper-V enables you to run both Microsoft and non-Microsoft operating systems (Windows, Linux, Unix, etc.). The operating systems can be both 32-bit and 64-bit versions.

Virtual Machine Migration   A very nice feature of Hyper-V is the ability to migrate virtual machines from one server to another without long periods of downtime. Let's say you have a server that is having hardware problems; you can switch the virtual machine to another server running Hyper-V without having to rebuild the bad machine immediately.

Network Load Balancing   Hyper-V allows you to use network load balancing (NLB) across multiple virtual machines even if they are on different physical machines.

Hardware Architecture   With the new Hyper-V hardware architecture, all hardware resources in a virtual machine (disk, network card, RAM, etc.) have access to resources on the physical machine.

Scalability   Hyper-V lets you place a large number of virtual machines on the same physical machine. In this way, you can grow a network without purchasing new hardware. If you need an additional server, you can add it as a virtual machine. Eventually, however, no matter how well your network is designed and created, we all need to purchase new hardware to keep up with the ever-changing software requirements.

Before we dive any further into Hyper-V, let's examine some basic networking terms and designs. Understanding how networking works and exploring some of the networking services needed to operate your environment will allow you to see the advantages of using Hyper-V. You can use Hyper-V to set up many of these services and networking models.

Microsoft Networking Models

The first topic we'll discuss is the network model types. The choices you make in designing your network are determined by many factors, such as the number of users on your network or the amount of money you can spend. Microsoft uses two networking models: peer-to-peer and domain-based.

> Since this is a Microsoft Hyper-V certification book, the network models that are discussed throughout this book are Microsoft Windows–related models.

Windows Peer-to-Peer Network

When setting up a Windows peer-to-peer network (also referred to as a workgroup network), you should understand that all computers on the network are equal. All of the peer-to-peer computers, also referred to as nodes, simultaneously act as both clients and servers.

This can be an advantage for small networks that have 12 or fewer users. It allows a small network to share resources without the need for a costly server. It also enables a small company to have a network setup without hiring an internal IT department.

Peer-to-peer networks are no more than Microsoft Windows XP and Vista machines connected by a centralized connection like a router or hub (see Figure 1.1).

Windows peer-to-peer networks have been out for many years in the industry. The two operating systems today that are commonly used for this type of network are Microsoft Windows XP and Vista. Windows Vista has included some new enhancements to the Windows peer-to-peer network:

- A feature called People Near Me
- A new application programming interface (API)
- Group Policy configuration support
- A new version of the Peer Name Resolution Protocol (PNRP)
- Windows Meeting Space

To learn more about Windows Vista peer-to-peer networks, see *MCTS: Windows Server 2008 Network Infrastructure Configuration Study Guide (70-642)* by William Panek, Tylor Wentworth, and James Chellis (Wiley, 2008).

FIGURE 1.1   Peer-to-peer model

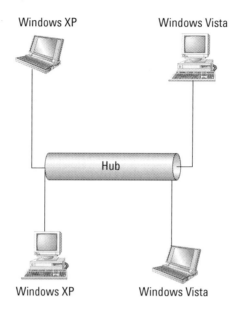

Using a Peer-to-Peer Network

One of the biggest debates among IT professionals is when to use a peer-to-peer network. These types of networks have their place in the networking world. Most of you at home use this type of network, in which all computers connect using a small internet router.

Well, it's the same for companies. You would use this network in a small environment with 12 or fewer users. This allows small organizations to share resources without using expensive equipment or server software.

But there is a downside to peer-to-peer networks related to manageability. Many new IT people like working on a small peer-to-peer network because of its size, but in fact a network with 10 users and 10 computers can be difficult to manage. Because there is no server to centralize user accounts, each Windows XP or Vista computer must have a user account and password. So, if you have 10 users with 10 computers and all 10 users must be able to access all 10 computers, you end up creating 100 accounts (10 accounts on each machine times 10 machines).

Another disadvantage of peer-to-peer networks involves backups. Most IT departments do not back up individual user machines, and since there is no centralized server for data storage, data recoverability can be an issue.

Windows Server 2008 Active Directory Network

Now that you have seen the advantages and disadvantages of a peer-to-peer network, let's discuss the domain-based network. A domain-based network is a network that uses Microsoft's Active Directory—a single distributed database that contains all the objects included within your network. Some of these objects are user accounts, group accounts, and published objects (folders and printers).

The first of many advantages to Active Directory is centralized management. As we just stated, the Active Directory database contains all the network information within a single, distributed data repository. Due to the fact that these objects are all located in the same database, an administrator can easily manage the domain from one location.

Another major advantage to using Active Directory is domain security. An administrator has the advantage of creating a single username and password for all users within the domain. This password can be used to access all resources that an individual has the proper rights to access. An administrator can determine, based on job function or position, which files or folders a user can obtain. In our earlier peer-to-peer example, you needed to create 100 accounts. Now with a domain, you would only need to create 10 accounts.

An Active Directory structure is made up of one or more *domains*. A domain is a logical grouping of objects within your organization. For example, in the Stellacon.com domain, all users in that domain should be members of the Stellacon.com organization. The objects that are contained within a domain do not need to be in the same physical location. Domains can span the entire globe even though they are part of the same organization.

A benefit to using domains is the ability to have child domains. A child domain is a subdomain of another domain. You can build child domains based on physical locations, departments, and so forth. Figure 1.2 shows the hierarchy structure of Stellacon.com with its child domains (based on geographic location).

> Microsoft domains are represented as triangles. It is important to remember that when taking any Microsoft exam.

By creating child domains, you achieve scalability. Active Directory lets you store millions of objects within a single domain, but child domains give you the flexibility to design a structure layout that meets your organizational needs.

When you're setting up child domains, the parent and child domains establish a *trust* relationship. Trusts allow users to be granted access to resources in a domain even when their accounts reside in a different domain. To make administration of trust relationships easy, Microsoft has made transitive two-way trusts the default relationship between domains. This means that, by default, all domains within the same forest automatically trust one another. As shown in Figure 1.2, Stellacon.com automatically trusts Boston.Stellacon.com, NY.Stellacon.com, and Dallas.Stellacon.com. This means that all child domains implicitly trust one another.

FIGURE 1.2   Domain structure

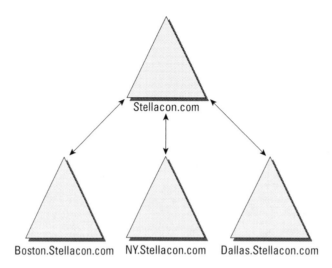

Boston.Stellacon.com   NY.Stellacon.com   Dallas.Stellacon.com

The final Active Directory advantage that we will discuss is an extensible schema. The Active Directory schema consists of the attributes of the database. For example, when you create a new user using the Active Directory Users and Computers snap-in, the system asks you to fill in the user's first name, last name, username, password, and so forth. These fields are the attributes of Active Directory, and that is the schema. An Administrator has the ability to change or expand these fields based on organizational needs.

🌐 **Real World Scenario**

An Example of Why You Might Change the Schema

You may be asking yourself why an organization may need to change the schema. Many years ago when I got out of the military and before I got into the computer industry, I used to cast toilets for American Standard. I made 50 toilets a day. When working for American Standard, I had an employee number of 343. All my toilets were stamped 343 (so they knew who made the product) on the bottom base. My time card did not even have my name—just my number.

This is an example of a field that you would need to add to your schema. I would have an account in Active Directory with my name, but there would need to be a field that showed my employee number. You may have to adjust your Active Directory schema based on your organization's requirements.

The major disadvantage to an Active Directory model is cost. When setting up an Active Directory domain, an organization needs a machine that is powerful enough to handle the Windows Server 2008 operating system. Also, most companies that decide to use a domain-based organization will require the IT personnel to manage and maintain the network infrastructure. To learn more about Microsoft Active Directory networks, See *MCTS: Windows Server 2008 Active Directory Configuration Study Guide (70-640)*, by William Panek and James Chellis (Wiley, 2008).

Microsoft Networking Terms and Roles

Now that we have seen the two networking models that Microsoft offers, let's talk about some basic networking terms and roles. Hyper-V can act as a server or domain controller (among other roles), so it makes sense to learn what these terms and roles mean.

Server   A server is a machine that users connect to so that they can access resources located on that machine. These resources can be files, printers, applications, and so forth. Usually the type of server is dependent on the resource that the user needs. For example, a print server is a server that controls printers. A file server is a server that contains files. Application servers can run applications for the users. Sometimes you will hear a server referred to by the specific application that it may be running. For example, someone may say, "That's our SQL server or Exchange server."

Domain Controller   This is a server that contains a replica of Active Directory. As I mentioned earlier in this chapter, Active Directory is your database that contains all the objects in your network. A domain controller is a server that contains this database. Years ago (when we used NT 3.51 and NT 4.0), we had a primary domain controller (PDC) and backup domain controllers (BDCs), but that's not true today. All domain controllers are equal in a Windows Server 2008 network. Some domain controllers may contain extra roles, but they all have the same copy of Active Directory.

Member Server   A member server is a member of a domain-based network, but it does not contain a copy of Active Directory. For example, Microsoft recommends that Exchange be loaded on a member server instead of a domain controller. Both domain controllers and member servers can act as file, print, or application servers. It just depends on whether you need that server to have a replica of Active Directory.

Stand-alone Server   A stand-alone server is not a member of a domain. Many organizations use this type of server for Hyper-V. For example, you load Windows Server 2008 with Hyper-V on a stand-alone server. You can then create virtual machines that act as domain controllers to run the network.

Client Machine   A client machine is a computer that normally is used for your end users in a company. The most common operating systems for a client machine are Microsoft Vista and XP.

DNS Server   The *Domain Name System (DNS)* server has the DNS service running on it. DNS is a name resolution service. DNS turns a hostname into a TCP/IP address (a process known as forward lookup). DNS also has the ability to turn a TCP/IP address into a name (known as reverse lookup). When you install an operating system onto a computer, you assign that computer a hostname. The problem is that computers talk to each other using the TCP/IP protocol (for example, 192.168.1.100). It would be difficult for most users to remember all the different TCP/IP addresses on a network. So normally you connect to a machine by using its hostname. DNS converts the hostname to a TCP/IP address for you.

The easiest way to understand how this works is to think of your telephone number. If someone wants to call you and they don't have your telephone number, they call information. They give information your name and they get your phone number. Well, this is how a network works. DNS is information on your network. You give DNS a hostname and it returns a network telephone number (TCP/IP address). DNS is a requirement if you want to install Active Directory. You can install DNS before or during the Active Directory installation.

DHCP Server   A *Dynamic Host Configuration Protocol (DHCP)* server runs the DHCP service. DHCP is the server on the network that assigns TCP/IP information to your computers dynamically. Every computer needs three settings to operate properly (with the Internet and intranet): a TCP/IP number, a subnet mask, and a default gateway (router number). Your computers can get this minimum information in one of two ways: manually (someone assigns the TCP/IP information) or dynamically (automatically configured). DHCP can assign more than just these three settings. DHCP can assign any TCP/IP configuration information (such as the DNS server, WINS server, or time servers).

Earlier, I told you that DNS consists of information on your network. Following this example, DHCP would be the phone company. DHCP is the component that assigns the phone number (TCP/IP number).

Global Catalog   The *Global Catalog* is a partial representation of the Active Directory objects. Think of it as an index. If you need to look something up in this book, you go to the index and find what page you need to turn to; you would not just randomly look through the book for the information. This is what the Global Catalog does on your Active Directory domain. When you need to find a resource in the domain (such as a user or published printer), you can search the Global Catalog to find its location.

Domain controllers need to use a Global Catalog to help with user authentication. Global Catalogs are a requirement on an Active Directory domain. All domain controllers can be Global Catalogs, but this is not always a good practice. Your network should have at least two Global Catalogs for redundancy, but too many can cause too much Global Catalog replication traffic.

Now that we have covered some of the basic Microsoft terms, let's turn our focus to the Windows Server 2008 operating system. Microsoft Windows Server 2008 is the core platform for the Hyper-V environment.

Understanding Windows Server 2008

It is important to understand Microsoft Windows Server 2008 and also how to install this operating system. Hyper-V has to run on Windows Server 2008. Hyper-V is new to the server operating system, so if you are running a previous version of Microsoft Windows Server, you must install Windows Server 2008 first.

This section discusses the various versions of Microsoft Windows Server 2008 (not all versions will run Hyper-V) as well as some of the new features. We will also do an exercise to install the Windows Server 2008 operating system.

New Features of Windows Server 2008

Microsoft Windows Server 2008 is the latest release of Microsoft's server operating systems. There are many new and upgraded features, and here are just a few:

Hyper-V   As I stated earlier, Hyper-V allows an organization to create and manage virtualized server environments. This is a new feature of Windows Server 2008 64-bit edition.

AD Rights Management Services (AD RMS)   Active Directory Rights Management Service (AD RMS) is a new feature included with Windows Server 2008. AD RMS gives network users or administrators the ability to determine the access level (such as open, read, or modify) they would like to assign to other users in an organization. By using Microsoft Office 2003 Professional or Microsoft Office 2007, users have the ability to secure email messages, internal websites, and documents.

The advantage to AD RMS is that any user can secure confidential or critical company information. To use AD RMS, an AD RMS client is required. The AD RMS client is included with Windows Vista by default.

Server Manager   Windows Server 2008 has included a new single-source utility for installing, configuring, and managing roles (see Figure 1.3) on a server. *Server Manager* also will display server status and system information as well as identify problems with server roles.

Server Manager has replaced several features that had been included with Windows Server 2003. These replaced features include Manage Your Server, Configure Your Server, and Add or Remove Windows Components.

A final issue that administrators face when deploying servers is the need to run the Security Configuration Wizard. Server Manager, by default, will allow an administrator to deploy servers without running the Security Configuration Wizard because Server Manager server roles are configured with Microsoft recommended security settings.

Network Access Protection (NAP)   Windows Server 2008 has a new security feature called Network Access Protection (NAP). You can now define network access, based on client requirements, using NAP. The advantage of using NAP is that you can define this access at the granular level. NAP also gives you the ability to allow network access based on compliancy with corporate governance policies. Here are some of the new features associated with NAP:

- Network layer protection
- DHCP enforcement
- VPN enforcement
- IPSec enforcement
- 802.1X enforcement
- Flexible host isolation

FIGURE 1.3   Server Manager

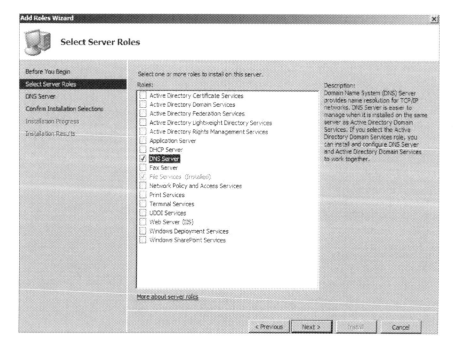

Read-Only Domain Controller (RODC)   Windows Server 2008 introduced a new type of secure domain controller called a *read-only domain controller (RODC)*. A read-only domain controller is a noneditable copy of Active Directory. Using an RODC allows an organization to place a domain controller in an area or off-site location that does not have much security.

As I explained earlier, all domain controllers are equal. They all have the same version of Active Directory. This is also true with a read-only domain controller. Replication between domain controllers is bidirectional (replication happens both ways) except for the use of read-only domain controllers. Replication traffic between domain controllers and RODCs is unidirectional (one way only). Other domain controllers have the ability to talk to the RODC, but the RODC does not have the ability to talk to other domain controllers.

Another advantage to using a RODC in a nonsecure location is that you can give a normal user the right to administer and maintain the RODC. This user would not require domain admin rights. They would be allowed to have the admin role for the one RODC only. This concept is known as administrator role separation.

Server Core Installation   Another new feature is the Server Core installation, which allows you to install Windows Server 2008 with minimal options. Server Core is a low-maintenance version of Windows Server 2008 and thus has limited functionality.

Windows Server 2008 Server Core has no graphical user interface (GUI) utilities. All commands have to be issued through the use of a command prompt. If you have been in the industry long enough, think of Unix or Cisco. You must know the command-line utilities to maintain the server. Server Core is a great security feature.

Think of a normal server. If you want to add or modify a user, you go to Active Directory Users and Computers (on domain-based networks) or the computer management system for workstations or nondomain servers. Once in the application, you can do what's needed. The problem with this is that it is easy to do. If a user gains access to your server room, it could be easy for them to wreak havoc on your network. In a Server Core environment, there are no GUI snap-ins. If users don't know the command-line utilities, they can't make changes.

Server Core is an installation option that allows you to set up only limited server roles: DNS, DHCP, File Server, Active Directory, Media Services, and Hyper-V. Many organizations choose this route to set up Hyper-V. Doing so provides extra security for the Hyper-V environment. By installing Server Core, you automatically create limitations:

- There is no Windows shell and very limited GUI functionality (the Server Core interface is a command prompt).
- There is no managed code support in Server Core (all code must be native Windows API code).
- **Microsoft** Installer Package (MSI) support is limited to unattend mode only.

Multiple editions of Windows Server 2008 are available. Table 1.1 shows which features are included with each version of the Windows Server 2008 operating system.

TABLE 1.1   Windows Server 2008 Editions Comparison

New Features	Enterprise Edition	Datacenter Edition	Standard Edition	Web Edition
Cryptography Next Generation (CNG)	X	X	X	X
Group Policy Preferences	X	X	X	X
Internet Information Services (IIS) 7.0	X	X	X	X
Read-only domain controllers	X	X	X	X

TABLE 1.1   Windows Server 2008 Editions Comparison *(continued)*

New Features	Enterprise Edition	Datacenter Edition	Standard Edition	Web Edition
Server Core installation	X	X	X	X
Server Manager	X	X	X	X
Network Access Protection (NAP)	X	X	X	
Hyper-V	X	X	X	
Active Directory Rights Management Services (AD RMS)	X	X	X	
Windows Deployment Services (WDS)	X	X	X	
Terminal Services Gateway and RemoteApp	X	X	X	

Enhancements	Enterprise Edition	Datacenter Edition	Standard Edition	Web Edition
Windows Server Backup enhancements	X	X	X	X
Network load balancing enhancements	X	X	X	X
Windows Reliability and Performance Monitor enhancements	X	X	X	X
TCP/IP Stack enhancements	X	X	X	X
Windows Firewall with Advanced Security enhancements	X	X	X	X
Windows Reliability and Performance Monitor enhancements	X	X	X	X
Windows Media Services enhancements	X	X	X	X
Active Directory Domain Services (AD DS)	X	X	X	
Active Directory Federation Services enhancements	X	X	X	
Terminal Services enhancements	X	X	X	

TABLE 1.1   Windows Server 2008 Editions Comparison *(continued)*

Enhancements	Enterprise Edition	Datacenter Edition	Standard Edition	Web Edition
DNS Server enhancements	X	X	X	
Public Key Infrastructure (PKI) enhancements	X	X	X	
Failover Clustering enhancements	X	X		

Requirements for Windows Server 2008 Installation

Now that you have seen what each version of Microsoft Windows Server 2008 has to offer, let's look at the requirements for installing Windows Server 2008. Even though these requirements will not be on the Microsoft Hyper-V exam, you need to know them to effectively create a Server 2008 base installation for Hyper-V. As the old saying goes, "You cannot build a good house unless you have a good foundation."

> These are not the requirements for installing Hyper-V. We will cover those in Chapter 2, "Installing Hyper-V." These requirements are the basics needed to install Microsoft Windows Server 2008.

Table 1.2 shows both the minimum and recommended requirements. I have been an IT manager and consultant for many years and from personal experience, I would use only the recommended requirements or higher. The minimum requirements will allow the Windows Server 2008 operating system to install, but it will not be practical for any real-world situation. To make sure the requirements have not changed, visit Microsoft's website at http://msdn.microsoft.com/en-us/windowsserver/cc196364.aspx.

TABLE 1.2   Windows Server 2008 Installation Requirements

Hardware Component	Requirements and Recommendations
Processor	Minimum: 1GHz (x86 processor) or 1.4GHz (x64 processor) Recommended: 2GHz or faster
Memory	Minimum: 512MB of RAM Recommended: 2GB of RAM or greater Maximum (32-bit systems): 4GB (Standard) or 64GB (Enterprise and Datacenter) Maximum (64-bit systems): 32GB (Standard) or 2TB (Enterprise and Datacenter)

TABLE 1.2 Windows Server 2008 Installation Requirements *(continued)*

Hardware Component	Requirements and Recommendations
Drive	DVD-ROM drive
Other hardware	Super VGA (800×600) or higher-resolution monitor Keyboard Microsoft Mouse or compatible pointing device

Activating and Installing Windows Server 2008

If you are interested in evaluating Windows Server 2008, you can do so for no cost; the installation does not require a product activation or product key. Microsoft allows you to install any Windows Server product without activating the software for 60 days.

At the end of the 60 days if you still need more time to finish your evaluation, you can reset your evaluation three more times (60 days each). This will allow an administrator or user to evaluate the product for up to 240 days. At the end of the 240 days, the Windows Server 2008 product will need to be uninstalled or a valid product key and activation will be required.

Real World Scenario

Microsoft Product Keys and Licensing

As a consultant, I have been in many IT departments throughout the United States and I have seen my fair share of organizations using illegal versions of operating systems. I cannot stress this enough: do not use illegal (copied) versions of any products. Your company should be using legal, valid copies and also have enough licenses to support the number of installations.

Remember, it is your job as an IT person to make sure your company stays legal, and it is also your job to make sure your organization understands the consequences that may be taken against them otherwise. Do not put your Microsoft certification on the line for any organization.

At this point, let's go ahead and install the product. Exercise 1.1 walks you through the steps for installing Windows Server 2008 Enterprise Edition.

> If you have already installed Windows Server 2008, you can skip the following exercise. Just make sure that Windows Server 2008 64-bit version was the version installed. Hyper-V must be run on a 64-bit version of Windows Server 2008. If you have a 32-bit version, please complete the exercise with a 64-bit version.

EXERCISE 1.1

Installing Windows Server 2008

1. Insert the Windows Server 2008 64-bit edition CD into the CD-ROM drive and reboot the machine. Make sure the computer can boot off the CD-ROM drive.

2. A window shows that files are loading onto the machine. Next, a screen will appear asking you to enter your language, time and currency, and keyboard settings. Choose the desired settings (just leave the defaults for US residents). Click Next.

EXERCISE 1.1 *(continued)*

3. At the Install Windows screen, click the Install Now arrow.

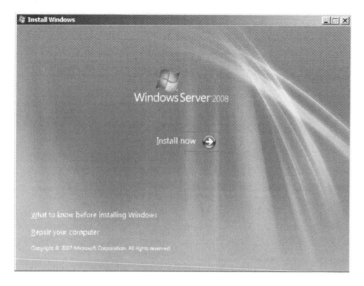

4. The next screen asks which version of Windows Server 2008 you would like to install. The choices you see may not be the same as shown here (depending on the CD you have). Choose Windows Server 2008 Enterprise (Full Installation) and click Next. If you do not have Enterprise Edition, choose Standard (Full Installation).

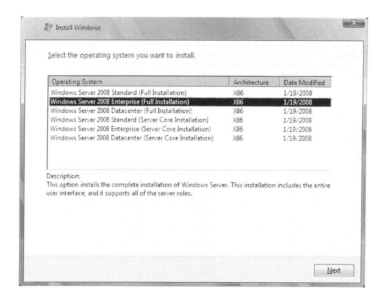

5. At the license terms screen, after reading the license, check the "I accept the license terms" check box and click Next.

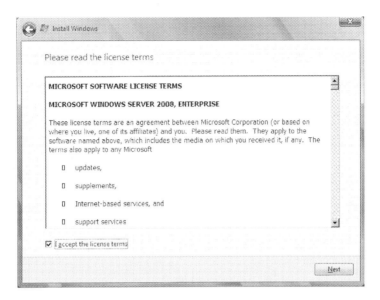

6. At the Which Type Of Installation Do You Want? screen, choose Custom (Advanced).

7. At the Where Do You Want To Install Windows? screen, choose the hard drive where you would like to install the operating system. Click Next.

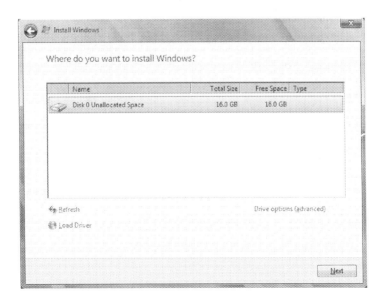

8. The Installing Windows screen appears, showing the status of your install. Reboot after the install is complete.

9. After you reboot, the system will ask you to change the Administrator password at first login. Click OK and then enter and reenter the password **P@ssw0rd**. Click the arrow to the right of the password boxes.

10. The Password Has Been Changed screen appears. Click OK.

Summary

In this chapter, we discussed some of the features of Microsoft Hyper-V. We explored the benefits of installing Hyper-V, which include reduced hardware costs, the ability to consolidate servers, reduced downtime and enhanced recoverability, the ability to test or develop software in a safe virtual machine operating system, and the Dynamic Datacenter feature.

Hyper-V has improved many features and offers new ones, such as symmetric multiprocessors (SMP) support, a new architecture design, operating system support, virtual machine migration, network load balancing, a new hardware architecture that allows hardware resources in a virtual machine to have access to resources on the physical machine, and scalability.

Microsoft networking has two models: peer-to-peer and domain based. Microsoft peer-to-peer networks have implemented many new features like People Near Me, a new API, Group Policy configuration support, a new version of PNRP, and Windows Meeting Space.

Domain-based networks take advantage of using an Active Directory database. This gives you many advantages over a peer-to-peer, such as centralized management, domain security, expandability, and scalability. Your infrastructure needs determine which Microsoft network model you will use.

To make a proper decision as to which networking model you will design, you must understand the various server roles and terms. Understanding how servers, domain controllers, member and stand-alone servers, clients, DNS servers, DHCP servers, and Global Catalogs operate is critical to successfully designing and creating your network infrastructure.

Windows Server 2008 is the platform that Hyper-V must reside on. Windows Server 2008 has many advantages over Windows Server 2003, including AD Rights Management Services (AD RMS), Server Manager, Network Access Protection (NAP), read-only domain controllers, and Server Core installations. This chapter included an overview of the Windows Server 2008 editions and requirements.

Exam Essentials

Understand the benefits of Hyper-V.   By installing Hyper-V, you can reduce your organization's hardware costs, help consolidate servers, reduce downtime and recoverability, use Hyper-V for testing and development in a safe virtual machine operating system, and build a dynamic datacenter for your IT environment.

Be able to describe the features of Hyper-V.   Hyper-V allows for symmetric multiprocessors (SMP) support and offers a new architecture design, operating system support, virtual machine migration, network load balancing, a new hardware architecture that allows hardware resources in a virtual machine to have access to resources on the physical machine, and scalability.

Be familiar with server roles and terms.   Understand the different types of domain and network servers (domain controllers, member and stand-alone servers). Hyper-V can be used for the different types of server roles (DNS servers, DHCP servers, Global Catalogs, etc.).

Know how to install and operate Windows Server 2008.   Hyper-V runs on the 64-bit version of Microsoft Windows Server 2008. Because of this, it is important to understand how Windows Server 2008 operates and the requirements that allow Windows Server 2008 to install.

Review Questions

1. Hyper-V allows an administrator to set up what feature?

    A. Monitoring Resources

    B. Virtualization

    C. Backups

    D. Security

2. What is an implementation of an operating system that runs in its own virtualization window called?

    A. Virtual window

    B. Virtual process

    C. Virtual machine

    D. Virtual host

3. Your manager has come to you because he has heard about the new Hyper-V feature. He asks you to explain some of the benefits that the company can gain by installing Hyper-V. Which of the following are benefits to installing Hyper-V? (Choose all that apply.)

    A. Server consolidation

    B. The ability to test or develop software in a safe virtual machine operating system

    C. Reduced hardware costs

    D. Faster and more efficient Internet connection speed

4. After you have explained some of the benefits of Hyper-V to your boss, he then asks you to explain some of the features. Which of the following are features of Hyper-V? (Choose all that apply.)

    A. New architecture design

    B. Symmetric multiprocessors (SMP) support

    C. Operating system support

    D. Scalability

5. You are the administrator for a small organization with five domains within a single tree. You need to get access to a resource in another domain in another company's tree. What do you need to have set up so that users can get access to the resources in the other tree?

    A. Your users would need accounts in the other company's domain.

    B. The users who need to use the resource must have Administrative rights.

    C. Trust must be established between companies.

    D. This cannot be done.

6. Windows Server 2008 has included a new single-source utility for installing, configuring, and managing roles on a server. What is this utility called?

   A. Add/Remove Programs

   B. Computer Manager

   C. Configuration Manager

   D. Server Manager

7. You are the network administrator for your organization. You need to define access for users based on client requirements and corporate policies. What new Windows Server 2008 feature can you implement?

   A. Network Access Protection

   B. Remote Access Protection

   C. Remote Access Permissions

   D. Network Access Permissions

8. You are the network administrator for a large organization with multiple smaller nonsecure locations. These locations have to go across a WAN line to authenticate with a domain controller. You want to implement a domain controller into these nonsecure remote locations. What type of domain controller can you install?

   A. Secure domain controller (SDC)

   B. Primary domain controller (PDC)

   C. Backup domain controller (BDC)

   D. Read-only domain controller (RODC)

9. As the system administrator for your company, you have decided to implement Hyper-V. You would like to install it onto a server that has limited functionality and no GUI snap-ins for better security. What type of server installation would you use?

   A. Limited Feature Installation

   B. Server Core Installation

   C. Normal Installation and then change the registry

   D. Server Limited Installation

10. You are the network administrator for a small network of 12 users. The company has decided to expand to 30 users over the next 6 months. You want to install a domain controller with Active Directory. You also need to install some type of server that does hostname resolution. What type of server would you install?

   A. DHCP server

   B. RAS server

   C. DNS server

   D. WINS server

11. What Windows Server 2008 server role allows a user to secure an email while using Microsoft Office 2007 Outlook?

   A. Active Directory Domain Services

   B. Active Directory Federation Service

   C. Active Directory Rights Management Service

   D. Active Directory Lightweight Directory Service

12. You are the administrator for a mid-sized organization. When you took the network over from the previous administrator, he had implemented all TCP/IP information manually. You have decided to switch Internet providers. You want to now implement a server to automatically assign TCP/IP information to all of your users. What type of server do you need to install?

   A. DHCP server

   B. RAS server

   C. DNS server

   D. WINS server

13. What component is a database of all Active Directory objects without all of the attributes and thus a partial representation of the Active Directory objects?

   A. Schema files

   B. Active Directory Index

   C. Schema index

   D. Global Catalog

14. Which of the following features of Active Directory allows information between domain controllers to remain synchronized?

   A. Replication

   B. Global Catalog

   C. The schema

   D. None of the above

15. You are the network administrator for a mid-sized company. You have decided to implement Hyper-V onto a new server. What editions of Windows Server 2008 can you install to install Hyper-V?

   A. Enterprise Edition

   B. Standard Edition

   C. Datacenter Edition

   D. Web Edition

16. Which of the following is a requirement of Active Directory?

    A. DHCP

    B. RAS

    C. DNS

    D. WINS

17. You are a consultant and have been asked by a new company to install a Microsoft network. They want to share folders and printers. What are the two types of Microsoft networks? (Choose all that apply.)

    A. AppleTalk network

    B. Domain-based network

    C. Peer-to-peer network

    D. Shared network

18. You are a network administrator for a small company. You are thinking about installing Windows Server 2008. You would like to install Server 2008 and see the features. How long can you evaluate the product before activating the server?

    A. 60 days

    B. 120 days

    C. 180 days

    D. 240 days

19. You are the system administrator for a large organization that just installed Windows Server 2008. All client machines are Windows XP and Vista. You are thinking of installing Network Access Protection (NAP). What are the features of NAP?

    A. Network layer protection

    B. DHCP enforcement

    C. VPN enforcement

    D. IPSec enforcement

20. You are the administrator of a mid-sized organization that has decided to install Windows Server 2008 Server Core. By choosing a Server Core installation, what characteristics should you expect? (Choose all that apply.)

    A. There is no Windows shell and very limited GUI functionality (the Server Core interface is a command prompt).

    B. There is no managed code support in Server Core (all code must be native Windows API code).

    C. Managed code support in Server Core for all coding.

    D. MSI support is limited to unattend mode only.

Answers to Review Questions

1. B. Hyper-V is the next-generation hypervisor-based virtualization technology. Hyper-V is a role-based feature that allows an organization to have multiple virtual machines on a Windows Server 2008 machine.

2. C. A virtual machine (VM) is an implementation of an operating system that runs in its own virtualization window. The advantage to using virtual machines is that you can have multiple VMs on the same Windows Server 2008 machine. Each VM can have its own unique resources running on its operating system.

3. A, B, C. Options A, B, and C are correct. Option D is not a benefit of installing Hyper-V.

4. A, B, C, D. All the options are correct. In addition, Hyper-V offers virtual machine migration and network load balancing.

5. C. Trust allows users to be granted access to resources in a domain even when their accounts reside in a different domain.

6. D. Server Manager is a new single-source utility for installing, configuring, and managing roles on a Windows Server 2008 machine. Server Manager also will display server status and system information as well as identify problems with server roles.

7. A. Windows Server 2008 has a new security feature called Network Access Protection (NAP). Administrators can now define network access, based on client requirements, using NAP. The advantage of using NAP is that administrators can specify this access at the granular level.

8. D. Windows Server 2008 introduced a new type of secure domain controller called a read-only domain controller (RODC). A read-only domain controller is a noneditable copy of Active Directory. It allows an organization to place a domain controller in an area or off-site location that does not have much security.

9. B. A feature new to Microsoft servers is the Server Core installation. This allows an administrator to install Windows Server 2008 with minimal options. Server Core is a low-maintenance version of Windows Server 2008 and has limited functionality.

10. C. A DNS server is a server that handles hostname resolution. DNS can turn a hostname into a TCP/IP address (forward lookup) or turn a TCP/IP address into a hostname (reverse lookup).

11. C. Active Directory Rights Management Service (AD RMS) is included with Microsoft Windows Server 2008. This service allows administrators or users to determine what access (open, read, modify, etc.) they give to other users in an organization. This access can be used to secure email messages, internal websites, and documents. Organizations can use AD RMS for confidential or critical information.

12. A. A DHCP server is a machine that will automatically assign TCP/IP addresses to your users. Not only can DHCP assign the IP address, subnet mask, and default gateway, but it can also assign all TCP/IP users configurations.

13. D. The Global Catalog is a database of all Active Directory objects without all of the attributes and is thus a partial representation of the Active Directory objects.

14. A Replication ensures that information remains synchronized between domain controllers. Replication can be bidirectional or unidirectional (for RODCs).

15. A, B, C. Hyper-V can be installed on Enterprise, Standard, or Datacenter editions of Windows Server 2008. Web and Itanium editions cannot install Hyper-V.

16. C. DNS does hostname resolution. DNS is a requirement of Active Directory. DNS can be installed and configured in a Hyper-V environment.

17. B, C. Microsoft networking allows for peer-to-peer networks or domain-based networks.

18. D. The activation allows for 60 days initially, but you can reset your evaluation three more times (60 days each). This will allow an administrator or user to evaluate the product for up to 240 days. At the end of the 240 days, the Windows Server 2008 product will need to be uninstalled or a valid product key and activation will be required.

19. A, B, C, D. NAP gives administrators the ability to allow network access based on compliancy with corporate governance policies. Some of the new features associated with NAP are network layer protection, DHCP enforcement, VPN enforcement, IPSec enforcement, 802.1X enforcement, flexible host isolation.

20. A, B, D. By installing Server Core, you automatically create limitations: there is no Windows shell and limited GUI functionality, there is no managed code support, and MSI support is limited to unattend mode only.

Chapter 2

Installing Hyper-V

MICROSOFT EXAM OBJECTIVES COVERED IN THIS CHAPTER:

✓ **Select and Configure Hardware to Meet Hyper-V Prerequisites**

  ※ May include but not limited to: Evaluate the existing environment, disk/logical unit number (LUN), memory requirements, correct CPU/BIOS, networking/Network Interface Card (NIC)

✓ **Configure Windows Server 2008 for Hyper-V**

  ※ May include but not limited to: Identify requirements, deploy Hyper-V with Virtual Machine Manager (VMM), Microsoft Assessment and Planning Tool, install on Full, install on Server Core

One the most important things to know when building any type of network is how to install the components on that network properly. This chapter walks you through the installation process for Hyper-V.

The information presented in this chapter is critical not only for the exam but for the real-world installation of Hyper-V. The Microsoft Hyper-V exam (70-652) covers many questions that are installation related.

In the first section of this chapter, you learn the requirements for Hyper-V installation. We also discuss the Microsoft Assessment and Planning Tool, an application that helps you prepare for the Hyper-V installation. We finish the chapter by installing Hyper-V on a full Windows Server 2008 installation and a Server Core installation.

Evaluating Your Network

When most people think of installation requirements, they think of what is physically needed to install the product. However, when determining software and hardware requirements you also need to take into account organizational requirements.

When setting up any new hardware or software on a network, consider the planned workload for the server or application. Can the hardware support the workload? Do you need multiple copies of the application running (load balancing)?

You also need to consider scalability when designing a network. Can the network grow with the organization? The last thing you want to do is redesign an entire network because the organization grew and you did not plan for it properly. These are factors you must think about when designing your Hyper-V network.

As we discussed in the first chapter, Hyper-V can consolidate many servers into one machine. To do this you must first design the network. Is this Hyper-V machine going to be on a domain? Is the Hyper-V virtual machine going to be a domain controller? These are all decisions that should be made before you even purchase hardware for the Hyper-V machine.

Now that you understand the importance of evaluating your organizational needs before you add any new hardware or applications to your network, let's discuss some utilities that will help you install Hyper-V properly in your network.

Real World Scenario

The Importance of Network Planning

I have been in this industry for almost 20 years, and I learned an important lesson early in my career: an hour of planning can save you a day of work!

Many years ago when I was working on an NT 4.0 domain, I got a new machine for my server room. I was so excited about getting the new server that I sat right down and started to build the machine. I loaded Microsoft NT 4.0 Server on the machine and set it up as a member server.

The box was being used as a remote access server (RAS) so I set up a card for multiple COM ports. I had to call the manufacturer of the card so we could get it to work with NT 4.0. I spent all day getting the machine up running. I tested my RAS connections and I was all set.

As I drove home, I realized that I needed another backup domain controller (BDC) on my network. Back then, you could not just promote a member server to a domain controller—you had to reinstall the software and rebuild the machine. Well, this started to eat at me all night. So the next day I decided to rebuild my server and make it a BDC and RAS server.

The point to this whole story is that if I would have stepped back and looked at my network when I first got the machine, I would have realized then that I needed a BDC. This would have saved me a whole day of rebuilding the machine.

When adding any new software or hardware to a network, the first thing you should always do is take some time to make sure that the machine or application is being added to the network the way your organization needs.

Microsoft Assessment and Planning Tool

When a software company releases a new product onto the market, you must ask whether your current IT infrastructure can meet the new hardware demands of that product. Microsoft Vista used a product called the Windows Vista Hardware Assessment Solution Accelerator to help administrators determine if the hardware they currently had was capable of running the new operating system.

Windows Server 2008 also has a similar utility called the Microsoft Assessment and Planning (MAP) tool. MAP will locate computers on a network and then perform a thorough inventory of these computers. To obtain this inventory, MAP uses multiple utilities, such as Windows Management Instrumentation (WMI), the Remote Registry Service, and the Simple Network Management Protocol (SNMP).

Once you have this inventory report, you can determine whether the machines in your infrastructure will be able to load Windows Vista or Server 2008, Microsoft Office 2007, and Microsoft Application Virtualization (formerly SoftGrid).

Microsoft Application Virtualization is the new version of SoftGrid, a product used to virtualize applications. SoftGrid allowed a client to have an application deployed and run on their machine without having to install the application locally on that machine. The SoftGrid client was the only software that had to be installed on the local client machine.

Anyone who has been in the industry for a while can see the potential of using MAP. A utility that discovers your network hardware and then advises you of needed resources to allow the system to operate properly is a tool that should be in every administrator's arsenal.

Here are the discovery options provided in MAP:

Using Active Directory Domain Services   Select this check box to find computer objects in Active Directory.

Using The Windows Networking Protocols   Select this check box to find computers in workgroups and Windows NT 4.0 domains.

Importing Computer Names From A file   Select this check box to import computer names from a file.

Scanning An IP Address Range   Select this check box to find computers within a specified IP address range.

Entering Computer Names And Credentials Manually   Select this check box to enter computer names individually.

As a network administrator, you may find it difficult to determine how many servers you need and where to place them on your network. MAP offers the ability to obtain performance metric data from the computers that you are considering for consolidation using Hyper-V. It will generate a report that recommends where you should physically place your servers in your virtual server environment.

MAP generates your report in both Microsoft Excel and Word. These reports can provide information to you in both summary and full detail modes. You can generate reports for scenarios such as the following:

- To identify currently installed client operating systems and requirements for migrating to Windows Vista

- To identify currently installed Windows Server systems and requirements for migrating to Windows Server 2008

- To identify currently installed Microsoft Office software and requirements for migrating to Microsoft Office 2007

- To assess server performance using the Performance Metrics Wizard

- To consolidate and place Hyper-V or Virtual Server 2005 servers

- To assess machines (clients and servers) for installation of Microsoft Application Virtualization

MAP System Requirements

To install the MAP toolkit, your hardware and software must first meet these minimum requirements.

Supported Operating Systems

- Windows Server 2008
- Windows Server 2003
- Windows Vista with Service Pack 1
- Windows XP Professional Edition with Service Pack 3

CPU Architecture

One advantage to MAP is that it can be installed on both the 32-bit and 64-bit versions of any of the operating systems listed.

Hardware Requirements

- 1.6GHz or faster processor minimum or dual-core CPU for Windows Vista
- 1.5GB of RAM minimum—2.0GB for Windows Vista
- Minimum 1GB of available hard disk space
- Network card that supports 10/100/1000Mbps

Additional Requirements

- Microsoft SQL Server 2005 Express Edition or higher
- Microsoft Word (Word 2003 with SP2 or Word 2007)
- Microsoft Excel (Excel 2003 with SP2 or Excel 2007)

You can download MAP from Microsoft's website and use it for free. Exercise 2.1 will walk you through the steps to download and install this tool.

EXERCISE 2.1

Downloading and Installing the Microsoft Assessment and Planning Tool

1. Go to http://www.microsoft.com/downloadS/details.aspx?familyid=67240B76-3148-4E49-943D-4D9EA7F77730&displaylang=en.

2. Scroll down to the bottom of the page and click the Download button for Microsoft_Assessment_and_Planning_Solution_Setup.x64.exe.

3. Click the Save button. Save the file to your hard drive.

4. After the file is downloaded to your hard drive, click the Run button.

5. The Microsoft Assessment and Planning Solution Accelerator Setup wizard will appear. Make sure the option Automatically Check For Device Compatibility is checked and click Next.

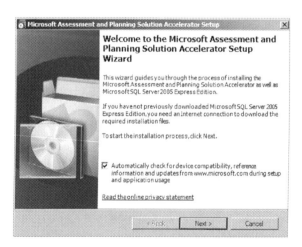

6. The License Agreement screen appears next. Click the I Accept The Terms Of The License Agreement radio button and click Next.

7. At the Installation Folder screen, accept the default location by clicking Next.

8. A screen will appear asking about SQL Server 2005 Express. If you have a previous version of SQL Server 2005 Express on your machine, click the radio button Install From Previous Downloaded Installation Files. If you do not have a previous copy of SQL, make sure that the radio button Download And Install is checked. Then, click Next.

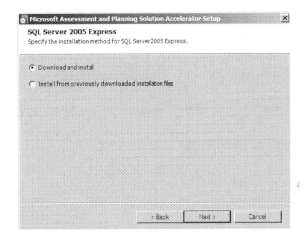

9. The SQL Server 2005 Express License Agreement screen appears next. Click the I Accept The Terms Of The License Agreement radio button and click Next.

10. At the Ready To Install screen, click the Install button.

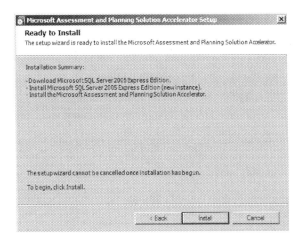

11. The Installing The Microsoft Assessment And Planning Solution Accelerator screen will appear and show you the status of the installation process.

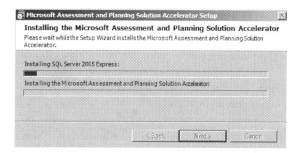

12. Once the installation is complete, you'll see the Installation Successful screen.

Now that you have installed MAP, it's time to configure and test your server. In Exercise 2.2, we create our database for testing.

Configuring the Microsoft Assessment and Planning Tool

1. Start MAP by clicking Start ➤ All Programs ➤ Microsoft Planning and Assessment Solution Accelerator ➤ Microsoft Planning and Assessment Solution.

2. The first thing we need to do is select our database. We are going to create our database at this time. To accomplish this, click Select A Database in either the center or right window pane.

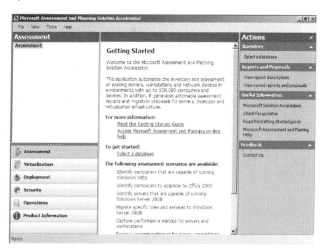

EXERCISE 2.2 *(continued)*

3. The Create Or Select A Database screen will appear. Make sure that the Create An Inventory Database radio button is selected. In the Name field, type **HyperV** and click OK.

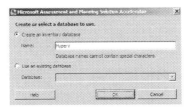

After your database is created, you have the ability to run the various options to test the machines and servers. This is where you decide which scenarios you would like to test for your network. A utility like MAP can not only detect your network and its operating systems but also recommend enhancements. Now that the database is created, it's time to run through some scenarios.

Exercise 2.3 walks you through the process of running the Migrate Specific Roles And Services To Windows Server 2008 utility. We will then look at the process of viewing the generated output report.

EXERCISE 2.3

Using MAP to Migrate Roles and Services to Windows Server 2008

1. Start MAP by clicking Start ➢ All Programs ➢ Microsoft Planning and Assessment Solution Accelerator ➢ Microsoft Planning and Assessment Solution.

2. To create the report, click Migrate Specific Roles And Services To Windows Server 2008 in either the center or right window panes.

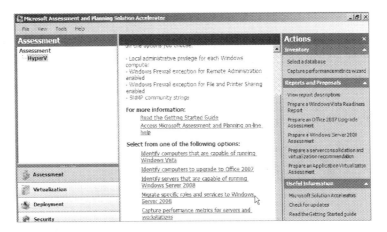

3. The Select Reports And Proposals screen appears. Make sure the Windows Server 2008 Readiness And Role Migration check box is selected. Click Next.

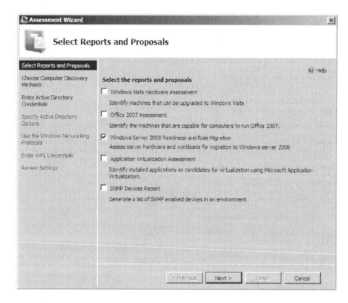

4. The Choose Computer Discovery Methods screen appears. Uncheck all boxes except for the Scan An IP Address Range check box. Click Next.

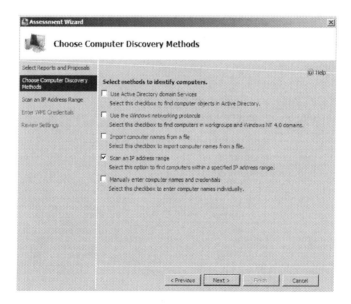

EXERCISE 2.3 *(continued)*

5. At the Scan An IP Address Range screen, type the TCP/IP address range for the server you want to scan. For example, my IP address is 192.168.1.100, so I scanned 192.168.1.0 through 192.168.2.250. Once you've entered the starting and ending TCP/IP addresses for your range, click Next.

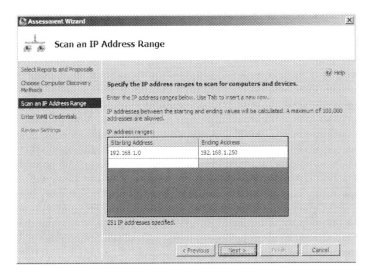

6. The Enter WMI Credentials page appears, where you will enter a username and password for the servers you are trying to generate the report on. Click the New Account button.

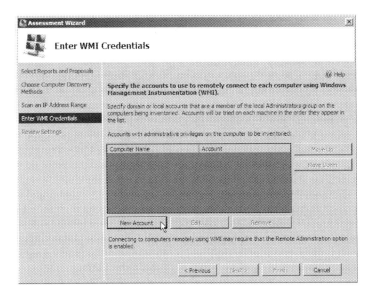

EXERCISE 2.3 *(continued)*

7. At the Inventory Account screen, enter a username and password for the credentials for the machine on which you are loading Hyper-V. If that machine is part of a domain, enter the domain name in the first field. For example, my machine is not part of the domain, so I just entered the username of Administrator with the password P@ssw0rd. Once you have entered your credentials, click the Save button.

8. You will return to the Enter WMI Credentials screen; just click Next.

9. At the Review Settings screen, click Finish.

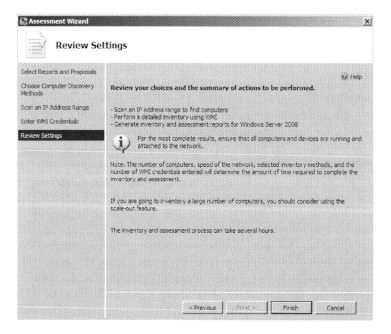

10. The Status window will appear while it is generating its information. Do not click anything during this process.

11. After the Status windows completes, click the Close button.

After the reports have been generated, you have the ability to view the different reports. By clicking the View Saved Reports And Proposals link, you can see the reports that you just generated for your machine.

Installing Hyper-V

Until now we have discussed the fundamentals of preparing for an installation of the Hyper-V role on a Windows Server 2008 machine. But before we dive any deeper into the Hyper-V installation, let's discuss a core component of Hyper-V called the *Windows hypervisor.*

The hypervisor is a thin layer of software that sits between the hardware and the Windows Server 2008 operating system. This thin layer allows one physical machine to run multiple operating systems in different Hyper-V virtual machines at the same time. The hypervisor is the mechanism that is responsible for maintaining isolation between the different Hyper-V partitions.

The hypervisor allows you to have multiple virtual machines running on the same machine at one time. You may be wondering how many virtual machines you can run at the same time. The answer depends on your machine's hardware. The physical memory and the processor are just two examples of hardware that will need to be increased depending on how many virtual machines you want to run. Also, other Hyper-V features, like failover clusters, may make even greater hardware demands. (Hyper-V failover clusters and their requirements will be discussed in full detail in Chapter 7, "Hyper-V and Failover Clusters.")

Once you have determined your machine's hardware specifications, Hyper-V allows you to define the amount of memory you can allocate to each individual virtual machine. In this way, each virtual machine has its own separate and distinct amount of RAM.

Another question you must answer before installing Hyper-V is whether the machine on which you are installing Hyper-V is going to be part of the domain. Hyper-V can act as a domain controller, so there may not be any reason to join the machine to the domain before installing Hyper-V.

A domain controller running within Hyper-V can be the domain controller that holds your organization's Active Directory database. This means that all client computers would have to join the domain that Hyper-V is running. A domain client can't tell the difference between a virtualized domain controller and a nonvirtualized domain controller. Also, the Hyper-V domain controller can be just another domain controller on an existing domain.

This is a decision that you must make based on your organization's current setup and requirements. Unless your Hyper-V server is going to be running as the only Active Directory domain controller, you should make the machine a member of the domain before you install Hyper-V.

There will be many instances where your Hyper-V system will not be a domain controller. For example, if you are going to install Hyper-V in a failover configuration, Microsoft recommends that the Hyper-V machines not be domain controllers. If the Hyper-V machine is not a domain controller, I highly recommend that you make it a member of the domain first before installing Hyper-V.

 **Real World Scenario**

Understanding Your Server Roles

As a system administrator, you should know what a server's responsibilities will be. Is the server going to be a domain controller or DNS server? Will it run Hyper-V?

The answers become very important because failing to plan the server's roles in advance can result in performance issues and downtime.

For example, let's say you decide to install a machine with Windows Server 2008 and you want to make it a DNS server. You purchase your hardware, you install your software, and you are up and running.

A month later you decide to install Hyper-V onto that same server. One of the requirements of Hyper-V is that the BIOS be able to support virtualization. The problem is that you already purchased your hardware. If the machine does not meet the basic requirements to support virtualization, you will need to purchase a new machine to handle this task.

Another potential problem of adding services or software after you purchase a machine relates to performance issues and bottlenecking. The more services and software you add to a machine, the more resources these items consume. This can slow down a machine, which in turn can slow down a network.

If you then need to increase hardware on these machines, you have to take live servers offline to add the new hardware. Many organizations lose money by having servers offline.

It is very important that you know the server's roles before you spend your organization's money to purchase the hardware. I know that in a real-world situation it is not always possible to know in advance everything that a server may handle. But the more you plan for in advance, the better you will be in the long run.

Hyper-V Hardware Requirements

To install Hyper-V, you must first meet the hardware requirements. Based on your organizational needs, these requirements may have to be increased to support your network properly. The hardware requirements are basically the same as the Windows Server 2008 requirements. There are just a few hardware issues that are different:

Disk/LUN (Logical Unit Number)   Storage devices (such as a disk, a portion of the disk, or an entire or a portion of a disk array in the subsystem) can be assigned a unique identifier called a *logical unit number (LUN)*. A logical unit number is just that: a logical reference to a particular section of a storage subsystem. A LUN can differentiate as many as eight devices.

LUNs allow a host computer to know which storage device in an array to access to gather the data that the system is looking to retrieve. For example, if your array has six devices attached and there is data on the last device, the array host can access that data by its LUN.

Microsoft's Storage Manager for SANs is a utility that allows an administrator to create and manage LUNs for fiber channel and iSCSI disk drive subsystems that support Virtual Disk Service (VDS). (LUNs will be discussed in further detail in Chapter 7, "Hyper-V and Failover Clusters.")

Memory (RAM)   Since Hyper-V runs on the 64-bit architecture, it allows for far more memory use than virtual platforms that are 32-bit based. Hyper-V requires a minimum of 512MB of RAM; Microsoft recommends 2GB of RAM or greater. Hyper-V can use a maximum of 4GB (Standard) or 64GB (Enterprise and Datacenter) for 32-bit applications and a maximum of 32GB (Standard) or 2TB (Enterprise, Datacenter) for 64-bit applications.

Network Interface Card (NIC) Adapters   Only one network card is technically required, but Microsoft strongly recommends the use of two minimum. They recommend that one network card be used for management and one or more cards used for virtual machine networking. Dedicated NICs when using iSCSI cards are also needed with Hyper-V.

CPU/BIOS   There are few major requirements for the CPU and BIOS when dealing with Hyper-V. The server must support a 64-bit environment as well as hardware-assisted virtualization (Intel VT or AMD-V) technology. The processor must be a minimum of 1.4GHz (x64 processor), but Microsoft recommends 2GHz or faster. Hardware-enabled Data Execution Prevention (DEP) is also required for Hyper-V. Hyper-V does not support Itanium-type processors.

> The listed hardware components are not all that is required to run Hyper-V properly. Your network subsystem (cable, routers, hubs, etc.) must be configured and running for Hyper-V to function properly.

Installing Hyper-V on a Windows Server 2008 Full Installation

When installing Hyper-V onto a server, you have two options for the way you install Hyper-V. You can install Hyper-V onto a Windows Server 2008 machine that has a full operating system installation, or you can install it onto a Windows Server 2008 Server Core installation (which we discuss later in this chapter).

When installing Hyper-V on a full installation of Microsoft Windows Server 2008, you can use the traditional full graphical user interface (GUI). This makes it easier for you to manage, configure, and maintain Hyper-V and the Windows environment. This is also a much more comfortable environment for newer administrators who may not be familiar with a command line–driven operating system.

But there is a drawback to the GUI: anyone, even if they have no experience, can manipulate the environment. Therefore, the GUI environment can be a security risk.

If you are in a non-GUI environment, you must know the actual commands to manage the environment. But since we are in a full GUI environment, anyone who can click on a mouse can hypothetically manipulate the environment.

Physical Security

We were just discussing the disadvantage of using a GUI environment. As a system administrator, part of your responsibilities is to teach others around you the benefits of network security. This does not only mean securing files, folders, and users; it also means physical security.

You should always try to avoid having servers in an unsecure area. Most server rooms are just that—rooms. These rooms have doors that normally have some type of locking system. Your organization should have some type of secure physical location for your servers to reside. If this is the case, it makes it very difficult for a user to just walk up to a server and make changes (even if it's a GUI).

If your server is a domain controller, you have to be a member of one of the following groups to log locally onto the machine: Account Operators, Administrators, Backup Operators, Print Operators, or Server Operators.

But if the machine is just a server (nondomain controller), you only have to be a member of the user group to log onto the machine. Normally the Hyper-V role will be installed onto a nondomain controller–based server. This means if the server is not located in a locked server room, most users would be able to make changes using the GUI environment.

Since the Windows Server 2008 full installation has a GUI environment, installing Hyper-V becomes a much easier task. Windows Server 2008 includes a new feature called *Server Manager*. Server Manager is a Microsoft Management Console (MMC) snap-in that allows an administrator to view information about server configuration, status of roles that are installed, and links for adding and removing features and roles (see Figure 2.1).

The following are some of the roles that you can install and manage using Server Manager:

- Active Directory Certificate Services
- Active Directory Domain Services
- Active Directory Federation Services
- Active Directory Lightweight Directory Services
- Active Directory Rights Management Services

- Application Server
- Availability and Scalability
- DHCP Server
- DNS Server
- Fax Server
- File Services
- Hyper-V
- Network Policy and Access Services
- Print Services
- Streaming Media Services
- Terminal Services
- Troubleshooting
- UDDI Services
- Web Server
- Windows Deployment Services

FIGURE 2.1   Windows Server 2008 server roles

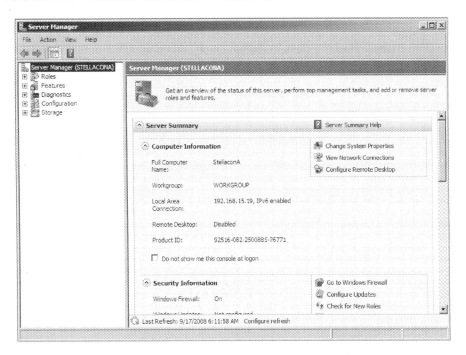

To learn more about all of these roles and services, see *MCTS: Windows Server 2008 Active Directory Configuration Study Guide* by William Panek and James Chellis (Sybex, 2008) and *MCTS: Windows Server 2008 Network Infrastructure Configuration Study Guide* by William Panek, Tylor Wentworth, and James Chellis (Sybex, 2008).

Before Server Manager, Windows Server 2003 administrators had to use many utilities such as Manage Your Server, Configure Your Server, and Add Or Remove Windows Components to install server roles and features. Server Manager lets you manage your server's features and roles from one central utility.

Server Manager is the utility that we will use to install the Hyper-V role. Exercise 2.4 walks you through the steps of installing Hyper-V onto a Windows Server 2008 full installation.

EXERCISE 2.4

Installing Hyper-V on a Windows Server 2008 Full Installation

1. Start the Server Manager application by clicking Start ➤ Administrative Tools ➤ Server Manager.

2. In the left pane, click Roles.

3. In the right pane, click the Add Roles link.

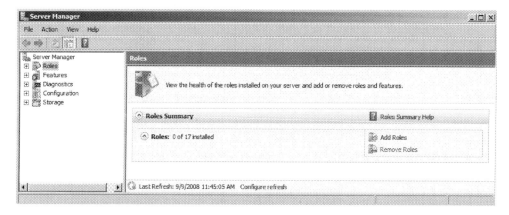

4. The Before You Begin window appears; click Next.

EXERCISE 2.4 *(continued)*

5. At the Select Server Roles screen, click the Hyper-V check box and then click Next.

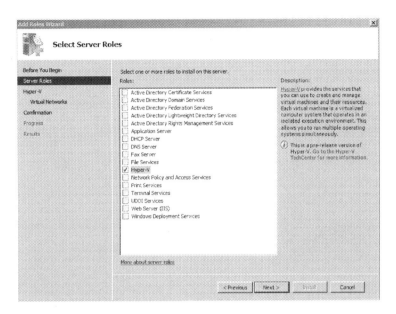

6. At the Introduction to Hyper-V screen, click Next.

7. At the Create Virtual Networks screen, select the check box for your network card.
    Then click Next.

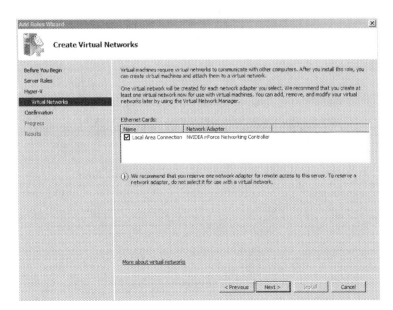

EXERCISE 2.4 *(continued)*

8. At the Confirm Installation Selections screen, click the Install button.

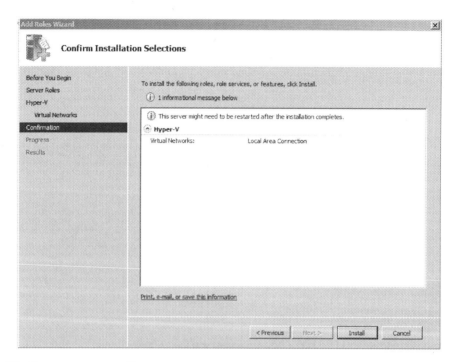

9. The Progress screen will appear next, showing you the progress of the installation. Once the Results screen appears, click Finished.

Now that you have just installed Hyper-V, you must verify that it is up and running. To do this, you will use the Hyper-V Manager. In Exercise 2.5 you will verify that the Microsoft Hyper-V role was installed onto your machine.

EXERCISE 2.5

Verifying the Installation of Hyper-V

1. Open the Hyper-V Manager by clicking Start ➢ Administrative Tools ➢ Hyper-V Manager.

2. The Hyper-V License Agreement will appear. Click the I Have Read And Agreed This Eula radio button for licensing. Then click the Accept button.

3. In the left window, click on your server name under Microsoft Hyper-V Servers.

4. If there are no errors or messages, close Hyper-V Manager.

5. We are now going to verify that the Microsoft Hyper-V services are up and running properly. To do this, click Start ➤ Administrative Tools ➤ Services.

6. Scroll down and verify that there are two services running under Microsoft Hyper-V (Image Management Service and Networking Management).

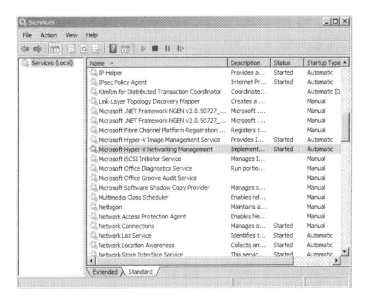

7. Close the Services snap-in.

Configuring and managing virtual machines by using the Hyper-V Manager will be discussed in full detail starting in the next chapter.

Installing Hyper-V on a Windows Server 2008 Server Core

A new feature in the Windows Server 2008 arsenal is called *Server Core*. The Server Core installation lets you have a minimal environment for running specific server roles, which, in turn, reduces the attack surface for those server roles. A smaller attack surface helps reduce the chances of being hacked by anyone inside or outside your organization.

> A well-known fact in the computer industry is that most hacks of a computer system come from within the organization of the hacked computer.

The following is a list of server roles that can be installed on a machine with the Windows Server 2008 Server Core installation:

- Active Directory Domain Services (AD DS)

- Active Directory Lightweight Directory Services (AD LDS)

- DHCP Server

- DNS Server

- File Services

- Hyper-V

- Print Services

- Streaming Media Services

- Web Server (IIS)

The Windows Server 2008 Server Core installation does not have an Explorer shell. Unlike the normal installation of Windows Server 2008, Server Core has no GUI. The default user interface for a Server Core installation is the command prompt; after the installation of Server Core, initial configuration at the command prompt is then required.

As explained in the previous section, an administrator for a Windows Server 2008 full installation does not need to know command-line commands to configure and maintain a server. This is not the case for a Server Core installation. In a Server Core installation, since there is no GUI interface you must know how to use command-line utilities. This is the downside to Server Core, but at the same time, it is also a benefit. This allows for better security for a server: most users cannot just sit down and change your server environment by typing in commands at the prompt.

Once Server Core is configured, you can manage the server either locally at the command prompt or remotely through the use of a Terminal Server connection or command-line utilities that support remote use.

There are many situations where the Server Core installation can be a useful tool in the deployment of your servers. Server Core can provide benefits to an organization in the following ways:

- Reduced maintenance

- Reduced attack surface

- Reduced management

- Less disk space required

Exercise 2.6 walks you through the installation of Windows Server 2008 Server Core. If you have a copy of Windows Server 2008 full installation, you can go ahead and install the Windows Server 2008 Server Core installation on the same machine. The machine will then dual-boot. This means that when the machine starts, it will give you an option of which operating system you want to start in. If possible, install the Server Core onto a partition or volume different from the one where the full installation resides.

Real World Scenario

Using Server Core When Physical Security Is Unfeasible

As explained earlier, you should always try to have your servers in a physically locked room. But there may be times when this is not possible.

Many years ago, I worked in the medical field as a network engineer. I worked with many doctors' offices, setting up networks and applications. Server Core would have been a useful tool back then because in many doctors' offices there is no secure server room.

Also, most doctors' offices do not have IT personnel on staff to do daily maintenance on the servers. These servers would sit in an unsecure location where anyone who could use a mouse could wreak havoc. If I'd had Server Core, those servers would have been more secure.

EXERCISE 2.6

Installing Windows Server 2008 Server Core

1. Insert the Windows Server 2008 64-bit installation DVD into your system.

2. Boot the machine up using the installation DVD.

3. At the first installation screen (where you pick a language to install), click Next.

4. The Install Now screen will appear. Click the Install Now arrow in the center of the screen.

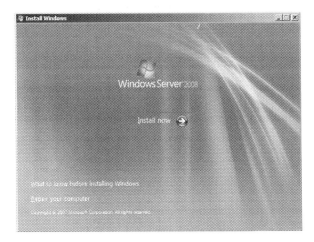

5. At the Select The Operating System You Want To Install screen, select the Server Core option (we are selecting Enterprise Server Core) and click Next.

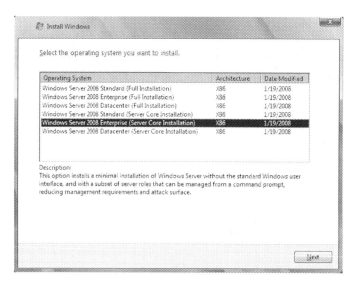

6. At the Accept License Agreement screen, check the I Accept The License Terms radio licensing button and click Next.

7. You will be prompted to choose a type of installation. Choose the Custom (Advanced) option.

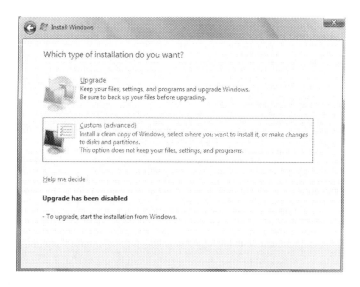

8. At the Where Do You Want To Install Windows? screen, choose the disk where you would like to install Server Core. After highlighting the disk, click Next.

9. The status screen will appear, showing you the progress of your install. The machine will need to be rebooted after installation.

10. After the machine reboots and finishes the installation, the CTL/ALT/DEL screen will appear. You will be required to set a password the first time you log in. Click OK, make the password **P@ssw0rd,** and confirm it. Click the arrow to the right or press Enter.

11. You'll see a screen stating that your password has been changed. Click OK.

If your machine now has two versions of Windows Server 2008 (full and Server Core), you can change the boot order or boot properties by using the **bcdedit /set** command at the command prompt.

Understanding Server Core Commands

We have now installed Windows Server 2008 Server Core onto our 64-bit computer system. Server Core, as explained earlier, has no GUI snap-ins to configure the operating system. The configuration is done through command-line commands. It is important to understand how and when to use these commands. In the next exercise, we will install Hyper-V onto the Server Core machine. If you do not understand what these commands are used for, doing your job will be very difficult. Table 2.1 lists many of the Windows Server 2008 Server Core commands and explains what these commands do.

TABLE 2.1   Server Core Command-Line Commands

Command	Syntax	Explanation
netdom join	netdom join <computer name> /domain: <DomainName> / userd:<UserName> /password:*	Joins a computer to the domain.
netdom remove	netdom remove	Removes the computer from the domain.
shutdown	shutdown /r /t 0	Shuts down the computer.
start ocsetup	start /w ocsetup DHCPServerCore (Other roles can be used here, like DFSN-Server or Microsoft-Hyper-V)	Starts an installation. The /w stops the command prompt from appearing until the process is complete.

TABLE 2.1 Server Core Command-Line Commands *(continued)*

Command	Syntax	Explanation
oclist	oclist	Lists all services and roles installed on the server.
/uninstall	start /w ocsetup DFSN-Server /uninstall	Removes the role from the server.
net start	net start dhcpserver	Starts a service. The net start command by itself will show you all the services running.
sc start	sc start dhcpserver	Starts a service.
sc config	sc config dhcpserver start=auto	Starts the service automatically each time a machine is restarted.
sc query	sc query type=drivers	Shows a specific item that is currently installed on the server. For example, this command shows all drivers installed on this machine.
DCPromo	DCPromo / unattend:<unattendfile>	Installs Active Directory. The /unattend allows you to install Active Directory using a file.
WinRM	WinRM quickconfig	Enables Windows Remote Shell on a server running Server Core.
NetSh	netsh show version	Utility used for scripting and command-line networking.
net user	net user administrator *	Modifies user accounts. The example given here sets the administrator password. You can also use the net user command to add or remove users.
net localgroup	net localgroup administrators /add <domain \username>	Modifies the members of a group. In this example we are adding a user to the administrators group. To remove a user, use the /remove command.
bcdedit	bcdedit /set hypervisorlaunchtype auto	Allows you to edit the Boot Configuration Data (BCD) files.

Most of the commands in Table 2.1 can be used with the /? switch. The /? switch is a help command switch that will normally show you all the commands that can be used with the command you are trying to use. For example, issuing bcdedit /? will show you all associated commands for the bcdedit command. For a thorough treatment of Server Core, see *Administering Windows Server 2008 Server Core* by John Paul Mueller (Sybex, 2008).

Now that you have an understanding of the Server Core commands, Exercise 2.7 lets you use some of these commands to install Hyper-V onto a Server Core machine.

EXERCISE 2.7

Installing Hyper-V on a Windows Server 2008 Server Core Installation

1. At the Server Core command prompt, type **oclist** and press Enter. Scroll up until you see the Microsoft Hyper-V entry.

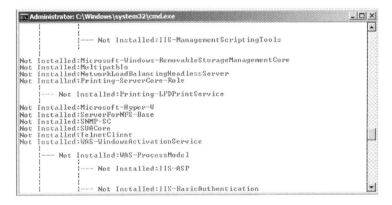

2. We now have to set the hypervisor to launch automatically. At the command prompt, type **bcdedit /set hypervisorlaunchtype auto** and press Enter.

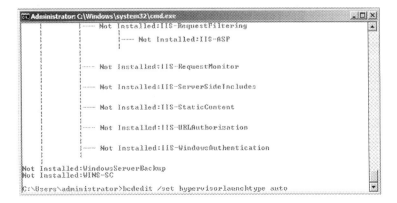

EXERCISE 2.7 *(continued)*

3. At the command prompt, type **start /w OCSetup Microsoft-Hyper-V** and press Enter.

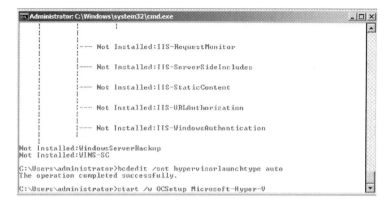

4. At the command prompt, type **oclist**. You will now see that Hyper-V is installed.

Hyper-V with Virtual Machine Manager

Microsoft has released a new version of System Center Virtual Machine Manager (SCVMM), a utility designed to help you manage your Hyper-V virtual machines and datacenter. It allows an organization to have centralized management and dynamic resource optimization among numerous multivendor platforms.

An average server operates at less than 15 percent capacity. SCVMM can help resolve this issue by consolidating server workloads using virtual machines. By allowing virtual servers to handle more of the workload, your organization will require fewer servers, thus saving on equipment, space, and power requirements. SCVMM will execute data analysis of several factors before making suggestions for the placement of server workload.

Another advantage of SCVMM is having one console that all administrators are familiar with. With all administrators using one application to handle virtual machines, an IT department can better manage and monitor the virtual environment.

SCVMM lets you create and manage virtual machine templates. You can use that template over and over, thus eliminating the need to reconfigure each virtual machine.

Since SCVMM is a Microsoft product, it will take advantage of the Windows Server 2008 server services, such as Active Directory. Here are some of the benefits of SCVMM:

- Support for VMs running on Windows Server 2008
- Multivendor virtualization platform support
- Performance and resource optimization
- Host cluster support for "high availability" virtual machines

> At the time of this writing, SCVMM 2008 was still in beta. You can download and evaluate a copy at http://technet.microsoft.com/en-us/evalcenter/cc793138.aspx.

Virtual Machine Manager will be discussed in greater detail in the next chapter, "Configuring Hyper-V."

Summary

In this chapter, we discussed how to evaluate your network using the Microsoft Assessment and Planning tool. We discussed the importance of taking your time and verifying your network requirements before installing new hardware or software on your network.

We then discussed the Windows hypervisor component of Hyper-V. We explained that this thin layer of software sits between the hardware and the Windows Server 2008 operating system.

Next we explored the requirements for installing Hyper-V. We discussed the two ways to install Hyper-V (Full or Server Core installation). We examined many of the Server Core command prompt commands and what they do. We also listed the pros and cons of both the Windows Server 2008 full installation and the Server Core installation.

Finally, we looked at the System Center Virtual Machine Manager and the benefits of using it to manage your Hyper-V virtual machines. In the next chapter, we will discuss configuring and optimizing Hyper-V.

Exam Essentials

Be familiar with the Microsoft Assessment and Planning tool. MAP is a utility that will locate computers on a network and then perform a thorough inventory of those computers. You can then use this inventory to determine if the machines on your network will be able to load Windows Vista or Server 2008, Microsoft Office 2007, and Microsoft Application Virtualization.

Understand the Windows hypervisor. The Windows hypervisor is a thin layer of software that sits between the hardware and the Windows Server 2008 operating system. This thin layer allows one physical machine to run multiple operating systems in various Hyper-V virtual machines at the same time.

Be able to list the Hyper-V hardware requirements. Know the hardware requirements for Hyper-V. The four major hardware items that need to be configured properly are disk/LUN (logical unit number), memory (RAM), network card (NIC), and CPU/BIOS.

Know the installation options. There are two ways to install Microsoft Hyper-V: onto a Windows Server 2008 full installation or onto a Windows Server 2008 Server Core installation.

Be familiar with SCVMM. SCVMM can help you manage your Hyper-V virtual machines and datacenter. It allows you to have centralized management and dynamic resource optimization among numerous multivendor platforms.

Review Questions

1. You are the network administrator for a fast-growing organization. The organization wants you to install Hyper-V. What's the first thing that you should do?

   A. Buy hardware for Hyper-V.

   B. Evaluate your network.

   C. Install Hyper-V on a machine that already has Windows Server 2008.

   D. Install Windows Server 2008 64-bit on a new machine.

2. You are a network administrator for a mid-sized company. Your organization currently uses Windows Server 2003 and Windows XP Professional. You have decided to upgrade the network to Windows Server 2008 and Microsoft Vista. You have also decided to use Hyper-V. Which application can help you determine which machines can be upgraded to Windows Server 2008 and Vista?

   A. Microsoft Migration tool

   B. Microsoft Upgrade tool

   C. Microsoft Assessment and Planning tool

   D. Microsoft 2008 Upgrade and Migration tool

3. You are a network administrator for a large legal firm. You have decided to use the Microsoft Assessment and Planning (MAP) tool to help you upgrade your machines. Which of the following are ways to locate the machines on your network? (Choose all that apply.)

   A. Use Active Directory domain services.

   B. Scan an IP address range.

   C. Use the Windows networking protocols.

   D. Import computer names from a file.

4. As a system administrator, you have decided to use the Microsoft Assessment and Planning (MAP) tool. You want to look at some of the reports that MAP generates. About which of the following can MAP generate a scenario report? (Choose all that apply.)

   A. Identify currently installed client operating systems and their requirements for migrating to Windows Vista.

   B. Identify currently installed Microsoft Office software and the requirements for migrating to Microsoft Office 2007.

   C. Evaluate server performance by using the Performance Metrics Wizard.

   D. Hyper-V or Virtual Server 2005 servers consolidation and placement.

5. You are the network administrator for a small insurance company. Your organization has decided to use the Microsoft Assessment and Planning (MAP) tool. Your boss has asked what other software the company needs to run the MAP utility. Which of the following are necessary requirements to run MAP? (Choose all that apply.)

   A. Microsoft Visual Basic

   B. Microsoft SQL Server 2005 Express

   C. Microsoft Word

   D. Microsoft Excel

6. You are the administrator for an organization with 450 users. Your organization has five servers, all running Windows Server 2003. Your organization has decided to implement Windows Server 2008 with Hyper-V. You are asked to explain Hyper-V to the executives during a proposal meeting. Someone in the meeting states that they have heard of a thin layer of software that sits between the hardware and the Windows Server 2008 operating system. This layer allows for multiple virtual machines to run at the same time on the same physical machine. What is this component called?

   A. Windows Hyper-V LOS

   B. Windows hyperlayer

   C. Windows virtualizor

   D. Windows hypervisor

7. You are a network manager and you have decided to implement Windows Server 2008 with Hyper-V. You have decided to buy new hardware for this implementation. When you build your specifications sheet for the new machine, what are the three items that are required for the CPU/BIOS to install Hyper-V? (Choose three.)

   A. 32-bit processor

   B. 64-bit processor

   C. Hardware-assisted virtualization

   D. Hardware-enabled Data Execution Prevention (DEP)

8. What is the name of the utility that allows an administrator to create and manage logical unit numbers (LUNs) for fiber channel and iSCSI disk drive subsystems that support Virtual Disk Service (VDS)?

   A. Microsoft Storage Manager

   B. Microsoft LUN Manager

   C. Microsoft Virtual Manager

   D. Microsoft SAN Manager

9. You are a network administrator for a large insurance company. Your company has decided to upgrade from Windows Server 2003 to Windows Server 2008. After you upgrade your servers to Windows Server 2008, you want to install DNS, DHCP, and Hyper-V. Which utility would you use to install these roles?

A. Server Roles

B. Server Manager

C. Server Organizer

D. Add/Remove Programs

10. You are the network manager for a large organization. You have some new junior IT members who have just been hired. You want them to start learning and managing Microsoft Hyper-V. You want to install Hyper-V onto a system that uses graphical user interface (GUI) snap-ins. How would you install Hyper-V?

A. Install Hyper-V onto a Windows Server 2008 Server Core installation.

B. Install Hyper-V onto a Windows Server 2008 full installation.

C. Install Hyper-V onto a Windows Server 2003 domain controller.

D. Install Hyper-V onto a Windows Server 2008 32-bit installation.

11. You are the network administrator for a large, multisite organization. You have one remote location that needs to have a domain controller. You want to install a domain controller in the site that requires the minimum amount of maintenance and has a reduced attack surface against security breaches. How would you install the domain controller?

A. Install the domain controller on a Windows Server 2008 Server Core installation.

B. Install the domain controller on a Windows Server 2008 full installation.

C. Install a Windows Server 2003 domain controller.

D. Install Hyper-V onto a Windows Server 2008 full installation and run the domain controller through Hyper-V.

12. You are a network administrator who has decided to install a version of Windows Server 2008 Server Core onto a new 64-bit machine. Your manager has asked you for a list of some of the server roles that can be installed on a Server Core installation. Which of the following apply?

A. DHCP

B. DNS

C. Hyper-V

D. Streaming Media Services

E. Web Services (IIS)

F. All of the above

13. You are the network administrator for an organization that has decided to install Hyper-V onto a machine loaded with Windows Server 2008 Server Core. You need to install Hyper-V from the command prompt. Which of the following is the proper way to install Hyper-V from the command prompt?

A. `start /x setup Microsoft-Hyper-V`

B. `start /i start Microsoft-Hyper-V`

C. `start /a srvsetup Microsoft-Hyper-V`

D. `start /w ocsetup Microsoft-Hyper-V`

14. Your organization has decided to purchase a new computer to install Microsoft Windows Server 2008 Server Core with Hyper-V. You currently have an older machine that is running Hyper-V. You install Hyper-V onto the new machine and you now need to remove Hyper-V from the previous computer. What is the command prompt command that removes the Hyper-V role?

A. `start /w ocsetup Microsoft-Hyper-V /uninstall`

B. `start /w ocsetup Microsoft-Hyper-V /remove`

C. `start /w ocsetup Microsoft-Hyper-V /delete`

D. `start /w ocsetup Microsoft-Hyper-V /kill`

15. You are the administrator of a large organization with multiple servers. You have decided to monitor the usage levels of your servers. You realize that your servers are working at an average of less than 15 percent capacity. You want to consolidate your server workload by using Hyper-V. Which Microsoft application can help you consolidate your servers by suggesting workload placement using Hyper-V?

A. System Control Machine Manager

B. Hyper-V Control Manager

C. System Center Virtual Machine Manager

D. Virtual Control Center

16. You are the network administrator for a small organization that has decided to upgrade all servers from Windows Server 2003 to Windows Server 2008. You purchase a new 64-bit computer system on which you need to load Active Directory. You install Windows Server 2008 Server Core as the operating system. What is the command to install Active Directory?

A. `ADInstall`

B. `ADPromo`

C. `DCInstall`

D. `DCPromo`

17. You are the network administrator for a mid-sized toilet maker. You have a server that has Windows Server 2008 Server Core installed as the operating system. You need to add a new user named Will Panek (wpanek) to the Stellacon domain. What is the command to create the new user in the Stellacon domain?

A. `net create <Stellacon \wpanek> /add *`

B. `net modify <Stellacon \wpanek> /add *`

C. `net user <Stellacon \wpanek> /add *`

D. `net account <Stellacon \wpanek> /add *`

18. You are a network administrator who is considering using SCVMM. The owner of the company asks you to list some of the benefits of this product. Which of the following are benefits of SCVMM? (Choose all that apply.)

A. Support for VMs running on Windows Server 2008

B. Multivendor virtualization platform support

C. Performance and resource optimization

D. Host cluster support for high availability virtual machines

19. You work for an organization that currently has 300 Windows Vista machines and 5 Windows Server 2003 machines. You have decided to add a new Windows Server 2008 Server Core machine that is going to be the DHCP server for the entire network. After you install Server Core and DHCP, you notice that the DHCP service did not start. How do you start the DHCP service from the command prompt?

A. `service start dhcpserver`

B. `net start dhcpserver`

C. `start service dhcpserver`

D. `start dhcpserver service`

20. You are the network administrator for a large organization that has decided to use Microsoft Hyper-V with failover clustering. You are trying to set up the machines for the cluster; how should you configure the operating system?

A. Windows Server 2008 domain controller

B. Windows Server 2008 member server

C. Windows Server 2003 domain controller

D. Windows Server 2003 member server

Answers to Review Questions

1. **B.** The first thing you should always do before installing any new hardware or software is evaluate your network. Based on network needs, this helps determine your hardware purchases.

2. **C.** The Microsoft Assessment and Planning (MAP) tool will locate machines on your network and do a full inventory of these machines. MAP will then tell you which computers can be upgraded and which computers cannot.

3. **A, B, C, D.** All four of these methods are used by MAP to help locate computers on your network. Also, you can manually enter computer names and credentials.

4. **A, B, C, D.** All of these answers can be scenario-generated reports. MAP gives you the ability to generate six scenario types. These scenarios allow you to determine how to upgrade or implement hardware and software.

5. **B, C, D.** To run MAP, you must have other supporting software, including Microsoft SQL Server 2005 Express, Microsoft Word (2003 with SP1 or 2007), and Microsoft Excel (2003 with SP1 or 2007).

6. **D.** The Windows hypervisor is a thin layer of software that sits between the hardware and the Windows Server 2008 operating system. This thin layer allows one physical machine to run multiple operating systems in different Hyper-V virtual machines at the same time. The hypervisor is the mechanism that is responsible for maintaining isolation between the various Hyper-V partitions.

7. **B, C, D.** The CPU/BIOS for a machine with Hyper-V needs to have some special requirements and settings before you install Hyper-V. Hyper-V has to be installed on a 64-bit processor, and the system has to support virtualization and enabled DEP. The processor also needs to be 1.4GHZ at minimum; Microsoft recommends 2GHz or faster.

8. **A.** Microsoft's Storage Manager for SANs is a utility that will allow you to create and manage logical unit numbers (LUNs) for fiber channel and iSCSI disk drive subsystems that support VDS.

9. **B.** Server Manager is a Microsoft Management Console (MMC) snap-in that allows an administrator to view information about server configuration and the status of roles that are installed. It also features links for adding and removing features and roles.

10. **B.** You must install Hyper-V onto a Windows Server 2008 full installation if you want to have the ability to use GUI snap-ins. Windows Server 2008 Server Core has no GUI interface. Hyper-V cannot be installed on Windows Server 2003 or 32-bit versions of Windows Server 2008.

11. **A.** A new feature to Windows Server 2008 is called Server Core. The Server Core installation gives an organization the ability to have a minimal environment for running specific server roles, such as a domain controller, which in turn reduces the attack surface for those server roles. A smaller attack surface helps reduce the chances of being hacked by anyone inside or outside your organization.

12. F. The Windows Server 2008 Server Core can have any of these services installed onto the machine. The Server Core installation can also include Active Directory Domain Services, Active Directory Lightweight Directory Services, File Services, and Print Services.

13. D. The `ocsetup` command sets up the Windows Server 2008 Hyper-V role from the Server Core command prompt. The switch /w prevents the command prompt from returning until the installation of Hyper-V is completed. Without the /w, you would not know when the role was installed completely.

14. A. If you need to remove any of the roles from the Windows Server 2008 Server Core installation, you can use the `/uninstall` switch at the end of the `ocsetup` command. The switch /w prevents the command prompt from returning until the command is finished being executed.

15. C. SCVMM can consolidate server workloads using virtual machines. By allowing virtual servers to handle more of the workload, you will need fewer servers, thus lowering equipment, space, and power requirements. SCVMM will execute data analysis of several factors before making suggestions for server workload placement.

16. D. DCPromo is the command that you need to use to install Active Directory onto a server. You can use `DCPromo` on a Server Core or full installation of Windows Server 2008.

17. C. You need to use the `net user` command to create and modify user accounts on computers. The `/add` command adds a user to the domain. You can also use the `/delete` command to remove a user. The * switch produces a prompt for the password.

18. A, B, C, D. Since SCVMM is a Microsoft product, it will take advantage of the Windows Server 2008 Server services, such as Active Directory. Some of the benefits of SCVMM 2008 are support for VMs running on Windows Server 2008, multivendor virtualization platform support, performance and resource optimization, and host cluster support for high availability virtual machines.

19. B. There are two ways to start a service from the command line. One way is with the `net start` command; the other is the `sc start` command.

20. B. Microsoft recommends that you make a failover server a member server and not a domain controller. Hyper-V needs to be installed on Windows Server 2008 and not Server 2003.

Configuring Hyper-V

MICROSOFT EXAM OBJECTIVES COVERED IN THIS CHAPTER:

✓ **Managing and Optimizing the Hyper-V Server**

   ※ This objective may include but is not limited to: VHD (virtual hard disk) location, snapshot location, System Center Virtual Machine Manager (SCVMM), Authorization Manager, release key.

✓ **Configure Virtual Networking**

   ※ This objective may include but is not limited to: Virtual Network Manager tool, SCVMM, virtual switches, VLAN tagging, external/private/internal switches.

✓ **Configure Remote Administration**

   ※ This objective may include but is not limited to: Hyper-V manager on Windows Server 2008 and Windows Vista, WMI, WinRM, firewall settings, RDP.

Hyper-V, like any other software product, should be configured after installation so that you can maximize the virtualization performance.

This chapter begins by exploring some of the Hyper-V terms and concepts needed to configure Hyper-V. We will also discuss the configuration of virtual networking, including how to configure your virtual and nonvirtual switches, the Virtual Network Manager, and the System Center Virtual Machine Manager (SCVMM).

Next you will learn how to configure Hyper-V remotely using Windows Server 2008 and Windows Vista. We will cover the Microsoft Windows Firewall and Remote Desktop Protocol (RDP). Finally, we will discuss Windows Management Instrumentation (WMI) and Windows Remote Management (WinRM), and you will learn how using these utilities can better help you configure and maintain your Hyper-V environment.

So let's begin by exploring some of the tools and techniques you need to configure the Hyper-V role properly.

Understanding the Configuration Tools and Techniques

It is always important to configure any application properly to allow that application to work at peak performance. Hyper-V is no different. By configuring Hyper-V, you are reducing the chances that any problems will occur down the road.

Configuring an application can be the most important and sometimes the most difficult task that you can complete. The time that you spend on the configuration now will be time that you save on fixing the application later.

Hyper-V has many variables that can you configure, from the virtual hard disk to the memory used for the virtual machine. First let's define some terms and concepts you should be familiar with.

Host Server (Parent Partition)   The host server is the Windows Server 2008 machine that hosts the Hyper-V role and executes the Hyper-V virtual machines. The host server is also known as the parent partition.

Guest (Child Partition)   These are the containers (virtual machines) that run the guest operating system. The virtual machines are referred to as the *guest*, or child, partition. These virtual machine systems can have operating systems running other than Microsoft.

Virtual Hard Disk (VHD)   When you're installing an OS onto a computer, you determine the size and location of the hard disk that you want to install the operating system on. A *virtual hard disk (VHD)* is the same for the virtual environment. When you install a guest system using Hyper-V, the VHD is the hard disk space you are using for that install.

VMBus   The parent and the child partitions use a new high-speed communication protocol for Hyper-V hardware called VMBus. As you learned in Chapter 1, the Microsoft hypervisor handles the interaction between multiple virtual machines running on the same host. VMBus handles many of the hardware communications, such as disk, networking, video, and input/output communications.

Host Clustering   To make Hyper-V more available on your network, you can install and run the clustering role on one or more Hyper-V servers. This type of clustering is called host clustering. An advantage of clustering is that if one of the servers goes down, the other servers in the cluster take up the extra load and continue to allow the cluster to run properly. (Hyper-V clustering is covered in full detail in Chapter 7, "Hyper-V and Failover Clusters.")

Operating System Partitioning   When setting up Hyper-V, you normally create two partitions: the parent and the child partitions. The parent partition manages the memory and virtual devices; the child partitions are the virtual machines. You can have as many child partitions as needed, but your Hyper-V can have only one parent partition. The child partitions can contain both 32-bit and 64-bit operating systems loaded on the virtual machine.

Now that you have a few basic terms and concepts down, let's start our Hyper-V configuration with VHDs.

Understanding Virtual Hard Disks

There are two main types of virtual hard disks (VHDs): fixed-size or dynamic. When setting up either of these VHDs, you determine the size of the VHD, and that will represent how large the disk will appear to the virtual machines. The maximum size that you can choose for either VHD is 2,040GB.

Fixed-size VHDs have a set amount of hard disk space and that amount does not change. For example, if I designate 16GB to a fixed-size VHD, then the VHD will take up all 16GB on the hard disk immediately—regardless of how much the system is actually using.

Dynamic VHDs only use the amount of space that is currently being used for the VHD. For example, if a dynamic VHD has 16GB allotted to it but it's only using 7GB, only 7GB will be used by the system. This is how you want to set up your VHD if hard drive space is limited on your server. However, the fixed-size VHD option offers better performance by eliminating the fragmentation associated with a growing file. Figure 3.1 shows the Choose Disk Type screen of the New Virtual Hard Disk wizard.

When setting up your VHD, there is a third option you can choose called *differencing*. A differencing disk is configured in a parent-child relationship with another disk that is left intact. This approach allows you to change the operating system or data without affecting the parent disk.

FIGURE 3.1   Choosing the VHD disk type

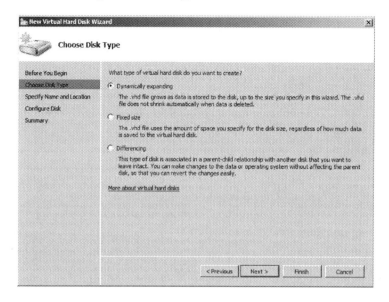

Differencing can help Hyper-V by reducing hard drive space on a host server but can be difficult to manage due to the parent-child relationship. The parent-child relationship may also cause performance issues. Figure 3.2 shows the Configure Disk screen of the New Virtual Hard Disk wizard. Differencing disks will be discussed in further detail in Chapter 4, "Creating Virtual Machines."

FIGURE 3.2   Configuring differencing to use a parent disk

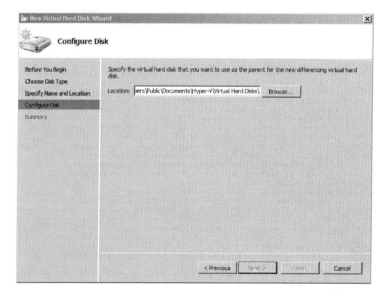

You need to establish a default location for storing your VHDs (see Figure 3.3). Depending on your network and your hard drive setups, this can be a critical decision. Do you want to store your VHDs locally on the server, or on the network? Keep in mind that the host system has the ability to store VHD files on an accessible file system, internal hard drive, or a storage area network (SAN).

FIGURE 3.3 Specifying the default storage location for VHDs

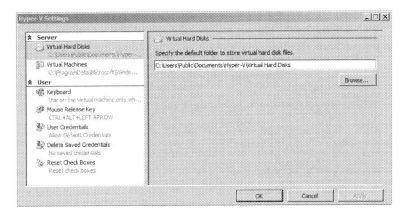

This setting will be your default location for all VHDs from this point on, but you have the ability to change the location of any VHD even after this setting is configured. Figure 3.4 shows the installation of a new VHD and the option to change the storage location of the VHD.

FIGURE 3.4 Setting a storage location for a new VHD

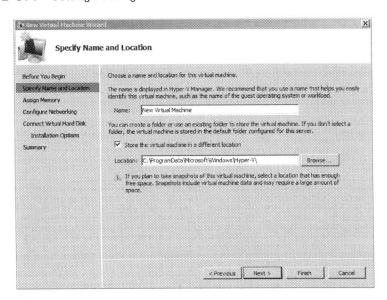

Exercise 3.1 shows you how to set the default VHD file location in the Hyper-V Manager.

EXERCISE 3.1

Setting the Default Storage Location for VHDs

1. Choose Start ≻ Administrative Tools ≻ Hyper-V Manager.

2. In the Hyper-V Manager, click on your Computer Name, and then in the Actions pane, click Hyper-V Server Settings

3. In the Hyper-V Settings dialog box, click Virtual Hard Disks.

4. In the field "Specify the default folder to store virtual hard disk files," type the folder name, such as **C:\Sybex\VHD**, and then click Apply.

5. In the Hyper-V Settings dialog box, click Virtual Machines.

6. In the field "Specify the default folder to store virtual machine files," type the folder name, such as **C:\Sybex\VM**, and then click OK.

Using Pass-Through Disk Access

You may be familiar with Microsoft's earlier virtualization products, Windows Virtual Server and Virtual PC. Hyper-V, Microsoft's newest virtualization technology, has many new features in the area of virtual machine storage. One such feature is called *pass-through disk access.*

This feature allows Hyper-V to work without the use of VHDs. Virtual machines can access a file system directly through the use of pass-through disk access, thus eliminating the need for VHDs. VHDs are inaccessible to nonvirtualized systems due to the VHD formatting. Pass-through disk access helps solve this problem by allowing the virtual machine to directly access the writable file system. Another advantage is that there is no 2040GB limitation as with VHDs.

So here is another decision for you to make when setting up the Hyper-V storage system: do you use pass-through disk access or VHDs? You must decide whether it's more important that virtual machines and applications be able to access the disk directly or that you take advantage of the VHD features, such as VHD snapshots (discussed further in this section), differencing, or dynamic VHDs.

After you make your decision, you have to specify how you want to show your host disks to your guest machines. You have the ability to show your disks as either virtual ATA devices or virtual SCSI devices (see Figure 3.5). The disk type does not have to match the way you decide to show the disk to the guest. For example, a SCSI disk can be shown to the guest as an IDE disk and an IDE disk can be shown as a SCSI disk.

FIGURE 3.5   Hard disk settings

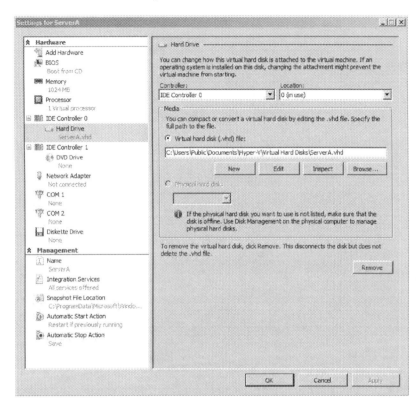

The requirements of the guest operating system determine how you will set the drive types. IDE hard drives are drives that the guest system can boot from, but with an IDE drive you can only have four virtual disks (two disks on two controllers). You can set up 256 SCSI virtual disks (64 disks on four controllers), but the system cannot boot up from the virtualized BIOS. If you need your guest systems to have more than four disks, you must use SCSI; if you need your guest systems to boot to the virtual disk, use IDE.

> When setting up your disk types, you have the ability to use both IDE and SCSI at the same time. If needed, you can boot off the IDE drive and use the SCSI drives for storage or applications.

Configuring Virtual Machine Snapshots

A feature that has become common in the Microsoft Windows world is volume shadow copies. Creating backups of open files is a challenge that all IT personnel have dealt with in their careers. Typically, backup software can't back up files while they are open.

Microsoft includes the Shadow Copy feature with most of its newer operating systems. Before this feature was released, if you ran your Microsoft Exchange mail server 24 hours a day, you had to purchase a special component of your backup software to back up your open Exchange files. Now, you can use the Shadow Copy feature to "take a picture" of the open files and then copy the picture to a location for recoverability.

Using Hyper-V, you can enjoy the advantages of shadow copies with your virtual machines. Hyper-V allows you to set up *virtual machine snapshots*. Hyper-V takes a "snapshot" of your virtual machine and places that copy in a specified location. Using the dialog box shown in Figure 3.6 (see Exercise 3.2 for a step-by-step), you specify the default location for these snapshots.

FIGURE 3.6 Snapshot File Location

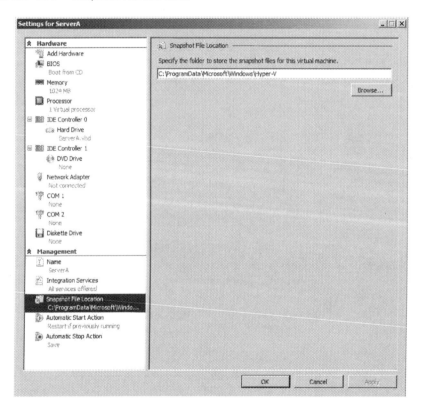

Having virtual machine snapshots gives you a few very important benefits. You have a backup copy of the virtual machine in case of a crash or error, and can quickly recover from any major problems. Also, this feature allows you to make major configuration changes to the operating system (such as adding new software or running updates) without worry. If the installation causes any problems, you can just revert back to a previous snapshot.

> ⊕ **Real World Scenario**
>
> ### Configuration Changes on Your Servers
>
> For all the years I've been in the IT field, one thing that has always amazed me about Micro-soft is their patches and updates. I like Microsoft products and I rarely complain about how they work, but one thing that has always bothered me is their product testing. There have been multiple times where I have loaded a patch from Microsoft and had my computer crash. These days, I wait until a patch or update has been out a while to make sure the bugs are worked out before I load the patch or update onto my network computers.
>
> Hyper-V and virtual machine snapshots can help in this situation. Having the ability to revert back to a snapshot if a patch or update causes a problem can solve these issues. Also, Hyper-V can help because, as mentioned in Chapters 1 and 2, you can use a Hyper-V virtual machine environment just for testing. This way, the patches won't be placed on a live server or workstation, and it gives you the advantage as an administrator to evaluate the update before taking it live.

Exercise 3.2 shows you how to set the default location for your snapshots. Keep in mind that once your snapshot is created, you can't change the folder location unless the snapshot is stopped.

EXERCISE 3.2

Setting the Default Snapshot Locations

1. Select Start ➤ Administrative Tools ➤ Hyper-V Manager.

2. In the Hyper-V Manager, click on your computer name in the console tree, and then in the Actions pane, click Hyper-V Server Settings.

3. In the Hyper-V Settings dialog box, click Snapshot File Location.

4. In the field "Specify the default folder to Virtual Machine Configuration files," type a folder name, such as **C:\Sybex\snapshot**, and then click Apply.

Hyper-V allows you to manipulate a virtual hard disk offline using a command-line utility called VHDMount. By using VHDMount, you can work directly on an offline VHD and do maintenance without having to power on the virtual machine.

When you use VHDMount, an undo disk is automatically created by the system. This undo disk records any changes that are completed to the mounted drive. You can use the undo disk to accept or reject the changes.

Configuring Hyper-V Server Settings

We just finished setting up our default snapshot locations and our default VHD locations, but there are many other server changes that can help optimize your Hyper-V environment.

BIOS   When setting up the BIOS for your Hyper-V server, the first thing you can specify is whether the numbers lock (Num Lock) is on or off by default when the Hyper-V server starts (see Figure 3.7).

You can also specify the Startup Order for the operating system. This is the order that your boot devices will be checked to start the operating system. You can boot from a CD, hard drive, network adapter, or a floppy disk.

FIGURE 3.7   Hyper-V server BIOS settings

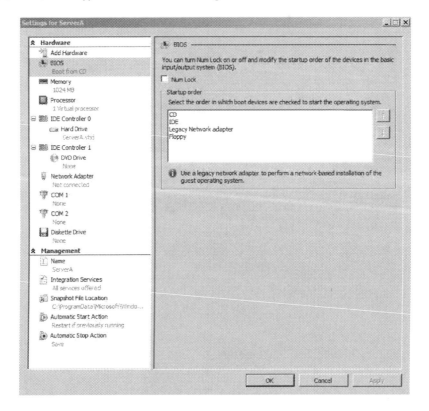

Memory   You need to have enough memory to handle the workload of the system and some extra for a buffer. A virtual machine only uses memory when it is either running or is paused. To configure the memory option, you must make sure the virtual machine is turned off.

Processors   The number of physical processors you have on your machine determines the number of virtual processors you can set on the Hyper-V server (see Figure 3.8). Other processor configuration options are related to resource control and process functionality. Again, to configure these options, make sure the virtual machine is turned off.

FIGURE 3.8   Processor settings

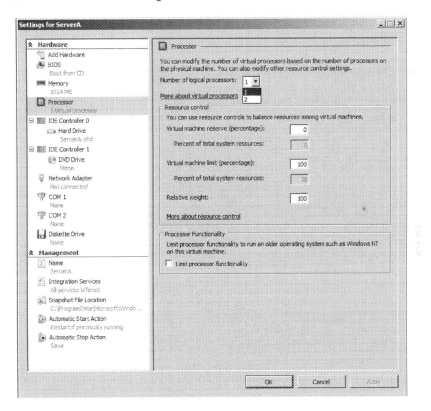

Virtual Machine Reserve (Percentage)   Here you specify how much of the hardware resources you want to reserve for Hyper-V. This setting will guarantee that the hardware that you reserve for Hyper-V will be available to the virtual machines.

Virtual Machine Limit (Percentage)   This option allows you to define the total maximum amount of resources that the virtual machine can use. No matter how many virtual machines are running, this setting always applies.

Relative Weight   This value specifies how resources will be allocated to the current virtual machine when more than one virtual machine is running. When multiple virtual machines are running at the same time, they are all competing for the use of the machine's hardware resources. The Relative Weight setting helps allocate these resources to the virtual machines.

Processor Functionality This option allows you to limit the processor functionality so that you can load an older operating system (such as Windows NT 4.0) on the virtual machine.

IDE Controller Here you specify your hard drive or DVD drive. You have the ability to add a controller at this screen. After the drive has been attached to one of your controllers, you can configure the hard drive to use either the virtual hard disk or the physical hard disk.

Hard Drive In this section you configure how the virtual hard disk is linked to the virtual machine. You can create, edit, remove, and inspect the VHD file (see Figure 3.9).

FIGURE 3.9 Hard disk configuration options

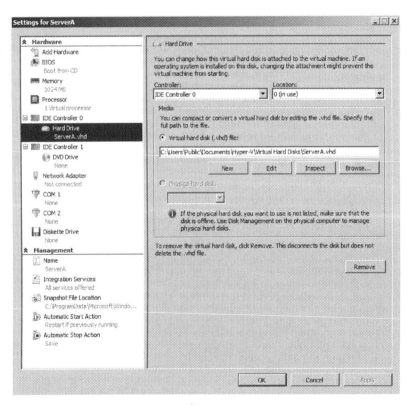

The Network Adapter section of the server settings will be discussed later in the chapter, in the section "Configuring Virtual Networking."

COM Ports This setting allows you to set up a named pipe that enables the physical computer to communicate through the use of a virtual COM port. There are two COM (COM1 and COM2) ports that you can configure in Hyper-V.

Diskette Drive   This setting allows you to set up a diskette drive in the Hyper-V environment.

Name   Name is the first option that you can configure under the management section. This screen (see Figure 3.10) allows you to rename the server and also record notes about the virtual machine.

FIGURE 3.10   The Name screen of the server settings

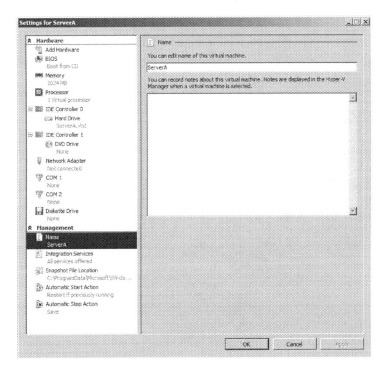

Integration Services   This screen (Figure 3.11) allows you to choose which services in Hyper-V you would like to offer to the virtual machines. Table 3.1 lists some of these services.

TABLE 3.1   Integration Services Options

Service	Explanation
Operating System Shutdown	Allows an administrator to properly shut down a guest operating system by using the Virtualization Management Console
Time Synchronization	Ensures that the time is synchronized between the host system and the guest operating system

TABLE 3.1   Integration Services Options *(continued)*

Service	Explanation
Heartbeat	Verifies that the guest operating system is working properly and is not currently locked up (hung up)
Backup (Volume Snapshot)	Helps create a backup or snapshot of the virtual machines

FIGURE 3.11   Integration Services screen

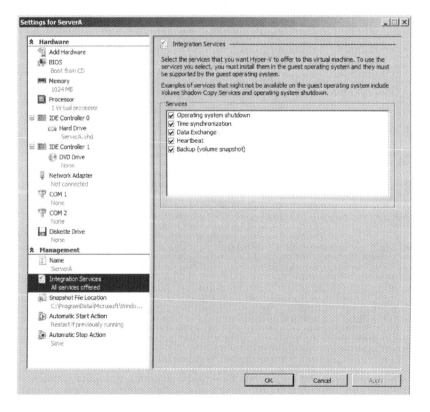

Automatic Start Action   This screen (see Figure 3.12) allows you to configure how the virtual machine is going to react when the physical machine is started. When the machine starts, you can have the virtual machine either do nothing or automatically start if it was running when the service stopped, or you can always start the virtual machine automatically. You also have the ability to set an automatic start delay. A start delay can help reduce resource contention among virtual machines.

FIGURE 3.12 Automatic Start Action screen

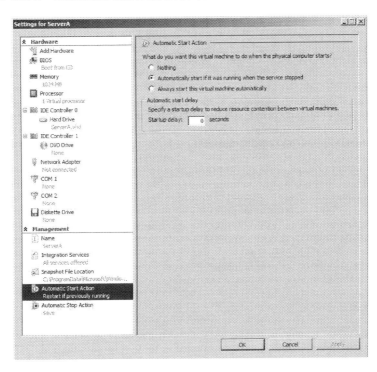

Automatic Stop Action This setting allows you to determine how the virtual machine will shut down when the physical machine shuts down. You can choose one of three options: Save The Virtual Machine State, Turn Off The Virtual Machine, or Shut Down The Guest Operating System.

Release Keys Release keys are the key combinations that release tasks. For example, pressing Ctrl+Alt+Delete starts the Task Manager or Windows Security box (logons), but that will not work in Hyper-V. To start the same tasks in Hyper-V, you need to press Ctrl+Alt+End. Table 3.2 shows you some of the Windows key combinations and what the corresponding Hyper-V key combinations are to start the same task.

TABLE 3.2 Key Combinations

Windows Key Combination	Virtual Machine Key Combination	Task Accomplished
Ctrl+Alt+Delete	Ctrl+Alt+End	Opens Task Manager or Windows Security dialog box
Alt+Esc	Alt+Insert	Cycles through open programs

TABLE 3.2   Key Combinations *(continued)*

Windows Key Combination	Virtual Machine Key Combination	Task Accomplished
Ctrl+Esc	Alt+Home	Displays Windows Start menu
None	Ctrl+Alt+Left Arrow	Releases the keyboard and mouse from virtual machine.
None	Ctrl+Alt+Pause	Opens virtual machine in full screen (also releases full screen)

Setting these configuration settings will help you manage your virtual environment more efficiently. Next, let's take a look at setting role-based access control.

Using Authorization Manager

Authorization Manager allows you to integrate role-based access control into applications. This gives you the flexibility to assign application access to users based on their job functions. Since Hyper-V is a server role, you can use Authorization Manager to work with Hyper-V. For example, users in your domain who are not administrators can still be given permissions to create and modify virtual machines in your organization. You also have the ability to specify certain users to manage only certain virtual machines.

To set up Authorization Manager, you must first create an authorization store, where the role-based access permissions will reside. The permissions can be stored in any one of the following:

- Active Directory Domain Services (AD DS)
- Active Directory Lightweight Directory Services (AD LDS)
- SQL databases
- XML files

If you choose to use AD DS, the function level must be at the Windows Server 2003 level. Function levels are discussed in detail in *MCTS: Windows Server 2008 Active Directory Configuration Study Guide* by William Panek and James Chellis (Sybex, 2008).

Because Authorization Manager provides role-based access to Windows applications, any application that needs role-based authorization can use this tool. Authorization Manager gives you a centralized location to record all your assigned access and their corresponding application.

After you have installed and configured Authorization Manager, you can use scripts to control how Authorization Manager works. These scripts, called authorization rules, allow you to configure specific control over the way access is given throughout your organization.

Depending on your network setup and how long you have been in the industry, you may have been in a situation where multiple applications have had multiple sets of permission or access. Years ago, there was no centralized application that showed you all your users and their corresponding role-based access to applications. You would have to go application to application and figure out which users had what access.

The problem becomes difficult when you have multiple administrators doing the same job. Now you may have different administrators assigning different access to multiple people. Also, if your IT department is like many around the world, your department almost never documents anything unless it's mandatory.

This is where Authorization Manager can be helpful. Authorization Manager gives you a centralized location for all administrators to record role-based application access.

Folks in the IT field often don't like to document IT issues or items. As a consultant and instructor, I have heard this many times: "I don't document; if they fire me, let them figure out their own network." I understand what many IT people are thinking, but it is important to document so that later you can go back and see what you did. You may fix an item and six months later come across the same item again; documenting what you did may save you many hours of work and frustration.

When setting up Authorization Manager's role-based application access, there are two categories of roles that are specifically used:

User Authorization Roles   These are roles set up through Authorization Manager that are based on the user's job function. You configure role-based access to users to allow them to perform their day-to-day tasks. For example, you might define an accountant role that would include the right to authorize transactions for the organization.

Computer Configuration Roles   These are roles set up through Authorization Manager that are based on the computer's function. You configure role-based access to a machine for specific tasks to be done. For example, you can configure a machine so that it can be designated as a domain controller, web server, or file server.

When setting up Authorization Manager, you can specify which groups can receive authorization policies. The types of groups are as follows:

Windows Users and Groups   This group includes the Active Directory users, computers, and built-in group objects. The Windows users and groups are used not only for Authorization Manager but throughout the Microsoft domain model.

Application Group   The Application group consists of users, computers, and other security groups in Authorization Manager. This group is an Authorization Manager group only; it is not a group of applications but a group of security objects.

LDAP Query Group   This is a type of Application group whose membership is dynamic. This group uses Lightweight Directory Access Protocol (LDAP) queries to help determine, as needed, the membership of the group.

Basic Application Groups   This is a type of Application group that is specific to Authorization Manager. This group type allows you to specify the members of the group, but it also allows you to specify who is not a member of the group.

Business Rule Application Group   This is a type of Application group whose members are created by a script (using VBScript or JScript, for example) at application runtime. This group allows you the flexibility to determine the criteria of the group membership through the use of a script.

Windows Server 2008 includes many new features for the Authorization Manager Microsoft Management Console (MMC) snap-in:

- Authorization stores that can be stored in SQL databases, AD DS, AD LDS, or an XML file

- Business rule groups (groups whose membership is configured by a script at application runtime)

- Custom object pickers

- API improvements

- Improved auditing

When you are using business and authorization rules in Authorization Manager, you set the rules by configuring registry settings. In earlier versions the rules were enabled by default, but this has changed in Windows Server 2008 Authorization Manager, where the rules are disabled by default. Authorization Manager is available for all editions of Windows Server 2008 in both 32- and 64-bit versions.

In Exercise 3.3 we will start using Authorization Manager by installing the MMC snap-in. MMC is the application that all other Microsoft applications run through. For example, there is an MMC snap-in for DNS, DHCP, and Active Directory. Knowing that most administrative tasks run using the MMC allows you to customize and configure custom administrative console windows. Let's say you are responsible for DNS, DHCP, and Authorization Manager; you can configure an MMC snap-in that has all of these applications in one location.

EXERCISE 3.3

Installing Authorization Manager

1. Start the Microsoft Management Console by clicking Start ➢ Run. Then type **MMC** and click OK.

EXERCISE 3.3 *(continued)*

2. Select File ➢ Add/Remove Snap-in.

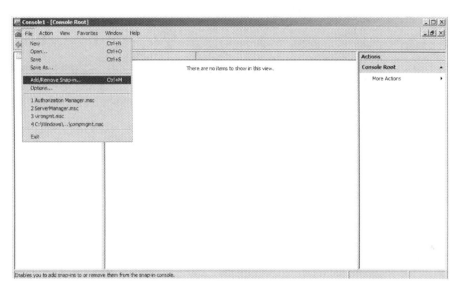

3. In the Available Snap-ins list on the left, select Authorization Manager and click the Add button. Authorization Manager should appear in the Selected Snap-ins window on the right. Click OK.

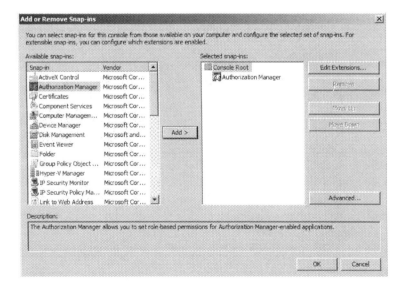

EXERCISE 3.3 *(continued)*

4.   In the window on the left, click on Authorization Manager. Once it's highlighted, select Action ≻ New Window From Here.

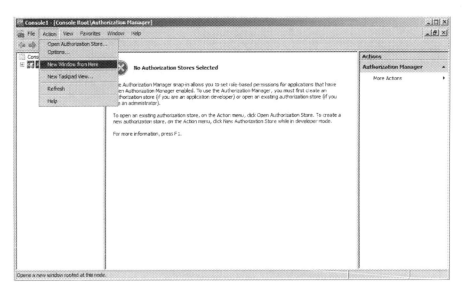

5.   Authorization Manager should now be the only item in the window on the left. Choose File ≻ Save. In the File Name box, type **Authorization Manager.msc**. Save the file in the Administrative Tools folder by choosing Administrative Tools from the Save In drop-down list.

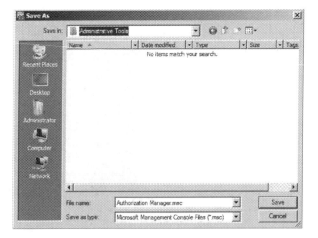

6.   Close all MMC windows.

Once the installation of Authorization Manager is complete, it's time to configure Authorization Manager. One of the first things that we have to do is create a new authorization store. To do this, we must be in the Developer mode of Authorization Manager. In Exercise 3.4 we begin by changing the mode type and then create a new authorization store.

EXERCISE 3.4

Configuring Authorization Manager

1. To start the Authorization Manager, click Start ➤ All Programs ➤ Administrative Tools, and then click `Authorization Manager.msc`.

2. Once the application opens, click on Authorization Manager in the window on the left. Right-click and choose Options.

3. Make sure that the Developer mode radio button is selected and click OK.

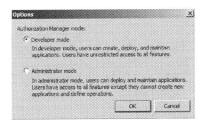

4. To use Authorization Manager, you must create an authorization store. Select Action ➤ New Authorization Store.

5. In the resulting dialog box, make sure the XML File and Schema Version 2.0 radio buttons are selected. In the Store Name box, append **TestStore** to the end of c:\users\Administrator\Documents\ and click OK.

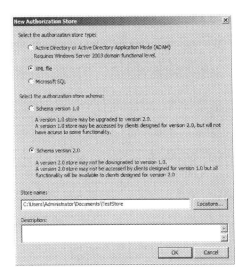

6. We need to now create an Application group. On the left-hand side, click the Groups folder under `TestStore.xml`. Right-click on the Groups folder and choose New Application Group.

7. In the Name field, type **TestGroup** and make sure the Basic Application Group radio button is selected. Click OK.

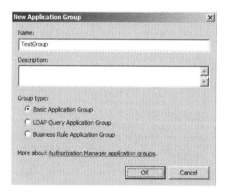

8. In the center window, select and then right-click the TestGroup group and choose Properties. Click the Members tab. In the Select Additional Members From box, make sure that Windows And Active Directory is selected, and click the Select button.

9. In the Enter The Object Names To Select box, choose a user on your machine and click the Check Names button. After the name is verified, click OK. As you can see here, we chose the Will Panek account for this example. Click OK again when you return to the TestGroup Properties screen.

10. Close the Authorization Manager MMC snap-in.

Authorization Manager can help any organization manage its virtual environment safely. But when it comes to the virtual environment, there are many more areas that we can configure to make virtualization run more efficiently. Let's take a look at one of the utilities that allows you to manage and configure your virtual world.

Introducing System Center Virtual Machine Manager

Microsoft has been using virtualization in the IT field for many years. To make it easier for IT personnel to do their jobs, over the years Microsoft has released applications that use wizards and templates.

Microsoft has also tried to improve the manageability of virtualization by implementing *System Center Virtual Machine Manager* (SCVMM). SCVMM is an easy-to-use and cost-effective application for administrators who are responsible for managing virtual networks. Since SCVMM works with the Windows Server 2008 technology, it allows you to configure and manipulate the physical and virtual machines, consolidate underutilized physical machines, and implement new virtual machines.

One of the advantages of SCVMM is that it provides a centralized location to manage your virtual environment. This allows administrators to manage and configure the virtual machines from one spot. The SCVMM has many other advantages including the following:

Windows Server 2008 Support   SCVMM takes full advantage of the Windows Server 2008 operating system and its advantages, which include Hyper-V and all of its benefits along with the Windows Server 2008 64-bit architecture. Windows Server 2008 also supports clustering support and attack hardening.

Multivendor Virtualization Support   One of the nice features of using SCVMM is the ability to support multivendor virtualization platforms. This allows the virtual machines to run operating systems other than Microsoft's. This gives your organization the flexibility to run applications that require non-Microsoft platforms.

Performance and Resource Optimization   A new feature is the Performance and Resource Optimization (PRO) utility. PRO can automatically react to failed or badly configured components. One nice advantage of PRO is that it also works with VMware, which allows you to manage your entire virtualized network no matter which virtualization platform you choose.

Clustering Support   SCVMM 2008 has new clustering support built in, which allows your organization to improve its availability for managing critical virtual machines. SCVMM can also detect Hyper-V host clusters and then manage those clusters as a single unit.

To install SCVMM, you must first install the .NET Framework (see Exercise 3.5).

EXERCISE 3.5

Installing the .NET Framework

1. Start the Server Manager application by clicking Start ➢ Administrative Tools ➢ Server Manager.

2. On the left-hand side, click the Features link.

3. On the right-hand side, click Add Feature.

4. Click the .NET Framework 3.0 Features check box.

5. An information box appears asking whether you want to install IIS as well. Click OK.

6. On the Select Features screen, click Next.

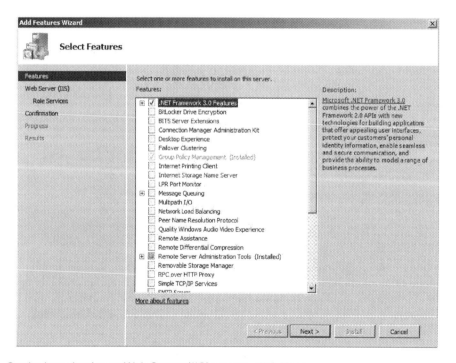

7. On the Introduction to Web Server (IIS) screen, click Next.

8. The Select Role Services screen appears; accept the defaults and click Next.

EXERCISE 3.5 *(continued)*

9. On the Confirmation screen, click Install.

10. On the Installation Results screen, make sure that all components installed success-
    fully and click Close. Close the Server Manager application.

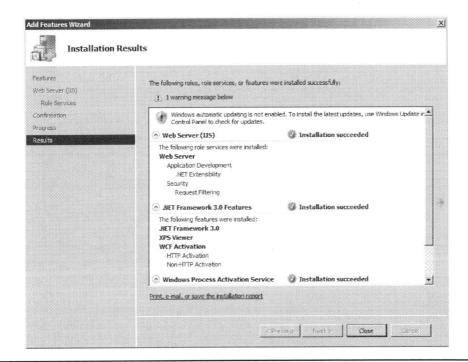

In Exercise 3.6 we will download and install SCVMM. Microsoft allows you to evaluate this product for 120 days. (The SCVMM will be discussed further throughout this
entire book.)

At the time that this book was written, the SCVMM 2008 version (vNext)
was just released in beta.

EXERCISE 3.6

Downloading and Installing SCVMM 2008

1. We need to download the SCVMM from Microsoft's website. On their web site you will need to register for the SCVMM download. Once you get to the download area, save the download to your computer . After the download is complete, run the SCVMM executable. Click the Install button, and files will begin to extract.

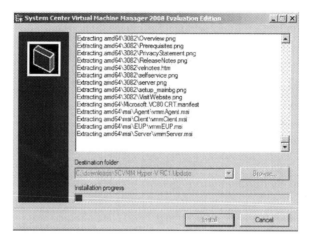

2. Once the files are extracted, the System Center Virtual Machine Manager 2008 Setup screen will appear. Click on the VMM Server setup link.

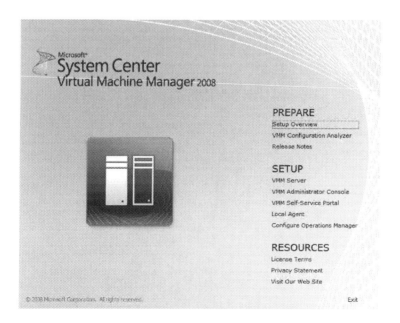

EXERCISE 3.6 *(continued)*

3. On the Microsoft License Terms screen, click the I Accept The Terms Of This Agreement radio licensing button and click Next.

4. You will see the Customer Experience Improvement Program screen next. This screen asks if you would like to participate in an improvement program to make the products better. You can decide how you want to respond. Read both questions and choose one of the radio buttons, and then click Next.

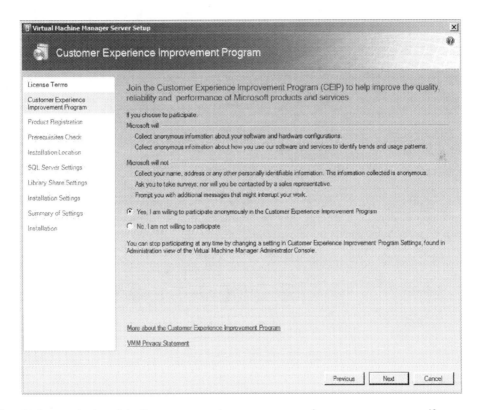

5. At the product registration screen, enter your name and your company name if you have one. Click Next.

6. The Prerequisites Check screen will appear next, and it will automatically check the hardware of your machine. After it verifies that you meet the minimum requirements, click Next.

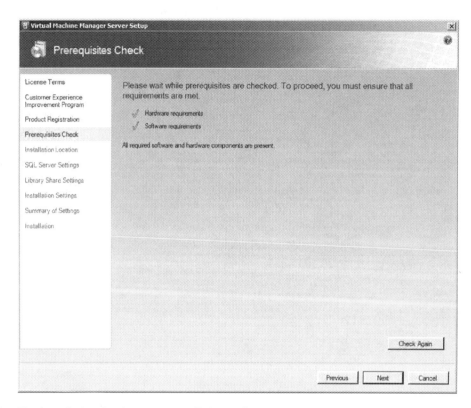

7. The Installation Settings screen will then ask you to choose an installation path for the install files. Accept the defaults and click Next.

8. The next screen asks you to either install SQL Server 2005 Express Edition or point to a previously installed version of SQL Server 2005. Click Install SQL Server 2005 Express Edition SP2 and then click Next.

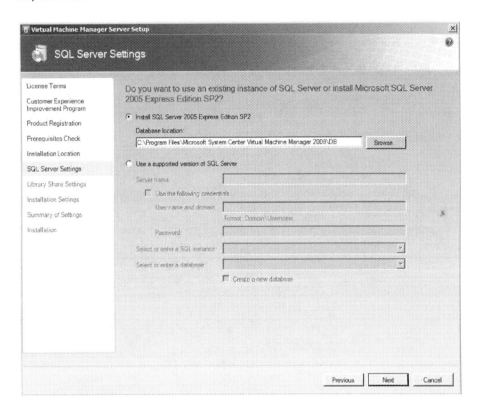

EXERCISE 3.6 *(continued)*

9. The Library Share Settings screen appears, which allows you to create a new library share or use an existing one. The library share is the location of the virtual machine library, and enables you to make resources available when creating new virtual machines. Choose the Create A New Library Share radio button and click Next.

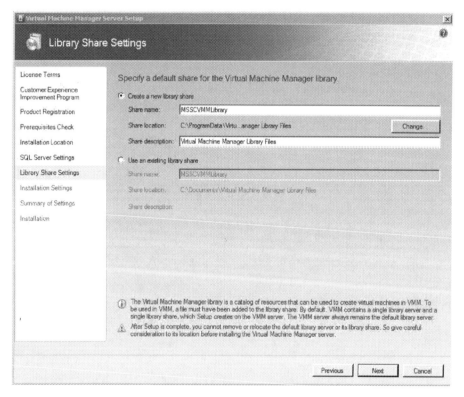

10. The Port Assignment screen asks you to choose which port numbers you want to use when setting up SCVMM. The default ports are 8100, 80, and 443. Port 80 is the HTTP default setting, and port 443 is secure HTTP (HTTPS). Accept the defaults and click Next.

EXERCISE 3.6 *(continued)*

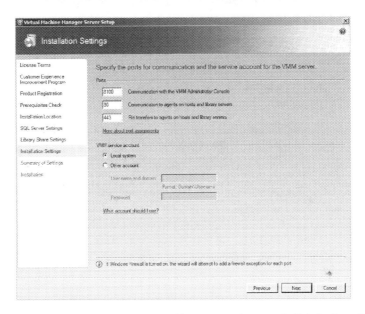

11. On the Summary Of Settings screen, verify your settings and click the Install button.

12. After the installation, make sure the Check For The Latest Virtual Machine Manager Updates check box is selected and then close the installation utility by clicking Close.

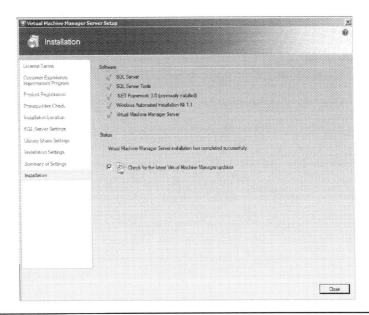

The SCVMM utility is a major component in your virtualization toolbox. It allows you to have one application that all administrators can use to configure your entire virtualized infrastructure. When you are setting up virtualization, one component that you must configure is your virtual network. So let's take a look at virtual networking.

Configuring Virtual Networking

When you set up virtualization, you are creating a virtual network. Before we discuss a virtual network, let's explore a normal network and see how it works. This will help you understand how a virtual network operates.

When setting up a network, you normally have a server machine and then you have client machines. The client machines connect to the server machine to access physical resources (files, folders, applications, etc.) or networking services (DNS, DHCP, etc.). You need physical machines to run the server operating systems. These machines must be able to handle the higher-end operating systems. When client machines connect to the server systems, they normally connect using the server name or the TCP/IP address of the server.

Virtual networking works a lot like normal networking except that you don't need as much hardware. You instead set up virtual servers that run on your network just like physical servers. The end users (clients) cannot tell the difference between a physical server and a virtual server.

When setting up virtual servers, you assign those virtual servers Ethernet adapters (just like a normal server) and give those Ethernet adapters TCP/IP addresses and Media Access Control (MAC) addresses. When setting up virtual network adapters, keep in mind that you can assign only one virtual network to a physical adapter. Also, wireless network adapters can't be used with Hyper-V virtual machines. You must be physically plugged into your network when setting up virtual networking. Your clients can still be wireless but not your Hyper-V virtual machines.

Utilities are available to help you with the configuration tasks. For example, Microsoft's *Virtual Network Manager,* shown in Figure 3.13, lets you add, remove, modify, and manage virtual networks from one location.

When discussing virtual networking, there are a few concepts that you need to understand. These concepts will not only help you set up a Hyper-V network, they are also covered in detail on the Hyper-V exam.

Virtual Local Area Network (VLAN)   A virtual local area network (VLAN) refers to the virtual network. It is the virtual network that the client machines access to get to their resources and network services.

Virtual Switches   Virtual switches help Hyper-V secure and control the network packets that enter and exit the virtual machines. You can limit the communications to or from a virtual machine and the VLAN. When setting up your network adapters, you can associate a single virtual switch with that adapter.

FIGURE 3.13 Virtual Network Manager

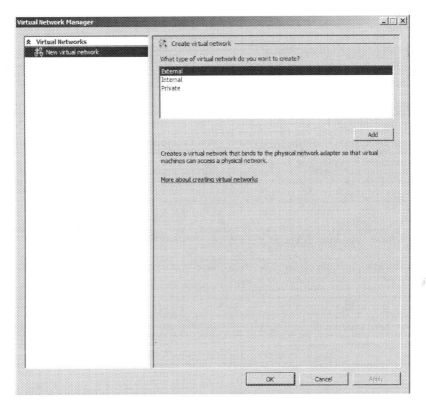

VLAN Tagging One problem that a virtual network could run into is that you have multiple virtual machines using the same physical network adapter. This is where VLAN tagging comes in handy. VLAN tagging allows multiple virtual machines on the same physical machine to use the same physical network adapter in that machine.

External/Private/Internal Settings When setting up your network adapters you have three choices. You can configure the communications to use the External setting, Internal setting, or the Private setting:

External This option creates a connection from the physical adapter and the virtual machine. It allows a virtual machine to access the network through the network adapter.

Internal This option allows communications between the virtualization servers and the virtual machines.

Private This option provides communications only among the virtual machines and allows the virtual machines to talk to each other only.

PXE Boot Hyper-V supports the Pre-Boot Execution (PXE) environment on the virtual network adapters that you configure. PXE booting allows a network card to be configured without the need of a hard drive or operating system. This enables the network cards to access a network without operating system assistance. The host network must be configured to use PXE if you want to take advantage of this feature.

Virtual Machine Quarantine One advantage to using Hyper-V on Windows Server 2008 is that you get to use many of the services offered with the Windows Server 2008 environment. One of those services is the Network Access Protection (NAP) feature. NAP enables you to quarantine machines that do not meet specific network or corporate policies. The noncompliant machines will not be permitted to access the network until they comply with the organization's policies. NAP is discussed in detail in *MCTS: Windows Server 2008 Network Infrastructure Configuration Study Guide* by William Panek, Tylor Wentworth, and James Chellis (Sybex, 2008).

In Exercise 3.7 we will use the Virtual Network Manager to configure a network adapter in Hyper-V. The Virtual Network Manager is included with the Hyper-V Manager.

EXERCISE 3.7

Creating a Virtual Network Connection

1. Start the Hyper-V Manager by clicking Start ➤ Administrative Tools ➤ Hyper-V Manager.

2. Open the Virtual Network Manager by clicking Virtual Network Manager in the right-hand window under Actions.

3. Make sure that External is highlighted under What Type Of Virtual Network Do You Want To Create? and click Add.

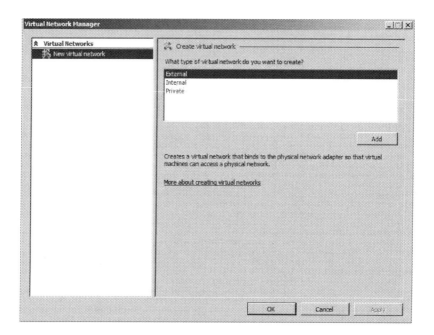

4. On the New Virtual Network screen, type **NIC1** in the Name field. In the Connection Type section, make sure the External radio button is selected and then choose your network adapter. Click OK.

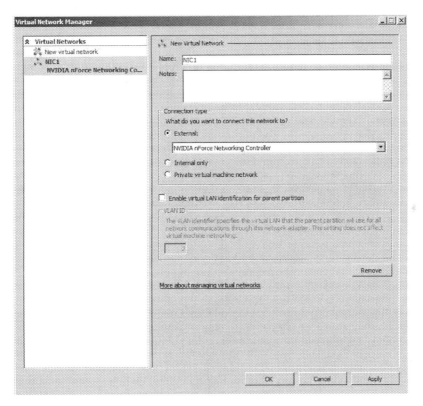

5. A warning box may appear stating that you are going to temporary lose your network connection while the virtual adapter is being configured. Click Yes.

6. Close the Hyper-V Manager.

We will discuss how to use and configure this new adapter we just created in Chapter 4, "Creating Virtual Machines."

A solid understanding of virtual networking is critical because the virtual environment runs within the virtual network. Being able to create virtual adapters and set up virtual networking are key components of setting up a virtual environment. Now let's take a look at configuring Hyper-V remotely.

Configuring Remote Administration

When you are working on a network, it may not always be possible to go directly to the Hyper-V server to make changes. You may have to connect to the server remotely instead.

In today's world, home is just an extension of work. In many organizations, working from home or being available on a 24-hour basis is a requirement. The last thing you want to do is drive all the way to the office because a service or server is not working properly. It is much easier to configure remote access.

You can configure the Hyper-V server in several ways. First, you can use another server to connect to the Hyper-V host server (see Figure 3.14). To do this, you just install the Hyper-V role to the server and then connect to the other server through the Hyper-V MMC snap-in.

FIGURE 3.14   Connecting to a Hyper-V server

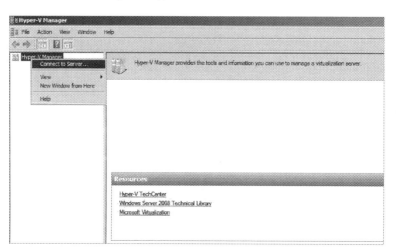

You can also install the Hyper-V Manager on the Windows Vista operating system as long as it has Service Pack 1 or higher installed. Once you install the Hyper-V management tool, it looks and feels just like the server's version of the Hyper-V Manager. To manage Hyper-V from Vista, you must download the Hyper-V management tools from the Microsoft website:

x86 Vista Update   Go to `http://www.microsoft.com/downloads/details.aspx?FamilyID=bf909242-2125-4d06-a968-c8a3d75ff2aa&DisplayLang=en`.

x64 Vista Update   Go to `http://www.microsoft.com/downloads/details.aspx?FamilyID=88208468-0ad6-47de-8580-085cba42c0c2&DisplayLang=en`.

Another way you can administer a Hyper-V server remotely is through the use of the Remote Desktop Protocol (RDP). RDP allows you to connect directly to the Hyper-V server and have an RDP session with the server. When using RDP, it looks as if you are sitting in front of the server console. Microsoft also offers a utility called the Virtual Machine Connection (`vmconnect.exe`) that uses the RDP protocol to establish a connection.

To use RDP, you may have to configure your router to allow port 3389. Port 3389 is the standard default RDP port. To connect to the server by using RDP, you need to use a RDP client. RDP is included with Windows Server, Windows Vista, and Windows XP.

An organization may also use the Virtualization Windows Management Instrumentation (WMI) tool to manage, create, and configure virtual machines. Virtualization WMI allows an administrator to:

- Manage server settings
- Control the status of virtual machines
- Create and configure virtual machines
- Create and configure virtual networking

To use the Virtualization WMI tool, you must use a scripting utility to configure and create WMIs. To write the WMI scripts, you can use C/C++, the Microsoft Visual Basic application, or a scripting language, including Windows PowerShell. If you are new to scripting or need additional scripting hints, go to Microsoft's website and visit the Script Center (http://www.microsoft.com/technet/scriptcenter/default.mspx).

Another utility that allows you to use scripts to configure Hyper-V is the Windows Remote Management (WinRM) utility. To configure Hyper-V, you can use the WinRM scripting objects, the WinRM command-line utility, or the Windows Remote Shell (WinRS) command-line utility.

No matter which way you decide to gain access remotely, one thing that you must configure is the Windows Firewall (see Figure 3.15). A firewall is a hardware or software device that helps stop unwanted intruders from accessing you network and doing any damage. The Windows Firewall application can stop you from connecting remotely if not configured properly. The Microsoft Firewall is included with the Windows Server 2008 operating system.

In Exercise 3.8 we will check the Windows Firewall and make sure that the Hyper-V and Remote Desktop Protocol (RDP) are both configured so that we can remotely connect to the Hyper-V server.

FIGURE 3.15   The Windows Firewall

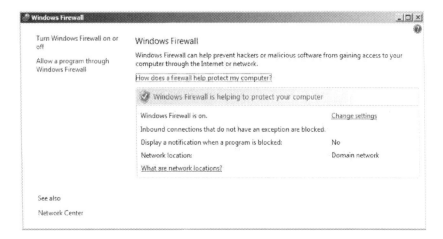

EXERCISE 3.8

Configuring the Windows Firewall

1. Open the Windows Firewall by clicking Start ➢ Control Panel ➢ Windows Firewall.

2. When the Windows Firewall opens, click the Change Settings link.

3. Make sure the Block All Incoming Connections check box is deselected. Click the Exceptions tab.

4. Select the Hyper-V and Remote Desktop check boxes.

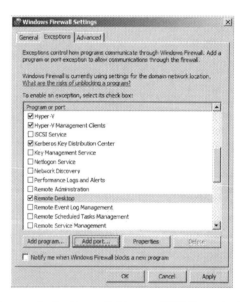

5. Click the Add Port button. In the Name field, type **RDP Port**. In the Port Number field, type **3389**. Select the TCP radio button and click OK.

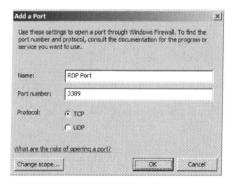

6. Click OK and close the Windows Firewall.

Real World Scenario

Configuring the Windows Firewall

Microsoft has included the Windows Firewall application on their operating systems for years now. I must admit that I am not the biggest fan of using the Windows Firewall on client machines. Many organizations will have their clients use the Microsoft Firewall throughout the company. I have had many issues with this in a real-world environment.

For example, I set up a printer a few years ago for a client, and once I installed the printer, it would not print. I worked on it for about an hour and no matter which drivers I installed and no matter what I did, I could not get the printer to print. While I was pulling my hair out for a simple printer issue, I decided to turn off the Windows Firewall on the client machine. As soon as I turned it off, the printer started to print. The printer needed to be bi-directional with the client machine and the Windows Firewall was stopping it from working properly. You can configure the firewall to allow this to work, but it's just an example of what can happen.

Firewalls are a must item in your organization (especially between your network and the Internet), but using the Windows Firewall on the client machines may cause issues when working with certain devices.

I want to make sure I stress that you *need* to have firewalls in your organization, but remember, you get what you pay for. Windows Firewall is free with the operating system. Invest in a good network firewall to protect your organization.

Summary

To configure Hyper-V properly, it is important to understand virtual hard disks (VHDs) and the various configuration options. There are three VHD types: fixed size, dynamic, and differencing. Fixed-size VHDs have a set amount of hard disk space, and that amount does not change. Dynamic VHDs only use the amount of space that is currently being used for the VHD. Differencing disks are configured in a parent-child relationship with another disk that stays intact.

Shadow copies are included with Hyper-V virtual machines, and they are called virtual machine snapshots. Virtual machine snapshots will take a copy of your virtual machine and place that copy in a specified location.

Pass-through disk access allows Hyper-V to work without VHDs. Virtual machines can access a file system directly through the use of this feature.

Authorization Manager allows administrators to integrate role-based access control to applications. The System Center Virtual Machine Manager (SCVMM) is an easy-to-use and cost-effective application for administrators who are responsible for managing virtual networks. SCVMM 2008 is a single application that allows you to configure and manage your entire virtual environment.

Virtual networking is the way you configure your virtual environment to work on the physical components to allow other machines to access your virtual resources through the physical network. In this chapter you learned about different virtual network concepts, such as VLANs, virtual switches, VLAN tagging, and the communication settings. One of the advantages that an administrator has is the ability to configure Hyper-V remotely.

In the next chapter we will discuss how to create and manage virtual machines.

Exam Essentials

Understand virtual hard disks (VHDs).   A VHD is a virtual hard drive that you install the guest operating system onto. During the installation of the guest operating system, you determine the size and location of the virtual hard disk that the virtual machine will use.

Be able to list the three VHD types.   There are three VHD types. Fixed-size VHDs have a set amount of hard disk space, and that amount does not change. Dynamic VHDs only use the amount of space that is currently being used for the VHD. The fixed-size VHD option offers better performance than the dynamic VHDs by eliminating the fragmentation associated with a growing file. Differencing disks are configured in a parent-child relationship with another disk that stays intact. This allows you to change the operating system or data without affecting the parent disk.

Be familiar with virtual machine snapshots.   Understand that Microsoft Hyper-V has also included the shadow copies advantages to your virtual machines and they are called Virtual Machine Snapshots. Understand that these virtual machine snapshots will take a copy of your virtual machine and place that copy in a specified location. Understand the recovery and rollback advantages of using virtual machine snapshots.

Understand pass-through disk access.   Pass-through disk access allows Hyper-V to work without the use of virtual hard disks (VHD). Virtual machines can access a file system directly, thus eliminating the need for VHDs. Be sure to know that VHDs are inaccessible to nonvirtualized systems due to the VHD formatting. Pass-through disk access helps solve this problem by allowing the virtual machine to directly access the writable file system. Using pass-through disk access allows you to surpass the 2040GB limitation of VHDs.

Know how to use Authorization Manager.   Authorization Manager allows you to integrate role-based access control to applications. This gives you the flexibility to assign application access to users based on their job functions.

Understand System Center Virtual Machine Manager.   Understand that System Center Virtual Machine Manager is an easy and cost-effective application for administrators that are responsible for managing virtual networks. Since SCVMM works with the Windows Server 2008 technology, understand that SCVMM allows you to configure and manipulate the physical and virtual machines, consolidate underutilized physical machines, and implement new virtual machines.

Know how to implement virtual networking.   Be familiar with VLANs, virtual switches, VLAN tagging, and the three communication settings that you can configure. Be able to set up a network adapter in the Virtual Network Manager tool.

Understand how to configure Hyper-V remotely.   Know how to remotely configure and maintain Hyper-V remotely. Understand how to configure the Windows Firewall and RDP settings to allow for the remote administration.

Review Questions

1. You are the network administrator for a large organization that uses Windows Server 2008 and Windows Vista. Your organization has decided to use Microsoft Hyper-V to help increase server productivity and reduce hardware costs. You have limited hard disk space for your Hyper-V virtual machines. How should you implement the VHDs?

    A. Use fixed-size VHDs.

    B. Use dynamic VHDs.

    C. Use VHD differencing.

    D. Use Virtual Server 2005 fixed size.

2. You are the network administrator for a large organization that has decided to use Hyper-V. Your manager has asked you to give a presentation on Hyper-V to all the executives. During the presentation someone asks you the maximum size of a VHD. What is your answer?

    A. 1750GB

    B. 1000GB

    C. 3400GB

    D. 2040GB

3. You are the network administrator for Panek Industries. Your organization has decided to implement Hyper-V. You have installed the Hyper-V role and you are getting ready to install your first virtual hard disk (VHD). During the installation of the VHD, a screen asks you what type of disk you want to configure. What are the three options that you have when installing a VHD?

    A. Fixed size

    B. Dynamic

    C. Differencing

    D. All of the above

4. You are the network administrator for a large organization that has decided to use Hyper-V. You decide to purchase new hardware for the installation. When setting up the virtual machines, you realize that you have to have nonvirtualized systems access the virtual machines. How would you configure the virtual machines?

    A. Fixed-size VHD

    B. Dynamic VHD

    C. Differencing

    D. Pass-through disk access

5. You are the network administrator for a mid-sized organization that has decided to use Hyper-V. You are trying to determine which type of hard drives you want to set up in the Hyper-V environment. The hard drive must have the operating system loaded and the machine will need to be booted up from the drive. What type of drive would you set up?

A. SCSI drive

B. IDE drive

C. Fixed-size VHD

D. Dynamic VHD

6. You are the network administrator for a large organization that has decided to implement Hyper-V. Your boss is concerned about making sure the virtual machines can be recovered in the event of a fatal error or in the event of a rollback. What feature can you tell your boss about to help relieve her concerns?

A. Virtual Machine VHD Backup tool

B. Virtual machine snapshots

C. Virtual Machine Recovery tool

D. VHDMount utility

7. You are the system administrator for a mid-sized organization. You need to start giving sales users role-based rights to use certain applications, including ASP.NET web applications. What application can you use?

A. Application Manager

B. Virtual Machine Manager

C. Authorization Manager

D. Hyper-V Manager

8. You are the IT manager for a large organization that has decided to implement Hyper-V. You currently have 25 servers that are all running Microsoft Windows Server 2008 and all of your clients are using either Windows Vista or Windows XP. You want to consolidate 50 percent of your servers to run as virtual machines in Hyper-V. You need to use one management utility to control the Hyper-V virtual machines. Which utility should you use?

A. System Center Hyper-V Manager

B. System Center Virtualization Manager

C. System Center Virtualization MMC

D. System Center Virtual Machine Manager

9. Your organization has decided to use SCVMM along with Hyper-V. Since you are the IT department head, you have been asked to give a presentation on SCVMM. During the conference with the IT personnel, one of the members asks you to list the advantages of SCVMM. Which of the following would be correct?

A. Multivendor support

B. Performance and resource optimization

C. Clustering support

D. All of the above

10. You are the network administrator for a large organization. You have implemented Hyper-V and you have decided to use SCVMM. You download and are ready to install the product. Before installing SCVMM, what is a requirement for proper installation?

    A. .NET Framework

    B. Visual Basic scripting

    C. PowerShell

    D. Routing and Remote Access (RRAS)

11. You have been hired as a consultant by a mid-sized organization that would like to install Hyper-V. You install Hyper-V and decide to install SCVMM. You first have to install the .NET Framework before installing the SCVMM program. From where do you install the .NET Framework in the Windows Server 2008 operating system?

    A. Control Panel

    B. Add/Remove Programs

    C. Server Manager

    D. Programs Manager

12. You have been hired as a consultant for a small real estate office. The organization wants you to set up a Windows Server 2008 machine along with 25 Windows Vista clients. They want you to be able to support the network remotely. You have decided to use RDP to connect and configure the server remotely. The office uses a small router for network connectivity to the Internet. You want to configure that router to forward the RDP port to the new server that you set up. Which port number would you use for port forwarding?

    A. 3390

    B. 3386

    C. 3398

    D. 3389

13. You have been hired as a consultant for a doctor's office. The office wants you to set up a Windows Server 2008 machine with the Microsoft Firewall. They want you to be able to support Hyper-V remotely using RDP. You need to configure the firewall to allow for remote Hyper-V and RDP. Which two services do you have to set exceptions on in the Windows Firewall?

    A. Remote Desktop

    B. Remote Assistance

    C. Virtualization

    D. Hyper-V

14. You are the network administrator for a large organization that has decided to start using Hyper-V. Your organization has many programmers on staff who are good at writing scripts. You want to use a scripting utility to manage and maintain your Hyper-V servers. Which scripting utility can you use?

    A. Virtualization WMD

    B. Virtualization WMI

    C. Virtualization WDS

    D. Virtualization WWF

15. You are the network manager for a small IT department. You have hired a new administrator who is going to be responsible for managing the Hyper-V environment. You do not want the new administrator to work in the computer room so all of his administration will be done remotely. Which operating systems can you install on his machine to allow him to manage Hyper-V remotely? (Choose all that apply.)

    A. Windows Vista with Service Pack 1

    B. Windows Server 2003

    C. Windows Server 2008

    D. Windows XP

16. You are the network administrator for a large organization. You have decided to implement Hyper-V and run all of your servers as virtual machines. You purchase the new server and install Windows Server 2008 and Hyper-V onto the machine. You need to install the network adapter card in Hyper-V. The adapter card will be the one used in the virtual machine that talks to the network. How would you set up the connection type?

    A. External

    B. Internal

    C. Private

    D. Network

17. You are the network administrator for a mid-sized organization that has just installed Hyper-V. You need to configure the network adapter for the Hyper-V console. Which application do you use?

    A. Add/Remove Programs

    B. Networking Services

    C. Virtual Network Manager

    D. WinNS

18. You are the operations manager for a large organization. You have decided to install Hyper-V. After you install the Hyper-V role, you need to set up a virtual machine where the network card gets configured without the need of an operating system. What feature allows this?

    A. PBX

    B. PXE

    C. PDF

    D. PRT

19. You are the network administrator for a large insurance company. Your organization has developed a corporate policy that requires all machines to use the IPSec security protocol. If the computer they are logging in from does not follow this corporate policy, they will be denied access to the network. What can you set up to help enforce the policy?

    A. Computer Access Protection

    B. Hyper-V Access Protection

    C. Network Access Protection

    D. Server Access Protection

20. You are the administrator for a large organization that has decided to use Hyper-V and virtual networking. Which of the following is not correct about Microsoft virtual networking?

    A. It supports VLAN tagging.

    B. It supports wireless adapters on virtual machines.

    C. It supports PXE boot.

    D. It supports virtual switches.

Answers to Review Questions

1. B. Dynamic VHDs only use the amount of space that is currently being used for the VHD. Use this approach to set up your VHD if hard drive space is limited on your server.

2. D. The maximum size of any virtual hard disk (VHD) is 2040GB.

3. D. You have three options when installing VHDs: fixed size, dynamic, and differencing. Fixed size and dynamic are the two most common settings for Hyper-V. Fixed size means that each VHD is set to a specific hard drive storage space and that space is taken by the system even if the VHD is less than what's set. Dynamic VHDs only use the space that is currently being used by the VHD. So if a dynamic VHD is set to 16GB but the VHD is currently using only 10GB, then 10GB is all that is currently being used by the dynamic VHD. Differencing allows for a child parent relationship of VHDs.

4. D. Virtual machines can access a file system directly through the use of pass-through disk access, thus eliminating the need for VHDs. VHDs are inaccessible to nonvirtualized systems due to the VHD formatting. Pass-through disk access helps solve this problem by allowing the virtual machine to directly access the writable file system.

5. B. IDE hard drives are drives that the guest OS can boot from, but with an IDE drive you can only have four virtual disks (two disks on two controllers). You can set up 256 SCSI virtual disks (64 disks on four controllers), but you can't boot up from the virtualized BIOS.

6. B. Hyper-V allows you to set up virtual machine snapshots. Hyper-V will take a copy of your virtual machine and place that copy in a specified location.

7. C. Authorization Manager allows you to integrate role-based access control to applications. You have the flexibility to assign application access to users based on their job functions.

8. D. System Center Virtual Machine Manager is responsible for managing virtual networks. SCVMM allows you to configure and manipulate the physical and virtual machines, consolidate underutilized physical machines, and implement new virtual machines.

9. D. All of these answers are advantages of using SCVMM. SCVMM also allows for centralized management of the virtual machines and includes Windows Server 2008 support.

10. A. A prerequisite for SCVMM is the installation of the .NET Framework. If this is not installed prior to installing SCVMM, the SCVMM installation will not complete.

11. C. The .NET Framework is required to install the SCVMM. To install the SCVMM you must use the Server Manager utility. The Server Manager utility is the application where you install all roles (including Hyper-V) along with the many features that are included with Windows Server 2008.

12. D. When setting up port forwarding for RDP, the standard RDP port number is 3389. You have the ability to change any port number, but by default this is the port that you need to forward.

13. A, D. The two exceptions that you need to make when setting up the Microsoft Firewall are the Hyper-V and the Remote Desktop settings.

14. B. An organization may also use the Virtualization Windows Management Instrumentation (WMI) tool to manage, create, and configure virtual machines. Virtualization WMI allows you to manage server settings, control the status of virtual machines, create and configure virtual machines, and create and configure virtual networking. To use the Virtualization WMI tool, you must use a scripting utility to configure and create WMIs.

15. A, C. You can use Windows Server 2008 and connect to the server through the Hyper-V Manager, or you can also install the Hyper-V Manager on the Windows Vista operating system as long as it has Service Pack 1 or higher installed.

16. A. You have three options when setting up the communications for the network adapter: External, Internal, and Private. External creates a connection from the physical adapter and the virtual machine. This option allows a virtual machine to access the network through the network adapter. Internal allows communications between the virtualization servers and the virtual machines. Private provides communications only between the virtual machines. This enables the virtual machines to talk to each other only.

17. C. Microsoft's Virtual Network Manager helps an organization set up, configure, and manage a virtual network. It allows you to add, remove, modify, and manage virtual networks from one location.

18. B. Hyper-V supports the Pre-Boot Execution (PXE) environment on the virtual network adapters. PXE booting allows a network card to be configured without the need of a hard drive or operating system.

19. C. One advantage to using Hyper-V on Windows Server 2008 is that you get to use many of the services offered with the Windows Server 2008 environment. One of those services is the Network Access Protection (NAP) feature, which allows you to quarantine machines that do not meet specific network or corporate policies. The noncompliant machines will not be allowed to access the network until they comply with the organization's policies.

20. B. Wireless network adapters can't be used with Hyper-V virtual machines. You must be physically plugged into your network when setting up virtual networking. Your clients can still be wireless, but not your Hyper-V virtual machines.

Chapter

4

Creating Virtual Machines

MICROSOFT EXAM OBJECTIVES COVERED IN THIS CHAPTER:

✓ **Create or Clone a Virtual Machine**

   ※ This objective may include but is not limited to: prepare guest operating system for duplication (Sysprep), differencing disks, copying Virtual Hard Disks (VHD), SCVMM vNext, PXE Boot (legacy network adapter), manage the Self Service portal, Windows Deployment Service (WDS)

✓ **Create a Virtual Disk**

   ※ This objective may include but is not limited to: pass-through disks, fixed vs. dynamic, differencing disks, IDE vs SCSI, Virtual Hard Disk Wizard

Installing the Microsoft Hyper-V role is an excellent beginning to creating our new virtualization environment, but we are still just crawling. Now it's time for us to stand up and walk.

Virtual machines are the core of the Hyper-V world, and they are the foundation that our guest operating system resides on. Knowing how to create virtual machines correctly is an essential part of building a Hyper-V virtual network. It is important to know—not only for the exam but for the real world—how to import, export, and deploy virtual machines throughout your Hyper-V network. It is also important to understand the Sysprep utility and the Windows Deployment Service (WDS), which will allow you to set up images for mass duplication for your client computers.

Before you can build virtual machines properly, you first have to understand how to build virtual hard disks. That's our first topic.

Creating Virtual Disks

Virtual disks are the "hard drives" that the virtual machines use to operate. The virtual disk is the drive that you install your operating system onto. Virtual hard disks (VHDs) provide the storage for your virtual network environment. The virtual machine looks at the virtual disk the same way a traditional machine looks at a hard drive. There are different ways that you can set up your virtual disk (see Figure 4.1):

Dynamic Virtual Disks   These are virtual disks that expand as needed. They usually start off very small and grow as the virtual machine continues to grow. When you set up a dynamic virtual disk, you establish a maximum amount that the virtual disk can expand to, but when the dynamic disk starts, it only uses the amount of space that is currently needed to make the system operate. As the virtual machine starts to grow, the dynamic virtual disk expands until it reaches its maximum amount. These disk types perform well in test and development environments.

The advantage of a dynamic virtual disk is that you only need the amount of hard disk space that is currently being used. The disadvantage to a dynamic virtual disk is performance. Also, as you delete files in a dynamic virtual disk, the size does not shrink down and resize.

Fixed Virtual Disks   These are virtual disks that are set to a specific size, and they acquire that amount of hard disk space as soon as they start to run. When you set a maximum amount of space on these fixed virtual disks, it does not matter how much actual space they use when operating—they always grab that maximum amount. This disk type works well in a production environment.

FIGURE 4.1   The Choose Disk Type screen

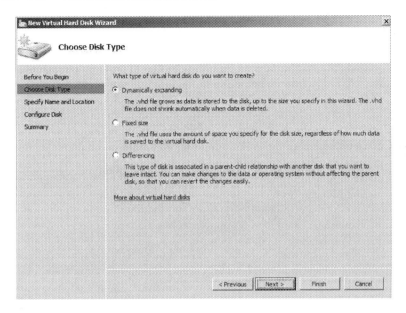

The advantage to fixed virtual disks is performance. Because these disks do not have to manage size during operation, they perform more efficiently. The disadvantage of fixed virtual disks is that regardless of the actual used amount, the fixed disk type always uses the maximum allowable amount.

Differencing Disks   This is a type of disk that uses a child-parent relationship. Differencing disks allow you to make changes to the virtual machine, and these changes do not affect the base image. Differencing disks store all of their changes to a separate file, and since all changes are stored on a different disk, this allows you to revert back to the original VHD quickly and easily.

The advantage to using a differencing disk is that all changes are isolated from the original VHD, thus protecting your original data. This is a good way for distributing base VHDs to different locations. The disadvantage to using differencing disks is that they have to be dynamic in size; they can't be compacted, and they require more system overhead.

Pass-through Disks   A new type of virtual machine storage in Hyper-V is called pass-through disks. Pass-through disks do not use any type of VHD. When using pass-through disks, the virtual machine accesses the storage device directly without the need of a VHD.

The advantage to using pass-through disks is that since there is no VHD and no VHD encryption, nonvirtualized machines can also access the pass-through disk directly. The disadvantage to using pass-through disks is that snapshots are not available. Also, whereas VHDs are portable and can be easily moved to other machines, pass-through disks are not portable.

Another decision you must make is how you want to set up the disk hardware types. There are two hardware types that you can use: SCSI and IDE. Table 4.1 shows the differences between using IDE and SCSI.

TABLE 4.1   Comparison of EIDE and SCSI Disks

IDE	SCSI
2 EIDE controllers	4 SCSI controllers
(Each controller can have two devices each.)	(Each controller can have 64 devices each.)
Virtual disks supported	Virtual disks supported
• Dynamic disks	• Dynamic disks
• Fixed disks	• Fixed disks
• Pass-through disks	• Pass-through disks
Supports emulated and synthetic	Synthetic only

One of the main differences between the two types of hardware disks is emulated or synthetic. Emulated works with older systems and allows the guest operating system to see and work with the BIOS. You need to use emulated when the device drivers that you have are designed for older hardware. Emulated systems are slower and consume more overhead than their synthetic counterparts.

Synthetic is new to Windows Server 2008 Hyper-V and it works with Windows Vista, Windows Server 2003, and Windows Server 2008. Synthetic works with a high-speed in-memory bus called VMBus. Because it works with VMBus, it is much faster and takes up less overhead than emulated.

There is an easier way to understand the difference between synthetic and emulated devices. Synthetic devices take requests made by the Hyper-V virtual machines and forward those requests through the high-speed VMBus to the physical devices, whereas emulated devices use software to emulate working with the physical device.

In Exercise 4.1 we will create new virtual disks by using the New Virtual Hard Disk wizard. The wizard allows you to create VHDs for new or existing virtual machines. The wizard is included with the Hyper-V Manager.

EXERCISE 4.1

Creating a Virtual Hard Disk

1.   Start the Hyper-V Manager by clicking Start ➢ Administrative Tools ➢ Hyper-V Manager.

2.   When the Hyper-V Manager opens, in the Actions section click the New, Hard Disk link.

3.   At the Before You Begin screen, click Next.

4. At the Choose Disk Type screen, click the Fixed Size radio button and click Next. Do not choose Dynamic at this point. In the next exercise we will convert this fixed disk to a dynamic disk.

5. The Specify Name And Location screen appears next. In the Name field type **TFixedVM.vhd**. Accept the default location and click Next.

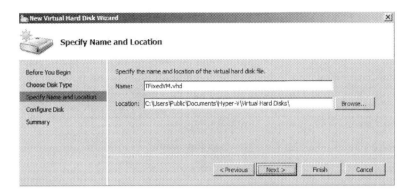

6. In the Configure Disk screen, click the "Create a new blank virtual hard disk" and make the size **20** GB. Click Next.

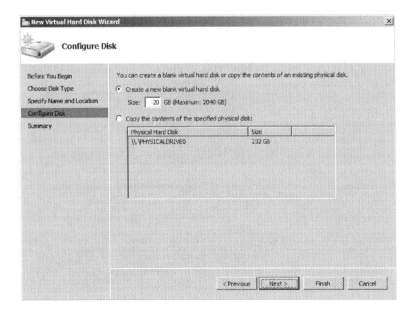

EXERCISE 4.1 *(continued)*

7. At the Summary screen, verify the settings and click Finish. A dialog box appears, showing that the VHD is being created.

8. Once the VHD is created, the New Virtual Hard Disk wizard closes. Keep the Hyper-V Manager open.

You can create a dynamic virtual disk as well by following the steps in Exercise 4.1. You have the ability to convert a fixed size disk to a dynamic disk. In Exercise 4.2 we will convert the VHD from a fixed disk to a dynamically expanding disk. You can convert VHDs using the Hyper-V Manager.

EXERCISE 4.2

Converting a Fixed Disk to a Dynamic Disk

1. In the Hyper-V Manager, click the Edit Disk link under Actions.

2. At the Before You Begin screen, click Next.

3. At the Locate Virtual Hard Disk screen, click the Browse button.

4. You should see the TFixedVM.vhd file. Click on TFixedVM.vhd so it populates the File Name field. Click the Open button.

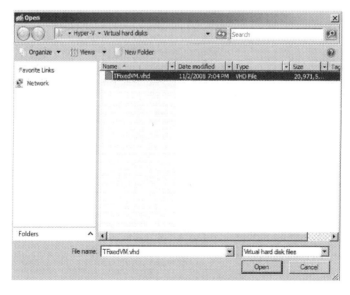

5. Clicking Open brings you back to the Locate Virtual Hard Disk screen. Click Next.

EXERCISE 4.2 *(continued)*

6. At the Choose Action screen, make sure the Convert radio button is selected and click Next.

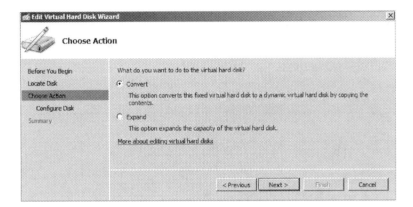

7. At the Convert Virtual Hard Disk screen, click the Browse button.

8. In the File Name field, type **TDynamic.vhd** and click the Save button.

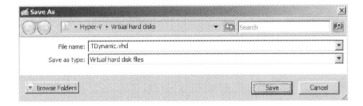

9. The Convert Virtual Hard Disk screen reappears; click the Next button.

10. At the Summary screen, click the Finish button. A dialog box will open telling you that the virtual disk is being edited.

11. When the conversion is complete, the dialog box automatically disappears. Leave the Hyper-V Manager Open.

Finally in this section we will create a differencing disk. In Exercise 4.3 we will create a differencing disk using the TDynamic.vhd file as the parent VHD.

EXERCISE 4.3

Creating a Differencing Disk

1. In the Hyper-V Manager, click the New, Hard Disk link in the Actions section.

2. At the Before You Begin screen, just click Next.

3. At the Choose Disk Type screen, click the Differencing radio button and click Next.

4. In the Name field, type **TDiffVM.vhd** and click Next.

5. At the Configure Disk screen, click the Browse button.

6. Click on the TDynamic.vhd file and click the Open button.

7. At the Configure Disk screen, click the Next button.

8. Click the Finish button.

9. We are now going to verify that all three disks are created. Click the Inspect Disk link under Actions.

10. All three disks should be showing. Click the Cancel button.

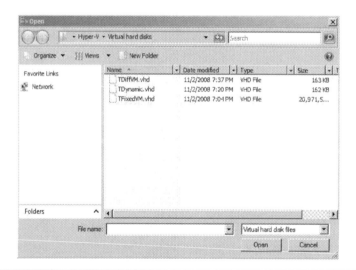

It is important to understand the concepts behind VHDs since they are the core of most virtual machines. As the old saying goes, "You can't build a strong house without a strong foundation." Virtual hard disks are the strong foundation for our virtual machine house.

> Remember, virtual hard disks are equivalent to physical hard disks, but in Hyper-V you have the ability to create virtual machines without the use of a virtual hard disk. This is not very common, but there is a possibility that the virtual machine will not have a virtual hard disk associated with it.

Creating Virtual Machines

Creating virtual machines is the single most important task that you can perform within the Hyper-V environment. Virtual machines run on a host Hyper-V server, but just as in a traditional network, you will most likely need to have more than one server. The Hyper-V hypervisor, a 64-bit mechanism, gives you the ability to run multiple virtual machines on the same physical Hyper-V machine. Its job is to create and manage the partitions between virtual machines. The hypervisor is a thin software layer that sits between the virtual machines and the hardware (Figure 4.2).

FIGURE 4.2   Hypervisor architecture

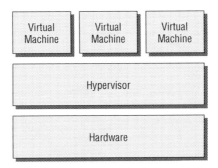

The end users who connect to the virtual machines do not know the difference between a normal Windows Server 2008 machine and a virtualized Windows Server 2008 machine. Because of this, you can set up your virtual machine environment the same way you would set up a normal server in your computer room.

An advantage to using virtual machines is that you can run many network services (DNS, DHCP, Active Directory, etc.) from multiple virtual machines on the same physical machine.

There are multiple ways to create virtual machines. One of the easiest ways is by using the New Virtual Machine wizard. It is included free with the Hyper-V Manager. When the wizard starts, it will take you through seven screens:

Before You Begin   This is a welcome screen that explains how the New Virtual Machine wizard operates.

Specify Name And Location   This screen allows you to specify the name of the new virtual machine and the location where you would like to store this new virtual machine.

Assign Memory   This screen lets you set the memory that this virtual machine will use. The default is 512MB.

Configure Networking   At this screen you can specify which network adapter this new virtual machine will use.

Connect Virtual Hard Disk   This screen gives you the option of using new or existing virtual hard disks. You also have the ability to attach a VHD at a later time.

🌐 **Real World Scenario**

Exchange Server and Your Infrastructure

A good example of some of the advantages of Hyper-V is using Microsoft Exchange Server. I am a big fan of Exchange and I have been configuring it for many years.

One rule of thumb, if possible, is that you should never load an Exchange server on the same machine as a domain controller. The reason for this is that the Exchange server will use just that domain controller for authentication and services. If that domain controller stops functioning properly, the Exchange server will also have errors. If you have to load Exchange onto a domain controller, that's fine. It's just not the best practice.

The problem here is that you should have at least two servers in this situation. You need one Windows Server 2008 domain controller and one server that has Exchange loaded on it.

Hyper-V can help with these types of issues. You can have two virtual machines, each loaded with its own version of Windows Server 2008, and make one a domain controller and make the other an Exchange server. This keeps the two components on two separate virtual machines while only using one physical machine.

Installation Options   At this point during the New Virtual Machine wizard, you can choose to install an operating system. You can install an operating system later, from a CD/DVD, boot floppy disk, or network-based installation server.

Summary   At this screen you can verify your choices before creating the new virtual machine.

In Exercise 4.4 we will use the New Virtual Machine wizard to create a new virtual machine. We will install Windows Server 2008 Enterprise Edition as the operating system. If you do not have a copy of Enterprise Edition, you can use a copy of Windows Server 2008 Standard Edition in its place. Before starting this exercise, insert the Windows Server 2008 DVD into your computer's DVD drive. If AutoPlay starts, close the application.

EXERCISE 4.4

Creating a New Virtual Machine

1. Start the Hyper-V Manager by clicking Start ➢ Administrative Tools ➢ Hyper-V Manager.

2. When the Hyper-V Manager starts, click the New, Virtual Machine link under the Actions section.

3. Click Next at the Before You Begin screen.

4. At the Specify Name And Location screen, type **S2008VM** in the Name field. Leave the default location. Click Next.

EXERCISE 4.4 *(continued)*

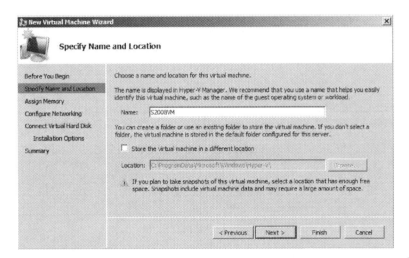

5. At the Assign Memory screen, type in **1024**MB and click Next.

6. At the Configure Networking screen, pull down the Connection Type drop-down and choose your network adapter. Click Next.

7. Choose "Use an existing virtual hard disk" at the Connect Virtual Hard Disk screen. Then click the Browse button.

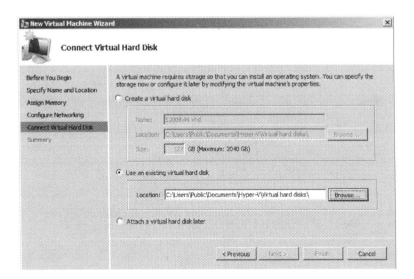

8. Choose the TDynamic.vhd file and click Open.

9. At the Connect Virtual Hard Disk screen, click Next.

10. At the Summary screen, check the "Start the virtual machine after it is created" check box and click Finish.

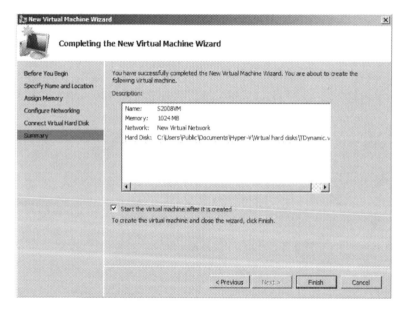

11. When the S2008VM starts, you will receive a boot failure. Click Media Ø DVD Drive ➢ Capture <your DVD drive letter>. Then press Enter.

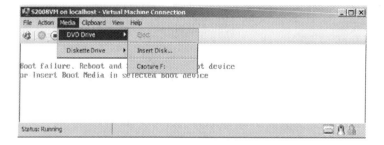

12. The Windows Server 2008 installation starts. Install the Windows Server 2008 Enterprise Full Edition.

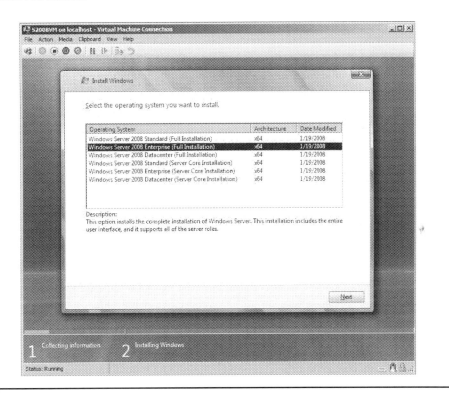

> If you need help installing Windows Server 2008, go back to Chapter 1 and perform Exercise 1.1, starting with step 2.

Another thing that you can do with virtual machines is move them from one server to another server. There are several different ways to copy a virtual machine from one location to another:

- XCopy
- Hyper-V Import/Export
- PowerShell Import/Export scripts
- SCVMM Migrate

Hyper-V Manager allows you to export a virtual machine to a location that you specify (local or network). You then have the ability to import the virtual machine into a different Hyper-V server or the same as the exported machine (recoverability).

In Exercise 4.5 we will use the Hyper-V Manager to export the S2008VM virtual machine to a network location. Then in Exercise 4.6 we will again use the Hyper-V Manager to import the S2008VM back to the same Hyper-V machine that we exported it from.

EXERCISE 4.5

Exporting a Virtual Machine

1. Start the Hyper-V Manager by clicking Start ≻ Administrative Tools ≻ Hyper-V Manager.

2. In the left-hand window, click the name of the Hyper-V server.

3. In the center window, right-click on S2008VM and choose Export.

4. In the Export Virtual Machine dialog box, click the Browse button.

5. In the Select Folder screen, choose a location that you want to export your virtual machine to. Click the Export button.

6. In the Hyper-V Manager, in the center window you will see that for S2008VM, Exporting appears in the Operations column.

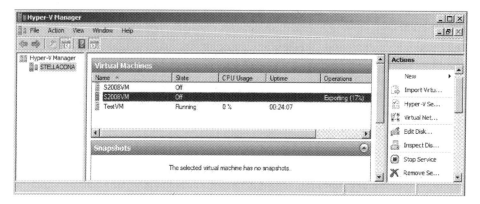

7. After the export completes, you can leave the Hyper-V Manager open for the next exercise.

EXERCISE 4.6

Importing a Virtual Machine into Hyper-V

1. With the Hyper-V Manager open, right-click on S2008VM and choose Delete.

2. At the Delete Virtual Machine dialog box, click the Delete button.

3. After S2008VM has been deleted, in the left-hand window right-click your server name.

4. Choose Import Virtual Machine.

5. On the Import Virtual Machine screen, click the Browse button and choose the directory that you exported your virtual machine to.

6. After you have the path to your exported file, click the Import button.

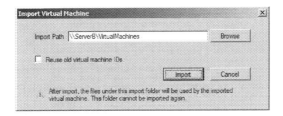

7. If you receive a warning dialog box, just click Close.

8. Click on S2008VM and choose Actions ➢ Start.

9. S2008VM should restore and start. After S2008VM boots up, close the S2008VM virtual machine by choosing Actions ➢ Turn Off.

Being able to move virtual machines from one server to another is a big advantage to an IT infrastructure. If you make sure that you export your virtual machine to a network location after it is completely set up and running, this will protect you against failures or network issues. If the virtual machine crashes and stops on the server or if the server itself has hardware issues, just import your virtual machine to another server and you are back up and running. (We will cover backing up and restoring virtual machines using tape backups and the Windows Server 2008 Backup utility in Chapter 8, "Backing Up and Restoring VMs.")

Now that we covered creating virtual hard disks and creating virtual machines, we will move our discussion to duplication and deployment of server and end-user machines.

System Preparation (Sysprep) Tool

Most of you reading this book are already in the computer industry. One task that many of us have tackled over the years is how to deal with operating system deployments. We have seen the many tools that have been released into the industry to help you make this task easier.

These tools allow you to set up a machine and then take a picture (called an image) of that setup and deploy that image to the other machines in your organization that need to be set up.

The *System Preparation (Sysprep)* tool is a Microsoft utility that allows you to get an image ready for transfer. The Sysprep utility prepares the machine and the image for transfer and then you use third-party software to physically transfer the image.

> Many third-party software products allow you to image a computer for deployment. This is a Microsoft-related book and I do not want to recommend any one imaging software over another. They all have their own pros and cons. On any search engine on the Internet, just type in **imaging software** and you will find all the information that you need to make an informative decision on which one is right for you. Microsoft has its own imaging utility called ImageX.

Sysprep is a utility that is good only for setting up a new machine. You do not use Sysprep to image a computer for upgrading a current machine. You can use a few switches in conjunction with Sysprep to configure the utility for your specific needs. Table 4.2 shows some of the switches and what they will do for you.

> These Sysprep switches are used at the command prompt or run line. When running the GUI version of Sysprep, many of these switches are pull-down options.

TABLE 4.2 Sysprep Switches

Switch	Explanation
/pnp	Forces a mini-setup wizard to start at reboot so that all plug-and-play devices can be recognized.
/generalize	This allows Sysprep to remove all system-specific data from the Sysprep image. If running the GUI version of Sysprep, this is a check box option.
/oobe	Initiates the Windows Welcome at the next reboot.
/audit	Initiates Sysprep in Audit mode.
/nosidgen	Sysprep does not generate a new SID on the computer restart. Forces a mini-setup on restart.
/reboot	Stops and restarts the computer system.
/quiet	Runs without displaying any confirmation dialog messages.
/mini	Tells Sysprep to run the mini-setup on the next reboot.

The Windows System Preparation tool is a free utility that comes on all Windows operating systems. By default, the Sysprep utility (Figure 4.3) can be found on the Windows Server 2008 operating system in the \Windows\system32\sysprep directory.

FIGURE 4.3   The Sysprep utility

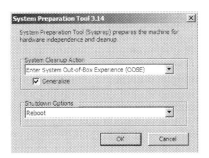

The Problems with Deployment Software

For many years when we had to create a number of machines with a Microsoft operating system on them, we would have to use files to help deploy the multiple systems.

Then, some third-party companies came out with software that allowed you to take a picture of the Microsoft operating system and you could deploy that image to other machines. One advantage of this approach is that all the software installed on the system could also be part of that image. This was a great way to copy an entire machine's software over to another machine.

There was one major problem for years: *Security Identification (SID)* numbers. All computers are assigned a unique number that represents them on a domain network. The problem for a long time was that when you copied a machine to another machine, the SID number was also copied.

When Microsoft released Sysprep, it helped solve this problem. Sysprep allows you to remove the SID number so that a third-party software program can image it to another machine. Many third-party image software products now also remove the SID numbers, but Sysprep was one of the first utilities to do so.

You may be wondering when you should use the Sysprep utility. Many IT departments and IT personnel just install a version of Windows when they buy new hardware, or they may keep the preinstalled operating system. As an IT consultant I do not recommend keeping the preinstalled version of Windows. Keeping the pre-installed version is good because it's easy and already created for you but the problem is that on most preinstalled operating systems, a lot of junk programs are included as well. I recommend clean installs for any new machine.

Installing a new operating system is great because you know what is being installed on the machine. But if you have to set up 25, 50, or 100 computers, this can be a huge task. This is where imaging can be a beautiful thing. Having an image with all preinstalled software like Microsoft Office, an antivirus program, and so forth can save you hundreds of hours of work. You just image the new machine(s) and you are done.

When you decide to use Sysprep to set up your images, follow these guidelines in order for Sysprep to work properly:

- You can use images to restart the Windows activation clock. The Windows activation clock starts to decrease as soon as Windows starts for the first time. You can only restart the Windows activation clock three times using Sysprep.

- The computer that you are running Sysprep on has to be a member of a workgroup. The machine can't be part of a domain. If the computer is a member of the domain, when you run Sysprep the computer will automatically be removed from the domain.

- When installing the image, the system will prompt you for a product key. You can use an answer file during the install, which in turn will have all the information needed for the install, and you will not be prompted for any information.

- A third-party utility or ImageX is required to deploy the image that is created from Sysprep.

- If you are using Sysprep to capture an NTFS partition, any files or folders that are encrypted will become corrupted and unreadable.

One new advantage to Sysprep and Windows Server 2008 is that you can use Sysprep to prepare a virtual machine for duplication. You can use Sysprep to image a virtual machine just as you would image a physical machine. The steps to image a virtual machine are as follows:

1. Create the virtual machine.
2. Install the guest operating system.
3. Install all components on the OS.
4. Run Sysprep /generalize to create the image.

When you image a computer using the Windows Sysprep utility, a Windows image (.wim) file is created. Most third-party imaging software products work with the Windows image file.

Windows Deployment Service (WDS)

Another method that many IT departments use to deploy operating systems is through the use of Remote Installation Services (RIS). RIS is a utility that allows an administrator to deploy an operating system remotely. On the client machine that is receiving the operating system, you use a set of disks (RIS client disks) that will automatically initiate a network card, connect to the RIS server, and download the operating system.

For Windows Vista and Windows Server 2008, a new version of RIS has been developed. Called *Windows Deployment Services (WDS)*, it allows an IT administrator to install a Windows operating system without using a CD or DVD (see Figure 4.4). Using WDS allows you to deploy the operating system through a network installation. WDS can deploy Windows XP, Windows Server 2003, Microsoft Vista, and Microsoft Windows Server 2008.

FIGURE 4.4   Windows Deployment Services MMC

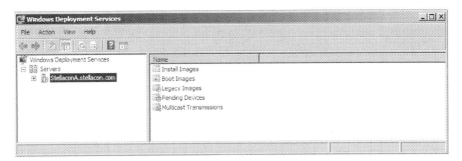

When setting up your infrastructure to use the WDS role in Windows Server 2008, you must set up the following on your network first:

- DHCP (must be configured to use PXE)
- DNS
- Active Directory
- NTFS partition set on the WDS server

The first step in setting up WDS to deploy operating systems to the clients is to install the WDS role. You do this by using Server Manager. You must make sure that DNS, DHCP, and Active Directory are installed before doing the next exercise. Exercise 4.7 will take you through the installation of WDS. (DNS and DHCP are discussed in detail in *MCTS: Windows Server 2008 Network Infrastructure Configuration Study Guide* by William Panek, Tylor Wentworth, and James Chellis [Sybex, 2008].)

EXERCISE 4.7

Installing Windows Deployment Services (WDS)

1. Start Server Manager by clicking Start ➢ Administrative Tools ➢ Server Manager.

2. On the left-hand window, click Roles.

3. In the right-hand window, click the Add Roles link.

4. In the Add Roles Wizard, click Next at the Before You Begin screen.

5. Select the Windows Deployment Services check box. Click Next.

EXERCISE 4.7 *(continued)*

6. On the Overview screen, click Next.

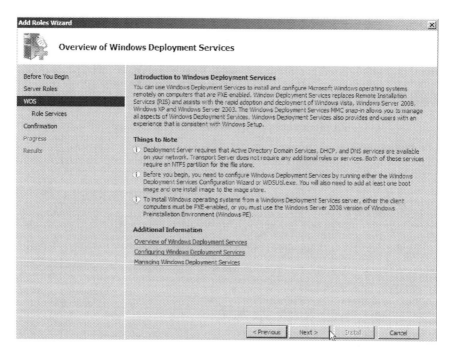

7. On the Select Role Services screen, make sure both check boxes (Deployment Server and Transport Server) are both selected and click Next.

8. On the Confirmation screen, verify the installation selections and click Install.

9. At the Installation Results screen, click Close.

10. Close the Server Manager MMC.

Now that we have installed the Windows Deployment Services role, we have to config-ure the server. Exercise 4.8 walks you through configuring the WDS server.

EXERCISE 4.8

Configuring the WDS Server

1. Start the WDS MMC by clicking Start ➢ Administrative Tools ➢ Windows Deployment Services.

2. In the left-hand window, expand the Servers link. Click on the name of your server and then right-click. Choose Configure Server.

EXERCISE 4.8 *(continued)*

3. The Welcome Page appears, explaining that you need DHCP, DNS, Active Directory, and an NTFS partition. If you meet these minimum requirements, click Next.

4. The Remote Installation Folder Location screen appears; accept the defaults by clicking Next.

5. A System Volume Warning dialog box appears; click Yes.

6. On the DHCP Option 60 screen, check both boxes and click Next.

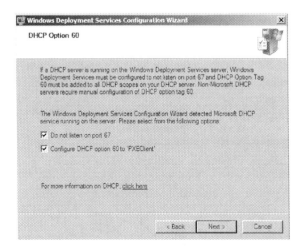

7. The PXE Server Initial Settings screen asks you to choose how PXE will respond to clients. Select the "Respond to all (known and unknown) client computers" radio button and click Finish.

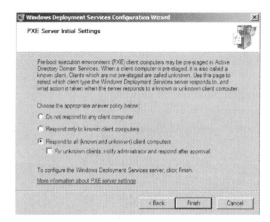

8. At the Configuration Complete screen, make sure the check box "Add image to the Windows Deployment Server" is unchecked. Click Finish.

An advantage of using the Windows Deployment Server is that WDS can work with Windows image (.wim) files. As stated in the previous section, Windows image files can be created through the use of the Windows Sysprep utility.

One component that you need to pay attention to when using the Windows Deployment Server is *Pre-Boot Execution Environment (PXE)* network devices. PXE Boot devices are network interface cards (NICs) that can talk to a network without the need for an operating system. PXE Boot NIC adapters are network adapters that have a set of pre-boot commands within the boot firmware.

This is important when using WDS because PXE Boot adapters connect to a WDS server and request the data needed to load the operating system remotely. Remember, most of these machines that you are using WDS for do not have an operating system on the computer. For WDS to work properly, you require NIC adapters that can connect to a network without the need of an operating system.

This is also why DHCP has to be set up to accept PXE machines. These machines require a valid TCP/IP address so that they can connect to the WDS server.

Configuring the System Center Virtual Machine Manager (SCVMM) 2008

Microsoft has a utility that allows us to work with Hyper-V virtual machines: System Center Virtual Machine Manager (SCVMM) 2008. SCVMM includes many tools that enable an administrator to create and manage virtual machines. The 2008 version, also referred to as SCVMM vNext, has many new features over SCVMM 2007, such as the following:

- Hyper-V support

- VMware ESX support

- Expanded delegated administration support

- Improved resource calibration and optimization

> SCVMM 2007 does not work with Hyper-V properly. You can't create or manage Hyper-V virtual machines using SCVMM 2007.

In Chapter 3 we downloaded and installed the System Center Virtual Machine Manager (Figure 4.5). In this chapter we will continue to use SCVMM by first installing the SCVMM Administrator Console. This administrative console will be the front-end application that we use to access SCVMM.

FIGURE 4.5   Virtual Machine Manager

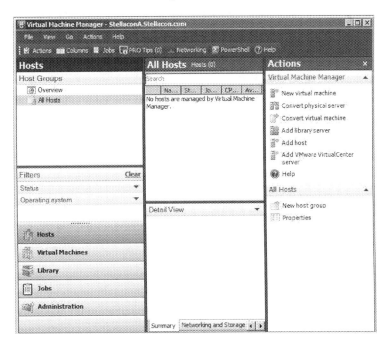

In Exercise 4.9 we will install the SCVMM Administrator Console. We will do this through the SCVMM installation utility that you downloaded in the previous chapter. You must have completed exercises 3.5 and 3.6 in Chapter 3 in order to do the following exercise.

EXERCISE 4.9

Installing the SCVMM Administrator Console

1. Start the System Center Virtual Machine Manager installation utility that you down-loaded in Chapter 3.

2. Click the Install VMM Administrator Console link.

3. On the License Terms screen, click the "I accept the terms of this agreement" radio button and click Next.

4. On the Customer Experience Improvement Program screen, click Next.

5. The Prerequisites Check screen will verify that you meet the hardware and software requirements. After it does its verification, click Next.

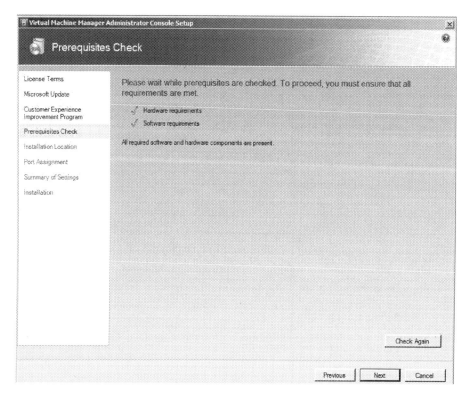

6. On the Installation Settings screen, just leave the default settings and click Next.

7. On the Configuration Settings screen, make sure the port number is the same as what you set in the Chapter 3 setup exercise. If you left the defaults in the previous chapter, it should state 8100. Click Next.

EXERCISE 4.9 *(continued)*

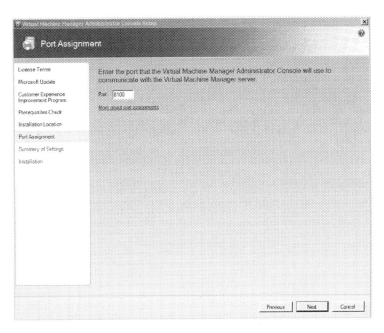

8. On the Summary of Settings screen, make sure everything is correct and click Install.

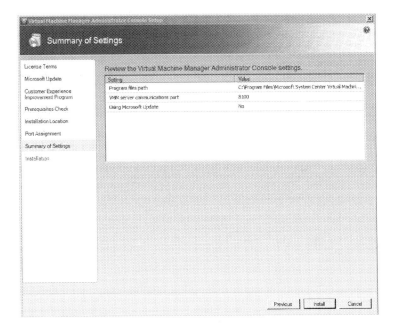

EXERCISE 4.9 *(continued)*

9. On the Installation Complete screen, it should show that all components were installed. Select the options "Create a shortcut to the VMM Administrator Console on my desktop" and "Check for the latest Virtual Machine Manager updates." Then click Close.

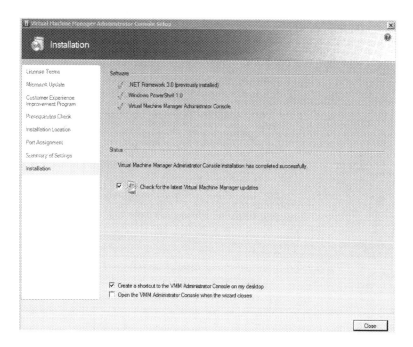

10. Close the System Center Virtual Machine Manager installation utility by clicking Exit.

SCVMM is a one-stop shop for creating and managing virtual machines. SCVMM allows an organization's IT department to have one centralized utility that everyone can use to manage your virtual datacenter. The following are just some of the actions that can be accomplished by using SCVMM:

New Virtual Machine   This action allows an administrator to create a new virtual machine by using the New Virtual Machine wizard (Figure 4.6). This wizard gives you the ability to create a virtual machine using an existing virtual machine, template, or virtual hard disk, or it lets you create a new virtual machine with a blank virtual hard disk.

Convert Physical Server   This action initiates a wizard that allows an organization to convert an existing physical computer into a virtual machine. This is known as a physical-to-virtual machine conversion (P2V conversion). When a P2V conversion starts (see Figure 4.7), an image of the hard drive is captured and then converted to a virtual machine for use with a virtualization server.

FIGURE 4.6   New Virtual Machine wizard

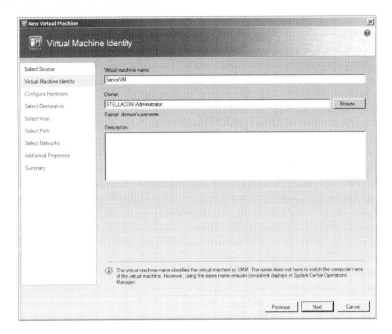

FIGURE 4.7   P2V conversion

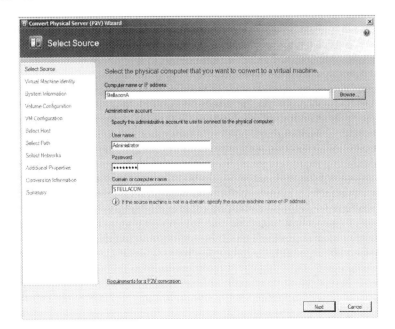

Convert Virtual Machine   This action allows you to convert a virtual machine from a non-Microsoft vendor (VMware ESX Server) and convert it to a virtual machine that Microsoft Hyper-V/Virtual Server can recognize.

Add Library Server   A virtual machine library is a central and secure location to store your virtual machines. A library server is a server in your infrastructure that stores the library shares. To create a new library, you first create the library shares on the server that you want to use and then add the library server using this action.

Add Host   This is a machine that is going to host a virtual machine. Using this action allows you to add a host server to SCVMM. Three types of virtual machine hosts can be added:

- Windows Server–based hosts that reside on an Active Directory Domain
- Windows Server–based hosts that reside on a perimeter network
- VMware ESX servers

Add VMware VirtualCenter   This action allows you to add a VMware VI3 environment to SCVMM. This allows you to manage your VMware environment alongside the Microsoft virtualized networks. SCVMM enables you to manage a VMware VirtualCenter 2.5 or VMware VirtualCenter 2.0.1. When adding a VMware VirtualCenter (see Figure 4.8), you can choose to use secure communications by using secure mode. A certificate and public key are required for each VMware ESX server that you are communicating with.

FIGURE 4.8   Adding a VMware VirtualCenter

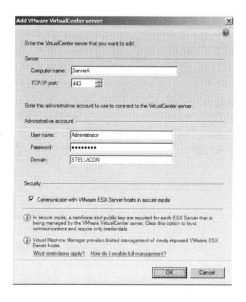

The first step in setting up SCVMM and configuring it for Microsoft Hyper-V is to add a host machine. In Exercise 4.10 we will install our first host server in the SCVMM admin console. This activity is necessary to complete in order to accomplish future exercises in this chapter.

EXERCISE 4.10

Configuring SCVMM Hosts

1. Start the SCVMM Admin Console by clicking on the SCVMM Admin Console on the desktop.

2. When the Connect to Server box appears, make sure that the Server Name field contains localhost:8100. Also make sure that the "Make this server my default" check box is selected. Click the Connect button.

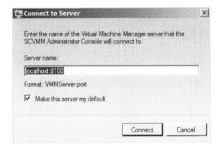

3. The first thing we need to do is add a host server to SCVMM. To do this, under the Actions sections click the Add Host link.

4. The Select Host Location screen appears; it asks for the credentials needed to connect to the host system. Enter an account that can connect to the host. Click Next.

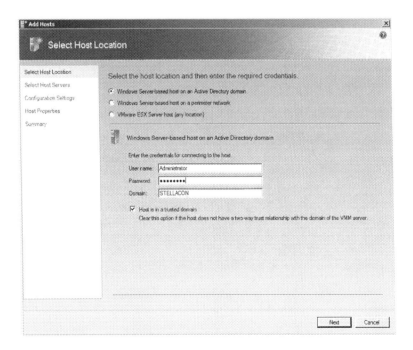

5. The Select Host Servers screen appears. Click the Search button.

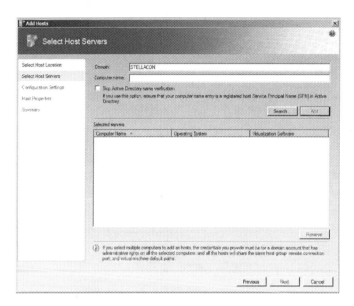

6. In the Computer Name box, type the name of the host machine and click Search. In the Search Results window, your host server should appear. Click on the host server and click the Add button. The host should appear in the Selected Computers section. Click OK.

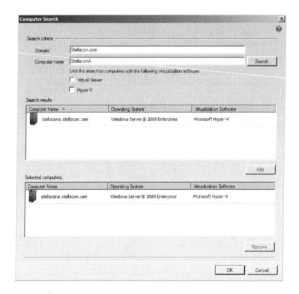

EXERCISE 4.10 *(continued)*

7. The Select Host Servers screen reappears. Click the Next button.

8. The next screen, Configuration Settings, asks which host group you would like to associate this host with. Keep the default of All Hosts and click Next.

9. On the Host Properties screen, just click Next.

10. On the Summary screen, verify all settings and click the Add Hosts button.

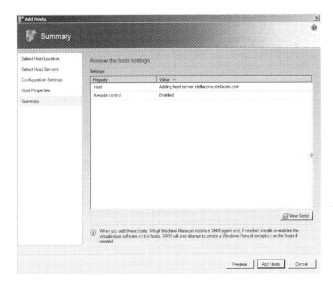

11. A Jobs screen appears while the host server is created. The status window shows you the status of the job.

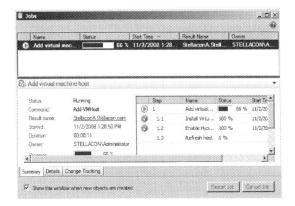

12. When the host server is added, the Jobs screen shows you a completed status. Close the box.

One of the many tasks that SCVMM can accomplish is the creation of a new virtual machine. With SCVMM, you can use one centralized familiar application for the management of your infrastructure's virtual network.

Now that we have installed the System Center Virtual Machine Manager Admin Console, it's time for us to add a virtual machine by using the console. Exercise 4.11 walks you through the creation of a virtual machine by using SCVMM.

EXERCISE 4.11

Adding a New Virtual Machine Using SCVMM

1. Open the SCVMM Admin Console.

2. In the Actions window on the right side, click the New Virtual Machine link.

3. On the Select Source screen, click the "Create the new virtual machine with a blank virtual hard disk" radio button. Click Next.

4. On the Virtual Machine Identity screen, type **TestVM** in the Virtual Machine Name box. Click Next.

5. The Configure Hardware screen opens. Make sure the following settings match. Then, click Next.

Setting	Configuration
Channel	Primary Channel (0)
Disk	Create a new virtual hard disk
Type	Fixed
Size	16 GB
File Name	TestVM_disk_1

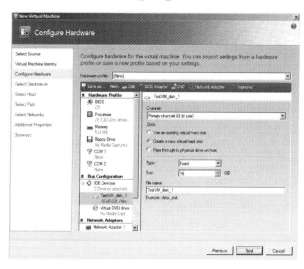

6. On the Select Destination screen, make sure the "Place the virtual machine on a host" radio button is selected. Click Next.

7. When the Select Host screen appears, make sure that the host server that you set up in the previous exercise is listed. Click on the host server and click Next.

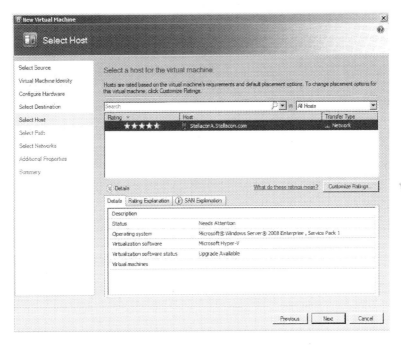

8. On the Select Path screen, accept the defaults and click Next.

9. When the Select Networks screen appears, choose your network adapter in the pull-down box and click Next.

10. On the Additional Properties screen, choose the following options and then click Next.

Setting	Configuration
Action When Physical Server Starts	Always Automatically Turn On The Virtual Machine
Action When Physical Server Stops	Save State
Specify The Operating System You Will Install In The Virtual Machine	64-Bit Edition Of Windows Server 2008 Enterprise

EXERCISE 4.11 *(continued)*

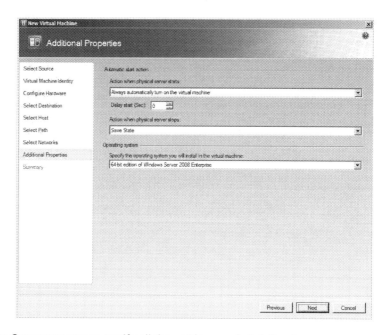

11. On the Summary screen, verify all the settings and click Create.

12. The Jobs screen appears, showing you the status of the creation. Once you see the process has completed, close the status screen.

In Exercise 4.12 we will add a *VMware* VirtualCenter to SCVMM. Only begin this exercise if you are currently using a VMware server that either runs VMware VirtualCenter 2.5 or VMware VirtualCenter 2.0.1. If you are not using a VMware server or neither of the above mentioned VMware server types, skip this exercise. If you do not have a matching VMware server and still want to try this exercise, in step 4 click Cancel instead of OK.

EXERCISE 4.12

Adding a VMware VirtualCenter Server

1. Start the System Center Virtual Machine Manager.

2. In the Actions section, click the Add VMware VirtualCenter Server link.

3. In the Server section, type the computer name of your VMware VirtualCenter server name and choose your communications port (default is Secure HTTP port 443). Enter the administrative credentials that are needed to connect to the VMware server. Make sure the option to communicate with the server in secure mode is selected. Click OK.

Another setting that you can configure within SCVMM is the Virtual Machine Manager Self-Service Portal. This web-based utility gives you the ability to allow a select set of users the right to create, manage, and operate virtual machines.

While using the VMM Self-Service Portal you can set Self-Service Portal policies that allow you to control how users can manipulate the virtual machine environment. The VMM Self-Service Portal (see Figure 4.9) is a part of SCVMM and can be installed from the same installation package as SCVMM.

FIGURE 4.9 VMM Self-Service Portal installation link

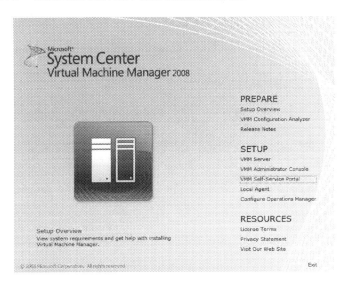

In Exercise 4.13 we will install the Virtual Machine Manager Self-Service Portal. To install the VMM Self-Service Portal we will use the SCVMM installation software that we downloaded in Chapter 3. To install the VMM Self-Service Portal, you will need to first install the Web Server (IIS) role and the IIS Management Compatibility role (Exercise 4.14).

EXERCISE 4.13

Installing the IIS Components

1. Start Server Manager by clicking Start ➢ Administrative Tools ➢ Server Manager.

2. Click the Roles link on the left-hand window.

3. On the right-hand window, click the Add Roles link.

4. When the Add Roles Wizard starts, click Next.

5. Choose the Web Services (IIS) role. Make sure the Common HTTP Features, Application Development, Security, and Management Tool check boxes are all selected. Click Next.

6. On the Confirmation screen, click Install.

EXERCISE 4.13 (continued)

---

7. On the Installation Results screen, click Close.

8. Close the Server Manager utility.

EXERCISE 4.14

Installing the VMM Self-Service Portal

1. Start the System Center Virtual Machine Manager 2008 installation utility that you downloaded in Chapter 3.

2. Click the VMM Self-Service Portal link.

3. On the License Terms screen, click the "I accept the terms of this agreement" radio button and click Next.

4. On the Prerequisites Check screen, make sure that both prerequisites are met and click Next.

5. On the Installation Location screen, accept the default location by clicking Next.

6. The Web Server Settings screen appears next. The name of the machine appears in the Virtual Machine Manager Server box. The TCP port number should be 8100 and the web port should be 80. Type **SSP** in the Portal Host Header field and Click Next.

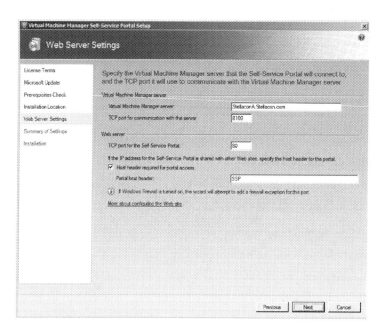

EXERCISE 4.14 *(continued)*

7. On the Summary screen, verify the settings and click Install.

8. After the VMM Self-Service Portal Setup screen shows that the components have been installed, click Close.

Summary

Virtual hard disks are the virtual equivalent to the physical hard drives in our traditional computers. When deciding which virtual hard disk to use, you have a few different choices: fixed-size disks, dynamic disks, differencing disks, and pass-through disks.

There are two main ways to create virtual hard disks. You can create a virtual hard disk first and then associate it with a virtual machine, or you can just create the virtual hard disk during the creation of the virtual machine. The two types of virtual hard disks that we use are EIDE and SCSI.

Virtual hard disks are just part of the virtual machine. Virtual machines are the core elements of the Hyper-V environment. Virtual machines are the platform on which the guest operating system will be located. When creating virtual machines, you can use the New Virtual Machine wizard.

You have the ability within Hyper-V to run multiple virtual machines on the same physical machine. The component that allows this to happen is called the hypervisor. The hypervisor is a thin software layer that keeps each of the virtual machines isolated so that they do not affect the other virtual machines on the same physical machine.

Microsoft's Windows Server 2008 operating system includes a utility called Sysprep. Sysprep allows you to prepare an image to be deployed by a third-party software package. Microsoft also has a deployment utility called the Windows Deployment Service (WDS). The WDS utility is the Windows Server 2008 replacement of RIS. WDS can deploy operating systems to remote clients.

Finally in this chapter we talked about the System Center Virtual Machine Manager 2008 (SCVMM), also known as vNext. The SCVMM utility is a downloadable tool that allows you to create, manage, and configure all of your virtual resources from one application. SCVMM allows you to manage not only your Windows virtual environments but also your VMware virtual environments. SCVMM is discussed in greater detail throughout the rest of this book. In the next chapter we discuss how to deploy virtual machines throughout your Hyper-V environment.

Exam Essentials

Be familiar with virtual hard disks (VHDs). A virtual hard disk (VHD) is a virtual hard drive that you install the guest operating system onto. Know the three types of VHDs: fixed-size, dynamic, differencing, and pass-through. Understand how each disk type works and in which situation you want to use these disks.

Know how to create VHDs. Be able to create VHDs using the New Virtual Hard Disk wizard. Understand the difference between IDE and SCSI hard drive types. Know how to convert disks from fixed size to dynamic.

Understand how virtual machines operate. The hypervisor is a 64-bit mechanism that allows Hyper-V to run multiple virtual machines on the same physical machine. Know how to copy virtual machines to other Hyper-V servers.

Be familiar with the Sysprep utility. The System Preparation (Sysprep) tool is a Microsoft utility that allows you to get an image ready for transfer. Sysprep prepares the machine and the image for transfer so that a third-party software program can image it to another machine.

Be familiar with the Windows Deployment Service (WDS). A new version of RIS has been developed; it's called Windows Deployment Services (WDS). WDS allows an IT administrator to install a Windows operating system without using a CD or DVD installation disc. Using WDS allows you to deploy the operating system through a network installation. Know how PXE Boot NIC devices work and why they are necessary for WDS.

Know how to use the Sysprep utility. The System Preparation (Sysprep) tool is a Microsoft utility that allows you to get an image ready for transfer. Sysprep prepares the machine and the image for transfer so that a third-party software program can image it to another machine.

Be able to use System Center Virtual Machine Manager (SCVMM). Microsoft has released a new version of the System Center Virtual Machine Manager, also referred to as SCVMM vNext. A major advantage of SCVMM 2008 over SCVMM 2007 is that SCVMM 2008 works with Hyper-V. Know how to create a server host and a virtual machine using SCVMM. Know how you can manage other virtualization environments like VMware. Users can log on through a website and create their own virtual machines using the VMM Self-Service Portal application.

Review Questions

1. You are the network administrator for a large organization that has decided to use Hyper-V to consolidate your network servers. You have decided to create a VHD using the New Virtual Hard Disk wizard. Performance is an issue with these virtual machines. Which type of virtual disk would you use?

   A. Fixed size

   B. Dynamic

   C. Pass-through

   D. Differencing

2. You are the network administrator for a mid-sized company that has decided to use Hyper-V. You need to set up Hyper-V in a test environment. You have decided to create a VHD using the New Virtual Hard Disk wizard. You need to minimize hard disk space. Which type of virtual disk would you use?

   A. Fixed size

   B. Dynamic

   C. Pass-through

   D. Differencing

3. You are the administrator for an organization that has been using virtualization for many years. You have migrated to Hyper-V and you need to create a new virtual machine that nonvirtualized machines can access. How do you set up the virtual machines?

   A. Using fixed-size VHDs

   B. Using dynamic VHDs

   C. Using differencing disks

   D. Using pass-through disks

4. You have been hired as a consultant for a small company that has asked you to migrate their servers to virtualization using Microsoft Server 2008 and the Hyper-V role. They have a small but new IT staff and they are worried about the staff causing problems with the virtual machines. You need to set up a way to roll back virtual machines to a previous state without the use of backups. How do you set up Hyper-V?

   A. Using fixed-size VHDs

   B. Using dynamic VHDs

   C. Using differencing disks

   D. Using pass-through disks

5. You are the network administrator for a large organization that has decided to use Hyper-V. The virtual machine has to work with older systems and has to allow the guest operating system to see and work with the BIOS. How do you set up the disk?

    A. Using an IDE disk

    B. Using a SCSI disk

    C. Using a pass-through disk

    D. Using a fixed-size disk

6. You are the network administrator for a mid-sized organization that has decided to implement Hyper-V. Your manager asks you to explain how you can have multiple virtual machines on your Hyper-V server. What would you do?

    A. Explain virtualization

    B. Explain disks

    C. Explain the hypervisor

    D. Explain SCVMM

7. You are the Hyper-V administrator for your organization. You have three Hyper-V servers and you need to make sure that you can copy virtual machines between the servers. What options do you have for copying virtual machines? (Choose all that apply.)

    A. XCopy

    B. Hyper-V Import/Export

    C. PowerShell Import/Export scripts

    D. Virtual copy

8. Paige, your IT manager, has asked you to set up 250 Microsoft Vista machines for a mass rollout. The 250 machines have to be completed within a short period of time. You decide to set up a Vista machine and then decide to make an image of the machine for mass duplication. Which Microsoft utility will allow you to create an image for mass duplication?

    A. Windows Deployment Service (WDS)

    B. System Preparation (Sysprep)

    C. Vista Preparation (Vprep)

    D. Windows Server 2008 image maker

9. You are the network administrator for a large search engine company. You have decided to use Sysprep to image all of your Windows Vista computers. You want to make the image as bare-bones as possible. You want all system information removed before imaging all the other computers. Which Sysprep switch would you use to make this happen?

    A. /oope

    B. /generalize

    C. /audit

    D. /pnp

10. Alexandria is your network administrator. She wants to use Sysprep to create an image that all of her client computers can use for operating system setups. She does not want any dialog boxes to appear during the Sysprep setup. How can she set this up?

    A. `/oope`

    B. `/quiet`

    C. `/nodialog`

    D. `/pnp`

11. You are the network manager for a small organization. You have decided to start using Sysprep for your image creations. You have one test box that you image and test on. You want to use Sysprep to reactivate the Windows activation when it expires. How many times can you reactivate the Windows activation using the Sysprep image?

    A. One

    B. Two

    C. Three

    D. Four

12. You are the administrator for a mid-sized candle maker. You have decided to use Sysprep to image your client computers. You need to use some other product to move the images to the client computers. Which Microsoft utility can you use to deploy your Sysprep image?

    A. ActiveX

    B. ImageX

    C. Image Maker

    D. Image Activate

13. You are a system administrator for a large organization that has decided to use Sysprep to image all of your client computers. You create an image for a third-party software to deploy. When using Sysprep, what type of file will you be creating?

    A. Windows image (`.wim`)

    B. System image (`.sim`)

    C. Server image (`.sim`)

    D. ImageX extension (`.imx`)

14. You are the network administrator for a large organization. You have been using Remote Installation Service (RIS) for many years and have decided to continue using it for Windows Server 2008 and Microsoft Vista. What new version of RIS would you use to do remote installations?

    A. Remote Installation Service v2

    B. Windows Deployment Service (WDS)

    C. Windows Installation Service (WIS)

    D. Remote Deployment Service (RDS)

15. You have decided to use Windows Deployment Services (WDS) for the remote installation of your client computers. You have started to set up the images and you are installing the different network services for your infrastructure. What besides a WDS server is needed to use WDS properly? (Choose all that apply.)

    A. DNS

    B. Active Directory

    C. WINS

    D. DHCP

16. You are the network administrator for a small yo-yo maker. You have decided to use Windows Deployment Services (WDS) to deploy your Microsoft Vista client operating systems. Your client computers must have a specific piece of hardware that is needed for the remote installation. What is the hardware that is needed?

    A. PXE Boot NIC adapter

    B. PBX Boot NIC Adapter

    C. PRE-Boot NIC Adapter

    D. PMX Boot NIC Adapter

17. You have been hired as a network consultant for a mid-sized company. You have decided to implement the Hyper-V role to help consolidate the network servers. You have decided to use the System Center Virtual Machine Manager to create and manage your virtual machines. Which versions can you use? (Choose two.)

    A. SCVMM 2007

    B. SCVMM 2008

    C. SCVMM vNext

    D. SCVMM V2

18. You are a network administrator for a large organization that has used virtualization for years. You have been using VMware VirtualCenter 2.5 and VMware VirtualCenter 2.0.1. You have decided to now implement Hyper-V. You need to be able to use one application that can manage the Hyper-V environment, the VMware VirtualCenter 2.5, and VMware VirtualCenter 2.0.1. Which application would you use?

    A. Hyper-V Manager

    B. SCVMM 2007

    C. SCVMM 2008 vNext

    D. VMM Manager

19. You are the network administrator for an organization that has decided to implement Hyper-V. You need to start by creating new virtual machines. Which two of the following will allow you to create Hyper-V virtual machines?

A. SCVMM 2008

B. SCVMM 2007

C. Hyper-V Manager

D. VMware Manager

20. You are the network administrator for a large organization that has decided to use Hyper-V. You want to set up a way so that a select group of users can create and manage their own Hyper-V virtual machines. You want them to be able to do this while using a web application. What would you set up to accomplish this goal?

A. SCVMM 2008 Internet Services

B. VMM Self-Service Portal

C. Hyper-V Internet Services

D. Hyper-V Self-Service Portal

Answers to Review Questions

1. A. Fixed-size disks work well in a production environment. The advantage is performance. Because these disks do not have to manage size during operation, they perform more efficiently.

2. B. Dynamic disk types perform well in test and development environments. The advantage is that you only need the amount of hard disk space that is currently being used.

3. D. A new type of virtual machine storage in Hyper-V is called pass-through disks. When using pass-through disks, the virtual machine accesses the storage device directly without the need of a VHD. The advantage is that since there is no VHD and no VHD encryption, nonvirtualized machines can also access the pass-through disk directly.

4. C. Differencing disks use a child-parent relationship. Differencing disks allow you to make changes to the virtual machine and these changes do not affect the base image. Differencing disks store all of their changes to a separate file, and all changes there are isolated from the original VHD. This allows you to revert back to the original VHD quickly and easily.

5. A. IDE disks support emulated disks that work with older systems and allow the guest operating system to see and work with the BIOS. You need to use emulated disks when the device drivers that you have are designed for older hardware.

6. C. The hypervisor is 64-bit mechanism that allows Hyper-V to run multiple virtual machines on the same physical machine. The hypervisor's job is to create and manage the partitions between virtual machines. The hypervisor is a thin software layer that sits between the virtual machines and the hardware.

7. A, B, C. There are many different ways to copy a virtual machine from one location to another. XCopy, Hyper-V Import/Export, and PowerShell Import/Export scripts are the three ways to copy a virtual machine from one server to another.

8. B. The System Preparation (Sysprep) tool is a Microsoft utility that allows you to get an image ready for transfer. The Sysprep utility prepares the machine and the image for transfer so that a third-party software program can image it to another machine.

9. B. The /generalize switch allows the Sysprep utility to remove all system-specific data from the Sysprep image. If running the GUI version of Sysprep, this is a check box option.

10. B. The /quiet mode runs without any confirmation dialog messages being displayed during the Sysprep setup.

11. C. You can use images to restart the Windows activation clock. The Windows activation clock starts to decrease as soon as Windows starts for the first time. You can only restart the Windows activation clock three times using Sysprep.

12. B. To load an image onto a client machine, you use a third-party utility or Microsoft ImageX to deploy the image that is created from Sysprep.

13. A. When you use the Sysprep utility you end up creating a Windows image (`.wim`) file. This file can be used by many third-party software packages to deploy the image to the client computers.

14. B. For Windows Vista and Windows Server 2008, a new version of RIS, called Windows Deployment Services (WDS), allows you to install a Windows operating system without a CD or DVD. Using WDS allows you to deploy the operating system through a network installation. WDS can deploy Windows XP, Windows Server 2003, Microsoft Vista, and Microsoft Windows Server 2008.

15. A, B, D. The four things that are needed for the Windows Deployment Services (WDS) to operate properly are DNS, DHCP, Active Directory, and a WDS server.

16. A. To use WDS, your client machines must support Pre-Boot Execution Environment (PXE) network devices. PXE Boot devices are network interface cards (NICs) that can talk to a network without the need for an operating system. PXE Boot NIC adapters are network adapters that have a set of pre-boot commands within the boot firmware.

17. B, C. One of the most important features of SCVMM 2008 is the ability to work with Hyper-V. SCVMM 2008 is also known as vNext. SCVMM 2007 does not work with Hyper-V properly. You can't create or manage Hyper-V virtual machines using SCVMM 2007. There is no such release called V2.

18. C. If you want to be able to manage both Hyper-V and VMware (VMware VirtualCenter 2.5 or VMware VirtualCenter 2.0.1) virtualization networks, you need to use the System Center Virtual Machine Manager 2008 (also referred to as vNext).

19. A, C. There are several ways to create virtual machines. SCVMM 2008 and Hyper-V Manager are the two ways listed here that will create virtual machines. SCVMM 2007 does not work with Hyper-V, and VMware Manager will not create Hyper-V virtual machines.

20. B. This web-based utility gives you the ability to allow a select set of users the right to create, manage, and operate virtual machines. While using the VMM Self-Service Portal, you can set Self-Service Portal policies that allow you to control how users can manipulate the virtual machine environment.

Chapter

5

Migrating and Converting Virtual Machines

MICROSOFT EXAM OBJECTIVES COVERED IN THIS CHAPTER:

✓ **Migrate a Computer to Hyper-V**

　　＊ May include but not limited to: from Virtual Server 2005, from third-party (Acronis), from VPC (Virtual PC), from Hyper-V (import/export), Intel to AMD virtual machine state, by using SCVMM vNext (P2V and V2V), Integrated Services/Virtual Machine additions, Assessment and Planning Tool.

Being able to migrate virtual machines from other virtualization environments can be a powerful tool in your virtualization arsenal. As a consultant and IT manager for many years, I tried to follow the wisdom of "Why re-create the wheel?" In other words, why re-create virtual machines that have been running fine in other virtualization environments? Being able to easily migrate these virtual machines to the Microsoft Hyper-V environment can save you time, which, in turn, saves money.

In this chapter we will discuss migrating a system to Hyper-V. We will explore the steps involved in migrating your Virtual Server 2005 and Microsoft Virtual PC virtual machines to a Hyper-V server and also the utilities needed to help migrate an infrastructure to Hyper-V.

We will explain how to convert physical computers to virtual computers (P2V), and we will also show you how to convert an existing VMware virtual machine, thus giving you the ability to manage them in an SCVMM environment (V2V).

Furthermore, we will show you how to transfer virtual machines from Microsoft Virtual Server and Microsoft Virtual PC to the new Hyper-V environment. So let's get started with physical-to-virtual conversions using the SCVMM utility.

Using Physical-to-Virtual (P2V) Conversion

In the previous chapters we started to work with System Center Virtual Machine Manager (SCVMM) 2008 vNext. We started by downloading and installing SCVMM, and then we installed the Admin console. In this chapter we will show you how to migrate a non-Microsoft virtualized machine into Hyper-V. We will also show you what is necessary to migrate a Microsoft Virtual Server and Microsoft Virtual PC virtual machine to a Hyper-V virtual machine.

Let's start this SCVMM discussion with migrating virtual machines to Hyper-V. The SCVMM 2008 vNext utility gives you two ways to migrate machines into Hyper-V virtual machines. The first is converting physical machines to virtual machines through a process known as *physical-to-virtual (P2V)* conversion. You may have used third-party software like Acronis (True Image 9.1) to do P2V conversions; the software you need is now included free with the SCVMM 2008 utility.

This function gives you the ability to convert servers that are already in production and running on your network. One advantage of using the P2V is that you can use the Windows PowerShell command line to convert multiple servers using the P2V conversion.

To use the *Windows PowerShell* command-line utility, you must script the commands that will allow the conversion to function properly. But when you convert the first machine using the SCVMM utility, you can copy the script from SCVMM, save it, and modify it for later use (we will show how to do this in Exercise 5.1).

P2V Conversions Using SCVMM

When using the System Center Virtual Machine Manager, the computer that you are converting with the P2V utility must meet a few minimum requirements before you convert it properly:

- You must have a minimum of 512MB of RAM.

- The computer must use the Advanced Configuration and Power Interface (ACPI) BIOS.

- The computer must be accessible by the SCVMM utility and the Hyper-V computer.

- The computer needs to be internal to your network. The computer you are converting can't be part of the perimeter network.

When you are deciding which machines you want to convert using the P2V utility, be aware of which operating systems SCVMM can convert using the P2V utility. SCVMM can convert the following operating systems into virtual machines:

- Windows 2000 Server SP4 or later (offline P2V only)

- Windows 2000 Advanced Server SP4 or later (offline P2V only)

- Windows Server 2003 (32-bit or 64-bit) SP1 or later

- Windows XP Professional (32-bit or 64-bit) SP2 or later

- Windows Vista (32-bit or 64-bit) SP1 or later

- Windows Server 2008 (32-bit or 64-bit)

> The SCVMM 2008 utility does not support converting a Microsoft Windows Server NT 4.0 machine to a virtual machine. If you need to convert an NT 4.0 server to a virtual machine, you can use the Microsoft Virtual Server 2005 Migration Toolkit (VSMT) or third-party solutions.

You may have noticed in the previous list that some entries specify *offline* next to the operating system. An offline conversion means that the machine's operating system that you are migrating must be taken offline before the conversion occurs. Online conversions mean that the system that you are converting can continue to operate normally during the conversion.

There are some other issues that you need to consider when choosing which machines you want to convert using the P2V utility. Windows Servers that are underutilized are an excellent choice for converting over to virtual machines.

Let's use an example of four servers in an organization. Three of those servers are being used at less than 25 percent utilization. Instead of having three physical machines not using their full hardware potential, you can create three virtual machines and place them all on the same physical machine. Now one machine will have its hardware used more efficiently, and that also frees up three physical machines to be used in a better way.

 Real World Scenario

Converting Servers

One thing I have learned over the years doing consulting is that being able to use preconfigured equipment is priceless. This is where the P2V conversion can be helpful. Think about it—you have servers prebuilt and running on the network. You can build new virtual machines, load the software, and configure them, or you can take a server that is already configured and convert it to a virtual machine.

Let's take the example I just used. You have four prebuilt running servers on your network; you can rebuild these servers from scratch as virtual machines, or you can convert these machines to virtual machines using the P2V conversion and get your network back up and running just as before.

Remember, another advantage to all of this is lower costs—due not only to less equipment but to time savings. If you had to rebuild four servers as virtual machines, this could take hours or even days. While you are building these servers, you are out of commission to do anything else. If you convert these prebuilt machines using the P2V conversion, then the SCVMM 2008 utility converts these machines while you do other work.

Let's start our exercises with the process of converting a physical machine to a virtual machine. In Exercise 5.1 you will take a machine physically located on your network and convert it into a format for use with Hyper-V. If you do not have a network configured while reading this book, you can skip this exercise. If you do not have a network and decide to not complete this exercise, it will not affect any other exercises in this chapter.

EXERCISE 5.1

Converting a Physical Machine to a Virtual Machine

1. Start the SCVMM 2008 Admin Console.

2. In the right-hand window under the Actions pane, click the Convert Physical Server link.

3. The Convert Physical Server wizard starts. At the Select Source screen you have several options you need to configure, as follows:

Field	Value
Computer Name or IP Address	The name or IP address of the computer on your network that you want to convert

Field	Value
User Name	Administrator
Password	Administrator's password for the chosen machine
Domain or Computer Name	If the computer you choose is part of a domain, the domain name field should be completed. If the machine is not part of a domain, type the computer name or IP address.

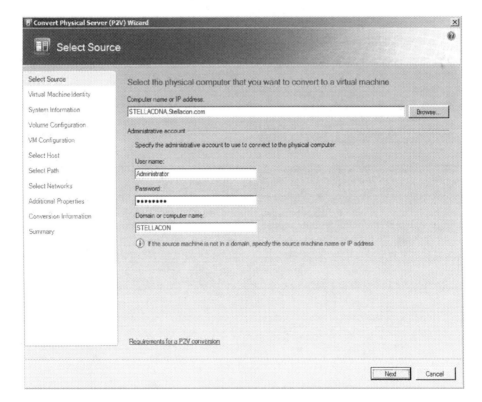

4. After you have filled in all the fields, click Next.

5. On the Virtual Machine Identity screen, configure these options:

Field	Value
Virtual Machine Name	TestMachine
Owner	Administrator
Description (optional)	Type a description here.

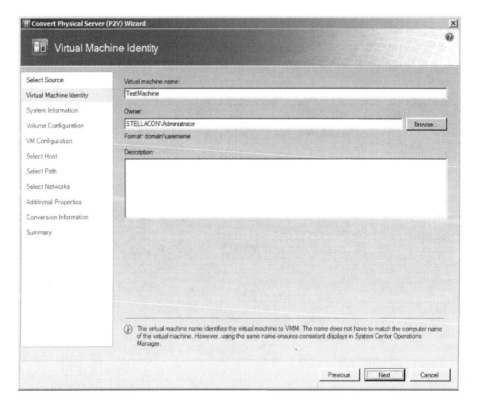

6. After you have filled in all the fields, click Next.

7. On the System Information screen, click the Scan System button. This begins a scan of the source machine and reveals if any components need to be installed before the P2V conversion. Click Next after the scan is complete.

8. The Volume Configuration screen is next. This screen shows you the volumes that you can convert. There are some settings that you can configure, as follows:

EXERCISE 5.1 *(continued)*

Field	Value
Select Volume check box	All volumes that can be converted will be shown. The system and boot volumes have to be converted. So if both volumes are on the C: volume, the volume will automatically be selected and grayed out. Choose any other volumes that you want to convert.
VHD Size	Choose the size of your VHD.
VHD Type	Dynamic or Fixed are your two options. Choose Dynamic to save hard disk space.
Channel	Choose Primary channel (0).
Conversion Options link	You can choose between Online or Offline conversion. The default is Online conversion. Accept the default.
Turn Off Source Computer After Conversion	This check box allows the system to shut down after the conversion is complete. Make sure this check box is not selected.

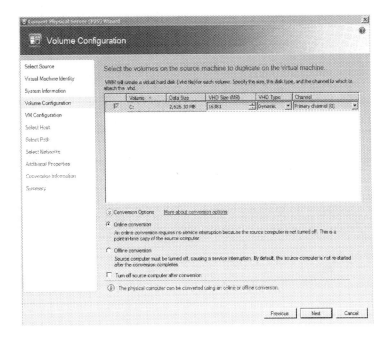

9. After you have filled in all the fields, click Next.

10. On the Virtual Machine Configuration screen, select the number of processors and the amount of memory you want to use for this new virtual machine. We have selected 1 processor and 512MB. Click Next.

11. On the Select Host screen, select which machine you want to deploy this virtual machine. All host servers appear in the Ratings box and a rating based on stars also appears (5 highest/0 lowest). Choose the host server where you want this virtual machine to reside and click Next.

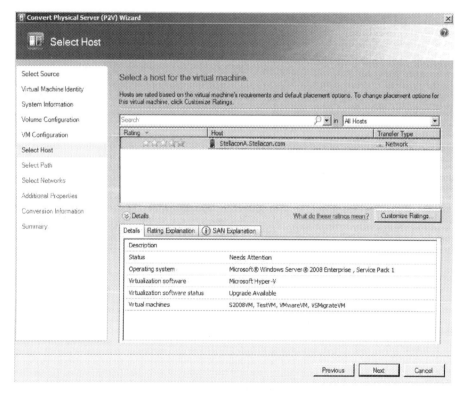

12. The Select Path page is next. This screen allows you to choose the path where the virtual machine files will be located. If you need to change the default settings, click the Browse button and choose the location for your files. We chose our D: drive due to hard drive space. After you set your path, click Next.

13. On the Select Networks page, choose New Virtual Network from the Network Adapter pull-down box. Click Next.

14. On the Additional Properties screen, set the following:

Field	Value
Action When Physical Server Starts	Always Automatically Turn On The Virtual Machine
Delay Start (Sec)	180
Actions When Physical Server Stops	Save State

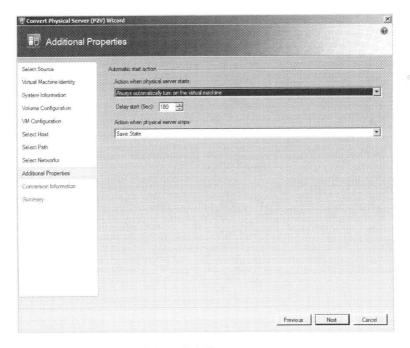

15. After you have filled in all the fields, click Next.

16. On the Conversion Information screen, you see any issues that your conversion may have. You see two main items:

- No Issues Detected

- Issues Reported By The Wizard

If problems are reported, you need to correct them and then click the Check Again button. Continue to do this until you get the message No Issues Detected. Click Next.

17. The next screen is the Summary screen. Verify all the settings and click the Create button. Optionally you can click the View Script button to view and then copy the script for use with the Windows PowerShell utility.

18. The Jobs screen appears, showing you the status of the conversion. If the job does not complete for any reason, an explanation appears on this screen. The conversion may take a while, so be patient.

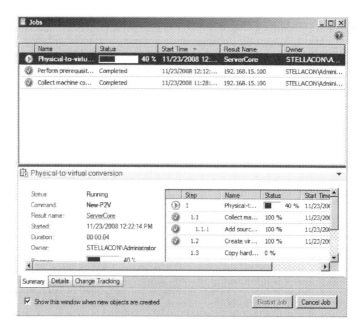

19. After the Jobs screen shows a completed conversion, close the Jobs screen.

20. When you are back at SCVMM 2008, right-click on the TestMachine virtual machine and click Start.

21. Right-click on TestMachine again and choose Connect To Virtual Machine.

22. After the TestMachine virtual machine starts, log in and verify that the conversion worked properly.

23. After you log on the machine and verify that everything is working properly, save the virtual machine by clicking Save State under the Actions section of SCVMM.

24. A Virtual Machine Manager dialog box appears; click Yes.

25. After the virtual machine is saved, close the Virtual Machine Viewer.

26. Close the SCVMM 2008 Admin Console.

The ability to convert a physical machine to a virtual machine can be a useful tool in your virtualization arsenal. Next, let's take a look at converting virtual machines from other vendors to Hyper-V.

Using Virtual-to-Virtual (V2V) Conversion

There may be times when it is necessary for you to convert a virtual machine from another virtual environment over to Hyper-V. SCVMM 2008 will also allow you to do this type of conversion.

Inside SCVMM, you can perform a *virtual-to-virtual machine conversion (V2V)*. A V2V conversion allows you to convert a VMware ESX server virtual machine to a Hyper-V or Virtual Server virtual machine.

There are only certain situations where a V2V conversion is necessary. In many situations, a virtual machine migration may be all you need to do to accomplish your transfer. Table 5.1 shows you when to migrate a virtual machine from another system or when to use the V2V conversion.

TABLE 5.1   Virtualization Conversion Chart

Current Virtualization Environment	Future Virtualization Environment	Use the Following Method
Hyper-V	Hyper-V	Migration
Virtual Server	Hyper-V	Migration
Virtual Server	Virtual Server	Migration
VMware ESX Server	Hyper-V	V2V conversion
VMware ESX Server	Virtual Server	V2V conversion

To use the virtual-to-virtual (V2V) conversion, the operating system that is on the machine that you are getting the virtual machine from (the source machine) must be one of the following:

- Windows Server 2008 (32-bit or 64-bit)
- Windows 2000 Server or Advanced Server with SP4 minimum
- Windows XP Professional (32-bit or 64-bit) with SP2 minimum
- Windows Vista (32-bit or 64-bit) with SP1 minimum

Exercise 5.3 walks you through the steps necessary to convert a VMware virtual machine to a Hyper-V virtual machine. If you do not have a VMware ESX Server, you can download an evaluation copy for free at VMware's website. If you do not have or do not want to download VMware, you can skip this exercise. There is nothing in this exercise that needs to be done for future exercises.

Before we can convert the VMware virtual machine, we need to add the VMware directory to the library share. To do this, we first have to share your VMware directory and then add it to the SCVMM Library share (Exercise 5.2).

EXERCISE 5.2

Sharing the VMware Files

1. Share the VMware directory that contains the VMware virtual machines that we are going to convert.

2. After the VMware folders have been shared, open the SCVMM Admin Console.

3. In the left-hand window, click the Library link (in the bottom section).

4. In the Resources section (left pane), expand Library Servers and then click on the name of your server.

5. Right-click the name of the server and choose Add Library Shares.

6. You should see the new share that you created. Check the check box for the shared directory and click Next.

7. Click the Add Library Shares button in the Summary screen.

8. The Jobs screen appears. After the job completes, close the Jobs screen.

9. You should see the shared directory under the server name. In our example, our share name was VMwareVM.

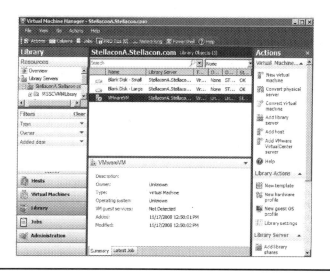

EXERCISE 5.3

Converting a VMware Machine to Hyper-V (V2V)

1. If SCVMM is closed, start the SCVMM 2008 Admin Console.

2. In the Actions pane, click the Convert Virtual Machine link.

3. On the Select Source screen, click the Browse button.

4. On the Select Virtual Machine Source screen, you should see the VMware virtual machine. Click on the virtual machine and click OK.

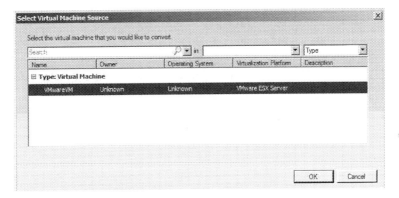

5. When you get back to the Select Source screen, click Next.

6. On the Virtual Machine Identity screen, accept the defaults and click Next.

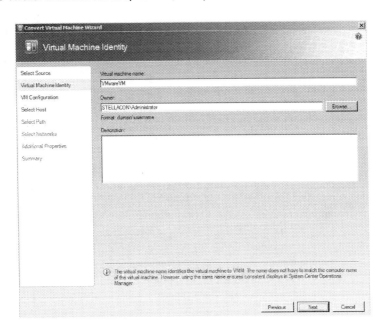

7. On the Virtual Machine Configuration screen, enter the number of processors and the amount of memory for the virtual machine.

8. The Select Host screen appears next. At this screen you can choose the host that you will deploy this virtual machine to. It grades the server based on a zero through five star system (five being the best). Select the Hyper-V server with the most stars. Click Next.

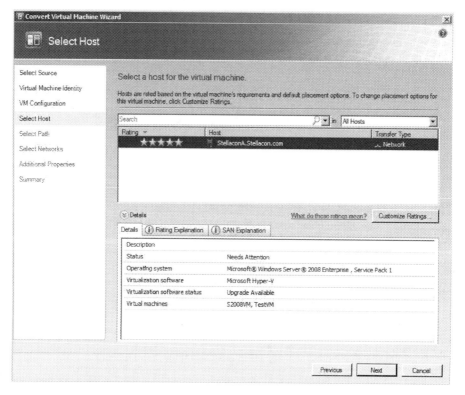

9. On the Select Path screen, accept the defaults and click Next. This screen is where you set the path to the folder where the configuration files reside.

10. On the Select Networks screen, pull down the Virtual Network menu and choose your virtual network. Click Next.

EXERCISE 5.3 *(continued)*

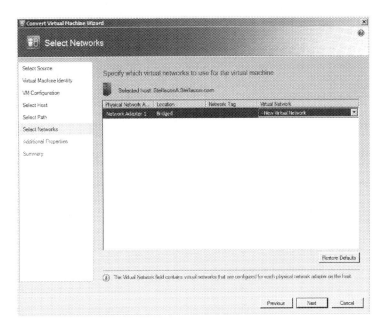

11. The Additional Properties screen is next. On this screen you choose which action to take when the physical server starts and stops. Make sure that Always Automatically Turn On The Virtual Machine and Save State are your two options and click Next.

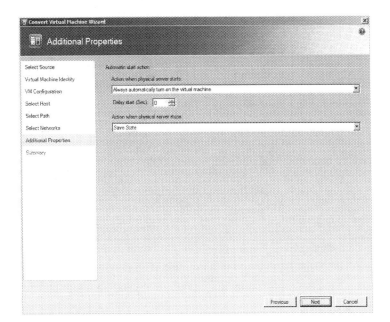

EXERCISE 5.3 *(continued)*

12. On the Summary screen, verify your choices and click the Create button. If you need to change an option, click the Previous button.

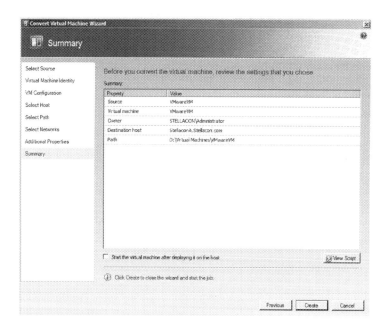

13. The Jobs screen appears and shows you the status of the conversion.

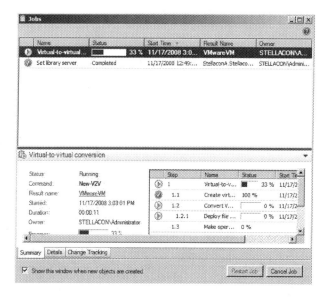

14. Close the Jobs screen. Click the Virtual Machines link in the left-hand window. You will see the new VMware virtual machine added as a Hyper-V virtual machine.

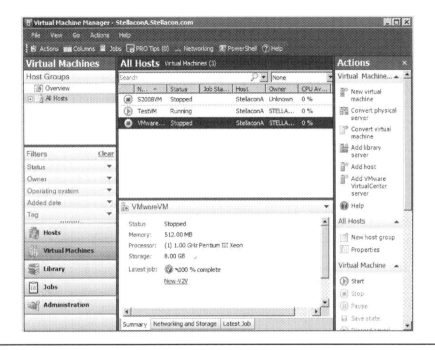

Many organizations have used VMware in the past, and it is important to understand how to convert a virtual machine from their software to Hyper-V. But what if you have used Microsoft virtualization in the past? Knowing how to convert virtual machines from previous versions to the current Hyper-V version is also an important step in moving your virtualization environment forward.

Converting Virtual Machines from Virtual Server and Virtual PC

Many years ago Microsoft threw their hat into the virtualization ring with Virtual Server. Along with Microsoft Windows Server 2003 or 2008, Virtual Server 2005 R2 enables most of your x86 operating systems to run in its own virtual environment. *Virtual Server* is a free download from Microsoft's website.

Microsoft also has a virtualization environment that can operate on its client software. Called Virtual PC, it allows you to create and manage virtual machines without the need of a server operating system. The advantage here is that you can run server operating systems in a client environment like Windows XP or Windows Vista.

Both Microsoft Virtual Server and Virtual PC used the .vhd extension types. Because the Virtual Server and Virtual PC use the .vhd virtual machine types, you only need to move the .vhd files to your library folders and then create a Hyper-V virtual machine using the Virtual Server or Virtual PC .vhd file.

You should be aware of some issues when moving Virtual Server and Virtual PC .vhd files. When starting a VHD from a previous version of virtualization, the processor type will not negatively affect the boot-up process but the chipset will. You may need to change your chip from Intel to AMD or AMD to Intel.

Here's another thing to keep in mind: after you move a VHD from Virtual Server or Virtual PC, when the system starts on Hyper-V for the first time, since the hardware has now changed from the previous virtualization, this may cause the activation feature to be reactivated (since the hardware has now changed from the previous virtualization).

When you are using Virtual Server or Virtual PC, you may have to include some enhancements to the virtual environment to allow operations within that virtualization environment to function properly. These enhancements are called *Virtual Machine Additions*. The Virtual Machine Additions offers these benefits:

- Improved mouse cursor tracking and control
- Greatly improved overall performance
- Virtual machine heartbeat generator
- Optional time synchronization with the clock of the physical computer

If you decide to migrate these virtual machines from Virtual Server or Virtual PC, you may need to uninstall the Virtual Machine Additions before migrating the virtual machines to Hyper-V. Depending on the version of the Virtual Machine Additions, you may be able to uninstall them after the migration. But I recommend just removing them before you migrate the virtual machine over.

Understanding Integration Services

Hyper-V has its own version of Virtual Machine Additions, called *Integration Services*. Integration Services (see Figure 5.1) are services that you want to offer to the Hyper-V virtual machine. To get the advantages of these services, they must be supported by the operating system that is installed on the virtual machine. Here are some of the services that are offered using Integration Services:

- Operating system shutdown
- Time synchronization
- Data exchange

- Heartbeat
- Backup (volume snapshot)

FIGURE 5.1   Integration Services

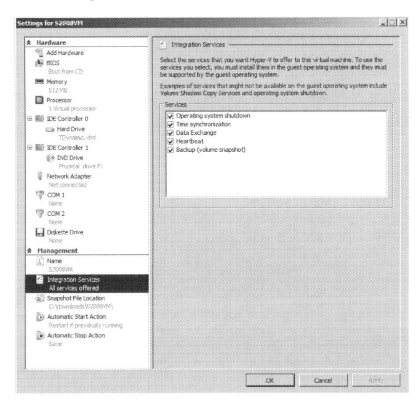

In Exercise 5.4 we will download and install Microsoft Virtual Server. Virtual Server is another virtualization product in the Microsoft lineup. Knowing how to install, configure, and create virtual machines in Virtual Server just adds another virtualization tool to your tool belt. You will have to complete this exercise to accomplish future exercises in this chapter.

EXERCISE 5.4

Downloading and Installing Virtual Server

1. Download and save Virtual Server 2005 from Microsoft's website: http://technet .microsoft.com/en-us/bb738033.aspx. You will need to register for the download.

2. Run the Setup file that you downloaded.

3. An Open File dialog box appears. Click Run to start the installation.

4. The Microsoft Virtual Server 2005 R2 SP1 Setup appears. Click the Install Microsoft Virtual Server 2005 R2 SP1 button.

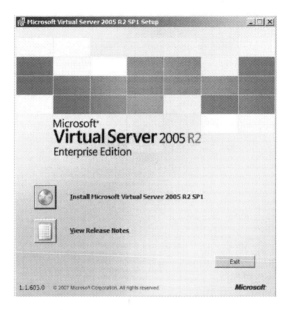

5. On the License Agreement screen, click the I Accept The Terms In This License Agreement radio button and click Next.

6. On the Customer Information screen, enter your name and organization. You will not have to enter a product key for the evaluation download. Click Next.

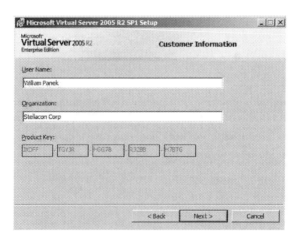

7. On the Setup Type screen, choose the Complete radio button and click Next.

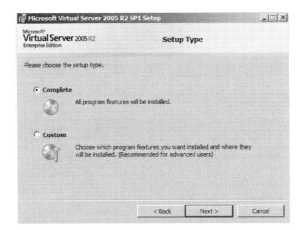

8. On the Configuration Components screen, accept the defaults of port 1024 and Configure the Administration Website to Always Run As The Authenticated User and click Next.

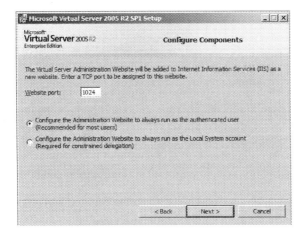

9. The next configuration screen will be for the Windows Firewall. To operate properly, the Virtual Server must be able to go through the firewall without error. If you are using the Windows Firewall, make sure the Enable Virtual Server Exceptions in Windows Firewall check box is selected. Click Next.

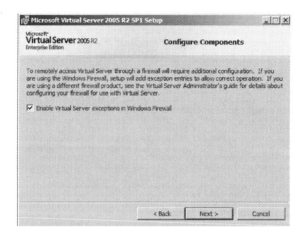

10. The Ready to Install screen appears next. Click the Install button.

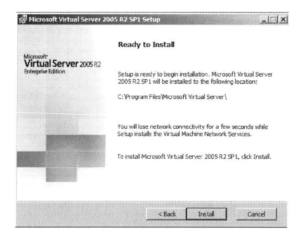

11. If an IIS dialog box appears, click Yes to install the required IIS components. Click the Install button again. The installation should start. A status bar will show you the status of the install.

EXERCISE 5.4 *(continued)*

12. After the installation finishes, a Setup Complete screen appears. Click the Finish button to close the window.

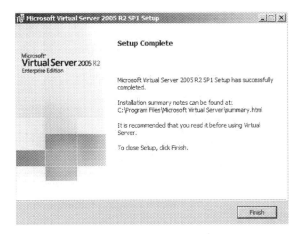

Now that Virtual Server 2005 is installed, we need to create a virtual machine in Virtual Server. In Exercise 5.5 we will create a virtual machine in Virtual Server 2005. Again, you will have to complete this exercise to continue to the other exercises in this chapter.

EXERCISE 5.5

Creating Virtual Machines in Virtual Server

1. Start the Virtual Server Administrative website by clicking Start ➤ All Programs ➤ Microsoft Virtual Server ➤ Virtual Server Administration Website.

2. The Connect To A Server login box will appear. Enter the Administrator username and password, and then click OK.

EXERCISE 5.5 *(continued)*

3. When the Virtual Server 2005 R2 Administrative website starts, click Create under the Virtual Machines section.

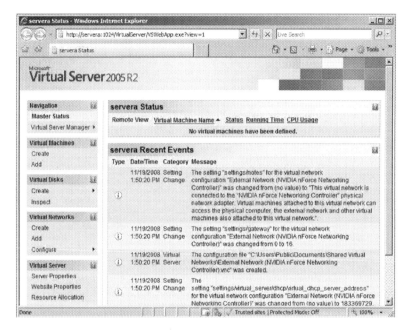

4. Use the following table to fill in all the appropriate fields:

Field	Entry
Virtual Machine Name	VirtualServerVM
Virtual Machine Memory	512
Virtual Hard Disk	Create A New Virtual Hard Disk
Hard Disk Size	10GB
Bus	IDE
Virtual Network Adapter	Choose Your Local Network Adapter

5. Click the Create button.

6. Do not close the Virtual Server Web Administrator.

So at this point we have downloaded and installed Virtual Server and in the previous exercise we created a virtual machine. In Exercise 5.6 we will load an operating system onto the Virtual Server virtual machine. After this exercise is complete, in future exercises we will import this virtual machine into Hyper-V.

EXERCISE 5.6

Installing an Operating System into a Virtual Server Virtual Machine

1. At the Virtual Server 2005 R2 Administration website, click the Configure link and choose the VirtualServerVM.

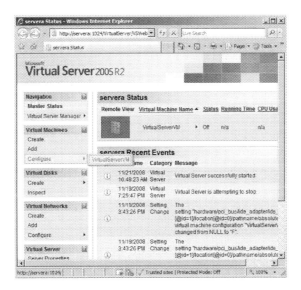

2. In the center window you will see the status of the VirtualServerVM. Click on the VirtualServerVM and choose Turn On.

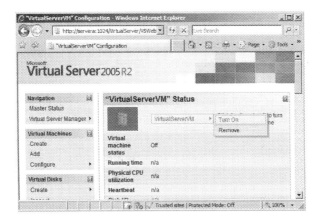

EXERCISE 5.6 (continued)

3. You will see a black thumbnail of the virtual machine. Click on the thumbnail.

4. A Virtual Machine Remote Control (VMRC) Server Properties screen appears. Click the Enable check box next to VMRC Server. Leave the rest of the settings at their defaults. Scroll down to the bottom and click OK.

5. If a Security Warning dialog box appears asking you to install the Virtual Server VMRC ActiveX Client Control, click the Install button.

6. If another dialog box appears warning you about the unencrypted connection, just click the Yes button to continue.

7. Enter the administrator's username and password on the credentials screen.

8. Another dialog box appears asking you to use NTLM Authentication. Click the Yes button.

9. The VirtualServerVM appears, and it should state that there is no boot device. Insert the Windows Server 2008 32-bit version DVD. Press the Enter key.

    If the system does not recognize the DVD, click the Configure Virtual-ServerVM link and change the DVD to the physical drive. Click OK. Then click on the thumbnail again and repeat beginning with step 6.

10. The Windows Server 2008 installation should start. Install Windows Server 2008 with a standard full installation. (If you need the steps to install Windows Server 2008, go back to Exercise 1.1 in Chapter 1.)

11. After Windows Server 2008 is installed, change the password to **P@ssw0rd**.

12. After you are logged in, click the Save State link (under the Control Virtual Machine section) on the VirtualServerVM screen.

13. After the VirtualServerVM system state saves, the VirtualServerVM will stop. Close the Virtual Server 2005 Administrator website.

Understanding Virtual PC

Now that you have installed and configured Microsoft Virtual Server, it's time to do the same with Virtual PC. As stated earlier in this chapter, Virtual PC is another virtualization weapon that allows you to set up virtualization without the need of server software.

Virtual PC lets you set up virtualization on a client operating system. This is beneficial for anyone in the industry who has to do testing or configuration. Virtual PC is not meant to run a network like Hyper-V and Virtual Server, but it does give you the ability to test software and patches before installing them live on a network. Also, it is valuable for researching problems in a controlled environment and not on a live server, where you could end up doing more damage than good.

Finally, Virtual PC gives you a training advantage. Think about having the ability to train users on a real product like Windows Server 2008 without having to purchase additional equipment. Virtual PC allows you to train users on products and software while using only one machine.

 **Real World Scenario**

Using Virtual PC

As an instructor and as a consultant, I can't begin to explain how valuable a tool Microsoft Virtual PC can be. I have used it on many occasions either to test a piece of software before installation or to find an answer to a problem in a controlled environment.

Currently, at the time of this writing, I use Microsoft Windows XP Professional on my laptop. On that same laptop I have a version of Virtual PC with both Windows Server 2008 and Windows Server 2008 operating system virtual machines.

While I am on a client site or while I am in the classroom, having a way to test and research problems using multiple operating systems on one client computer system is an invaluable resource.

To run Virtual PC, you need a minimum of a 400MHz Pentium-compatible processor (1.0GHz or faster is recommended) and at least 35MB of free disk space. You can load Virtual PC on Windows Vista with SP1 (Enterprise, Business, Ultimate) or on Windows XP with SP3.

In Exercise 5.7 we will download, install, and configure Virtual PC. We will create a virtual machine and show you how to configure Virtual PC. We are going to do all these steps in the same exercise. You will need to do this from a Microsoft Windows XP or Vista machine (I am using Windows XP in this example).

EXERCISE 5.7

Downloading and Configuring Virtual PC

1. Download Microsoft Virtual PC (currently version 2007) at http://www.microsoft
   .com/downloads/details.aspx?FamilyId=28C97D22-6EB8-4A09-A7F7-
   F6C7A1F000B5&displaylang=en.

2. After the download completes, install the application to your system.

3. Once the product is installed, open the Virtual PC application by clicking Start ➤ All
   Programs ➤ Virtual PC.

4. When you start Virtual PC, the New Virtual Machine Wizard automatically appears.
   Click Next.

5. On the Options screen, click the Create A Virtual Machine radio button.

6. On the Virtual Machine Name And Location screen, type **VirtualPC_VM** and then click Next.

7. On the Operating System screen, choose Other in the pull-down box (we are going to install Windows Server 2008 32-bit). Click Next.

8. On the Memory screen, choose the Adjust The RAM radio button and set it to 512. Click Next.

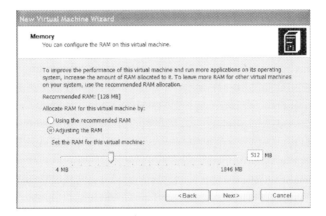

9. On the Virtual Hard Disk screen, click the New Virtual Hard Disk radio button option and click Next.

10. The Virtual Hard Disk Name and Location screen is next. Accept the default location and click Next. You can change the name or location if needed.

11. On the Completing The New Virtual Machine screen, verify the settings and click Finish.

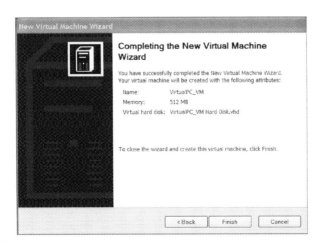

EXERCISE 5.7 *(continued)*

12. The Virtual PC Console now shows the VirtualPC_VM virtual machine. Click on the virtual machine and choose Settings under the Actions menu.

13. The Settings for VirtualPC_VM screen appears. Here is where you can change or verify your settings for this virtual machine. Click on the CD/DVD drive and verify that you are using the local DVD drive. Click OK.

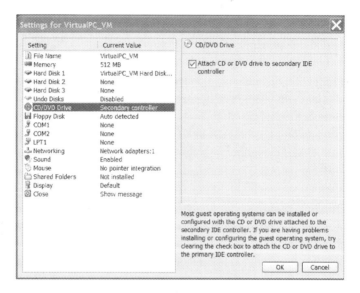

14. Put the Windows Server 2008 32-bit DVD in the physical drive. On the Virtual PC Console screen, click on the VirtualPC_VM and click Start.

15. Install Windows Server 2008 onto the virtual machine. If for any reason the DVD is not recognized, click on the CD menu and choose the Use Physical CD option. Press Enter and finish the installation.

16. After Windows Server 2008 is installed, close the VirtualPC_VM virtual machine and save the changes.

Migrating Microsoft Virtual Server

Now that we have installed both Microsoft Virtual Server and Virtual PC, in Exercise 5.8 we will migrate a Virtual Server 2005 virtual machine to a Hyper-V virtual machine. This exercise will use the virtual machine created in Exercise 5.5. You need to copy the VHD file created by Virtual Server in the previous exercise to a location that the Hyper-V server can access. If you did not complete Exercise 5.5, you need to do so before continuing.

EXERCISE 5.8

Migrating a Virtual Server VM to a Hyper-V VM

1. Open the Hyper-V Manager.

2. In the Actions window in the right-hand side, click the New Virtual Machine link.

3. When the New Virtual Machine Wizard appears, click Next.

4. On the Specify Name And Location screen, type **VSMigrateVM** in the Name field and click Next.

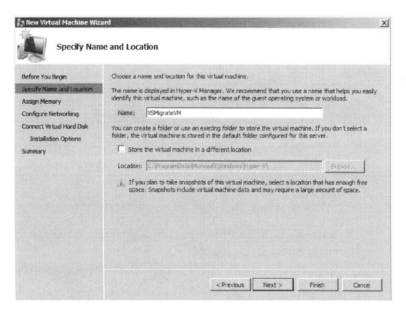

5. On the Assign Memory screen, type **512** and click Next.

6. On the Configure Networking screen, choose your network connection and click Next.

EXERCISE 5.8 *(continued)*

7.   The Connect Virtual Hard Disk screen is next. On this screen click the Use An Existing Virtual Hard Disk radio button. Click the Browse button and choose `VirtualServerVM` `.vhd`. Click the Open button.

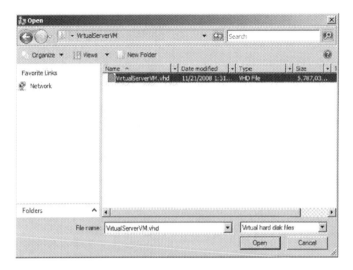

8.   The Connect Virtual Hard Disk screen reappears. Click the Next button.

9.   The Completing the New Virtual Machine Wizard screen is next. Verify your settings and make sure the "Start the virtual machine after it is created" check box is deselected. Click the Finish button.

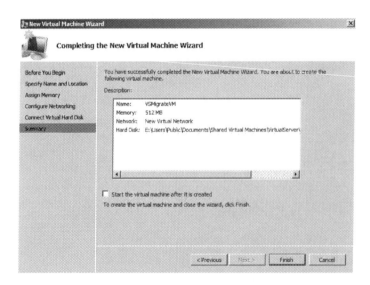

10. After the wizard completes, you will return to the Hyper-V Manager. Click on the new VSMigrateVM virtual machine and click the Start link under Actions.

11. Click the Connect link under VSMigrateVM. The VSMigrateVM virtual machine should start up.

12. Log in. If the machine asks you to reboot the computer, click the Reboot Now button.

13. After the machine starts up, log in and then close the VSMigrateVM virtual machine.

Knowing how to convert older or third-party virtual machines to Hyper-V is something that all IT virtualization administrators need to understand and accomplish. Having these skills not only makes you more valuable in the virtualization industry but also allows you to convert any type of virtualized network to Hyper-V.

Microsoft Assessment and Planning Toolkit

In Chapter 2 we talked about the Microsoft Assessment and Planning (MAP) Toolkit. As we stated in Chapter 2, MAP is a utility that will find machines on your infrastructure and then perform a secure, agent-less, and enterprise-wide inventory of those machines. MAP generates your inventory report in both Microsoft Excel and Microsoft Word.

The inventory that MAP creates will allow you to organize computer resources and device information from a single networked computer. One of the advantages to using MAP is that no software agent needs to be installed on the client machine.

Having an inventory like this will help you determine if the machines on your infrastructure will have the capability of loading Microsoft Windows Vista or Server 2008, Microsoft Office 2007, and Microsoft Application Virtualization. Another advantage of using MAP is that it will help you determine how to deploy your servers based on utilization.

If you're using Hyper-V or Virtual Server, you can use MAP to generate an inventory report that will also provide server consolidation recommendations. This report will also state which servers are good candidates for server virtualization. The MAP report will also provide recommendations on how to physically place your virtualization servers on your infrastructure.

We installed and configured the Microsoft Assessment and Planning (MAP) Toolkit in Chapter 2. If you want to test your network and run the inventory report, refer to the Chapter 2 exercises on MAP.

Using the MAP toolkit to determine which servers and how to place these servers on your infrastructure can help you reduce network congestion and avoid problems down the road.

Summary

In this chapter we discussed many ways to do conversions and migrations from other virtualization environments to the Hyper-V environment. We started our discussion with using the SCVMM 2008 utility to accomplish physical-to-virtual (P2V) conversions. We explained the benefits of taking live preconfigured running servers and running the P2V conversion and turning them into virtual machines. We also explained how the P2V conversion can save you time by doing the conversions while you have the ability to do other tasks.

We then continued our conversion discussion by exploring virtual-to-virtual (V2V) conversions using the SCVMM utility. You saw how this conversion gives you the ability to convert a third-party virtual machine like VMware to a Hyper-V virtual machine.

Our focus then turned to converting Microsoft Virtual Server and Microsoft Virtual PC virtual machines to Hyper-V virtual machines. We discussed how both Virtual Server and Virtual PC programs used the .vhd files and how to migrate these files after you move them to a Hyper-V library location.

We then finished our chapter with a discussion on using the Microsoft Assessment and Planning Solution Accelerator (MAP) utility and how this utility could help any administrator who is trying to determine which servers to virtualize and where to place them.

In the next chapter we will explore managing templates, profiles, and the image library using the SCVMM 2008 utility. We will also discuss managing virtual machine settings like DVD/ISO, NIC, and many others. You will learn how to configure these settings in both the Hyper-V Management utility and the SCVMM 2008 utility.

Exam Essentials

Understand physical-to-virtual (P2V) conversion.   The physical-to-virtual (P2V) conversion allows you to convert servers that are already built and running on your network. You can do a P2V conversion by using the System Center Virtual Machine Manager 2008 utility or with the Microsoft Windows PowerShell command-line utility.

Be familiar with virtual-to-virtual (V2V) conversion.   The SCVMM 2008 utility can also perform a virtual-to-virtual machine conversion (V2V). A V2V conversion allows you to convert a third-party virtual machine (e.g., VMware ESX server) to a Microsoft Hyper-V or Virtual Server virtual machine. Be able to identify which virtual environments need to be converted using the V2V conversion and which environments just need to be migrated to the Hyper-V environment.

Know how to convert Virtual Server and Virtual PC.   Both Microsoft Virtual Server and Virtual PC use the .vhd file extension types. Understand how to move these files to a shared library directory and then how to migrate the files into the Hyper-V environment. Know the issues that you need to address when moving Virtual Server and Virtual PC .vhd files. Before you migrate these files to Hyper-V, you may need to uninstall the Virtual Machine Additions. Know how to change your chip from Intel to AMD or AMD to Intel.

Be familiar with Integration Services.   Integration Services are services that you want to offer to the Hyper-V virtual machine. Some of these services are Operating System Shutdown, Time Synchronization, Data Exchange, Heartbeat, and Backups (volume snapshot). Understand how to configure the Integration Services.

Know how to use Microsoft Assessment and Planning Solution Accelerator (MAP).   MAP allows you to use Hyper-V or Virtual Server to generate an inventory report that will also provide server consolidation recommendations. This report will show you which servers are good candidates for server virtualization and where to physically place these servers on your infrastructure.

Review Questions

1. You are the administrator of a mid-sized organization with four servers. You have decided to monitor the usage levels of your servers. You realize that your servers are averaging at less than 25 percent capacity. You want to consolidate your server workload by using Microsoft Hyper-V virtualization. Which Microsoft application can help you consolidate your servers using Hyper-V?

   A. System Control Machine Manager

   B. Hyper-V Control Manager

   C. System Center Virtual Machine Manager

   D. Virtual Control Center

2. You are the manager of an IT department that has four servers and 400 Windows Vista and Windows XP machines. You have decided to use Hyper-V in your organization to help reduce equipment costs. You need to set up four virtual machines the same as the four servers that you have set up. What is the best way to create four virtual machines with the same settings as the four already created servers?

   A. P2V conversion

   B. V2V conversion

   C. V2P conversion

   D. P2P conversion

3. You are an IT manager for a mid-sized company. Your company has decided to start using virtualization. You want to use the System Center Virtual Machine Manager to do P2V conversions on some of the machines within your infrastructure. The machines have to have which operating systems loaded to do the conversion? (Choose all that apply.)

   A. Windows NT 4.0 with Service Pack 4

   B. Windows Server 2000 with Service Pack 2

   C. Windows Server 2003 with Service Pack 2

   D. Windows XP with Service Pack 2

4. Crystal, your IT manager, has been using virtualization for many years. She has been using a VMware ESX Server to run her network. She has started looking at migrating her entire network to Windows Server 2008. She wants to also migrate her virtual machines from VMware ESX Server to the Windows Server 2008 Hyper-V role. Which utility can she use to migrate her VMware ESX Server to Hyper-V virtual machines?

   A. P2V conversion

   B. V2V conversion

   C. V2P conversion

   D. P2P conversion

5. You are the network administrator for a large organization that has been using various version of virtualization for years. Your organization has used Virtual Server and VMware to help virtualize your network. You have decided to use Hyper-V to run your network. You have heard about a utility that can help you convert your virtual machines from Virtual Server and VMware to Hyper-V. Which of the following need to be converted using the V2V utility? (Choose all that apply.)

   A. Virtual Server to Hyper-V

   B. Virtual PC to Hyper-V

   C. Hyper-V to Hyper-V

   D. VMware to Hyper-V

6. Your company has been using Microsoft Virtual Server for three years for its entire virtualized environment. One of the managers has asked you to give a presentation on virtualization. During this lecture, someone asks you what Virtual Machine Additions do. Which of the following does Virtual Machine Additions accomplish? (Choose all that apply.)

   A. Improved mouse cursor tracking and control

   B. Greatly improved overall performance

   C. Virtual machine heartbeat generator

   D. Optional time synchronization with the clock of the physical computer

7. You are the network administrator for a large organization that has decided to switch from Virtual Server to Hyper-V. When you were using Virtual Server, you used Virtual Machine Additions. Now that you are switching to Hyper-V, you need to use a similar service. What is the Hyper-V equivalent to Virtual Machine Additions?

   A. Virtual Machine Additions

   B. Integration Services

   C. Virtual Integration

   D. Integrated Machine Additions

8. You are the administrator of a mid-sized glass company who has decided to switch from Virtual Server to Microsoft Hyper-V. You have created a Hyper-V virtual machine with Windows Server 2008. You are having issues when the machine's operating system shuts down. You need to help correct the operating system shutdown problem. What do you need to install to solve your problem?

   A. Virtual Machine Additions

   B. Run a V2V conversion

   C. Virtual Integration

   D. Integration Services

9. Your company has decided to use Hyper-V for its entire virtualized environment. You are trying to learn about all the issues surrounding Hyper-V. You start reading about Integration Services. You want to know all the services offered by this feature. Which of the following apply? (Choose all that apply.)

    A. Time Synchronization

    B. Data Exchange

    C. Heartbeat

    D. Backup (volume snapshot)

10. Your organization has decided to start using virtualization throughout the network. You would like to use a client-based virtualization throughout the organization for testing and learning purposes. Which of the following should you use on the client machines?

    A. Virtual Server

    B. Hyper-V

    C. Virtual PC

    D. VMware Server

11. You are the network administrator for a large organization. Your manager has asked you to come up with a way to allow end users to be able to test and train on multiple operating systems. You have decided to use Virtual PC 2007 as the solution to your manager's problem. Which operating systems can you load Virtual PC onto?

    A. Windows 2000 Professional w/SP4

    B. Windows Vista with SP1

    C. Windows XP with SP3

    D. Windows NT Server with SP2

12. You are the network administrator for a large organization that has decided to use Hyper-V. You have been using other versions of virtualization for years and you need to use the P2V and V2V utilities. What utility do you have to use to use the P2V and V2V utility?

    A. SCVMM 2008

    B. Hyper-V Web Admin Tool

    C. Server Manager

    D. Virtual Machine Admin Console

13. You are a network administrator for a large organization that has used both Virtual Server and VMware. The version of VMware that you have been using is VMware VirtualCenter 2.5. You are now moving the organization to Hyper-V. You want to use one application that can manage the Hyper-V environment and the VMware applications. Which application would you use?

A. Microsoft Hyper-V Manager

B. SCVMM 2008 VNext

C. SCVMM 2007

D. VMM Manager

14. You are the administrator of a large company that has decided to switch from Virtual Server to Hyper-V. You have created a Hyper-V virtual machine with Windows Server 2008. You want to be able to do volume snapshots. What do you need to install to get the volume snapshots?

A. Virtual Machine Additions

B. Integration Services

C. Virtual Integration

D. Virtual Machine Services

15. You are the network administrator for a large organization that has decided to migrate from Virtual Server to Hyper-V. What are the steps needed to convert the Virtual Server to Hyper-V? (Choose all that apply.)

A. Move the files to a library share.

B. Uninstall any Virtual Machine Additions.

C. Use the V2V utility.

D. Create a new virtual machine with the Virtual Server VHD as the virtual hard disk.

16. You are the administrator for a large company that has decided to implement Windows Server 2008 and Hyper-V. You have some machines that you would like to make virtual machines from. You have decided to use the P2V conversion utility. What are some of the minimum requirements on the source computer in order to use the P2V utility? (Choose all that apply.)

A. Minimum of 512MB of RAM.

B. The computer must use the Advanced Configuration and Power Interface (ACPI) BIOS.

C. The computer must be accessible by the SCVMM utility and the Hyper-V computer.

D. The computer needs to be internal to your network. The computer you are converting can't be part of the perimeter network.

17. You are a network administrator for a large university. You have decided to use the Microsoft Assessment and Planning Solution Accelerator (MAP) tool to help you upgrade your machines. Which of the following are ways to locate the machines on your network? (Choose all that apply.)

   A. Use Active Directory domain services.

   B. Scan an IP address range.

   C. Use the Windows networking protocols.

   D. Import computer names from a file.

18. You are the network administrator for a small company. Your organization has decided to use the Microsoft Assessment and Planning Solution Accelerator (MAP) tool. You need to put in an order for additional software. Which of the following are necessary requirements to run MAP? (Choose all that apply.)

   A. Microsoft Visual Basic

   B. Microsoft SQL Server 2005 Express

   C. Microsoft Word

   D. Microsoft Excel

19. As a system administrator you have decided to use the Microsoft Assessment and Planning Solution Accelerator (MAP) tool. You want to look at some of the reports that MAP generates. Which of the following can MAP generate a scenario report about? (Choose all that apply.)

   A. Currently installed client operating systems and their requirements for migrating to Windows Vista

   B. Currently installed Microsoft Office software and their requirements for migrating to Microsoft Office 2007

   C. Server performance by using the Performance Metrics Wizard

   D. Hyper-V or Virtual Server 2005 server consolidation and placement

20. You are a network administrator for a mid-sized company. Your organization currently uses Windows Server 2000 and 2003 and Windows XP professional. You have decided to upgrade the network to Windows Server 2008 and Microsoft Vista. You have also decided to use Hyper-V. Which application can help you determine which machines can be upgraded to Windows Server 2008 and Vista?

   A. Microsoft Migration tool

   B. Microsoft Upgrade tool

   C. Microsoft Assessment and Planning Solution Accelerator tool

   D. Microsoft 2008 Upgrade and Migration tool

Answers to Review Questions

1. C. System Center Virtual Machine Manager can consolidate server workloads using virtual machines. By allowing virtual servers to handle more of the workload, your organization will require fewer servers, thus saving on equipment, space, and power requirements.

2. A. Creating the four servers by converting the physical machines to virtual machines is easiest through a process known as physical-to-virtual (P2V) conversion. P2V conversions are now included free with the SCVMM 2008 utility. This gives you the ability to convert servers that are already built and running on your network.

3. C, D. The SCVMM utility can convert the following operating systems into virtual machines: Windows 2000 Server SP4 or later (offline P2V only), Windows 2000 Advanced Server SP4 or later (offline P2V only), Windows Server 2003 (32-bit or 64-bit) SP1 or later, Windows XP Professional (32-bit or 64-bit) SP2 or later, Windows Vista (32-bit or 64-bit) SP1 or later, and Windows Server 2008 (32-bit or 64 bit).

4. B. A virtual-to-virtual (V2V) conversion allows you to convert a VMware ESX server virtual machine to a Hyper-V or Virtual Server virtual machine.

5. D. The V2V utility is only necessary in specific situations. If you are migrating Virtual Server or Virtual PC, the V2V conversion is not needed, since both Virtual Server and Virtual PC use .vhd files and they need to be just migrated into Hyper-V. Only VMware ESX Servers need to use the V2V conversion utility.

6. A, B, C, D. Virtual Machine Additions are improvements to the virtual machine. They allow for better performance and provide all four of the above features.

7. B. Integration Services are services that you want to offer to the Hyper-V virtual machine. To get the advantages of these services, they must be supported by the operating system that is installed on the virtual machine.

8. D. Integration Services are services that you want to offer to the Hyper-V virtual machine. One of the services that the Integration Services offers is the operating system shutdown.

9. A, B, C, D. Integration Services are services that you want to offer to the Hyper-V virtual machine. To get the advantages of these services, they must be supported by the operating system that is installed on the virtual machine. The following services are offered using Integration Services: Operating System Shutdown, Time Synchronization, Data Exchange, Heartbeat, and Backup (volume snapshot).

10. C. Virtual PC is a client version of virtualization, and it allows you to do local testing and is also useful as a learning tool.

11. B, C. To run Virtual PC 2007, you need a minimum of a 400MHz Pentium-compatible processor (1.0GHz or faster recommended) and at least 35MB of free disk space. You can load Virtual PC on Windows Vista with SP1 (Enterprise, Business, Ultimate), or Windows XP with SP3.

12. A. You can use the SCVMM 2008 utility to use both the P2V and V2V utility. The SCVMM utility also lets you create and manage virtual machines. The SCVMM 2008 utility is a one-stop shop for all of your Hyper-V management tools.

13. B. If you want to be able to manage both Hyper-V and VMware (VMware VirtualCenter 2.5 or VMware VirtualCenter 2.0.1) virtualization networks, you should use the System Center Virtual Machine Manager 2008.

14. B. Integration Services are services that you want to offer to the Hyper-V virtual machine. One of the services that Integration Services offers is Backup (volume snapshots). The following other services are provided as well: Operating System Shutdown, Time Synchronization, Data Exchange, and Heartbeat.

15. A, B, D. To convert a virtual machine from Virtual Server to Microsoft Hyper-V, you need to copy the VHD files to a shared library folder, uninstall and Virtual Machine Additions, and then just create a new virtual machine with the existing VHD file.

16. A, B, C, D. When using the System Center Virtual Machine Manager, the computer that you are converting with the P2V utility must meet a few minimum requirements before you convert it properly. You need a minimum of 512MB of RAM; the computer must use the Advanced Configuration and Power Interface (ACPI) BIOS; the computer must be accessible by the SCVMM utility and the Hyper-V computer; and the computer needs to be internal to your network.

17. A, B, C, D. All four of these methods are used for MAP to help locate computers on your network. Also the final option you can use is to manually enter computer names and credentials.

18. B, C, D. To run the Microsoft Assessment and Planning Solution Accelerator (MAP) tool, you must also have other supporting software. This software includes Microsoft SQL Server 2005 Express, Microsoft Word (2003 with SP1 or 2007), and Microsoft Excel (2003 with SP1 or 2007).

19. A, B, C, D. All of these can be scenario-generated reports. MAP gives you the ability to generate six different scenario types. These scenarios let you determine how to upgrade or implement hardware and software.

20. C. The Microsoft Assessment and Planning Solution Accelerator (MAP) tool will locate machines on your network and do a full inventory of these machines. MAP will then tell you which computers can be upgraded and which computers can't be upgraded.

Chapter

6

Managing Virtual Machines

MICROSOFT EXAM OBJECTIVES COVERED IN THIS CHAPTER:

✓ **Managing Virtual Machine Settings**

    ※ May include but not limited to: DVD/ISO, NIC, Integration Services, state of virtual machines, Hypercall adapter availability requirements, reboot/start options, BIOS, memory, processor (Windows NT 4.0)

✓ **Managing Templates, Profiles, and the Image Library by using SCVMM vNext**

    ※ May include but not limited to: ISOs, VHDs, deployment from library

At this point in the book, you should be feeling pretty comfortable with creating virtual machines. We are now going to move into the realm of managing virtual machines and templates.

By managing virtual machines properly, you can help your organization reduce its chances of having any problems in the future. Also, you ensure that your virtual machines will operate at peak performance.

Another helpful task that you can manage in Microsoft Hyper-V is setting up Hyper-V templates, profiles, and the image library. Templates allow you to have a copy of a virtual machine that you can use to create other copies of virtual machines.

We will start the chapter with managing the virtual machine variables. You will learn how to manage these variables in the System Center Virtual Machine Manager 2008 (SCVMM) 2008 utility.

Another useful tool in your virtualization tool belt is the template. Templates allow you to create a virtual machine that can be copied over and over again to create new virtual machines with the same hardware and software settings.

You can use image libraries to help organize all of your virtual machines. Organizing your virtual machines into libraries allows you to find virtual machines quickly and easily. But before we show you how to organize your virtual server and virtual machines, let's talk about configuring the virtual machines and servers properly.

Managing Virtual Machine Settings

In Chapter 3, "Configuring Hyper-V," we started talking about some of the Hyper-V configuration options and how to set them using the Hyper-V Manager. In this chapter we will discuss all the configuration options for both the virtual machine and the server using the SCVMM 2008 utility.

Establishing virtual machine settings is one of the most important tasks that you can perform while using Hyper-V. By configuring the virtual machine properly, you are ensuring that your virtual network runs properly and more efficiently.

Application configuration helps us truly become IT professionals. Most people can take a DVD and start an installation, but knowing how to properly configure the application is what separates the professionals from the amateurs.

Configuring Virtual Machines with SCVMM

The SCVMM 2008 utility allows you to manage and configure all of your virtual machines from one location. The first thing that you can check in SCVMM is the status of your virtual machines (see Figure 6.1). By knowing the status of the virtual machines, you can see if any virtual machines need attention or if the virtual machines are stopped or running.

FIGURE 6.1   You can check the status of your virtual machines on this screen.

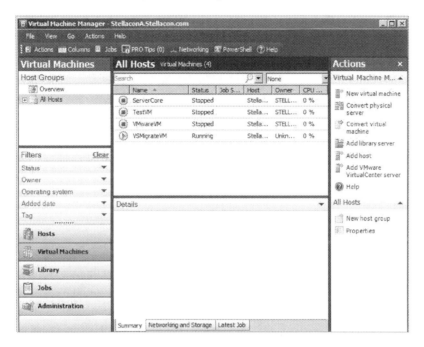

Once you have viewed the status of the virtual machines, you can right-click on any of the virtual machines and then choose from different configuration options (see Figure 6.2). Let's take a look at the different options:

Start   This option allows you to start a virtual machine that is currently stopped.

Stop   This option allows you to stop a virtual machine that is currently started.

Pause   This option allows you to suspend the virtual machine and save the virtual machine state in memory. To restart the virtual machine, you would then choose Start.

Save State   This option allows you to currently save the present state of the virtual machine. When choosing this option, the virtual machine will be stopped and saved. After you save the virtual machine state, you must restart the virtual machine by clicking the Start option.

FIGURE 6.2 Virtual machine options

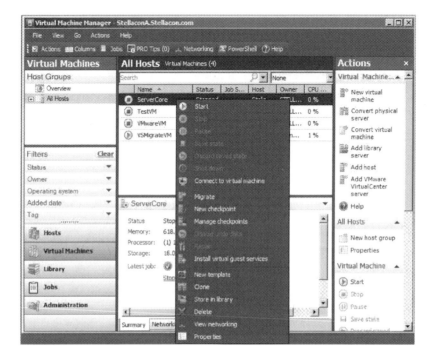

Discard Saved State This option deletes the saved state of the virtual machine and then the virtual machine is stopped.

Shut Down This option allows you to shut down the operating system on the virtual machine.

Connect To Virtual Machine This option allows you to connect to a virtual machine by using the Remote Desktop Protocol (RDP). When you double-click on the thumbnail screen or choose the Connect To Virtual Machine option, a larger virtual machine screen appears, allowing you to log on and work on the virtual machine.

Migrate This option allows you to move a virtual machine from one Hyper-V server to another Hyper-V server.

New Checkpoint Creating checkpoints allows you to save a virtual machine at a specific spot and then restore to that spot later. You can create multiple checkpoints, which will allow you to return a virtual machine to any point in time where the checkpoint was created. When a checkpoint is created, all of the virtual machine state is saved, including the hard disk content and application data files.

Manage Checkpoints This option allows you to edit, create, or merge checkpoints.

Disable Undo Disks In Hyper-V, you can use Undo Disks to help return a virtual machine to its previous state. The problem is that Undo Disks is not supported in SCVMM. To return a virtual machine to a previous state, you would use checkpoints. SCVMM lets you disable Undo Disks so that you can manage previous states more properly. You can use Undo Disks in Hyper-V Manager.

Repair   This option helps you fix a virtual machine that has failed. The Repair option tries to fix the action that caused the failure, and then it restores the virtual machine to a previous state before the failure.

Install Virtual Guest Services   This option installs the virtual guest service on the virtual machines. Hyper-V uses the Integration Components and virtual servers use Virtual Machine Additions.

New Template   This option allows you to create a new template. Templates let you create new virtual machines with standardized hardware and software settings.

Clone   This option allows you to create a double or clone virtual machine from an existing virtual machine.

Store In Library   SCVMM gives you the ability to store a virtual machine in a virtual machine library. You can then organize the virtual machines by the virtual machine libraries.

Delete   This option deletes all of the virtual machine components, including the configuration files and the virtual hard disk.

View Networking   This option brings up a dialog box (see Figure 6.3) with a graphical view that you can click on to explore and configure your NIC adapter.

FIGURE 6.3   View Networking option

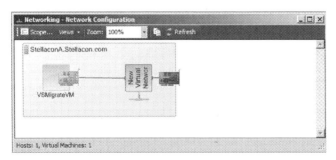

Properties   This option allows you to configure the properties of the virtual machine.

Using these options, you can configure your virtual machine to perform at its best. Now let's take a closer look at some of the configuration options and how they can be set.

Configuring Virtual Machine Properties

The virtual machine properties are another set of configuration items that you can configure to help increase the reliability and performance of your virtual machines.

When using SCVMM, you can configure the virtual machine properties by right-clicking on the virtual machine and choosing the Properties option. When the Virtual Machine Properties window appears, you will have multiple tabs that you can configure.

> We are configuring the virtual machine properties using the SCVMM 2008 utility. You can also configure these properties using the Hyper-V Manager.

General Tab

The first tab that appears when you open the Virtual Machine Properties window is the General tab (see Figure 6.4). The General tab has a few of the basic virtual machine properties that you can set, such as name and description, but it also contains values that can help you when you look at costs and filters. Let's take a look at each value:

FIGURE 6.4   The General tab of the Virtual Machine Properties window

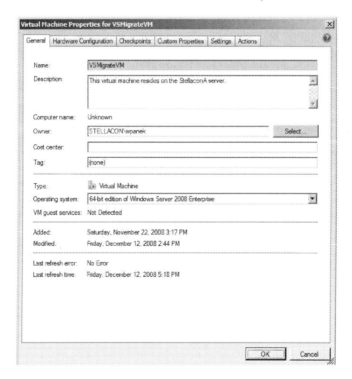

Name   This is a unique name that identifies the virtual machine to SCVMM. If you give two virtual machines the same name, this will cause virtual machine failures. The virtual machine name does not have to be the same as the name of the computer in the operating

system. But it is a good rule of thumb to assign the same name to both the operating system that is deployed in the virtual machine and the virtual machine.

Description The description section is an area where you can put in some details that make it easy to recognize the location and description of the virtual machine.

Owner This option allows you to determine the owner of the virtual machine. The owner of the virtual machine must have an Active Directory account in the domain. If the virtual machine is going to be in the self-service user mode, you need to put in the self-service user or group in this location.

Cost Center The cost center value is a value that you can enter to help you track resources used. This information can then be given to a cost center so they can calculate a charge for the use of these virtual machines. Many organizations need the ability to charge departments or companies for the use of their resources. The cost center value helps a cost center determine the charges for virtual machine usage.

Tag You set up the tags value to help you filter result lists in the virtual machine view. For example, you want to be able to filter virtual machine views by tags. You can add a Tag column in the virtual machine results pane and then filter the results using these tags.

Operating System This is the location where you can list which operating system is been installed onto the virtual machine.

The rest of the General tab shows you if any errors have occurred, the last time the virtual machine was modified and added, and the last time the virtual machine was refreshed. Now let's take a look at the next tab in the Virtual Machine Properties window: the Hardware Configuration tab.

Hardware Configuration Tab

The Hardware Configuration tab is where you set up the hardware settings for this virtual machine (see Figure 6.5). For example, you can specify how the machine's BIOS will start up, set the virtual machine memory, and specify the number of processors that this virtual machine is going to use. To configure the options on this tab, make sure the virtual machine is not running. If it is running, the values will be grayed out.

BIOS This setting lets you determine how your virtual machine BIOS Startup Order is configured. You can have the virtual machine first try to boot up using a CD, then IDE Hard Drive, then PXE Boot, and finally Floppy. It does not have to be in this order. You can choose the order in which you want the virtual machine to boot up.

Processor The Processor section allows you to set up the number of processors that this virtual machine is going to use. The maximum number of processors will be determined by the virtualization platform of the host server (see Figure 6.6). You can also set the CPU type in this section. Finally, you have the ability to limit processor functionality. You only need to limit processor functionality if you are loading Windows Server NT 4.0 on the virtual machine as the operating system.

FIGURE 6.5   The Hardware Configuration tab of the Virtual Machine Properties window

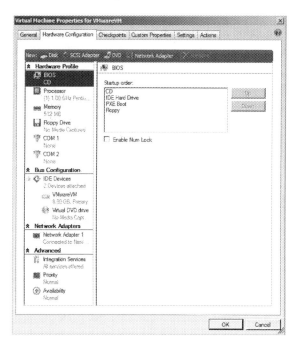

FIGURE 6.6   Processor configuration

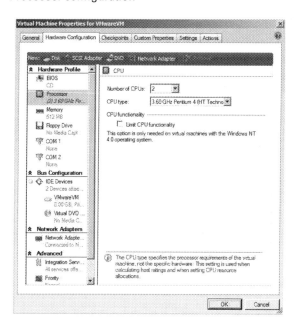

Memory   This section allows you to set the virtual machine memory. This setting only applies to this virtual machine. This gives you the ability to allocate more memory to a virtual machine that requires it due to a heavy workload and less memory to virtual machines that will not have a heavy load placed on the virtual server. Hyper-V will allow you to allocate 64GB of memory as a maximum amount to a virtual machine.

Floppy Disk   This is the section where you configure the use of a floppy drive. You have three options that you can set:

- No Media
- Physical Floppy Drive
- Existing Virtual Floppy Disk File

COM 1 and COM 2   There are two sections here. You have the ability to configure two virtual communication (COM) ports. COM ports used to be the ports that all of us hooked external modems to. They can be used for other types of older hardware, and they may still be needed depending on your network configuration. There are two settings when choosing a virtual COM port:

- None
- Named Pipe

IDE Devices   There are two different types of IDE devices that the virtual machine will use: virtual hard drive and CD/DVD. You can have up to four IDE devices connected to a virtual machine. Each one has its own fields that can be configured:

> **Virtual Hard Disk**   In the Virtual Hard Disk section of the hardware configuration settings, the first value that you need to configure is the Channel field. The Channel field allows you to select the channel on which the IDE device is attached. The next field that you can configure is Fully Qualified Path to File. This is the path that points to the virtual hard disk. Finally, you can do some maintenance in this section to the virtual hard disk:
>
> - Convert to Fixed Type Virtual Hard Disk
> - Compact Virtual Hard Sisk
> - Expand Virtual Hard Disk
>
> **Virtual CD/DVD Drive**   This configuration section also has a Channel field that you can configure. It also has a Capture mode. The Capture mode gives you three choices that you can make:
>
> - No Media
> - Physical CD/DVD Drive
> - Existing Image File (ISO image)
>
> Virtual CD/DVD drives can be linked to an ISO image file or a physical drive.

SCSI Adapter   If you are going to use SCSI devices, you can add a SCSI adapter in the SCVMM utility. The one drawback to using SCSI adapters is that you can't boot up your virtual machine using a SCSI adapter. You can only boot up using IDE.

Network Adapters   This section allows you to configure the network (NIC) adapter (see Figure 6.7). The NIC makes it possible for the virtual machines to talk to the physical network. The first setting you can configure is whether or not the network adapter is connected to this virtual machine:

FIGURE 6.7   Network adapter configuration

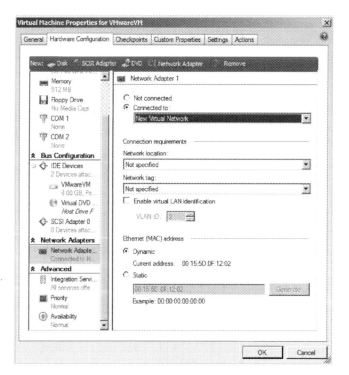

Connection Requirements   In the middle section of the Network Adapter section is the connection requirements. In this section you can configure a network location, network tag, and VLAN identification.

- The Network Location field allows you to select which network that you want to connect your virtual machine adapter. Setting this field allows you to differentiate between the virtual network connection and the physical network connection.

- The Network Tag field allows you to define what the virtual machine does. For example, say you have a virtual machine that has two virtual adapters but one of the adapters is going to be used primarily for DNS name resolution. The tag for this adapter could then be "DNS." This lets you determine what this virtual adapter is doing.

- The Enable Virtual LAN Identification field allows you to configure the VLAN identification number.

Ethernet (MAC) Address   This section allows you to configure a MAC address for the virtual network adapter. You can dynamically configure the MAC address, which means that the system will assign a MAC address to the virtual network adapter, or you can manually configure a MAC address. Two adapters can't have the same MAC address associated to them. This will cause network packet problems on your network.

Integrated Services   Integrated Services are the extra services that you want your virtual machine to complete while running in Hyper-V. There are five services that you can choose for your virtual machine:

- Operating System Shutdown
- Time Synchronization
- Data Exchange
- Heartbeat
- Backup (Volume Snapshot)

Priority   When you create your virtual machines, some virtual machines may run more important tasks (like Active Directory) than other virtual machines. The Priority section gives you the ability to assign a virtual machine a higher priority to the host machine's CPU. There are four priority settings that you can choose from:

- High
- Normal (the default)
- Low
- Custom

Availability   In the Availability section you have only one check box to configure: Make This VM Highly Available. Choose this option if you want this virtual machine to run on a clustered Hyper-V Host server. We will discuss Hyper-V and clustering in Chapter 7, "Hyper-V and Failover Clusters."

The Hardware Configuration tab is important to understand and configure properly if you want to avoid problems in the future. Now let's move on to the next tab, Checkpoints.

Checkpoints Tab

The Checkpoints tab allows a Hyper-V administrator to create and restore virtual machine checkpoints (see Figure 6.8). Checkpoints give you the ability to save the state of each virtual hard disk that is associated with a virtual machine. Checkpoints save all of the virtual hard disk data, including the hard disk content, hardware configuration information (Hyper-V server only), and data files.

The advantage to using checkpoints is that you are making a backup of the virtual machine. This allows you to restore a previous checkpoint if the operating system fails.

FIGURE 6.8 The Checkpoints tab of the Virtual Machine Properties window

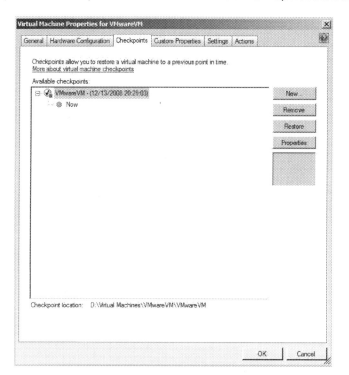

 Real World Scenario

Using Checkpoints for Recoverability

Checkpoints are a very important part of using Hyper-V and the SCVMM utility. There have been many times in my career where I needed to install services or applications to a live server. This is where checkpoints can save you in the event of an error.

Very early in my IT years I needed to install a Microsoft server service pack. I received the service pack by CD and loaded the CD at the end of the business day. Back then, we only had backups and we did not have checkpoints. After I installed the service pack, the server crashed and stopped responding. I had to reload my server from my previous tape backup.

Now looking at that same scenario today, before I start the install of the service pack on the virtual machine, I do a new checkpoint and save the virtual machine. If I load the service pack and get some type of error, I just restore the checkpoint from before the installation and I am back up and running without the need of backups or rebuilds.

You have the ability to create multiple virtual machine checkpoints, but you need to remember that every time you create a new checkpoint, you use hard disk space. Using Hyper-V, you can create up to a maximum of 50 checkpoints. You should always remove unused checkpoints from the Checkpoints tab.

Checkpoints are not meant to be a backup but they are a temporary solution for when changes have to be made to a virtual machine. Checkpoints are stored on the virtual machine host, and if the Hyper-V host server fails, you can lose both the virtual machine and the checkpoints.

Custom Properties Tab

The Custom Properties tab allows you to set up 10 custom fields for a virtual machine (see Figure 6.9). You can then use these custom fields to identify, track, and monitor virtual machines. You can set these custom fields by location, department, or groups. That's the advantage of using these custom fields; you get to customize your fields based on organizational necessity.

FIGURE 6.9   The Custom Properties tab of the Virtual Machine Properties window

Settings Tab

This tab lets you set up this virtual machine for the self-service role (see Figure 6.10). The self-service role gives an administrator the ability to grant users the right to create their own virtual machines. An administrator has the ability to control the user's environment and give them control over only the actions that the administrator wants to assign.

FIGURE 6.10   The Settings tab of the Virtual Machine Properties window

The SCVMM administrator determines the rights and responsibilities of the self-service users and then the SCVMM administrator can assign these roles. These roles determine how the users can access their virtual machines. To create, modify, and operate their virtual machine, the users would then use the self-service portal website. The administrator can then choose which Hyper-V host server group the virtual machine is placed on. When the virtual machine is created by the user, the virtual machine will automatically get placed on the most suitable administrator-assigned server group host based on host ratings.

After the self-service roles are set up, an administrator can add any Active Directory user or group to the role. If you assign a group to the role, then all users of the group receive the role. If a single user owns a virtual machine, then they can administer the virtual machine, but if a group owns a virtual machine, the entire group can administer the virtual machine.

You may have noticed in Figure 6.10 a field named Quota Points. Quota Points is the setting that you configure to specify how many virtual machines a self-service user can deploy. The Quota Points setting only applies to virtual machines on a host.

Actions Tab

The Actions tab has only two configuration items, but they are two of the most important items that you can set in a virtual machine (see Figure 6.11). These settings relate to how the virtual machine reacts when the host system boots up or shuts down. This is very important because if the physical system shuts down, do you want to save the virtual machine or delete changes that you made?

FIGURE 6.11   The Actions tab of the Virtual Machine Properties window

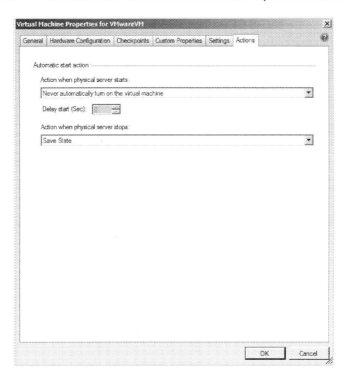

Action When the Physical Server Starts   This item allows you to decide how you want the virtual machine to react when the physical system starts. There are three options that you are allowed to choose from:

- Never Automatically Turn On the Virtual Machine
- Always Automatically Turn On the Virtual Machine
- Automatically Turn On the Virtual Machine if It Was Running When the Physical Server Stopped

Action When Physical Server Stops   This item allows you to decide how you want the virtual machine to react when the physical system stops. There are three options that you are allowed to choose from:

- Save State
- Turn Off Virtual Machine
- Shut Down Guest OS

Well, now that you have seen all the different properties of a virtual machine, it's time to walk through configuring all these different properties. In Exercise 6.1 we will specify the configuration settings of a virtual machine. We will configure a virtual machine that we created in Chapter 4 called TDynamic.vhd.

EXERCISE 6.1

Configuring Virtual Machine Properties

1. Start the SCVMM 2008 utility.

2. In the bottom-left window, click the Virtual Machines box. You should see the TDynamic virtual machine in the center window.

3. Right-click on the TDynamic virtual machine and choose Properties.

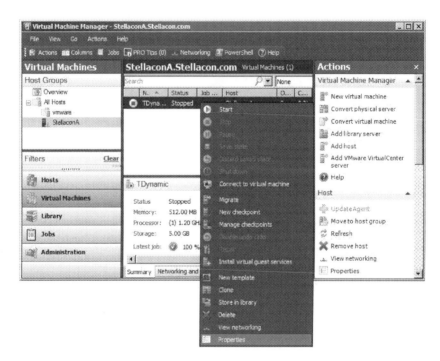

4. On the General tab, make sure all the following are configured:

Field	Value
Description	Dynamic virtual machine
Owner	Your account name
Cost Center	25

Field	Value
Tag	None
Operating System	Choose the Windows Server 2008 version that you installed.

5. Click the Hardware Configuration tab. On the Hardware Configuration screen, configure the following options:

Field	Value
BIOS	CD, IDE Hard Drive, PXE Boot, and Floppy (in that order)
Processor	Number = 1 CPU Type = Your machine's CPU
Memory	1024 MB
IDE Devices - VHD	Primary Channel = 0 Expand Virtual Hard Disk = Add 1GB to whatever you originally made the number.
IDE Devices - DVD	Second Channel = 0 Choose the Physical CD/DVD drive radio button and put in your drive letter.
Integrated Services	All radio buttons checked

6. Click the Checkpoints tab and click the New button.

7. The New Checkpoint dialog box appears. In the Name field, type **TestCheckPoint**, followed by a hyphen and the current date.

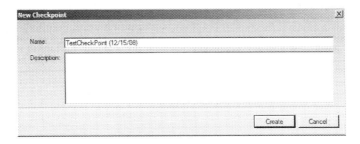

EXERCISE 6.1 *(continued)*

8. Click the Create button. You will see that the new checkpoint is created.

9. Click the Custom Properties tab. Fill in the following custom fields:

Field	Value
Custom 1	Sales
Custom 2	Marketing
Custom 3	Finance
Custom 4	New Hampshire
Custom 5	Dallas

10. Click the Settings tab and change Quota Points to 5.

11. Click the Actions tab and fill in the following fields:

Field	Value
Action When Physical Server Starts	Always Automatically Turn On the Virtual Machine
Delay Start (Sec)	60
Action When Physical Server Stops	Save State

12. Click OK.

Virtual machines that are configured properly will be worth their weight in gold. It is very important to take the time and properly configure your virtual machines so that they can function at peak performance. Now that we have configured the virtual machine, let's take a look at how to configure the virtual server.

Configuring Hyper-V Host Properties

The SCVMM 2008 utility gives you the ability to configure the virtual machines as well as the virtual servers that you manage. When you configure your virtual machines properly, your network resources run properly within those virtual machines. When you configure your virtual servers properly, your virtual machines can then run properly. To get to the Properties window of the virtual machine, right click on the virtual machine and choose Properties.

Summary Tab

The Summary tab gives you a summary of the virtual server and shows the system information for the computer (see Figure 6.12). The only option we can configure is the Description field.

FIGURE 6.12 The Summary tab of Server Properties

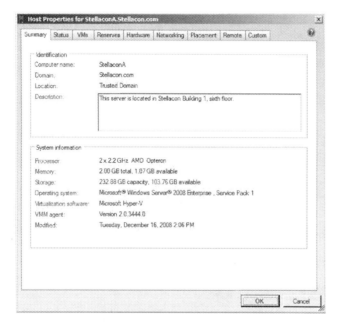

Status Tab

The Status tab is an informational tab that has only one configurable check box (see Figure 6.13). The Status tab shows how the server is currently operating. You can use this tab to monitor five items, as shown in Table 6.1. Each of the five monitored items displays a status value that lets you know what, if anything, needs to be done.

TABLE 6.1 The Items Monitored by the Status Tab

Status Type	Value
Overall Status	OK—No problems or errors.
	OK (limited)—Requires security credentials.
	Needs Attention—A problem needs fixing.

TABLE 6.1 The Items Monitored by the Status Tab *(continued)*

Status Type	Value
Connection Status	Responding—Communications are working properly. Not Responding—No communications. Access Denied—Agent is no longer associated with the SCVMM server.
Agent Version	Up-to-Date—The agent version is current. Upgrade Available—The agent has an upgrade that can be downloaded. Unsupported—The agent is not supported by the SCVMM functions.
Virtualization Service Status	Running—The virtualization service is running. Stopped—The virtualization service is stopped.
Virtualization Service Version	Up-to-Date—The virtualization software is current. Upgrade Available—An upgrade to the virtualization software is available. Unsupported—The version of virtualization is not supported by SCVMM.

FIGURE 6.13 The Status tab of Server Properties

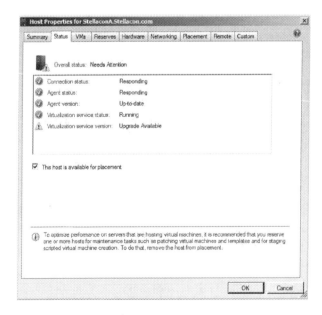

As you may have noticed, there is a check box on this tab: This Host Is Available For Placement. When selected, this option shows that the server is ready to go into a live environment and ready to host virtual machines. If you want to use a Hyper-V server just for templates and staging, uncheck the option.

VMs Tab

The VMs tab allows you to register your virtual machines with the virtual server (see Figure 6.14). When you build a virtual machine in the SCVMM 2008 utility, the virtual machine is automatically registered with the virtual server.

FIGURE 6.14   The VMs tab of Server Properties

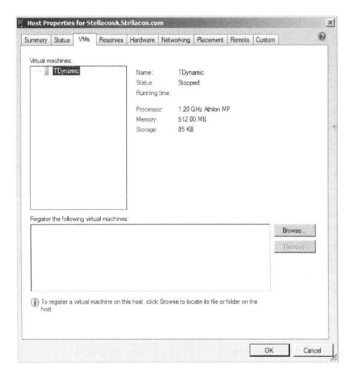

There may be times when you need to register a preexisting virtual machine. This basically lets the server know that the virtual machine is out there, and it allows the SCVMM to manage and maintain the virtual machine.

Reserves Tab

The Reserves tab allows an administrator to reserve resources for the operating system on the host (see Figure 6.15). This section allows you to set aside resources for the Windows Server 2008 operating system. As you are creating and running virtual machines, these virtual machines will take resources away from the host operating system. By setting aside resources just for the host operating system, this guarantees that the host operating system will continue to function properly. There are five different reserved resources that you can configure (see Table 6.2).

FIGURE 6.15   The Reserves tab of Server Properties

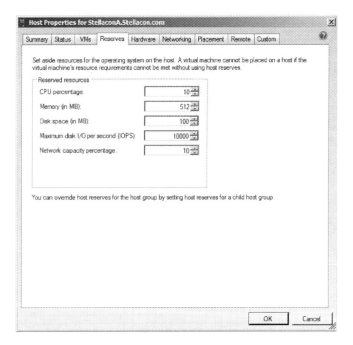

TABLE 6.2   The Resources Configured on the Reserves Tab

Reserved Resource	Value Explanation
CPU Percentage	This is the percentage of CPU that the host server will always have access to.
Memory (in MB)	This is the amount of RAM that will be dedicated to the host operating system.
Disk Space (in MB)	This specifies the amount of hard drive space reserved for the host system.
Maximum Disk I/O per Second (IOPS)	This setting is the maximum disk input/output capacity that the host operating system has reserved.
Network Capacity Percentage	This setting specifies the amount of network usage reserved just for the host operating system.

Hardware Tab

The Hardware tab has only a few configurable options. This tab summarizes your current hardware settings (see Figure 6.16). The advantage of the Hardware tab is the ability to go to one location and view all of the hardware settings for the virtual server.

FIGURE 6.16   The Hardware tab of Server Properties

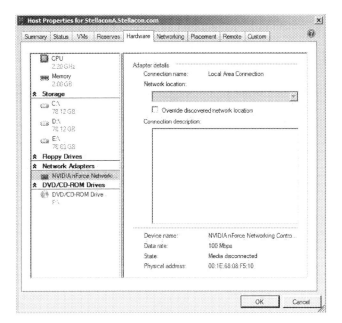

Networking Tab

The Networking tab lets you set up the network adapters (see Figure 6.17) in your virtual network. The virtual network allows a virtual server to communicate with the physical network through the NIC adapter.

When setting up your virtual network, you can decide how the network bindings are configured. You have three options:

- Private Network
- Internal Network
- Physical Network Adapter

Placement Tab

The Placement tab of Server Properties allows you to set up paths to store virtual machines. Use the options on this tab to specify the default paths to be used for the storing of virtual machines. To add paths to the default section, click the Add button and choose the path where you would like to store the virtual machines.

FIGURE 6.17 The Networking tab of Server Properties

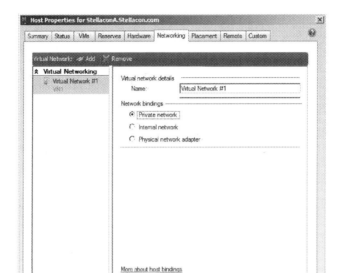

Remote Tab

The Remote tab allows you to set up the port that enables remote connections to the virtual server (see Figure 6.18). Remote connections to the virtual server are enabled by default.

FIGURE 6.18 The Remote tab of Server Properties

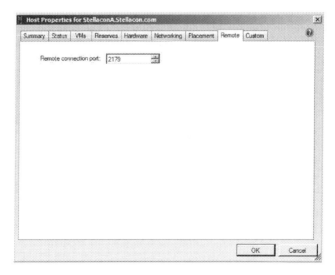

Custom Tab

The Custom tab for the virtual server works the same as it does for the virtual machine. The options allow you to create up to 10 custom fields for a virtual server. You can then use your custom fields to identify, track, and monitor virtual servers. You can set these custom fields by location, department, groups, and so on.

Configuring the virtual server and the virtual machines is an important part of managing and maintaining Hyper-V. Proper configuration is a key element in ensuring the longevity of the Hyper-V server and the virtual machines that run on that server.

HyperCall Adapter

A nice advantage of using the Hyper-V role is the ability to run multiple platforms from a single physical server. As you learned in previous chapters, you have the ability to run a VMware environment from SCVMM, and you can also convert a VMware virtual machine into a Hyper-V virtual machine.

There are many third-party virtualization solutions on the market today. One technology used throughout the virtualization world is the Xen hypervisor. The Xen hypervisor is a fast virtualization method that includes security. The Xen hypervisor works with multiple guest operating systems, such as Windows, Solaris, Linux, and BSD operating systems. The Xen hypervisor is open source, which means other vendors can program code that allows their virtualization system to work with Xen.

Microsoft's Hyper-V works with the Xen hypervisor by using the HyperCall adapter. The HyperCall adapter is a thin software layer that allows Xen virtualization function calls to be converted to Hyper-V. In this way, Hyper-V improves performance for your virtual machines that are running the Linux and Citrix server environments.

The HyperCall adapter, created in Cambridge, Massachusetts, was a collaboration of engineers from two of the networking giants: Microsoft and Novell. Because of this teaming, you can contact either Microsoft or Novell to get technical support on the HyperCall adapter.

Configuring Hyper-V properly is one of the most important tasks that you can undertake when setting up your virtual environment. Any configuration issues will bound to appear sooner or later. Once you have your virtual network configured properly, you can create easier ways to manage virtual machines.

Managing Templates, Profiles, and the Image Library

In previous chapters we have discussed how to create virtual machines from scratch. What if you want to create multiple virtual machines over and over? You don't want to re-create the virtual machine every time. This is where templates come into play.

Image libraries are also a useful tool. They allow you to organize your virtual machines so that you can quickly access and reuse them again in the future.

Hardware profiles help in the creation of virtual machines. Hardware profiles allow you to set up a standardized hardware configuration that you can use when creating new virtual machines or when using virtual machine templates. But before we dive into hardware profiles, we'll show you how to use templates.

Creating and Managing Templates

A *template* is a version of a virtual machine that you can reproduce time after time with the same hardware and software settings. It allows you to create a virtual machine from a copy, thus eliminating the need to rebuild the virtual machine from scratch.

Templates can be helpful not only because of the time that you save but also because it is difficult at times to re-create a virtual machine with the same hardware and software settings as a different virtual machine. Also, if you want to use the self-service role for your users, templates are required for users to create virtual machines.

When you create a template, you must understand that the source virtual machine (the machine you get the template from) can be destroyed. This is because the system information is stripped off the virtual machine during the Sysprep preparation. So if you want to create a machine to use as a template, you have two options. First, create a virtual machine and do not use it as a live production server; just use it as a template-making machine. Second, before turning the virtual machine into a template, clone (make a duplicate copy) the virtual machine so it can be used again without damage.

There are a few rules to keep in mind. Let's go over some of the template ground rules.

- SCVMM 2008 must manage the virtual machine for it to be a template.

- The virtual machine has to be on a host server.

- The Administrator's password on the source's virtual machine should be blank.

- The Windows system partition and the boot partition need to be on the same partition.

- All operating systems on the virtual hard disk must be supported by Hyper-V.

- All hardware on the target server must meet the minimum Hyper-V requirements to receive the template.

When you start creating a template, a new template wizard appears. You will need to answer some questions about how you would like to create the template. Let's take a look at some of the items you need to configure during the wizard:

Template Identity Page   This page allows you to state the name of the template, who the owner will be, and the description. The description is important when you're creating the templates. The template should be informative enough for you to go back to the template later and still know enough about the template that you can decide if it's the correct one to copy. For example, let's say you create five different templates with five different operating systems on the virtual machines. You want to make sure that you can choose the correct one down the road to copy. A properly written description lets you do just that.

Configure Hardware Page   This page allows you to configure the hardware setting for this template. This is the page where you can configure the BIOS, processor, memory, hard disk, DVD, network adapter, priority, and availability.

Guest Operating System   This is probably the most important page on the wizard. This is where you configure all of the guest system settings, as shown in Table 6.3.

TABLE 6.3   The Guest System Settings

Setting	Value
Identity Information	Specifies the computer name.
Admin Password	Contains the administrator password.
Product Key	Contains the 25-digit Windows product key.
Time Zone	Specifies the time zone your virtual machines will reside in.
Operating System	Specifies the operating system of the virtual machine.
Domain/Workgroup	You can specify here whether the virtual machine will be part of a domain or workgroup. If it's going to be part of a domain, you can specify the username and password credentials required to join the virtual machine to the domain.
Answer File	This file can answer normal installation questions. You can associate an answer file with the virtual machine template in the event that you want to install other products.
GUIRunOnce	You run this file once after the first user login. This file will run only once.

Select Library Server Page   Library servers are a way to organize virtual machines in a centrally located and secure location. You can organize your virtual machines for an easy way to track and reuse approved configurations. Library servers will be discussed in greater detail later in this chapter.

Select Path and Summary Pages   The first of these two pages is the Select Path page. This page allows you to enter the share path of where the virtual machines will be stored. You can also store these virtual machines to a storage area network (SAN). The Summary page lets you verify your choices before you create the template.

Creating templates is an easy way to reproduce virtual machines with the same hardware and software settings. Now that you know what the new template wizard will ask, let's go ahead and create a new template. In Exercise 6.2 we will walk through the process of creating a new virtual machine and then converting that virtual machine into a master template.

EXERCISE 6.2

Creating a Master Template

1. Open the SCVMM 2008 utility.

2. Click the New Virtual Machine Wizard under Actions.

3. The New Virtual Machine Wizard starts. At the Select Source screen, choose the "Create the new virtual machine with a blank hard disk" radio button.

4. On the Virtual Machine Identity page, type **TemplateVM** in the Virtual Machine Name field. Click Next.

5. On the Configure Hardware screen, click on the VHD section under the Bus Configuration section. Change the size to 10GB. Click Next.

6. On the Select Destination screen, choose the "Place the virtual machine on a host" radio button. Click Next.

7. On the Select Host screen, choose the name of your server and click Next.

8. On the Select Path screen, leave the default and click Next.

9. On the Select Network screen, pull down the Virtual Network list and choose your network adapter. Click Next.

10. On the Additional Properties screen, choose the Windows Server 2008 server (whichever version you have) and click Next.

11. On the Summary screen, verify the settings and click Create.

12. Close the Jobs dialog box after the virtual machine has been created.

13. Install the Windows Server 2008 operating system.

14. After the Windows Server 2008 operating system is loaded, in the center window click on the TemplateVM virtual machine and then under the Actions window, click the New Template link.

15. A Virtual Machine Manager dialog box appears. Just click Yes.

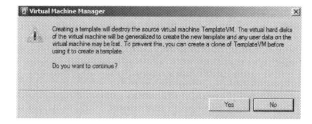

16. On the Template Identity screen, type **2008TemplateVM** in the Template Name field. Click Next.

17. On the Configure Hardware screen, leave the defaults and click Next.

18. On the Guest Operating System screen, click the Admin Password link and type in the administrator's password. Click the Product Key link, and then type in your product key from the Windows Server 2008 CD. Click on the time zone and enter your time zone. Click Next.

19. On the Select Library Server screen, just click Next.

20. On the Select Path screen, choose a shared location in which to place your virtual machine template. After choosing your path, click Next.

21. On the Summary screen, verify your settings and click Create.

22. If any errors appear, the Job dialog box will state what is missing or needs to be done. Fix any errors and repeat starting at step 14. If the template had no errors, close the Jobs dialog box.

Creating templates can be a valuable weapon in the virtual networking world. It allows a Hyper-V administrator to quickly and easily create the same templates over and over. But you may want to organize the way these templates are stored on the server. This is where creating and managing virtual machine libraries can help.

Creating Image Libraries

Being an IT manager and consultant for many years has taught me a few things about making the IT job easier. One of the lessons that I learned over the years is that organization is a key component to any successful IT department.

Organization allows you to quickly and reliably find resources that are necessary to make an IT department run smoothly. It doesn't matter what is being organized—just making sure that you are organized in all aspects of the department will pay off in the long run.

Let's take a look at a few examples. Take your software CDs and DVDs. If you have them organized in a CD case, you will always be able to find them quickly. I have been in IT departments where CDs and DVDs are laying all over the IT department. That disorder makes it difficult to find discs when they are needed.

Another example is software licenses. Keeping them organized in a secure lock box or file cabinet makes it easy to access them if you are audited. Again, if the software licenses (they are just paper certificates) are thrown into a box or left around the office, you will never find them when you need to. It's Murphy's Law—they will be lost when you need to find them. Organization can help in all aspects of the IT department.

Virtual machines can also be organized. You can organize your virtual machines into image libraries. Image libraries are a secure centrally located location in which all of your virtual machines can reside. Using image libraries helps you reuse images that have been properly configured and approved by your Hyper-V administrators.

The first thing that we need to do before creating your shares is to add your library server. This is a server that will contain your library shares for all of your Hyper-V servers to use.

In Exercise 6.3 we will begin by adding a library server to the SCVMM 2008 utility. We will add another server to the SCVMM utility to place our shared libraries onto. If you have only one server, just add that server. If you have multiple servers, just choose one to add during this exercise.

EXERCISE 6.3

Adding a Library Server

1. Start the SCVMM utility.

2. In the right window under Actions, click the Add Library Server link.

3. The Enter Credentials screen appears. You need to add the Administrator username and password. If you are part of a domain, the domain name should already be filled in. After you enter the password, click Next.

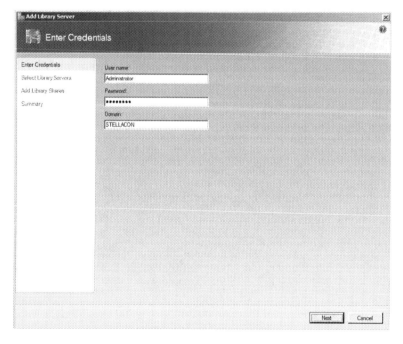

4. The Select Library Server screen appears next. Type the name of the server you are going to use and click the Add button. Click Next.

5. The shared folders will all be shown. Click Next.

6. On the Summary page, verify your settings and click Finish.

Now that we have added the library server, let's walk through the steps for adding library shares to the server. In Exercise 6.4 we will walk through the steps.

EXERCISE 6.4

Adding a Share to the Library

1. We need to create and share a folder. Start Windows Explorer (right-click the Start button and choose Explore).

2. Right-click on the C drive and choose New ➢ Folder.

3. Name the new folder **Virtual Machine Storage**.

4. Right-click on the Virtual Machine Storage folder and choose Share.

5. Add the Everyone group and make them co-owners. Click the Share button.

6. Click the Done button.

7. Start the SCVMM utility if it's not started.

8. In the right windows under Library Server, click the Add Library Share link.

9. When the Add Library Share window appears, click the Virtual Machine Storage check box and click Next.

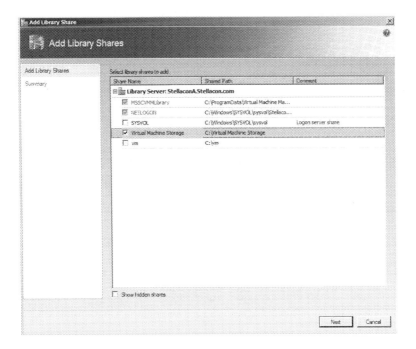

10. On the Summary screen, verify the settings and click the Add Library Shares button.

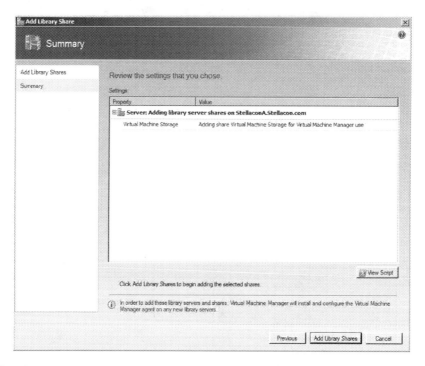

11. After the job is completed, close the Jobs dialog box.

Another advantage of creating libraries is the ability to create hardware profiles. *Hardware profiles* are preset hardware specifications that can be applied to a new virtual machine or a virtual machine template. The hardware specifications that can be set are items like the CPU, memory settings, and network adapters.

Hardware profiles are easily created in the SCVMM utility by using a new hardware profile wizard. Then when you create a new virtual machine or template, you can pull down the existing hardware profile and all the hardware items will be preconfigured.

In Exercise 6.5 we will develop a hardware profile and then create a new virtual machine using that profile.

Creating Hardware Profiles

1. Start the SCVMM utility if it's not started.

2. In the right window under Library Actions, click the New Hardware Profile link.

3. The New Hardware Profile dialog box appears. On the General tab type **Hardware Profile Test** in the Name field. Then select the Hardware Settings tab.

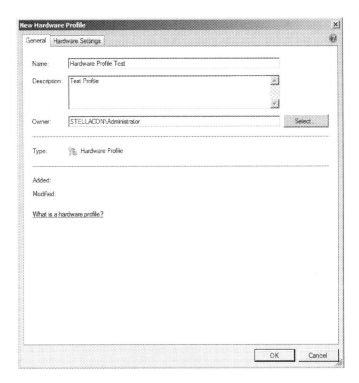

4. On the Hardware Settings tab, set the following:

Field	Value
BIOS	CD, IDE Hard Drive, PXE Boot, and Floppy (in that order)
Processor	Number = 2 (if you have 2, if not 1) CPU Type = Your machine's CPU
Memory	1024MB
IDE Devices - DVD	Second Channel = 0 Choose the Physical CD/DVD Drive radio button.
Priority	High

5. Click OK.

6. Now we will create a virtual machine using this hardware profile. Click the New Virtual Machine link under Actions.

7. Click the "Create the new virtual machine with a blank virtual hard disk" radio button.

8. On the Virtual Machine Identity screen, type **ProfileVM** in the Virtual Machine Name field and then click Next.

9. On the Configure Hardware screen, click the Hardware Profile pull-down menu and choose Hardware Profile Test. Change the hard drive size to 10GB. Click Next.

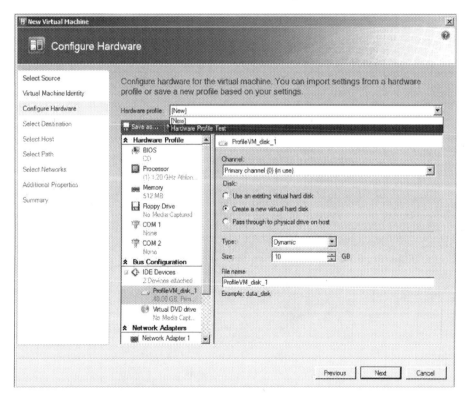

10. On the Select Destination screen, choose the "Place the virtual machine on a host" radio button. Click Next.

11. On the Select Host screen, choose your server and click Next.

12. On the Select Path screen, just click Next.

13. On the Network Adapter screen, choose your network adapter and click Next.

EXERCISE 6.5 *(continued)*

14. On the Additional Properties screen, choose your operating system and click Next (leave the other fields set at their defaults).

15. On the Summary screen, verify the settings and click the Create button.

16. Close the Jobs dialog box.

Creating hardware profiles is an excellent way to preset hardware configurations before you create the virtual machines. Hardware profiles allow you to associate a hardware configuration to both the virtual machine and your virtual machine templates.

Summary

Configuring virtual servers and virtual machines are some of the most important tasks that a Hyper-V administrator can perform. Properly configuring your virtual servers and machines will help ensure the longevity of your virtual network.

The SCVMM utility is a one-stop shop for all of your virtualization management utilities. Using SCVMM you can configure the virtual machine's settings, including starting and stopping the virtual machine, discarding the virtual machine, and migrating.

SCVMM also lets you set up checkpoints. Checkpoints allow you to create a temporary backup for your virtual machines so that you can recover the virtual machines in the event of a failure. Checkpoints are not meant to replace backups, but they are a quick way to save a virtual machine before making any major changes.

You have the ability to set up the virtual machine properties using SCVMM, using the options on the General, Hardware Configuration, Checkpoints, Settings, Custom, and Actions tabs. You can set up cost center values so that a cost center can report the use of resources to be billed.

Creating templates is another useful ability SCVMM gives you. Templates allow you to create multiple virtual machines with the same hardware and software settings.

In addition, you can create and manage image libraries. Libraries help an IT department organize their virtual machines in a safe, central location. Organizing the virtual machines also makes it easy for other administrators to locate virtual machines without searching an entire network. This is helpful for avoiding redundancy among your IT staff.

Hardware profiles are a way for you to preset hardware configurations for new virtual machines or virtual machine templates. Using hardware profiles is a quick way to configure the hardware settings without re-creating them every time you create a new virtual machine.

In this chapter we discussed the various configuration options for the virtual environment. In the next chapter we will discuss ways to recover from hardware or software failures.

Exam Essentials

Know how to assign virtual machine properties.   Understand the importance of configuring the virtual machine properties properly. Know how to configure the options on the General, Hardware Configuration, Checkpoints, Settings, Custom, and Actions tabs.

Know how to assign virtual server properties.   Understand the importance of configuring various properties for the virtual servers. Know how to set the default values, such as the default virtual machine path location. Be able to quickly view the hardware settings for the virtual server.

Understand how to create checkpoints.   Checkpoints are a quick and easy way to set up saved states at a given period in time. You can use them to recover from a failure or error. Know to create checkpoints before you do any major updates or improvements to the Hyper-V virtual machines. Be able to manage and recover using these checkpoints.

Understand how to use templates.   Templates are a way to produce virtual machines with the same hardware and software settings. Using templates allows you to quickly create a virtual machine without having to create the virtual machine from scratch.

Know how to create and use an image library.   Know the purpose of an image library does and how to configure it. Know how to add a library server and how to add library shares to the library server. Understand the benefits of creating libraries and keeping all of the virtual machines organized for future use.

Understand hardware profiles.   Know how to configure a hardware profile. A hardware profile can be used for a new virtual machine or a virtual machine template. A hardware profile allows you to preset the hardware configuration in advance.

Review Questions

1. You are the IT manager for a large food distributor who has decided to implement Microsoft Hyper-V to help control resources. Your organization has 10 Windows Server 2008 machines, 1,500 Windows Vista client computers, and 250 Windows XP clients. Your company wants to be able to bill all the various departments based on how much access they have to the virtual machines. You have set up and installed Hyper-V and the SCVMM 2008 utility. What field do you have to fill in to be able to bill all the departments?

   A. Billing Center

   B. Cost Center

   C. Management Center

   D. Tracking Center

2. You are the IT manager for your organization. You have installed two Windows Server 2008 machines with the Hyper-V role. You have built four virtual machines on each Hyper-V server, all with the Windows Server 2008 operating system. You need to install Microsoft Exchange 2007 on one of the virtual machines. What is the easiest procedure to do before installing Exchange on the virtual machine to ensure that you can recover the virtual machine if any errors occur during the install?

   A. Create a new backup before installing Exchange Server.

   B. Save the virtual machine to another Hyper-V server.

   C. Create a new checkpoint before installing Exchange Server.

   D. There's no need to do anything. Virtual machines can automatically revert back to the previous state.

3. You are the administrator for a large organization that has recently implemented Hyper-V. The company has written policies that all applications need to be monitored by using reports and monitoring. Your organization wants to be able to quickly locate fields based on geographic locations when they do searches. Where can you set up your virtual machines to show geographic location in the view window?

   A. Geographic field

   B. Location field

   C. Custom tab field

   D. General field

4. You are the administrator for a large IT team that has 10 servers and 2,500 client machines. Your organization has implemented Hyper-V, and the IT team has started converting servers into virtual machines. You need to move one of the virtual machines from one Hyper-V server to another. What command do you use to move the virtual machine?

   A. Move

   B. Migrate

   C. Copy

   D. XCopy

5.   You are the network administrator for your organization. You have recently implemented Microsoft Hyper-V. You have started migrating your servers over to virtual machines. You have one virtual server that needs to access the processor more than the other virtual machines. What configuration setting would you configure to give the one virtual machine greater access to the processor?

    A.   Processor

    B.   Availability

    C.   Infinity

    D.   Priority

6.   Ricky, your organization's IT manager, has decided to implement Hyper-V throughout the company. Your organization does a lot of training and testing in the Windows Server 2008 environment. Ricky wants to allow normal users to build and manage their own virtual machines. What can your organization implement to allow your users to create and manage their own virtual machines through the use of Hyper-V?

    A.   Microsoft Virtual Server

    B.   Microsoft Virtual PC

    C.   Self-service role

    D.   User creation role

7.   You are the network administrator for a large organization. Your organization has decided to implement Hyper-V to help consolidate your servers. The vice president of the company has asked you to give a presentation to the IT staff from all locations. You present all the facts about Hyper-V, and then a staff member asks you why you would need to use an IDE hard drive instead of a SCSI hard drive. What is one of the main reasons to choose IDE over SCSI?

    A.   IDE can have more devices than SCSI.

    B.   IDE can be booted from.

    C.   IDE can have larger partition sizes.

    D.   IDE has built-in security.

8.   You are the network administrator for a large organization that has decided to migrate all of its servers to Hyper-V. In the past, every Friday afternoon your IT department has updated all the servers with the latest service packs and security updates. Your typical routine consists of a full backup on Mondays and incremental backups the rest of the week. Before loading the service packs and security patches, your organization always does a daily backup, which does not affect your backup routine. You do this in case the update causes any errors or failures. When your organization switches to Hyper-V, you would still like to do the updates on Fridays, but you would like to find a better way to back up the virtual machines without actually doing a backup. What is something that you can do before you run your updates on Fridays to ensure that you can recover your virtual machines in the event of a failure due to the updates?

    A.   Checkpoints

    B.   Differential backups

    C.   Snapshots

    D.   Virtual machine backup

9. You are the network administrator for a mid-sized company that switched to Hyper-V last year. You have been building virtual machines and slowly filtering out your Windows Server 2008 physical machines. You are trying to use one physical machine for every four virtual machines. You have noticed that the Hyper-V host server is responding slower than before. When you start monitoring the server, you realize that all of the virtual machines are taking the resources away from the physical server. You want to guarantee that the server has at least a minimum amount of access to the resources. How can you guarantee this?

   A. Placement tab

   B. Availability tab

   C. Reserves tab

   D. Hardware configuration

10. Denise, your IT manager, has decided to implement Hyper-V throughout your organiza- tion. After Denise implements the Hyper-V role on all three organizations' Windows Server 2008 machines, she starts to build the virtual machines. Denise wants to make sure that whenever the host system is shut down that the virtual machine will be saved. How would Denise configure the virtual machine action?

   A. At the Server Stops action, choose Save Virtual Machine.

   B. At the Server Stops action, choose Save State.

   C. At the Server Stops action, choose Shut Down Guest OS.

   D. At the Server Stops action, choose Turn Off Virtual Machine.

11. You are the network administrator for a large organization that uses Hyper-V for all of its networking services. You need to start allowing remote connections to the Hyper-V servers. You have configured your firewalls to allow port 9740 for your remote connections. Where in SCVMM would you configure the port for remote communications?

   A. Remote tab

   B. Port tab

   C. General tab

   D. Availability tab

12. You have been hired as a consultant by a large organization that wants you to migrate their servers over to Hyper-V. You want to set up the Hyper-V so that after you leave, the admin- istrators on staff can continue to create virtual machines. The administrators will need to create many virtual machines. These virtual machines will be rolled out throughout the country and require the same hardware and software settings. What can you implement to help the IT staff do these tasks?

   A. Create images for them to copy.

   B. Create templates.

   C. Create virtual machine duplication.

   D. Use the Migrate utility.

13. You are the administrator for a large organization that has implemented Windows Server 2008 and the Hyper-V role. You have to create multiple virtual machines with the same hardware and software settings. You have decided to use templates to create the virtual machines. Which of the following are requirements when setting up virtual machine templates? Choose all that apply.

   A. SCVMM 2008 must manage the virtual machine for it to be a template.

   B. The virtual machine has to be on a host server.

   C. The Administrator's password on all the Hyper-V servers should be blank.

   D. The Windows system partition and the boot partition need to be on the same partition.

14. You are the network administrator for a large plumbing company. You have decided to implement Windows Server 2008 and the Hyper-V role. You've implemented all of your Hyper-V servers, and you've started creating your virtual machines. You have decided to store all of your virtual machines on a separate file server. You need to add the file server into the SCVMM utility so that you can start storing your virtual machines onto the file server. What do you need to do in the SCVMM utility?

   A. Add a new share.

   B. Add a new library server.

   C. Add a new file server.

   D. Add a new Hyper-V file server.

15. You are the network administrator for a large organization that makes computer chips. Your IT department has decided to migrate all of its servers over to Hyper-V. You want to preset the hardware configuration in advance for all of your virtual machines. What can you set up to preset hardware configurations in advance?

   A. Hardware profiles

   B. Configuration profiles

   C. Machine profiles

   D. Virtual machine profiles

16. You are the network administrator for a large whiskey manufacturer. You were hired to migrate all of the servers to Hyper-V. You installed Windows Server 2008 with the Hyper-V role. You need to set up your virtual machines so that when the host server turns on, the virtual machines automatically start. How would you set the Start Virtual Machine action?

   A. Never Automatically Turn On The Virtual Machine

   B. Always Automatically Turn On The Virtual Machine

   C. Automatically Turn On The Virtual Machine If It Was Running When The Physical Server Stopped

   D. Always Start All Virtual Machines

17. You have been hired as a Hyper-V consultant to consolidate the organization's servers to Hyper-V. You have decided to use templates to make it easier on the existing IT staff to re-create virtual machines in the future. After you set up the virtual network, you add an Active Directory domain controller to the virtual environment. You want to ensure that all the templates are automatically joined to the new domain. Where in SCVMM do you preset the domain that all templates will be joining?

    A. Template Identity page

    B. Hardware Configuration page

    C. Guest Operating System page

    D. Settings page

18. You are the network administrator for your organization. You have implemented Windows Server 2008 with the Hyper-V role. You have a virtual machine named ServerA. ServerA's MAC address has been configured in the firewall so that anything with that MAC can properly be routed through the firewall. ServerA starts to encounter errors, and you decide to replace ServerA with ServerB. You want to configure ServerB to have the same MAC address as ServerA so that you do not have to reconfigure the routers. ServerA will be taken offline to guarantee that two machines will not have the same MAC address. Where do you configure the MAC address on ServerB?

    A. Network Adapter section

    B. Hardware Adapter section

    C. Layer3 Adapter section

    D. Layer2 Adapter section

19. You are the network administrator for a large organization that makes snowmobile parts. The company has six Windows Server 2008 machines all running the Hyper-V role. You have migrated some of the virtual machines from Virtual Server to Hyper-V. You want to implement some of the extra services that you get with Integrated Services. Which of the following are parts of Integrated Services? Choose all that apply.

    A. Operating System Shutdown

    B. Time Synchronization

    C. Data Exchange

    D. Heartbeat

20. You are the network administrator for a large organization that has implemented Hyper-V. You have started creating virtual machines and virtual machine templates. You have other administrators who would like to locate your virtual machines easily. What can you implement that would make it easy for administrators to locate and organize virtual machines?

    A. Image libraries

    B. Catalog sheets

    C. Database listings

    D. Virtual machine organizer

Answers to Review Questions

1. B. You can enter cost center values to help you track resources used. You can then give this information to a cost center so they can calculate a charge for the use of these virtual machines.

2. C. Checkpoints are a way to temporarily save your virtual machine. This is a great way to have recoverability if you need to load software or do testing. Backups would also work here, but a backup is a longer process and much more complex. You would not want to move or save the virtual machine to another Hyper-V server, and virtual machines can't automatically recover.

3. C. The Custom tab fields give you 10 custom fields that you can configure to be anything that your organization needs including departments and geographic location.

4. B. The Migrate link is the way to move a virtual machine from one Hyper-V server to another. You can migrate a virtual machine by clicking the Migrate link in the Actions section.

5. D. The Priority section gives you the ability to assign a virtual machine a higher priority to the host machine's CPU. There are four priority settings that you can choose from: High, Normal (the default), Low, and Custom.

6. C. The self-service role allows an administrator to give users the right to create and manage their own virtual machines. Users can create and manage their own virtual machines by using the self-service web portal.

7. B. The biggest advantage of IDE compared to SCSI is that IDE can be booted from. You can't boot the machine up from a SCSI drive. SCSI drives have greater performance than IDE and they are primarily used for storage. Hyper-V virtual machines can use SCSI devices, but they can't be booted from SCSI devices.

8. A. Checkpoints are a quick and easy way to set up saved states at a given period in time. Checkpoints are used for recoverability from a failure or error. Create checkpoints before you do any major updates or improvements to the Hyper-V virtual machines.

9. C. The Reserves tab allows an administrator to reserve resources for the operating system on the host. The options allow you to set aside resources for the Windows Server 2008 operating system. As you are creating and running virtual machines, these virtual machines will take resources away from the host operating system. By setting aside resources just for the host operating system, you guarantee that the host operating system will continue to function properly.

10. B. When configuring the virtual machine, you can specify how you want the virtual machine to react when the physical system stops. There are three options that you are allowed to choose from: Save State, Turn Off Virtual Machine, and Shut Down Guest OS. Save State guarantees that when the host system shuts down, the virtual machine will be saved.

11. A. The Remote tab allows you to set up the port that enables remote connections to the virtual server. Remote connections to the virtual server are enabled by default, but you may need to configure your port number.

12. B. Templates allow you to create multiple virtual machines with the same hardware and software settings. Using templates allows you to quickly create a virtual machine without the need to create the virtual machine from scratch.

13. A, B, D. All of the answers are correct except for C. Administrator passwords should not be blank on a server. The administrator password should be blank in the template but servers should *never* have blank administrator passwords.

14. B. This is a server that will contain your library shares for all of your Hyper-V servers to use. After you add the new library server to the SCVMM utility, you need to share folders on that server. After the folders are shared, you add a share into the SCVMM utility. This will then give you the ability to place virtual machines onto the shared server.

15. A. Hardware profiles can be used for a new virtual machine or a virtual machine template. Hardware profiles allow you to preset the hardware configuration in advance, and then you can choose these hardware profiles during the creation of the virtual machines.

16. B. By choosing the Always Automatically Turn On The Virtual Machine radio button, you ensure that whenever the physical machine starts, the virtual machine will automatically start. This guarantees that if the machine reboots or restarts, the virtual machine restarts.

17. C. You'd use the Guest Operating System page if this template is going to be a member of the workgroup or domain. Here you would also set the Administrator's password and the user credentials needed to properly add the computer to the domain.

18. A. In the Network Adapter section is the Ethernet (MAC) Address settings. This section allows you to configure a MAC address for the virtual network adapter. You can dynamically configure the MAC address, which means that the system will assign a MAC address to the virtual network adapter, or you can manually configure a MAC address.

19. A, B, C, D. All of the answers are part of Integrated Services. Integrated Services are the extra services that you want your virtual machine to complete while running in Hyper-V. There are five services that you can choose for your virtual machine: Operating System Shutdown, Time Synchronization, Data Exchange, Heartbeat, and Backup (Volume Snapshot).

20. A. Image libraries are an easy way to organize your virtual machines. After setting up a library server, you just share the folders where you want to place the virtual machines.

Chapter 7

Configuring Hyper-V for High Availability

MICROSOFT EXAM OBJECTIVES COVERED IN THIS CHAPTER:

✓ **Configure Hyper-V to be Highly Available**

 ※ May include but not limited to: failover clustering, disk structure (RAID, quorum, shared storage), network.

✓ **Configure a Virtual Machine for High Availability**

 ※ May include but not limited to: quick migration, storage redundancy, perform a manual failover, live migration if available, networking redundancy.

One of the most important preemptive tasks that you can perform is to ensure recoverability from hardware or software failures. Regardless of how well you plan and set up your network, if there is a machine or software crash and you can't get the network back up and running in a timely manner, your organization loses money and many times IT personnel lose their jobs.

There are many ways to make sure your network has recoverability. First and most important is a network backup (discussed in Chapter 8, "Backing Up and Restoring Hyper-V"). Failover clustering is another way to ensure that your network continues to function properly when there is a hardware or software failure.

In the Hyper-V environment, not only can we make sure that our servers are protected against failure but we can also make sure that we protect our virtual machines from failure. One of the advantages of using Hyper-V over traditional servers is when a traditional server goes down, we have to rebuild and restore the server. When a Hyper-V server goes down, we just migrate the virtual machine to another Hyper-V machine and we are back up and running.

Setting up a failover strategy is one of those tasks that is never fun to setup and configure, but it's one of those things that is well worth the time and effort when you can recover from a hardware or software failure in a minimal amount of time. In this chapter we will discuss the many ways to try to make your Hyper-V server, and the hard disks that it resides on, redundant. We will discuss the different types of software RAID and failover clusters that can be configured to help make your Hyper-V servers reliable and recoverable.

Configuring Hyper-V to Be Highly Available

Hyper-V is an excellent way for an organization to save money by running multiple virtual machines on one Hyper-V physical server. At the same time, having multiple virtual machines on a single physical Hyper-V server also gives you a single point of failure. If the physical machine crashes, none of your virtual machines will be running. If you store the virtual machines on a SAN or backup, at least you will still have the virtual machines after the physical crash.

⊕ **Real World Scenario**

The Price of Not Having High Availability

A few years back I was reading an article about how a giant telephone corporation in 1990 had a major network failure. The failure was due to a software upgrade. The article stated that over 75 million calls were unanswered during 9 hours of downtime.

This company lost millions of dollars due to the fact that it took them so long to recover from this crash. It also caused a lot of embarrassment throughout the industry. This telephone giant has changed the way they now operate, and they also changed their network failure recovery procedures.

Many large organizations now have duplicate facilities so that if one location goes down, a duplicate facility in another state will automatically take over and continue to allow the network to operate properly. We are all familiar with the statement "Time is money"—well this can be major money depending on the time and severity of the network crash.

Due to the importance of high availability, Microsoft Hyper-V was designed with high availability in mind. High availability is basically defined as the amount of time that the system should be operational for use. Depending on where you set your high availability level determines how much downtime you are willing to experience. Table 7.1 shows a high availability chart and the amount of downtime that should be expected.

TABLE 7.1 Availability Chart

High Availability Target	Expected Amount of Annual Downtime
90%	36.5 days
99%	87 hours and 36 minutes
99.9%	8 hours 46 minutes
99.99%	52 minutes 34 seconds
99.999%	5 minutes 15 seconds

Even though you set up your servers for high availability, there will most likely be times when the server is down. Normally these events are planned downtime. All servers, no matter how well they are set up, will have planned downtime for maintenance. You can work around this while using Hyper-V.

For example, let's say that you need to take a server offline for normal maintenance, and this downtime is expected to last a couple of hours. You can move your Hyper-V virtual machines to another Hyper-V server temporarily while you do your maintenance. This way, your network continues to run without interruption. After the maintenance is completed, you can migrate the virtual machines back to their original Hyper-V location, and you are back in business. Let's take a look at how you can set up high availability both with Hyper-V and by using RAID.

Understanding RAID

Making sure that your servers are always available also means that you have the ability to recover quickly from a system failure. The less amount of downtime that your servers have translates to greater productivity for your organization.

One way that Microsoft helps with recoverability is through the use of *Redundant Array of Inexpensive* (sometimes also stated as *Independent*) *Disks* (RAID). RAID allows you to have redundancy through the use of multiple disks. Redundancy is the ability to recover data from a single failed disk.

There are two types of RAID that we can use: hardware and software. Hardware RAID means that the RAID is built into the physical hardware. Software RAID is handled through the Windows Server 2008 operating system. Microsoft supports both hardware and software RAID.

There are different levels of software RAID. Some of the levels are redundant and some are not. The basic levels of software RAID that Microsoft Windows Server 2008 supports are as follows:

RAID 0   RAID 0 is also referred to as disk striping. Disk striping uses a minimum of two physical hard drives and can have a maximum of 32 hard disks. Let's say you have two physical disks (disk 0 + disk 1) that you want to write data to. A piece of the data is written to disk 0, then disk 1, then disk 0, then disk 1 until all of the data is completely written to the machine. The advantage to this is that both hard drives use their own read/write heads. This gives you better performance. The downside is if you lose one of the hard drives, you lose the entire RAID 0 volume. RAID 0 is *not* fault tolerant.

RAID 1   RAID 1 is also referred to as mirroring. RAID 1 allows two volumes or disks to duplicate each other (like looking into a mirror). If one of the disks fails, then you can use the duplicate disk to recover or continue normally. RAID 1 is fault tolerant. This is the most expensive RAID options due to the fact that it uses a one-to-one hard disk or volume, meaning you lose one hard disk or volume for the mirror but it has the fastest recoverability time from a failure. The reason that the recoverability time is quicker is due to the fact that when one half of the mirror fails, you just point everything to the other half to continue normal operations until the mirror is fixed. This is an excellent form of RAID to protect your system and boot partitions.

RAID 0+1   This is a combination of both RAID 0 and RAID 1. This gives you the benefits of greater read/write performance (RAID 0) along with the fault-tolerant mirror (RAID 1).

RAID 5   A RAID 5 volume (which used to be called a stripe set with parity) works like RAID 0 except that there are a minimum of three physical disks and a single parity block is created for fault tolerance. This allows you to recover your data from a single hard disk failure. RAID 5 is an excellent choice for protecting data from a single disk failure. RAID 5 volumes can't include the system or boot partition as part of the RAID 5 volume. Table 7.2 shows you four hard disks and how the data and parity block is placed onto the drives.

TABLE 7.2   RAID 5 Example

DISK 0	DISK 1	DISK 2	DISK 3
DATA 0A	DATA 1A	DATA 2A	Parity
DATA 0B	DATA 1B	Parity	DATA 3B
DATA 0C	Parity	DATA 2C	DATA 3C
Parity	DATA 1D	DATA 2D	DATA 3D
DATA 0E	DATA 1E	DATA 2E	Parity

RAID 6   RAID 6 works like RAID 5 except you get even better redundancy due to the fact that it uses two parity blocks for fault tolerance instead of a single parity block like RAID 5.

When you are creating software RAID on a Windows Server 2008 machine, the hard disk has to be configured to support volumes. This is where disk storage types are applied.

Disk Storage Types

You must follow some rules when setting up software-based RAID. First, you need a minimum of two hard disks to set up even the most basic of RAID. Second, the hard disk storage type must be set to dynamic. The two disk storage types that you can use are as follows:

Basic Storage Type   A disk that is set up for the basic storage type is called a basic disk. Basic disks can be used on any Windows operating systems, including older systems like MS-DOS. Basic storage disks use partitions, and you can have up to four partitions on a basic disk. These four partitions can be three primary partitions (partitions you can boot the machine from) and one extended or four primary partitions. Windows Server 2008 partitions can be formatted either using the Fat32 or NTFS disk structures.

Basic partitions can't be extended using the Windows operating system. Once you configure the partition size and you fill the partition up with data, there is no way to make the partition larger. You can use third-party utilities to increase the size of the partition.

The one major advantage to using basic disks is the ability to dual-boot. Dual-booting involves loading multiple operating systems on a machine and then choosing which operating system you want to start when the machine turns on.

Dynamic Storage Type   A disk that is set up for the dynamic storage type is called a dynamic disk. Dynamic disks use dynamic volumes instead of partitions. Dynamic volumes are a lot like partitions in the sense that using Windows Server 2008 allows you to format the volumes using either FAT32 or NTFS. But if the volumes are NTFS, they can be extended if space is available.

Dynamic disks have many advantages over a basic disk. First, as we just explained, volumes can be extended. Second, you can set up software RAID on a dynamic disk. Third, you do not have the four-partition limit when using dynamic volumes. Remember, when it comes to setting up Microsoft Windows Server 2008 software RAID, the hard disks have to be configured as dynamic disks.

Exam Tip

When taking any Microsoft exam, make sure you pay attention to the word *partition* or *volume*. Microsoft expects you to understand that if they use an example with the word partition, you should know that you are on a basic disk. This is the same for the word volume. Volumes automatically let you know that you are on a dynamic disk.

So the real question is whether to choose basic or dynamic disks. Unless you are dual-booting the machine, you should use dynamic disks. Having the ability to increase the volume is worth its weight in gold. The benefits of dynamic disks are too beneficial not to use. You have the ability to convert a basic disk to a dynamic disk without losing any data. But to convert a dynamic disk to a basic disk, you have to delete all volumes on the disk.

There are two ways to convert a basic disk to a dynamic disk. First, you can use the convert command at a command prompt. Second, you can convert the disk in the Disk Management utility by right-clicking the disk and choosing the Convert option.

One important detail that you should keep in mind is that the RAID we have been discussing is Windows Server 2008 operating system software RAID. It's a good, inexpensive way to set up RAID, but hardware RAID is the way to go if you can afford it. There is no comparison. I can't stress this enough: if possible, choose hardware RAID over software RAID.

🌐 Real World Scenario

The Key Benefit of Dynamic Disks

One feature that most IT departments give their users is the advantage of using home folders. Home folders are a location on the servers that your users can use to save their important documents. Most companies do not have the ability to back up all of their users' computers, so they give their users space on the server to store items that can then be backed up when the servers complete their nightly backup.

Over the years, one of the major problems that IT departments faced was when the partitions on which the home folders resided filled up. IT personnel would then have to have their users clean up or remove older documents. This could cause issues with users deleting crucial documents.

When basic disks were our only disk type, unless we used a third-party utility, we did not have the ability to expand our partitions. Also, third-party utilities were not always safe to use, and sometimes they would cause more damage than good.

We can now use Windows Server 2008 operating system and make our storage types dynamic disks. If the home folder volumes start to fill up (as long as they're formatted as NTFS), we can just add another hard disk, make it dynamic, and then expand our home folder volume onto the new hard disk.

Anyone who has been in a similar situation can see the immediate advantages of using dynamic disks over basic disks.

Understanding the Disk Management MMC

Hardware RAID is built into the physical machine and has many advantages over software RAID. Most companies do not use software RAID, but since it is included with the Windows Server operating system, it will be covered on the exam. Software RAID is an excellent option for a small company with limited money to spend on RAID.

To configure RAID, we use the Disk Management utility within the Computer Management snap-in. When you create the RAID using the Disk Management utility, it walks you through the creation of the RAID process.

Before we do an exercise to set up RAID, let's discuss the Disk Management utility (see Figure 7.1). The Disk Management utility displays your hard drive configuration. As you can see in Figure 7.1, we have three hard disks in this system: Disk 0, Disk 1, and Disk 2.

FIGURE 7.1   The Disk Management utility

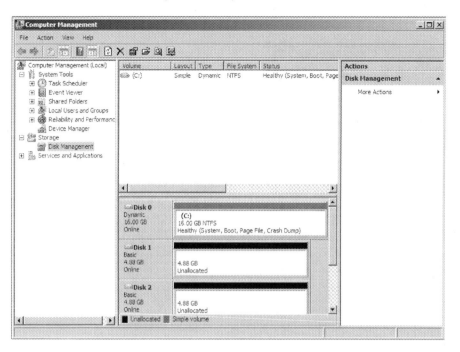

In the bottom-center left section, you will notice the three hard disks and their names (Disk 1, Disk 2, and Disk 3). Under the names you will see how the disk storage type (basic or dynamic) is configured. Under the disk storage type, the size of the hard disk is listed. Finally, you see the status of the hard disk. The statuses of these three hard disks are online.

To the right of this information is the drive letter and status of the volumes or partitions. If there is no volume or partition created, it will mark the section as Unallocated. This Unallocated section can be turned into a partition, volume, or RAID volume (if the minimum RAID requirements are met). The top-center section also shows your volumes and partitions as well as the details about those volumes and partitions.

In Exercise 7.1 we will convert our basic disks to dynamic. If all of your disks are already set with the dynamic storage type, just skip this exercise. Your hard disks will need to be set up as dynamic to complete future exercises in this chapter.

EXERCISE 7.1

Configuring Dynamic Hard Disks

1.   Start the Computer Management utility by clicking Start ➢ Administrative Tools ➢ Computer Management.

2. In the Computer Management snap-in, click the Disk Management item under the Storage section.

3. Right-click on one of your basic disks and choose Convert To Dynamic Disk.

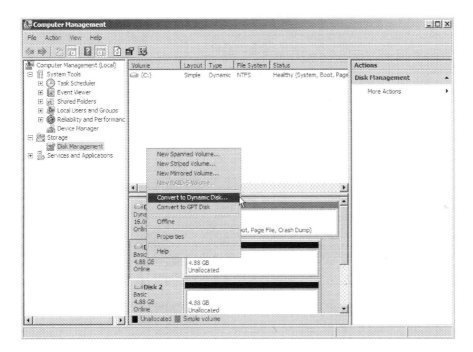

4. The Convert To Dynamic Disk dialog box appears. Choose all the drives that you want to convert and click OK.

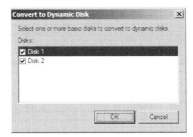

EXERCISE 7.2 *(continued)*

5. After the hard disks are converted to dynamic, you will see that the storage types for these disks are now Dynamic.

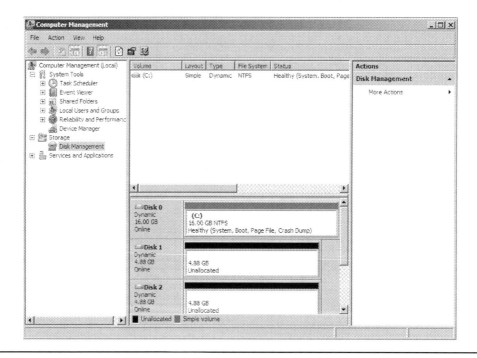

The Disk Management section of the Computer Management utility can be a useful tool when you are trying to diagnose hard disk errors. By checking the status of your hard disks and volumes (or partitions), you can see if the hard disks are encountering any errors. Now that we have changed the storage disk types, let's go ahead and configure RAID.

In Exercise 7.2 we will set up RAID by configuring RAID1 mirroring. To accomplish this exercise, you must have a minimum of two physical hard disks and unformatted free space on one of the disks. If you would like to mirror an existing volume, the available free space must be greater than or equal to the existing volume.

EXERCISE 7.2

Configuring RAID 1 Mirroring

1. Click Start ➢ Administrative Tools ➢ Computer Management.

2. In the Computer Management snap-in, click the Disk Management item under the Storage section.

EXERCISE 7.2 *(continued)*

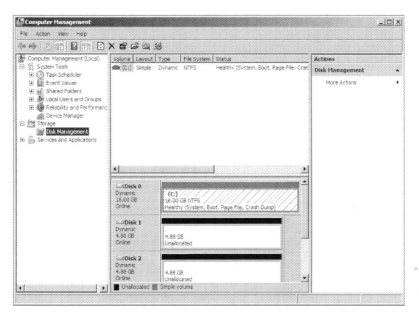

3. In the Disk Management section, right-click on the unformatted free space of one of your disks and choose New Mirrored Volume.

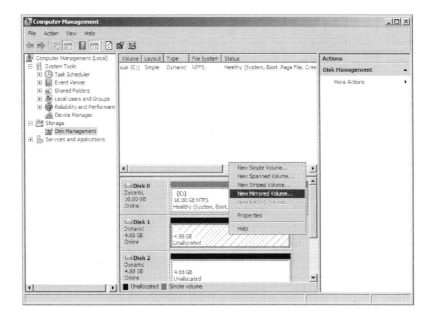

4. The New Mirrored Volume wizard appears. On the Welcome screen, click Next.

5. When the Select Disks screen appears, choose the two disks that you want to mirror and click Next.

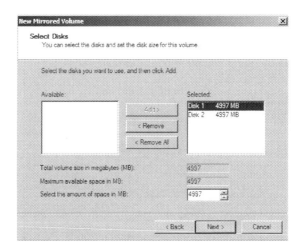

6. On the Assign Drive Letter or Path screen, choose a drive letter for your mirrored volume and click Next.

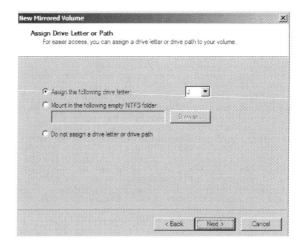

7. On the Format Volume screen, choose the following options and then click Next:

EXERCISE 7.2 *(continued)*

Field	Value
Format This Volume With The Following Settings	Radio button selected
File System	NTFS
Allocation Unit Size	Default
Volume Label	Test Mirror
Perform A Quick Format	Checked
Enable File And Folder Compression	Unchecked

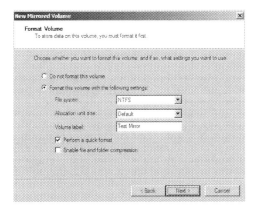

8. At the Completing The New Mirrored Volume Wizard screen, verify the settings and click the Finish button.

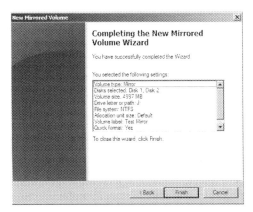

9. After the mirrored volume is created, you will see it appear in a different color. Close the Computer Management utility.

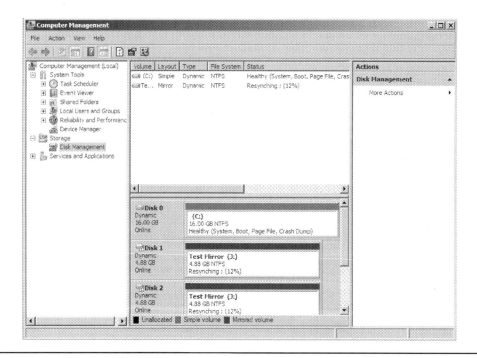

Besides configuring your hardware or software RAID, there are other ways to configure your Hyper-V environment to be redundant. Let's take a look at how to configure your Hyper-V and non-Hyper-V networks to be more reliable.

Configuring Failover Clustering

As a member of an IT department, part of your job is to try to build redundancy into your infrastructure and also try to eliminate the possibility of having a single point of failure. To help eliminate these concerns for your organization, Microsoft has built failover clustering into the Windows Server 2008 operating system.

Clusters are a group of individual computers (called cluster *nodes*) that work together as one unit. You can have up to 16 nodes in a failover cluster running on a 64-bit version of the Enterprise or Datacenter edition of Windows Server 2008. Your end users think they are connecting to just one machine when in fact they are dealing with multiple machines that work as one.

The advantage of using a cluster is if one of the nodes fails, the other nodes take up the load (known as failover). *Failover clusters* (formally known as server clusters) help provide high availability to servers that run mission-critical applications or services.

For example, if you have only one email server handling all the email for your organization and that server goes down, the company loses a critical application. With failover clusters, if an email server goes down, another server takes up the load and the organization continues to function properly. Two goals that we are always trying to achieve as IT personnel are minimum downtime and no data loss. Failover clusters help us achieve both goals.

Failover Cluster Management

Failover clusters are installed by using the Server Manager snap-in, and you can manage your server cluster by using the Failover Cluster Management snap-in (see Figure 7.2). Failover Cluster Management allows you to create clusters, manage clusters, and validate a configuration.

FIGURE 7.2   Failover Cluster Management

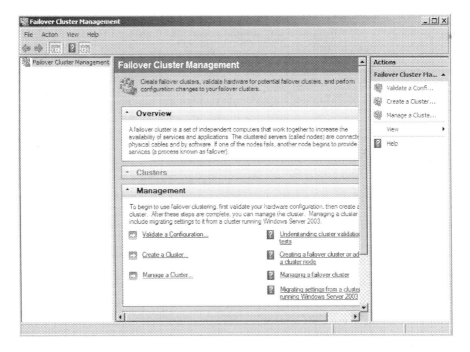

When setting up a failover cluster, you need to follow some recommendations and rules. When setting up this cluster, some cluster settings may be different than the way you would set up an application cluster (like Microsoft Exchange Server) due to the fact that we will be setting up this cluster for Hyper-V.

Software Requirements for Failover Clustering with Hyper-V Windows Server 2008 Enterprise or Datacenter editions need to be loaded on the physical machines. The same version must be loaded on all of the machines in the cluster. If you load Server Core Enterprise edition onto one server in the cluster, then all servers in the cluster must have Server Core Enterprise edition.

Hyper-V will also need to be installed onto these servers. This means that the servers on which you are setting up the cluster would also have to meet the minimum requirements for installing Hyper-V. The failover clusters feature should just be installed onto your Hyper-V servers to allow for high availability.

Network Settings and TCP/IP Addresses When setting up your network adapters for the cluster, you want to use all the same hardware settings for all machines within the cluster (Speed, Duplex Mode, etc.). The machines within the cluster must also all use the same protocol (TCP/IP) and be configured properly.

Shared Storage The best practice is to set up the cluster using a storage area network (SAN) for storage. You should try to avoid using the hard disks from the machines in the cluster. If you use the machine's hard disk and the machine fails, you lose the storage disks and the data on the disks. The idea of a cluster is to allow network resources to continue to work if you have a machine failure. But if you use the machine's hard drive as storage, you still have a single point of failure.

Domain Role All the machines within the cluster must belong to the same Active Directory domain. All machines within the cluster must have the same domain role (member server or domain controller). Microsoft recommends that all the servers in the cluster be member servers and not domain controllers.

DNS All of the machines within the cluster must be using the Domain Name System (DNS) for name resolution. DNS resolves a hostname into a TCP/IP (forward lookup) address and also turns a TCP/IP number into a hostname (reverse lookup). Proper DNS configuration is one of the most important tasks that you can complete on your network infrastructure.

Many of the services that run on your network require DNS to be set up properly. For more information on configuring DNS, refer to *MCTS: Windows Server 2008 Network Infrastructure Configuration Study Guide* by William Panek, Tylor Wentworth, and James Chellis (Sybex, 2008).

Account Credentials To add machines to or manage the cluster, the domain account that you use must have administrative rights and permissions on all the servers within the cluster. The account that you use only needs to be part of the Administrators group, and the account does not need to be a domain admin or higher.

> Windows Server 2003 clustering used a cluster service account for the cluster. Windows Server 2008 clustering no longer uses the cluster service account, but instead the cluster automatically runs in a special context to allow the cluster to operate properly.

In Windows Server 2008 there are a few types of cluster configurations that you can choose from. Use these options to define how you are setting up your clusters (geographic location of the cluster, number of nodes in the cluster) in your organization.

Local Two-Node Cluster   A local two-node cluster is just as it states: two nodes in the cluster. If one node fails, the other node takes up the slack and continues to operate. These two nodes are commonly attached to a shared storage device (such as a SAN), and because of this shared storage device the cluster is allowed to continue to operate properly if one of the nodes fails.

Single-Node Cluster   A single-node cluster (also referred to as a stager) is a single-machine cluster normally used for testing purposes in a staging area. This type of cluster allows you to test your products in a clustered environment before deploying your applications into your production (live) network.

Cluster with No Shared Storage   Cluster with no shared storage is a cluster that does not use a shared storage device like a SAN. The cluster is stored on the nodes that are part of the cluster. This approach can cause issues if one of the nodes fails. Not only do you lose the node, you also may lose the data that is stored on the node.

Multisite or Geographically Dispersed Cluster   This cluster type allows you to have nodes within the cluster in different geographic locations or different sites. Multisite clusters normally have a storage location at each physical location. This way, if one of the sites fails, the other site can continue to function properly. Data is replicated or mirrored between the sites, thus keeping the data synchronized between the multiple sites.

In Exercise 7.3 we will start setting up our high-availability servers by installing the Failover Cluster feature on our servers. You need to have at least two servers both with Hyper-V installed. It should be the same machines that you have been using for Hyper-V. If you do not have two 64-bit servers to set Hyper-V with failover, you can still install the Failover Cluster support on two 32-bit Windows Server 2008 Enterprise machines. This will allow you to learn how to set up the clustering features on your servers.

If you do not have two machines, you can download Microsoft Virtual PC and load two virtual machines with Windows Server 2008 Enterprise. You can then set up the Failover Clustering feature and learn how to cluster. You will not be able to load Hyper-V onto the Virtual PC virtual machines (Hyper-V can't run within a virtual environment), but at least you can play around with the clustering feature.

EXERCISE 7.3

Installing a Failover Cluster

1.   Start the Server Manager application by clicking Start ➢ Administrative Tools ➢ Server Manager.

2.   In the left pane, click Features.

3.   In the right pane, click the Add Features link.

EXERCISE 7.3 *(continued)*

4. The Add Features Wizard appears. Click the Failover Clustering check box and click Next.

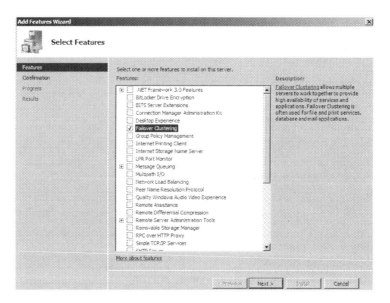

5. On the Confirm Installation Selection screen, verify that it's the Failover Server you are installing. Click the Install button.

6. When the installation is completed, the Installation Results screen appears. Click Close.

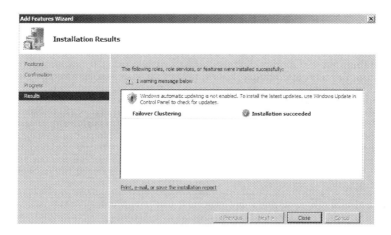

7. Repeat this process on all servers that are going to be part of the cluster.

In Exercise 7.4 we will create a two-node cluster using the Failover Cluster Management snap-in. When you create the new cluster, a Create Cluster wizard will walk you through the steps. This exercise will install a normal two-node cluster.

EXERCISE 7.4

Creating a Cluster

1. Open the Failover Cluster Management snap-in by clicking Start ≻ Administrative Tools ≻ Failover Cluster Management.

2. In the center window under the Management section or the right window under the Actions section, click the Create a Cluster link.

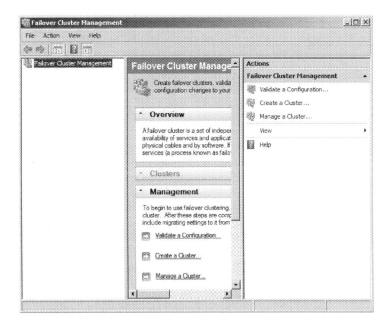

3. The Create Cluster Wizard Before You Begin screen will be the first to appear. At this welcome screen, click Next.

4. On the Select Servers screen, enter the names of the servers that will be part of the cluster.

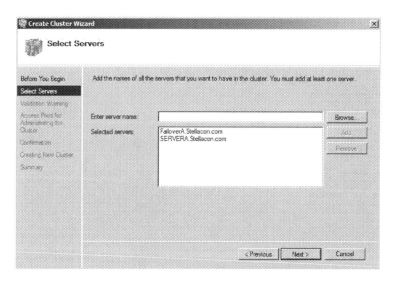

5. On the Validation Warning screen, if you would like to run a validation check to see if your setup meets Microsoft's recommendations, make sure the Yes radio button is selected and then click Next.

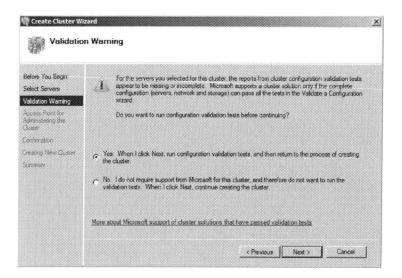

6. The Validate a Configuration Wizard starts. On the Before You Begin screen, click Next.

7. On the Testing Options screen, you can allow the validation wizard to test all clustering options, or you can choose what you want tested. Click the Run All Tests radio button and click Next.

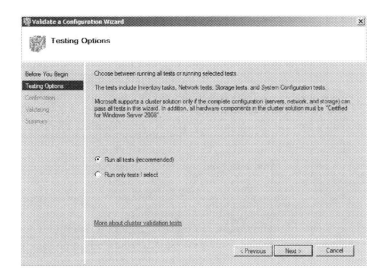

8. On the Validate Conformation screen, verify your settings and click Next. The tests will begin validating.

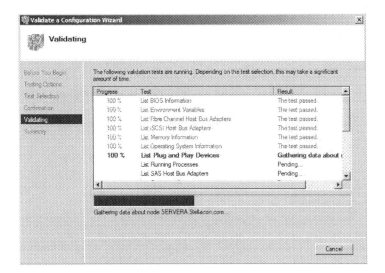

9. On the Validation Summary screen, verify that you passed the validation tests. If there were any warnings or errors, fix the errors and restart this exercise. Continue to fix any errors until your systems are ready to be clustered.

10. When the Validation Warning screen reappears, make sure that the No radio button is selected and choose Next.

11. The Access Point for Administering the Cluster screen appears. Type **TestCluster1** for the name and make sure your network check box is checked on the network that the cluster resides on. Click Next.

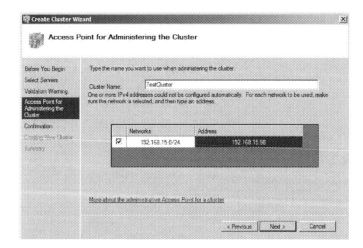

12. On the Confirmation screen, verify that the settings are correct and click Next.

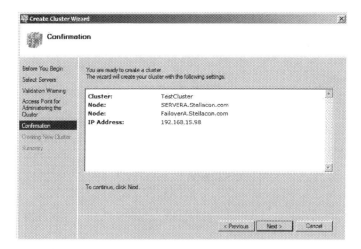

13. The Summary page should appear, showing that the cluster has been created. Click the Finish button.

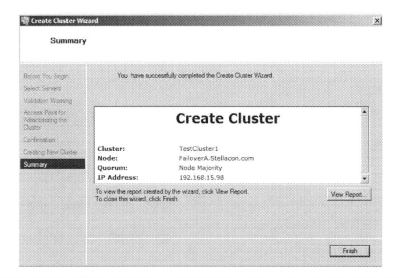

When it comes to clustering, another piece of the puzzle that is very important to understand is *quorums*.

Configuring Quorums

Cluster quorums are the number of pieces that must remain online for the cluster to continue to operate properly. Each piece in the quorum gets to vote on whether the cluster continues to operate online.

The pieces of the cluster that get to vote are the nodes, a disk witness (this is a disk in cluster storage), or a file share witness (this is a file share). The nodes and the disk witness also contain a replica copy of the cluster configuration, and the cluster service keeps all replicas of the configuration synchronized.

The easiest way to understand how quorums operate is to think of a small town of five residents only. At a town meeting, three have to be present to allow the meeting to function properly. As long as three people are at the meeting to vote, the meeting can take place.

This is how quorums operate. If you have five servers in a cluster and the majority vote is three, two of your servers in the cluster can fail and the cluster will continue to operate properly. As long as there are enough pieces to vote, the quorum and cluster will operate properly. If the number of pieces doesn't equal the quorum vote, the cluster stops operating properly.

Microsoft recommends that you use the quorum mode selected by the cluster software. You have the ability to change the quorum mode by configuring the Cluster Quorum Wizard (see Figure 7.3). You should only change the quorum if you are certain that another quorum is best for your cluster.

FIGURE 7.3   The Cluster Quorum Wizard

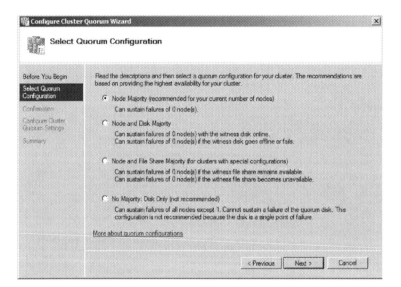

There are four types of quorum modes that Microsoft Windows Server 2008 clustering can work with:

Node Majority Quorum Mode   In this quorum mode, the majority of votes (more than half) constitute the quorum. Each node is allowed to vote as long as they can communicate with the other nodes. If more than half of the nodes vote, the cluster continues to function properly.

Node and Disk Majority Quorum Mode   In this quorum mode, the majority of votes (more than half) constitute the quorum. In this quorum, not only does each node that can communicate get to vote, but also the cluster storage device (disk witness) gets to vote.

Node and File Share Majority Quorum Mode   In this quorum mode, the majority of votes (more than half) constitute the quorum. Each node is allowed to vote as long as they can communicate with the other nodes along with the file share (file share witness) that the administrator creates for the cluster. If more than half vote, the cluster continues to function properly.

No Majority: Disk Only Quorum Mode   This is the quorum that was the equivalent of what was used in Windows Server 2003. In this quorum, there is no majority vote. The cluster continues to operate properly as long as one node is available with the cluster storage disk. The problem with this quorum is that there is a single point of failure. If the only node in the cluster fails, you have a single point of failure.

In Exercise 7.5 we will change the quorum mode type. We will choose the Node and File Share Majority mode type. Normally you will point this to a SAN storage device, but we assume that you don't have a SAN next to your computer while reading this book, so we will just share a folder on your machine and then we will point to that share.

EXERCISE 7.5

Changing the Quorum Mode

1. Share a folder on the C drive and name it **Failover Share**. Give the Administrators and Everyone groups full control.

2. Open the Failover Cluster Management snap-in by clicking Start ➢ Administrative Tools ➢ Failover Cluster Management.

3. In the left window, right-click the TestCluster1 cluster, choose More Actions, and then choose Configure Cluster Quorum Settings.

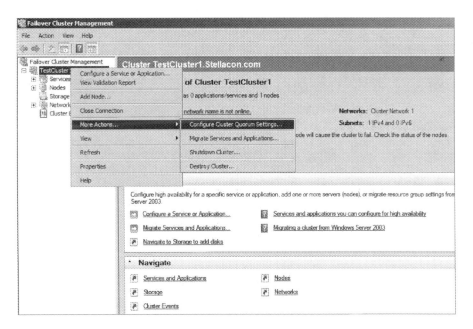

4. On the Before You Begin screen, click Next.

5. On the Select Quorum Configuration screen, click the Node and File Share Majority radio button and click Next.

6. On the Configure File Share Witness screen, click the Browse button.

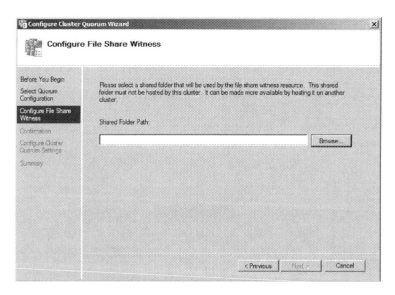

7. In the Browse for Shared Folders dialog box, type the name of the server where you shared the Failover Share folder and click the Show Shared Folders button. The Failover Share folder should appear in the Shared folders section. Click on Failover Share and click OK.

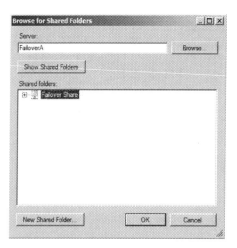

8. When you return to the Configure File Share Witness screen, click Next.

9. On the Confirmation screen, verify the settings and click Next.

10. When the Configure Cluster Quorum Settings screen appears, watch the progress of the configuration.

11. On the Summary screen, after the configuration is complete, click the Finish button.

Now that we have set up a cluster, it's time to set up Hyper-V so that your virtual machines get the advantages of high availability through failover clusters.

Understanding Quick Migration

An important part of Hyper-V and failover clusters is making sure that you have as little downtime as possible. One of the reasons that we install and configure failover clusters is to make sure that if we have a failure, we can get back up and running as soon as possible.

Microsoft *quick migration* gives you the ability to easily migrate a virtual machine from one host server to another with as little downtime as possible. One of the nice advantages to quickly migrating virtual machines from one host server to another is the ability to do maintenance on a server and not be worried about downtime. Remember, you have to plan not only for unscheduled downtime but for downtime for normal server maintenance.

Windows Server 2008 clustering has made a few enhancements when it comes to working with virtual machines. If you used clustering for Windows Server 2003 and Virtual Server 2005, you may recall that the cluster could only see the LUN and the cluster did not know that the LUN was a virtual machine. An administrator had to use scripts to shut down, restart, or migrate virtual machines. One new advantage is that Windows Server 2008 failover clusters can automatically see the virtual machines, making quick migration much more easily configurable.

When you use quick migration for a planned outage, the migration saves the virtual machine, moves the virtual machines to the other host server, and then restores the virtual machine on the other host server. The amount of data that needs to be written to the new host server will determine how long the migration process will take.

If the outage is unplanned (a system error or failure), the virtual machine would not be saved (due to the failure), but the virtual machine would be failed over from the shared cluster storage.

In Exercise 7.6 we will make a virtual machine highly available. To do this, you must make sure that your virtual machines folder is shared with appropriate permissions. If the folder is not shared, you will receive an error during the exercise stating that the virtual machine is not available. You need to have at least two servers running failover for this exercise to work properly.

EXERCISE 7.6

Making a Virtual Machine Highly Available

1. Open the Failover Cluster Management snap-in by clicking Start ➤ Administrative Tools ➤ Failover Cluster Management.

2. In the left window, click on the TestCluster1 cluster.

3. In the right window under the Actions section, click the Configure a Service or Application link.

4. The Before You Begin screen will appear. Click Next.

5. Scroll down and click on Virtual Machine. Click Next.

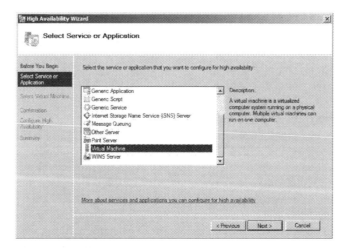

6. On the Select Virtual Machine screen, choose one of the virtual machines that we created in previous exercises. We chose TFixedVM. Click Next.

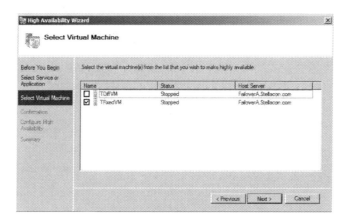

EXERCISE 7.6

7. On the Confirmation page, verify all settings and click Next.

8. After the virtual machine becomes highly available, close the wizard.

After you have set up virtual machines for high availability, there may be a time when you have to manually migrate your virtual machines from one Hyper-V server to another. Other virtualization products in the industry have the ability to automatically, without administrator intervention, switch to another virtualization server when there is a machine failure. Microsoft is designing Hyper-V to use live migration.

Live migration is the ability of a Hyper-V virtual machine to automatically switch from one host server to another with no downtime or problems. If one of your Hyper-V servers fail, the virtual machine would automatically, without administrator intervention, switch to another running Hyper-V server. This would keep the virtual machine running in the event of a Hyper-V server failure.

At the time this book was written, Hyper-V live migration had not been released by Microsoft. It is scheduled to be released when Windows Server 2008 R2 is released.

Since Microsoft Hyper-V does not have an automatic way to migrate a highly available virtual machine from one clustered Hyper-V server (that has a failure) to another, the Hyper-V administrator will have to manually migrate the virtual machine. To have the ability to do this, you have to first set up your cluster and then make the virtual machine highly available (see Exercise 7.6). After the virtual machines are configured for high availability, you would then use the Failover Cluster Manager to migrate the virtual machine from one clustered Hyper-V node to another clustered Hyper-V node.

Exercise 7.7 walks you through the steps required to manually migrate a highly available Hyper-V virtual machine from one clustered server to another. To complete this exercise, you must have two nodes in your cluster, and both nodes must have Hyper-V installed and running.

EXERCISE 7.7

Manually Migrating a Virtual Machine

1. Open the Failover Cluster Management snap-in by clicking Start ➢ Administrative Tools ➢ Failover Cluster Management.

2. In the center console, right-click on the virtual machine you made highly available in Exercise 7.6. Click Move This Service or Application to Another Node and choose the name of one of the other nodes in the cluster that is running Hyper-V.

3. You will see the virtual machine go into a Pending state. After the Pending state is complete, the virtual machine will be migrated to the other node in the cluster.

Knowing how to manually migrate your virtual machine from one clustered node to another is an important step in ensuring that your virtual machines stay up and running.

You should also understand that part of making your virtual machine highly available means making your network redundant. This means that your network components also need to have redundancy in the event of a network hardware failure. This includes having redundancy on your switches, routers, and so forth.

Summary

One important task that an administrator must try to accomplish is the ability to keep the network infrastructure up and running with minimum downtime. It is also important to an administrator to be able to recover data in the event of a hard disk failure.

This is where RAID comes into play. RAID (except RAID 0, which does not provide fault tolerance) allows you to recover from a single hard disk failure so that you do not lose any of your data. RAID 0 is not a fault-tolerant option, but it gives a machine better read and write performance since both hard drives use their own read/write heads.

To configure software RAID on your Windows Server 2008 machine, the hard disk must be configured as a dynamic disk. Compared to using a basic disk, dynamic disks have a few benefits over using a basic disk. Dynamic disks: you can extend volumes (if they are NTFS), you can use RAID, and you can exceed the four-partition limit of basic disks. Basic disks are required, however, if you want to dual-boot the server.

Another way to help protect your organization from downtime is to implement failover clusters. Failover clusters are multiple servers (called nodes) that work as one unit. The advantage of using a failover cluster is if one node fails, other nodes take up the load (known as failover). Failover clusters (formerly known as server clusters) help provide high availability to servers that run mission-critical applications or services.

It is also important to understand failover cluster quorums. Cluster quorums are the number of nodes or devices that must remain online for the cluster to continue to operate properly. Each node or device in the quorum gets to vote (depending on the quorum) on whether or not the cluster continues to operate online.

Microsoft failover clusters and Hyper-V give you the advantage of using the quick migration. Quick migration lets you quickly and easily migrate a virtual machine from one host server to another with as little downtime as possible.

In the next chapter we will discuss the benefits and requirements of using backups and restores. You will learn how to protect your Hyper-V virtual machines from major failures or disasters.

Exam Essentials

Be familiar with RAID.   RAID 1, RAID 0+1, RAID 5, and RAID 6 help you recover from a single hard disk failure. Understand the different types of RAID, how they are configured, and how they work.

Know the benefits of basic disks and dynamic disks.   Understand the differences between a basic disk and a dynamic disk. Understand the main benefits of using a dynamic disk (the ability to use RAID and expand volumes, and no 4-partition limit) and know when to use a basic disk (when you are dual-booting).

Know how to set up failover clusters.   Failover clusters are multiple servers that work as one unit. Know how quorums work and be able to identify the four types of quorums that you can configure.

Understand how quick migrations work.   Hyper-V and failover clusters allow you to quickly and easily migrate a virtual machine from one host to another in the event of a planned or unplanned outage.

Review Questions

1. You are the administrator for a small organization that has just implemented two Windows Server 2008 operating systems. Your manager has asked you to implement a way to recover your data in the event of a single disk failure. You currently have two hard disks in each server. You decide to implement software RAID on the two servers. Which RAID can you implement that allows for two hard disks and that will recover from a single hard disk failure?

   A. RAID 0

   B. RAID 1

   C. RAID 5

   D. RAID 6

2. You have been hired as a consultant for a small real estate office. The office wants you to install a new Windows Server 2008 machine, and they also want you to install a way to recover from a hard disk failure. The office cannot afford to purchase hardware RAID. The RAID will protect only data from a single hard disk failure. You have purchased a new server machine with four hard disks. You install the operating system and boot files on the first hard disk. You want to use the other three disks to set up RAID for data. Which software RAID will you install?

   A. RAID 0

   B. RAID 1

   C. RAID 0+1

   D. RAID 5

3. You are the network administrator for a small printing company. Your company has just purchased a new machine, and you install the Windows Server 2008 operating system onto the computer. You install the operating system with the default settings. The new server has two hard disks and you have decided to implement a software RAID 1 (mirroring) volume onto the system. You go to the Computer Management snap-in, but the RAID 1 option is grayed out and it does not allow you to create the RAID 1 volume. What needs to be done first before creating the RAID 1 volume?

   A. Install a third hard disk.

   B. Install the drivers that allow RAID 1.

   C. Convert the disks to dynamic.

   D. Format both hard disks to set up the RAID.

4. You are the network administrator for a small organization that needs to cut costs in the IT department. You purchase a new Windows Server 2008 machine without hardware RAID. The new machine only has two hard disks installed, and you do not have the ability to insert another disk. Your organization wants to implement RAID to help make retrieving data faster. The data is mostly temp files and log files. Fault tolerance is not necessary on this RAID volume, but better performance and speed is required. What type of RAID would you implement?

    A. RAID 0

    B. RAID 1

    C. RAID 0+1

    D. RAID 5

5. You are the IT administrator for a small ski lodge that has computerized all of its lift tickets and employee files. Money is always an issue, and it's part of your job to keep expenses down. You have a Windows Server 2003 test machine that you have decided to install Windows Server 2008 on, but you do not want to upgrade the machine. You decide to dual-boot the machine so that you can test Windows Server 2008 and verify that all current applications will continue to run properly. You need to decide how to set up the disk storage type for this server. How would you configure the disk storage type?

    A. Dynamic disk type

    B. Basic disk type

    C. Volume disk type

    D. Partition disk type

6. You are the IT administrator for a small organization that has two Windows Server 2008 machines and 45 Windows Vista machines. Your organization has decided to implement RAID 1 mirroring on both Windows Server 2008 servers. Which application would you use to create the RAID 1 mirroring?

    A. Machine Management

    B. Server Management

    C. Computer Status Manager

    D. Computer Management

7. You are the IT manager for a large organization that has decided to use failover clusters. Your organization has five Windows Server 2008 machines that will all be part of the failover cluster. You are trying to decide which type of quorum you would like to configure. You have decided that in the quorum, only the nodes will get to vote on the quorum. Which type of quorum would you configure?

    A. Node Majority Quorum mode

    B. Node and Disk Majority Quorum mode

    C. Node and File Share Majority Quorum mode

    D. No Majority: Disk Only Quorum mode

8. You are the IT manager for a large organization that has decided to use failover clusters. Your organization has five Windows Server 2008 machines that will all be part of the failover cluster. You are trying to decide which type of quorum you would like to configure. You have decided that in the quorum, the nodes and the shared file system that the administrator sets up will get to vote on the quorum. Which type of quorum would you configure?

   A. Node Majority Quorum mode

   B. Node and Disk Majority Quorum mode

   C. Node and File Share Majority Quorum mode

   D. No Majority: Disk Only Quorum mode

9. You are the network administrator for a large organization that develops computer chips. Your organization has decided to use failover clusters. You would like to set up a cluster node in your staging area so that you can test your configurations before creating a full cluster for all your nodes. What type of cluster set up are you using?

   A. Local two-node cluster

   B. Single-node cluster

   C. Multisite cluster

   D. Cluster with no shared storage

10. You are the network administrator for your organization. You have five servers and 450 Windows XP and Vista users. You have decided to implement Hyper-V on all five servers. After the Hyper-V role is installed, you create virtual machines on all five servers. You then decide to implement failover clusters. You install failover clusters on all five servers, and you want to make your virtual machines highly available. What application would you configure to make the virtual machines highly available?

   A. SCVMM 2008

   B. Hyper-V Manager

   C. Failover Cluster Management

   D. Computer Management

11. You are the IT manager for a large organization that has decided to use failover clusters. Your organization has five Windows Server 2008 machines that will all be part of the failover cluster. You are trying to decide which type of quorum you would like to configure. You have decided that in the quorum, both the nodes and the cluster storage device will get to vote on the quorum. Which type of quorum would you configure?

   A. Node Majority Quorum mode

   B. Node and Disk Majority Quorum mode

   C. Node and File Share Majority Quorum mode

   D. No Majority: Disk Only Quorum mode

12. You are the network administrator for a large organization that produces yo-yos. Your organization has locations in New York and Boston. Your organization has decided to use failover clusters for both locations. To set up clustering so that both locations work together, what type of cluster do you use?

    A. Local two-node cluster

    B. Single-node cluster

    C. Multisite cluster

    D. Cluster with no shared storage

13. You have been hired as a consultant to a small watch company. The company wants you to configure two different tasks for them. They want to be able to expand volumes on their servers, and they also want to set up software RAID. The hard disks are still configured with the default setting of a basic disk. You need to change the basic disk to a dynamic. Which utility can you use to accomplish this goal?

    A. Active Directory Sites and Services

    B. Active Directory Domains and Trusts

    C. Disk Management Utility

    D. Computer Configuration utility

14. You are the IT manager for a large organization with 20 Windows Server 2003 machines and 4,000 Windows XP and Vista users located throughout the United States. You want to implement failover clusters for the organization. You decide to upgrade all servers to Windows Server 2008 and use Hyper-V. You are getting ready to purchase the Windows Server 2008 editions needed to set up the clusters and Hyper-V. Which editions of Windows Server 2008 can you install? (Choose all that apply.)

    A. Standard edition

    B. Enterprise edition

    C. Web edition

    D. Datacenter edition

15. You are the network administrator for your organization. You have decided to implement failover clusters throughout the organization. You want to make sure that all required services are configured properly to allow clustering on your network. What services or applications are required to configure clustering properly?

    A. WINS

    B. GlobalNames

    C. DNS

    D. RDP

16. You are the network administrator for a small organization. You have been asked by the owner of the company to give a presentation on dynamic disks. You need to explain the characteristics and benefits of using a dynamic disk. Which of the following are characteristics and benefits of using a dynamic disk? (Choose all that apply.)

    A. Uses volumes

    B. Uses partitions

    C. Can have RAID installed

    D. Can be dual-booted

17. You are the network administrator for a large organization. You want to set up failover clusters and Hyper-V. You need to have the ability to quickly and easily transfer a virtual machine from one host server to another for planned and unplanned downtime. What feature of failover clusters and Hyper-V can you use?

    A. VMotion

    B. VM migration

    C. Quick migration

    D. Virtual machine migration

18. You are the network administrator for a large organization that has eight Windows Server 2008 machines along with 450 Windows Vista users. Your organization has decided to implement failover clusters. You would like to cluster all of the servers, but you are not sure what the maximum number of nodes in a cluster can be. What is the maximum number of nodes that you can have in a Windows Server 2008 cluster?

    A. 4

    B. 8

    C. 16

    D. 32

19. You are the IT manager for a large organization that has decided to upgrade its Windows Server 2003 server cluster to a Windows Server 2008 failover clusters. You have decided that in the quorum, no votes will be cast by any nodes or devices. You want the cluster to operate just as it did in Windows Server 2003. Which type of quorum would you configure?

    A. Node Majority Quorum mode

    B. Node and Disk Majority Quorum mode

    C. Node and File Share Majority Quorum mode

    D. No Majority: Disk Only Quorum mode

20. You are the network administrator for a large organization that creates clothing. Your organization has two Windows Server 2008 machines that you would like to cluster. What type of cluster setup are you using?

    A. Local two-node cluster

    B. Single-node cluster

    C. Multisite cluster

    D. Cluster with no shared storage

Answers to Review Questions

1. B. RAID 1, also known as mirroring, allows you to implement RAID with only two hard disks. This RAID is also a fault-tolerant option that will allow you to recover from a single hard disk failure.

2. D. RAID 5 is an excellent way to protect data against a single disk failure. RAID 5 requires a minimum of three hard disks, and the RAID 5 volume can't include the system or boot partitions. This is not a problem here since all of the system files (boot partition) are installed onto the first hard disk.

3. C. To create software RAID onto a Windows Server 2008 operating system, the hard disks have to be converted from the basic storage disk type to a dynamic storage disk type. Any new RAID on Windows Server 2008 has to be on a dynamic disk. Only machines that were upgraded from a previous version can have RAID on a basic disk, but even if the machine was upgraded, the disks have to be converted to dynamic if you want to create a new RAID volume.

4. A. RAID 0 is also referred to as disk striping. Disk striping uses a minimum of two physical hard drives and can have a maximum of 32 hard disks. The advantage of RAID 0 is that both hard drives use their own read/write heads. This gives you better performance. RAID 0 is not fault tolerant, but in this question it is not a requirement.

5. B. Basic disk types have to be used in this situation because you have decided to dual-boot the operating systems. Dynamic disk types are not allowed if you dual-boot operating systems.

6. D. To implement RAID in Windows Server 2008, you would use the Computer Management mmc snap-in. You would then click on the Disk Management section to configure the RAID.

7. A. In this quorum mode, just like many of the other quorums, the majority of votes (more than half) constitute the quorum. But in the Node Majority Quorum mode, the node is only allowed to vote as long as it can communicate with the other nodes. As long as more than half of the nodes vote, the cluster continues to function properly.

8. C. In this quorum mode, just like many of the other quorums, the majority of votes (more than half) constitute the quorum. But the Node and File Share Majority Quorum mode allows the node and the shared file system to vote as long as they can communicate. As long as more than half of the nodes and shared file systems vote, the cluster continues to function properly.

9. B. Single-node clusters are also known as a "stager." You use this approach to set up a single-node cluster for testing your network configuration and applications.

10. C. To make a virtual machine highly available, you would first create a cluster in the Failover Cluster Management snap-in. Then you would configure an application or service (virtual machines) for high availability. After the virtual machine is configured for high availability, you can use quick migrations for any planned or unplanned outages.

11. B. In this quorum mode, the majority of votes (more than half) constitute the quorum. But in this quorum, both the nodes and the cluster storage device (disk witness) get to vote.

12. C. This cluster type allows you to have nodes within the cluster in different geographic locations or sites. Multisite clusters can have storage at each physical location of each site. This way, if one of the sites fails the other site can continue to function properly. Data is replicated or mirrored between the sites, thus keeping the data synchronized between the multiple sites.

13. C. There are two ways to convert a basic disk to a dynamic disk. First, you can use the convert command at a command prompt, or you can convert the disk in the Disk Management utility by right-clicking the disk and choosing the Convert option.

14. B, D. If you are going to be using failover clusters with Hyper-V, Windows Server 2008 Enterprise or Datacenter editions must be loaded on the physical machines. The same version must be loaded on all of the machines in the cluster. If you load Server Core Enterprise edition onto one server in the cluster, then all servers in the cluster must have Server Core Enterprise editions.

15. C. All of the machines within the cluster must be using the Domain Name System (DNS) for name resolution. DNS resolves a hostname into a TCP/IP (forward lookup) address and also turns a TCP/IP number into a hostname (reverse lookup).

16. A, C. Dynamic disks have many advantages over a basic disk. First, dynamic disks use volumes, and volumes can be extended. Second, you can set up software RAID on a dynamic disk. Third, you do not have the four-partition limit using dynamic volumes.

17. C. Microsoft's quick migration feature gives you the ability to easily migrate a virtual machine from one host server to another with as little downtime as possible. One of the nice advantages to quickly migrating virtual machines from one host server to another is the ability to do maintenance on a server and not be worried about downtime.

18. C. Clusters are a group of individual computers (called cluster nodes) that work together as one unit. You can have up to 16 nodes in a failover cluster running on a 64-bit version of Enterprise or Datacenter edition of Windows Server 2008.

19. D. This is the quorum that was the equivalent of what they used in Windows Server 2003. In this quorum, there is no majority vote. The cluster continues to operate properly as long as one node is available with the cluster storage disk. The problem with this quorum is that there is a single point of failure.

20. A. A local two-node cluster is just as it states: it's two nodes in the cluster. If one node fails, the other node takes up the slack and continues to operate. These two nodes are commonly attached to a shared storage device (such as a SAN), and it's because of this shared storage device that the cluster can continue to operate properly if one of the nodes fails.

Chapter

8

Backing Up and Restoring VMs

MICROSOFT EXAM OBJECTIVES COVERED IN THIS CHAPTER:

✓ **Monitoring and optimizing virtual machines.**

    ※ This objective may include but is not limited to: not limited to: Tool: Reliability and performance monitor, Tool: SCVMM, processor, optimize memory, network, disks.

✓ **Manage snapshots and backups**

    ※ This objective may include but is not limited to: live backups of a VM by using VSS Data Protection Manager (DPM), backup within a virtual machine, snapshots.

✓ **Manage and Optimize the Hyper-V server.**

    ※ This objective may include but is not limited to: performance monitoring of 2k8.

The performance of servers should be monitored on a day-to-day basis, and Microsoft has included tools in the Windows Server 2008 operating system that allow us to monitor the daily performance. Not only do we need to monitor the Hyper-V role running on our server, but we also have to monitor the physical performance of the machine that Hyper-V is running on.

Network recoverability is vital and that is why knowing how to properly back up and restore your Hyper-V servers and virtual machines is so critical. Windows Server 2008 includes a free backup software utility called Windows Server Backup.

Microsoft also provides a tool for backing up and restoring Hyper-V servers known as the System Center Data Protection Manager. The Data Protection Manager (DPM) allows you to back up many of the Microsoft software packages (such as Exchange, SQL, and Hyper-V) from one utility.

Let's start by diving into one of the tasks that can help you determine problem areas on your network infrastructure. Monitoring your network allows you to identify any issues you are having on your network.

Monitoring and Optimizing Virtual Machines

One feature that you can achieve while using Microsoft Windows Server 2008 is the ability to fine tune the performance of your servers. Think about owning a car; if you want to get the best mileage out of your automobile you would check tire pressure, oil levels, etc. It works the same for computers. If you want to get the best performance out of your servers, you have to do the maintenance and tuning. Maintenance and performance tuning is a task that many IT administrators do not perform on a daily basis. Many times, administrators begin monitoring servers when they start to experience problems. By choosing that route, you are already starting behind the curve. It's always better to be proactive instead of reactive.

Reliability and Performance Monitor

Server performance issues can greatly affect how your overall network performance is operating. When servers have problems and start to operate slower than normal, this can cause bottlenecks on your network. Servers can't answer requests fast enough, and the requests build up until your network is no longer operating properly.

There are many tools, Microsoft or third-party, that you can use to fine-tune your servers. Before you can optimize performance, you have to find the source of the problems. Gathering data is an important part of configuring and optimizing any server.

One of the first steps in monitoring is establishing a *baseline*. A baseline is a readout of how the server is running when you first install all the services on your server and the machine has just gone into a live production environment.

When you first install the operating system and then install the services that are going to run on that machine, this should be when the system is running at its best and you can set your baseline. Once you have your baseline, you now have captured statistics to compare against when you are monitoring in the future.

Windows Server 2008 allows you to gather data using the Reliability and Performance Monitor (see Figure 8.1). The Reliability and Performance Monitor is an MMC snap-in that includes multiple tools that you can use to help monitor your servers.

FIGURE 8.1   Reliability and Performance Monitor

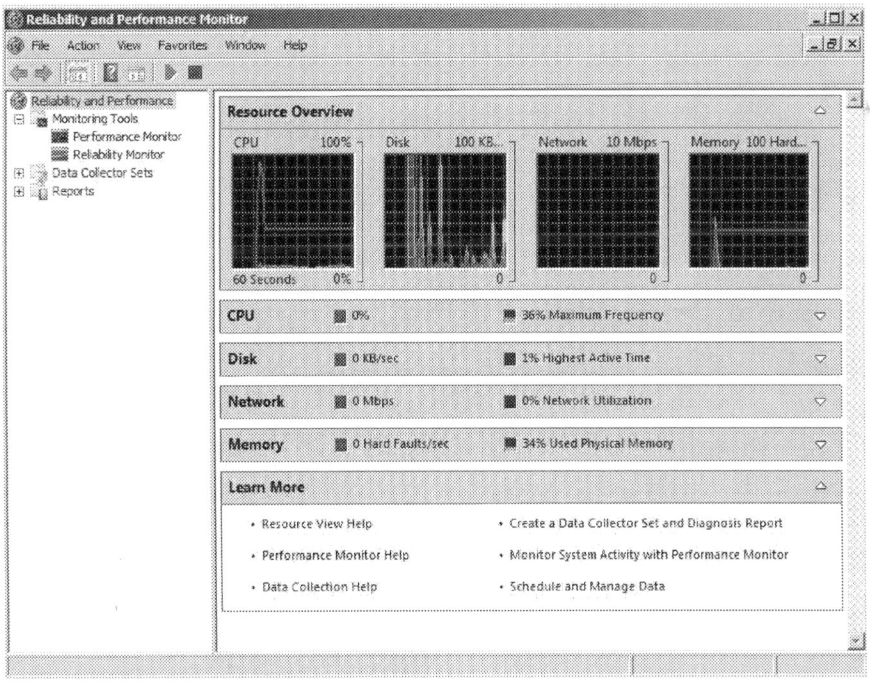

When monitoring your servers, there are many different items, called *counters*, that you can check to determine the performance of the machine. There are four main resources that you need to keep an eye on. When you first open the Reliability and Performance Monitor, you will see four monitor windows in the resource overview.

CPU   The CPU window will show you the total percentage of the CPU being used in a green color, and it will show you the Maximum Frequency of the CPU value in blue.

Disk   The Disk windows will show you the total current input/output in green, and will show you the highest activity time in blue.

Network   The Network window shows you how the network traffic is operating. The window will show you the percentage of network capacity in blue and the total current network traffic in green.

Memory (RAM)   This section will show you how much memory is being used. When looking at the Resource Overview Memory window, you should monitor two colors. The current physical memory that is being used will be shown in blue. The hard faults (also referred to as page faults) per second are shown in green.

When an application is opened, the application is loaded into RAM. If part of the application is referenced and that part is not in RAM, the system will read that part of the application from the physical disk. This is called a hard fault, or page fault. Too many hard faults per second will show you that you do not have enough RAM to support the applications running on the machine.

This resource overview is just a quick look at some of the main components that should be monitored. The Reliability and Performance Monitor allows you to monitor many other counters and the objects within those counters. You can monitor the following:

Counters   *Counters* are the specific data that is being measured with the Reliability and Performance Monitor. Counters are added to the monitor as the different services get added to a specific machine.

Performance Objects   A *performance object* represents data that you can monitor on specific components of the system. For example, the Hyper-V Hypervisor counter has objects that include Logical Processor, Monitor Notification, Partitions, Total Pages, and Virtual Processors. You can monitor the entire counter and its objects, or just specific objects within a counter.

Instances   *Instances* allow you to further specify which component you are measuring. For example, if you have multiple CPUs, instances allow you to show which CPU you are monitoring.

One of the advantages of using the Reliability and Performance Monitor is that you can monitor counters for services and roles that you install onto the server. For example, when you install Hyper-V onto the server, many new counters for Hyper-V will become available for you to monitor. Some of the counters that get installed with Hyper-V:

- Hyper-V Hypervisor
- Hyper-V Hypervisor Logical Processor
- Hyper-V Hypervisor Partition
- Hyper-V Hypervisor Root Partition
- Hyper-V Hypervisor Root Virtual Partition
- Hyper-V Hypervisor Virtual

- Hyper-V Legacy Network Adapter Processor
- Hyper-V Task Manager Details
- Hyper-V Virtual IDE Controller
- Hyper-V Virtual Machine Bus
- Hyper-V Virtual Machine Summary
- Hyper-V Virtual Network Adapter
- Hyper-V Virtual Storage Device
- Hyper-V Virtual Switch
- Hyper-V Virtual Switch Port

The Reliability and Performance Monitor tool (see Figure 8.2) allows you to easily add counters to the view. You can choose from three different views when monitoring your systems:

FIGURE 8.2   Graph view of Reliability and Performance Monitor

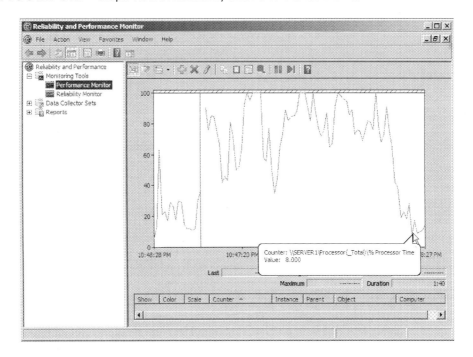

Graph View   Graph is the default view when you start the Windows Server 2008 Reliability and Performance Monitor. This chart represents the percentage of usage by using colored lines for the various counters. These lines represent the values by vertical and horizontal movements. Graph views are useful when you're capturing data over a long period of time.

Histogram View   The Histogram view represents the percentage of usage by using colored bar graphs (see Figure 8.3). Histogram views are a good way to grab a point-in-time value of a counter. The Histogram view can offer you an average measurement or a minimum and maximum value of a counter.

FIGURE 8.3   Reliability and Performance Monitor, Histogram view

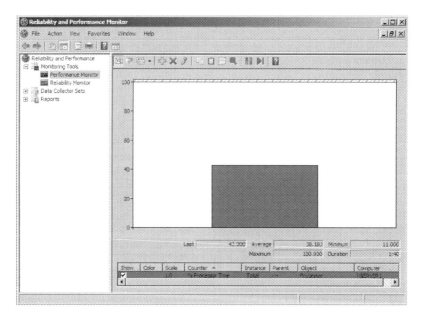

Report View   The Report view shows you all the statistical data in an easy-to-read numeric report (see Figure 8.4). The Chart and Histogram views show you lines and bars whereas the Report view shows you numeric data. This helps you get a clear representation of the items you are monitoring.

In Exercise 8.1 we will walk through the steps of monitoring your server. We will add counters and objects to the Reliability and Performance Monitor and also show the different views that you can monitor.

FIGURE 8.4   Reliability and Performance Monitor, Report view

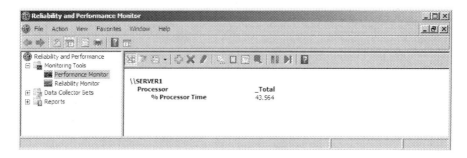

Adding Counters to Performance Monitor

1. Start the Reliability and Performance Monitor by clicking Start ➢ Administrative Tools ➢ Reliability and Performance Monitor.

2. In the left window, click Performance Monitor.

3. In the right window, click on the plus sign (or press Ctrl+L) to add a counter.

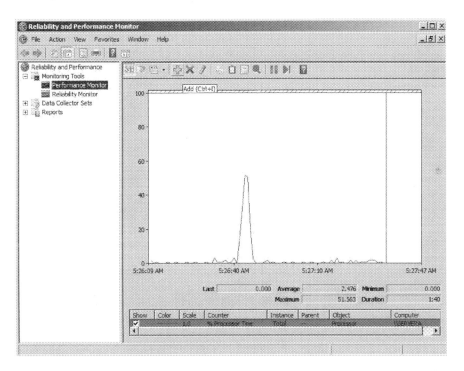

4. The Add Counters screen will appear. Under Available Counters, choose <Local Computer> and Hyper-V Processors. Click the Add button.

5. Again under Available Counters, choose <Local Computer> and this time choose Processor. If you have multiple processors, under the Instances box choose <All Instances> and click the Add button.

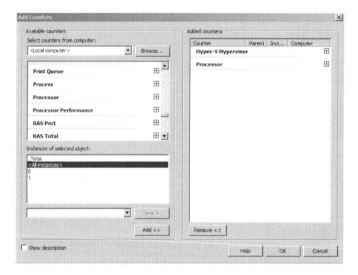

6. Click OK to add the counters. You will see that the Graph view has many new objects being monitored.

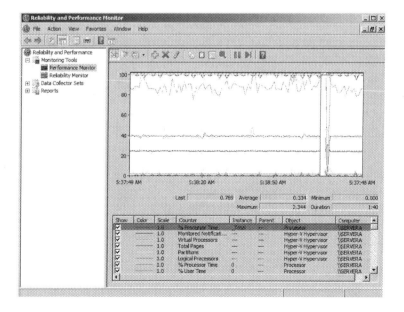

7. After monitoring the graph for a few minutes, click Ctrl+G to switch between views.

8. Make sure that your virtual machines are now running. If they aren't, start a virtual machine and you will see your numbers change. Once you have finished watching these counters, close the Reliability and Performance Monitor.

Once you have captured this data, you can view the outcome and decide if you need to add or change any components of the server. The data that you capture can help you fine-tune your server to run at peak performance. Now let's take a look at how to configure the Reliability and Performance Monitor properties.

Managing the Reliability and Performance Monitor Properties

The Reliability and Performance Monitor gives you the ability to configure various properties that will allow you to get the most out of your monitoring. You can configure these properties two ways: by clicking the Properties button in the taskbar or by right-clicking the Reliability and Performance Monitor and choosing Properties. The Properties dialog box has five tabs that you can configure:

General   The General tab (see Figure 8.5) allows you to specify several different options that relate to the Reliability and Performance Monitor view. You have the ability to enable or disable display elements such as the legends, the value bar, and the toolbar.

FIGURE 8.5   The General tab lets you enable or disable display elements such as the legends, the value bar, and the toolbar.

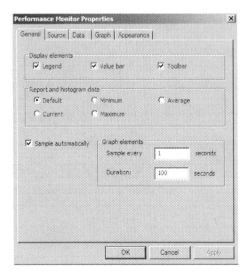

In the Report and Histogram data section, you can choose how much of the information is displayed. Choose Default, Current, Minimum, Maximum, or Average.

You also have the ability to configure the graph elements. This setting lets you specify how often (Sample Every) and the duration of the view that your counters will be monitored.

Source   The Source tab (see Figure 8.6) allows you to specify where the data from the Reliability and Performance Monitor will be placed and how it can be viewed. The Data Source section allows you to determine if the data will be placed in the current activity (the default setting), log file, or a database. If you choose to analyze information from a log file, you can also specify the time range for which you want to view statistics.

FIGURE 8.6   The Source tab lets you specify where the data will be placed and how it can be viewed.

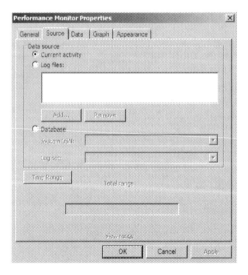

Data   The Data tab (see Figure 8.7) allows you to set the properties for the data that you are currently monitoring. You can change the color, scale, width, and style of the data you are capturing. You also have the ability to add data in the section of the properties.

Graph   The Graph tab (see Figure 8.8) allows you to customize the way the Reliability and Performance Monitor displays its captured data. On this tab you can specify if the view will be Graph, Histogram, or Report. You can add a title to the graph and specify a label for the vertical axis. You can also choose to display grids and specify the vertical scale range.

Appearance   The Appearance tab (see Figure 8.9) allows you to set the appearance of the data. You can specify the colors for the display, such as the background and foreground. You can also specify the fonts that you want to use to display the counter. You also have the ability to set up the properties for a border.

FIGURE 8.7 On the Data tab, you set the properties for the data that you are currently monitoring.

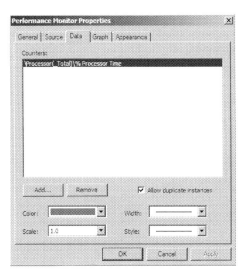

FIGURE 8.8 The Graph tab lets you customize the way the Reliability and Performance Monitor displays its captured data.

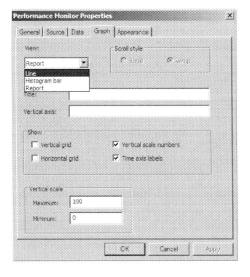

Now that you know the types of information Reliability and Performance Monitor tracks and how this data can be used to fine-tune your server, let's take a look at protecting your data in the event of hardware failure or accidental deletion.

FIGURE 8.9   The Appearance tab lets you specify the appearance of the data.

Understanding Backups and Recoverability

One of the most important tasks that any administrator must perform is backing up data. Backups allow you to make a copy of your data on a media other than your servers. This allows you to recover that data in the event of accidental data loss or machine failure.

 **Real World Scenario**

The Importance of Backups

As a consultant, I have been hired by many IT companies. Many times I have been impressed by how well many IT departments function and perform their duties. But on the other side of that coin, on many job sites I just shake my head in disbelief.

But no matter how the IT department is performing, they all must have one thing in common: backups. Many companies will allow IT personnel to make mistakes, but very few will allow those mistakes to involve backups. I have seen people fired on the spot because they didn't make proper backups.

Could your company survive if you lost all of your data? How would you know who owes you money? If you lost all of your clients, you would most likely lose your business. Backups are an essential part of all IT departments.

Knowing how important backups are to your organization, it is also important to know the different types of backups and when to use each type of backup.

Configuring Backup Types

Which backup method you choose is based on the backup strategy you want to create for your organization. Your backup strategy determines when and what is going to be backed up every day. Your backup strategy also has to include your restore strategy. When choosing a backup strategy, you have to make sure that your restore strategy can recover any data, from any time period, that may be lost.

Your backup strategy also depends on your backup software. If you are using third-party software, your options may be different than if you are using the Windows Server 2008 Backup utility.

Before we talk about the different types of backups, you must first understand how files work when they are changed. Files use an archive bit (1s and 0s) to show when a file has been modified and saved. Think of the data as a house mailbox. When you put something in your mailbox, you raise the flag to show that there is mail. This is the job of the archive bit. When data changes, the flag (archive bit) is raised. The type of backup that you choose will determine whether or not the archive bit is reset.

Five main types of backups are available, and not all are supported by the Windows Server 2008 Backup utility:

Full Backup *Full backups*, also referred to as normal backups, involve backing up the entire machine's hard disks and files. When you set up your full backup type, you choose which files, folders, and hard disks are to be backed up.

After a full backup is performed, all archive bits are reset to 0. Full backups are available using the Windows Server 2008 Backup utility.

Incremental Backup *Incremental backups* are backups of any files that have changed since the last full or incremental backup (see Figure 8.10). The incremental backup finds all files that have an archive bit set to 1 and then proceeds to back up those files. After the backup is complete, all archive bits are reset to 0. Incremental backups are available using the Windows Server 2008 Backup utility.

FIGURE 8.10 Incremental backup

The advantage of using an incremental backup is speed. Since you are only backing up files that have changed since the previous full or incremental backup, nightly backups are smaller and take less time to back up. The disadvantage is longer recovery. Using

Figure 8.10 as an example, if you have a crash on Friday, you must load Monday's full backup and then Tuesday's incremental, Wednesday's incremental, and Thursday's incremental to recover back to Friday.

Differential Backup   *Differential backups* are backups of any files that have changed since the last full backup (see Figure 8.11). Differential backups find all archive bits that are set to 1 and then it performs a backup of all those files. When the backup process finishes, the archive bits do not get reset. This is why differential backups back up from the last full backup.

The Windows Server 2008 Backup utility does not support differential backups. Previous versions of Windows Server did support differentials. Many third-party backup utilities do support the differential backup process.

FIGURE 8.11   Differential backup

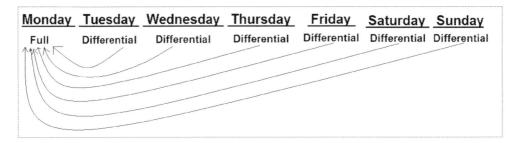

The advantage of using differential backups is faster recovery times. Since differentials are backing up from the last full backup; to recover you need to load just the last full tape and then the last differential tape. The disadvantage to differential backups is that the backup process is slower than an incremental backup.

Copy Backup   *Copy backups* are the same as a full backup except for the archive bit. Copy backups do not reset the archive bits. You normally use copy backups to do a backup in the middle of the day and you do not want to affect your nightly backups by changing the archive bit.

Say you want to install Microsoft Exchange Server after lunch. You want to do a backup before doing the installation. If the installation causes any issues or errors, you can recover quickly using the backup.

Daily   *Daily backups* back up all files that have changed during a single day. This operation uses the file time/date stamps to determine which files should be backed up and does not mark the files as having been backed up.

Table 8.1 shows all four main backup processes and the advantages and disadvantages of each one of the processes.

TABLE 8.1   Backup Processes

Backup Type	Description	Advantage	Disadvantage	Archive Bit
Full	Backs up all selected files	All files backed up, not just changed ones	Longer backups	Reset
Incremental	Backs up only files that have changed since last full or incremental backup	Shorter backups, since it's only backing up changed files from last backup	Longer recovery time (you must load all tapes since last full backup)	Reset
Differential	Backs up only files that have changed since last full backup	Shorter recovery time	Longer backups than incremental	Not Reset
Copy	Backs up all Selected files	All files are backed up. Useful for backups during working hours.	Longer backups	Not Reset
Daily	Backs up only files that have changed during that day	Allows you to back up daily changes only	Not part of a normal backup schedule	Not Reset

In Exercise 8.2 we will start by installing the Windows Server 2008 Backup Features. To use the Windows Server 2008 Backup utility, you must first install the feature to the server.

EXERCISE 8.2

Installing the Windows Backup Feature

1. Start the Server Manager MMC by clicking Start ➢ Administrative Tools ➢ Server Manager.

EXERCISE 8.2 *(continued)*

2. In the Server Manager MMC, click the Features link under the Server name.

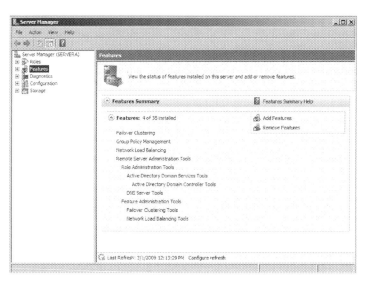

3. In the right window, click the Add Features link.

4. When the Select Features screen appears, scroll down and check the Windows Server Backup Features box. Click Next. (A message box asking to install the Windows PowerShell may appear; if it does, click Yes to install the PowerShell command-line utilities for the Backup Features.)

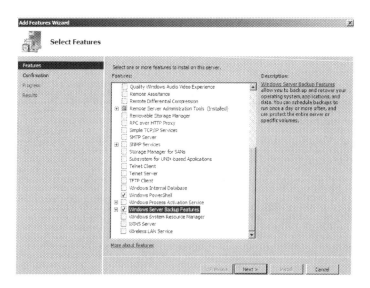

5. On the Confirm Installation Selection screen, verify your settings and click Install.

6. After the installation is complete, an Installation Results screen appears. Click Close.

7. Close the Server Manager MMC utility.

In this chapter I emphasize the importance of backing up your data for recoverability. Many times when I am on site as a consultant I ask the administrator why they do not have backups. Many administrators have stated that backups are very expensive. This is not a good excuse! A backup utility is included with the server operating system. Let's talk about an inexpensive way to do backups.

Using Windows Server 2008 Backup

Microsoft Windows Server 2008 includes a free backup utility with the operating system (see Figure 8.12). The *Windows Server 2008 Backup utility* gives you the ability to create full or incremental backups from a single interface.

FIGURE 8.12   Windows Server 2008 Backup

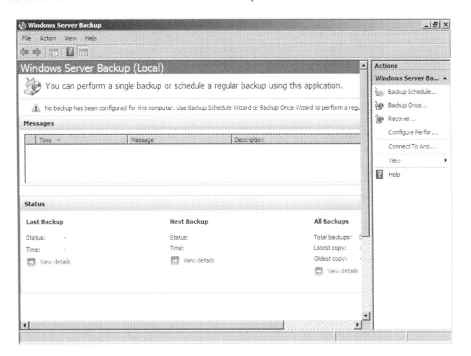

There are advantages and disadvantages to using the Windows Server 2008 Backup utility. The first advantage is that it is free—the utility is included with the operating system. But, as the old saying goes, you get what you pay for. Because it is a free backup utility, it has many limitations that third-party backup software does not have.

An advantage of using the Windows Server 2008 Backup utility is that it automatically works with Active Directory and many other Microsoft products such as Exchange Server. Many third-party backup software requires you to purchase additional services to back up products such as Exchange.

The biggest disadvantage to using the Microsoft Backup utility is that it is an all-or-nothing backup. Many third-party backup utilities allow you to back up or restore only specific files and folders. For example, let's say that you are using Microsoft Exchange Server and you accidentally delete a mailbox. Many third-party utilities let you restore that one mailbox. The Windows Server 2008 Backup utility only allows you to recover the entire Exchange Server and not just the one mailbox.

 **Real World Scenario**

Using Backup Software

In the real world, most IT people do not use the Windows Server Backup utility. The reason for this is that it has more limitations than benefits. But there are times when the Windows Server 2008 Backup utility can work.

I have done many consulting jobs for smaller companies where there are financial strains. I recently finished a contract job for a small flight school that wanted to implement a server in their office. I decided to implement Windows Server 2008 and use the Windows Server Backup utility to back up the server and all of its data.

I set it up so that a full backup was done on a normal schedule and then the tapes would be taken offsite. No matter what backup software or technology that you use, always use off-site backups. Even if this means putting a tape in a safety deposit box, you should not have your recovery method in the same location as your servers. If you have a fire or natural disaster, you can lose both your servers and your recovery.

The Windows Server 2008 Backup utility is better than having no backup at all and should be used in the event that an organization can't afford to purchase third-party software.

When using the Windows Server 2008 Backup utility, you can back up your data to a hardware device (such as a tape device) or to a network or local drive.

Another feature of using the Windows Server 2008 Backup utility is that you can schedule backups to take place at specific times. It is important to set the backup schedule properly. When a server gets backed up, it will reduce the performance of the system.

If you schedule your backups too early in the evening, you may still have users working on the network. If you schedule the backups too late, the backup may run into the following day, and that would cause performance issues. You have to decide when to schedule your backup based on how much data you normally back up each evening. To add a backup to the schedule, you simply click the Add button on the Specify Backup Time dialog.

Authoritative Restore vs. Nonauthoritative Restore

The easiest way to explain the difference between an authoritative restore and a nonauthoritative restore is to explain how the backup process works.

Let's say we have an Active Directory network with five domain controllers. Your organization has two IT members who have the rights to modify Active Directory. One of the members accidentally deletes an organizational unit (OU). He is informed that the OU needs to be restored.

The IT member reboots one of the domain controllers and enters the Directory Services Restore Mode and restores the OU. This is considered a nonauthoritative restore. The problem here is if the IT member reboots the server and the domain controller that he loaded the OU onto replicates with another domain controller, the other domain controller will erase the OU again. The reason is that the domain controller that had the OU reloaded onto it would have a time stamp from the previous night's backup. So when that machine replicates with another domain controller, the other domain controller will have a time stamp that is current and it will remove the OU again.

The way to solve this problem is to do your nonauthoritative restore and then go into the command prompt and run NTDSUTIL.exe. After you enter NTDSUTIL, you perform an authoritative restore (by typing in the command **Authoritative restore**). Doing so creates a setting on the machine that basically states that no matter what the time stamp states, it is the machine you are supposed to listen to.

You do not always want to do an authoritative restore. If a domain controller crashes and you restore the domain controller, after you restore the domain controller you would want it to replicate with other domain controllers and get the current Active Directory database. If you are responsible for restoring servers, it is important to know when to perform a nonauthoritative backup only and when to perform an authoritative backup.

In Exercise 8.3 we will walk through the steps of setting up and performing a full backup using the Windows Server 2008 Backup utility. We will back up the server data to a network location. Before completing this exercise, create a folder named Test Folder on the C: hard disk.

EXERCISE 8.3

Completing a Full Backup

1. Create a folder called Test Folder on the C: drive. Create a file within that folder called TestFile.txt.

2. Start the Windows Server 2008 Backup utility by clicking Start ➢ Administrative Tools ➢ Windows Server Backup.

3. In the right window under Actions, click the Backup Once link.

4. The Backup Options screen appears. If this is the first time you have used the Windows Backup utility, you should see only one option. Make sure the Different Options radio button is selected and click Next.

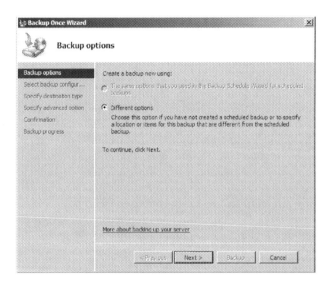

5. On the Select backup configuration screen, click the Custom radio button and click Next.

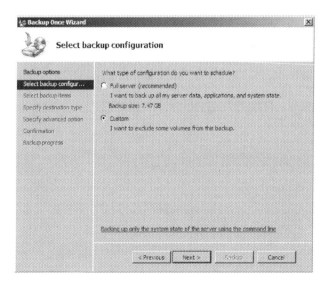

EXERCISE 8.3 *(continued)*

6. On the Select Backup Items screen, choose the Local Disk (C:) check box only. Also make sure the check box Enable System Recovery is selected. Click Next.

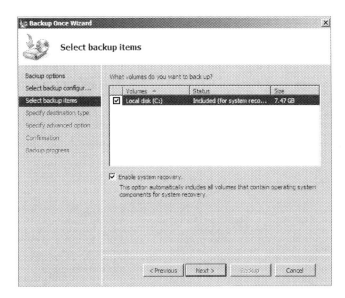

7. On the Specify Destination Type screen, choose the Remote Shared Folder radio button and click Next.

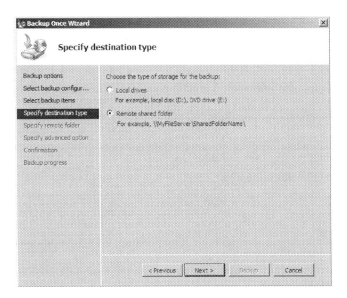

EXERCISE 8.3 *(continued)*

8. On the Specify Remote Folder screen, type the path of a network location for the placement of the backup. Make sure the Inherit radio button is selected and click Next.

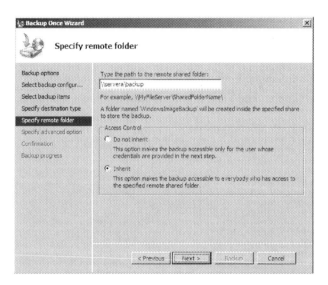

9. On the Specify Advanced Options screen, make sure the VSS Full Backup radio button is selected. VSS stands for Volume Shadow Copy Service, and since we are not using any other products to back up this server, we want the VSS fully backed up. Click Next.

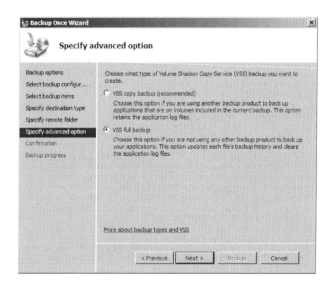

10. On the Confirmation screen, verify that all settings are correct and click the Backup button.

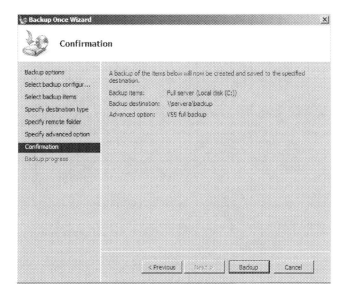

11. The Backup Progress screen appears. This screen will let you know the status of the backup progress.

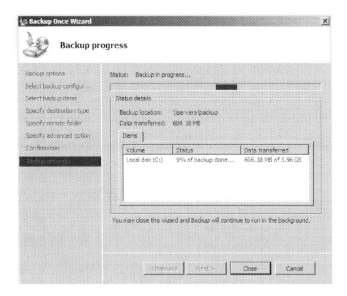

12. When the backup completes, the status should state Backup Completed. Click the Close button.

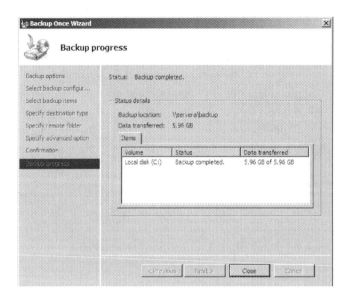

Once the backup is completed, you must ensure that you could recover the data in the event of a failure or accidental deletion. The best way to verify that the backups will be able to recover your data is to test the recovery. You do this by moving a folder (do not delete it just in case the test does not work) to another location and then recover your data and make sure the folder is there.

In Exercise 8.4 we will walk through the steps of recovering data using the backup we created. We will first move a folder to another location and then we will recover our data. After the data is recovered, the folder should be back in its original location.

EXERCISE 8.4

Recovering Data Using the Windows Backup

1. Open Windows Explorer and delete the Test Folder that you created in Exercise 8.3.

2. If the Windows Server 2008 Backup utility is not open, open it by clicking Start ➢ Administrative Tools ➢ Windows Server Backup.

3. In the right Actions window, click the Recover Data link.

4. On the Getting started screen, click the This Server radio button and click Next.

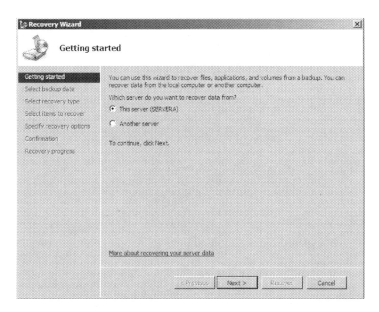

5. On the Select Backup Date screen, choose the date that you did the backup on and click Next.

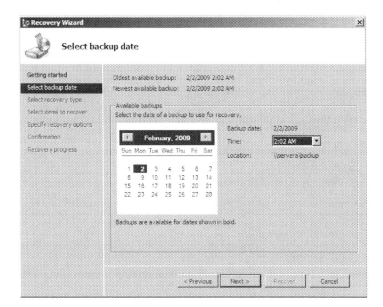

6. On the Select Recovery Type screen, choose the Files and Folders radio button and click Next.

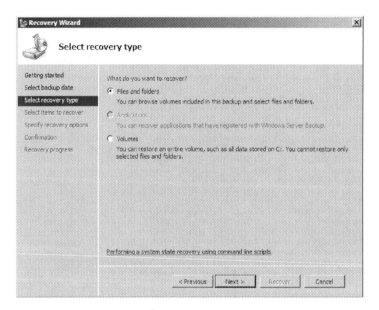

7. On the Select Items to Recover screen, expand the Local Disk (C:) drive and choose Test Folder. Click Next.

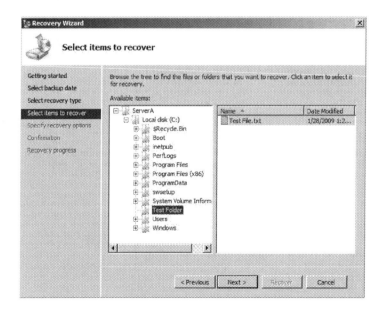

8. On the Specify Recovery Options screen, choose the Original Location radio button. Make sure that the "Overwrite existing files with recovered files" radio button is also selected. Leave the Restore Security Settings check box selected and click Next.

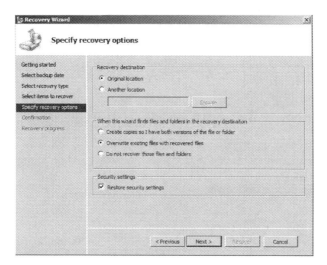

9. On the Confirmation screen, verify all settings and click the Recover button.

10. The Recovery process screen appears. After the restoration is complete, close the Recovery Progress screen by clicking the Close button.

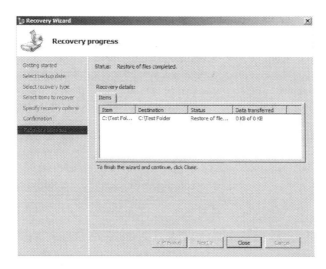

11. Check the Hard Disk (C:) and verify that the Test Folder has been recovered.

If you are running a version of Microsoft Windows Server as the operating system on a virtual machine, you have the ability as a Hyper-V manager to run these backups on the virtual machine. You can use the Windows Server Backup utility to back up the data in the virtual machine.

There is one drawback to backing up the virtual machine's files on Hyper-V; most backup software requires that you shut down the virtual machine and then perform a backup. You may even be able to shut down the machine for only a few minutes, but there is still downtime while doing the backup.

If you are running Microsoft Server 2003 or Microsoft Server 2008 operating systems on your virtual machines, Microsoft has solutions to allow you to back up your Hyper-V and virtual machines without having to shut down those machines.

Understanding the Data Protection Manager

Microsoft System Center *Data Protection Manager (DPM)* is a utility from Microsoft that allows you to back up certain Microsoft servers such as Hyper-V, Exchange Server, and SQL Server.

One advantage to using DPM is that you can back up both your virtual and nonvirtual servers. This gives you one application that allows you to back up all the different servers on your infrastructure.

One of the newer features of DPM is the ability to back up a virtual machine without having to shut down the machine. As long as the operating system is Windows Server 2003 or Windows Server 2008, the virtual machine will be backed up without you having to shut it down.

If the guest operating system is not a Windows Server version, the DPM will temporally shut down the guest operating system, take a snapshot to back up, and then restart the operating system to accomplish the backup. This shutdown only results in downtime normally less than five minutes.

For Windows Servers 2003 and 2008, when you install DPM, a VSS writer is placed on the guest Windows operating system, which in turn makes sure that all backups are data consistent without the need to shut down the virtual machine.

For example, if you are running SQL Server on a Windows Server 2008 guest system, the VSS writer will make sure that the SQL Server database is consistent. Once this is done, the Hyper-V service will turn over the data to DPM for backup. This verifies that the data in the virtual machine is consistent before the backup is done on the physical machine.

Another advantage of using DPM is that no third-party backup software is required to protect your virtual machines. DPM will automatically back up your virtual machines and protect your data. For more on DPM, see *Mastering System Center Data Protection Manager 2007* by Devin L. Ganger and Ryan Femling (Sybex, 2008).

Data Protection Manager Requirements

When you decide to install DPM onto your servers, you must meet certain requirements for a proper installation. First you must be logged into the system as a member of the local administrators group. The server that you install DPM onto must be a member of a Windows Server 2003 or Windows Server 2008 domain.

DPM can be installed on the following Microsoft operating systems:

- Windows Server 2008 (Standard and Enterprise Editions)
- Windows Server 2003 with Service Pack 2 (SP2) or later
- Windows Server 2003 R2 with SP2 (Standard or Enterprise Editions)
- Windows Advanced Server 2003 with SP2 or later
- Windows Storage Server 2003 with SP2 or later (Standard, Enterprise, and Express Editions)
- Windows Storage Server 2003 R2 with SP2

> You can't install DPM onto a server that is running the clustering service. You must first remove the clustering service before installing DPM.

When installing DPM, your hardware must not only support the Hyper-V installation but it must also meet the minimum requirements needed to install DPM. Table 8.2 shows the minimum and recommended hardware requirements for DPM.

TABLE 8.2   Hardware Requirements for DPM

Component	Minimum	Recommended
Processor	1GHz or greater	2.33GHz quad-core CPUs
Memory (RAM)	2GB	4GB
Hard Disk Space	Program files drive: 410MB Database files drive: 900MB System drive: 2650MB	Program files drive: 3GB Database files drive: 900MB System drive: 2650MB
Disk Space for Storage	1.5 times the size of the protected data	3 times the size of the protected data
Logical unit number (LUN)	N/A	Maximum of 17TB for GUID partition table (GPT) dynamic disks 2TB for master boot record (MBR) disks

To install DPM properly, you must first meet these software requirements:

- Windows PowerShell
- Web Services (IIS)
- Single Instance Storage (SIS)

In Exercise 8.5 we will install the software needed to install DPM. These features must be installed on the server that you are installing DPM onto. We will install these features using the Server Manager MMC.

EXERCISE 8.5

Installing Features Needed for DPM

1. Start Server Manager by clicking Start ➢ Administrative Tools ➢ Server Manager.

2. In the left window, click the Features link.

3. In the right window, click Add Feature.

4. Select Windows PowerShell and then click Next.

5. On the Confirm Installation Selection screen, click Install.

6. After the install is complete, click the Roles link and click Add Role.

7. When the Add Role Wizard begins, click Next on the Before You Begin screen.

8. On the Select Server Roles screen, select Web Service (IIS). Make sure the following IIS services are installed:

   - Static Content
   - Default Document
   - Directory Browsing
   - HTTP Errors
   - HTTP Redirection
   - ASP.NET
   - .NET Extensibility
   - ISAPI Extensions
   - ISAPI Filters
   - Server Side Includes
   - IIS 6 Metabase Compatibility
   - IIS 6 WMI Compatibility
   - IIS 6 Scripting Tools
   - IIS 6 Management Console
   - Windows Authentication

9. Close the Server Manager MMC.

EXERCISE 8.6 *(continued)*

10. We need to also install the Single Instance Storage (SIS). To do this, open a command prompt (Start ➤ Run and enter **CMD.exe**).

11. At the command prompt type the following command and press Enter: **OCSetup SIS-Limited**.

12. The command prompt will return but the process is still running. When the process finishes, a dialog box appears, stating that you need to reboot the machine. Click Yes.

In Exercise 8.6 we will download the System Center Data Protection evaluation product from Microsoft's website. You will be required to sign in to Microsoft's Download Center. If you do not have an account, create one at this time.

This download is around 1.69GB and depending on your download speed may take a couple of hours to complete. Be sure to also download any available service packs for DPM. After the downloads are complete, we will walk through the configuration of DPM.

EXERCISE 8.6

Installing DPM

1. Download the evaluation version of System Center Data Protection Manager at http://technet.microsoft.com/en-us/evalcenter/bb727240.aspx.

2. Execute the downloaded file. The file should start to extract to the hard disk.

3. After the extraction has completed, a completion dialog box appears. Click OK.

4. In the directory where the extraction takes place, click the setup.exe file.

5. The System Center Data Protection Manager installation screen appears. Click the Install Data Protection Management link.

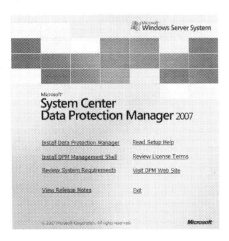

EXERCISE 8.6 *(continued)*

6. On the Microsoft Software License Terms screen, click the "I accept the license terms and conditions" radio button and click Next.

7. On the Welcome screen, click Next.

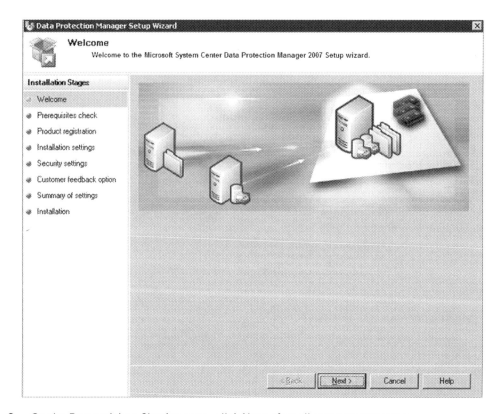

8. On the Prerequisites Check screen, click Next after all components pass.

9. On the Registration screen, type your username and company and click Next.

10. On the Installation Settings screen, leave the default settings for the DPM Program Files. Choose the "Use the dedicated instance of SQL Server" radio button. Click Next.

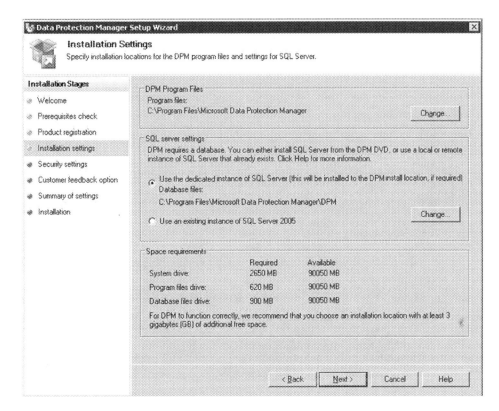

11. On the Security Settings screen, type **P@ssw0rd** and confirm the password. Click Next.

12. On the Customer Experience Improvement Program screen, click the No radio button and click Next.

13. On the Summary screen, verify your settings and click Install.

14. After the DPM software installs, click the Close button.

15. Install any patches or updates for DPM before starting the application.

Backing up your virtual machines and your servers is a priority when designing your infrastructure. When using Hyper-V in your organization, you must ensure that data recoverability is established and configured properly to protect against data loss or hardware failure.

Summary

It is very important to monitor your servers and virtual servers. Monitoring allows you to determine the problem areas of your network. Monitoring can you help you fine-tune performance and allow your network to run at its peak performance.

Before you set up monitoring, first establish a baseline when the machine is first installed and running at peak performance. After you have your baseline, you can determine what areas are causing performance problems on the servers.

Microsoft Windows Server 2008 helps you monitor your systems by including a utility called the Reliability and Performance Monitor. This tool allows you to monitor the counters and objects of your system. Four items that need to be monitored daily are the CPU, Disk, Network, and Memory (RAM).

Another important task to complete every day is your system backups. Backing up data is one of an IT person's most critical tasks. Not only can protecting your data save your organization money, but it can also save jobs. If your organization loses all of its data, you could go out of business.

Microsoft includes tools to help you back up critical data. The Windows Server 2008 Backup utility is a good solution for a small organization with limited financial means.

Another tool in the Microsoft arsenal is the System Center Data Protection Manager (DPM). The DPM tool allows you to back up Microsoft applications (SQL, Exchange, Hyper-V) from a single application.

DPM is an excellent way to back up Hyper-V virtual machines. If the virtual machines have Microsoft Server software as the guest operating system, the virtual machine does not need to be stopped first before accomplishing the backup. Recoverability should be one of your main goals.

Exam Essentials

Be familiar with the Reliability and Performance Monitor.   Monitoring is vital part of your job. The Reliability and Performance Monitor is a tool that is included with Windows Server 2008.

Know which components to monitor.   By monitoring four components on a daily basis (CPU, Disk, Network, and Memory [RAM]), you can determine if the machine or network can handle the load placed upon it. It is important to monitor Hyper-V components to determine if you need to increase the virtual environment components to help enhance performance.

Understand the importance of recoverability.   Recoverability is one of the most critical goals for an IT person. Microsoft helps you set up recoverability when using Windows Server 2008 with its free backup utility. When you create your backup schedule, you should also create your restore strategy to make sure that you can recover data from any time period.

Know how to use System Center Data Protection Manager.   The System Center Data Protection Manager allows you to back up both your virtual and nonvirtual servers. This gives you one application that allows you to back up all the different servers on your infrastructure. The DPM can help protect your Hyper-V server, Exchange Server, and SQL Server.

Review Questions

1. You are the network administrator for a large IT consulting firm. You have decided to implement monitoring on a new Windows Server 2008 machine that is going to be running Hyper-V with four virtual machines. You create the server and load Hyper-V. You create your four virtual machines and you are getting ready to take the server live into your production environment. What is the first thing you should do to set up the monitoring on the new server?

    A. Turn off all unnecessary services.

    B. Create a baseline.

    C. Install the Reliability and Reliability and Performance Monitor.

    D. Nothing; you just start monitoring.

2. You are the network administrator for a large organization that has decided to start monitoring its servers. You decide to use the Reliability and Performance Monitor. What key factors should you always monitor? (Choose all that apply.)

    A. CPU

    B. Network

    C. Disk

    D. Memory (RAM)

3. You are the network administrator for Stellacon Training Center. You have five Microsoft Windows Server 2008 operating systems. You have decided to implement the Reliability and Performance Monitor for all of your monitoring. What are the types of things that you can monitor? (Choose all that apply.)

    A. Counters

    B. Performance objects

    C. OUs

    D. Instances

4. You are the network administrator for a small company that has decided to use the Reliability and Performance Monitor on their Windows Server 2008 operating system. You want to capture the data in an easy-to-read numeric format. What type of view should you use?

    A. Graph view

    B. Histogram view

    C. Report view

    D. Output view

5. You are the network administrator for a mid-sized company that has decided to use the Reliability and Performance Monitor on their Windows Server 2008 operating system. You want to capture the data in bar format and also make a point-in-time capture. What type of view should you use?

    A. Graph view

    B. Histogram view

    C. Report view

    D. Output view

6. You are the network administrator for a large organization that has decided to use the Reliability and Performance Monitor on their five Windows Server 2008 operating systems. You want to capture the data in color-lined view. What type of view should you use?

    A. Graph view

    B. Histogram view

    C. Report view

    D. Output view

7. You are the IT manager for a small company that has just installed a Windows Server 2008 operating system. You have decided that you want to start monitoring the server. You want to use a Microsoft product to monitor your server. What application can you use to monitor your server?

    A. Windows Server 2008 Backup utility

    B. Reliability and Performance Monitor

    C. Windows Server 2008 Monitor utility

    D. Server Monitoring Agent

8. You are the network administrator of a small organization that has implemented a new Windows Server 2008 operating system with Hyper-V installed. You load Windows Server 2008 as the virtual machine guest operating system. You want to be able to back up the data within the virtual machines. What application can you use to back up the data within the virtual machines?

    A. Windows Server 2008 Backup utility

    B. System State Backup utility

    C. Differential Backup utility

    D. Incremental Backup utility

9. You are the administrator for a small company that has only one Windows Server 2008 operating system machine. You decide that you want to back up the server every night. You purchase an external tape drive and multiple tapes. You decide to use the Windows Server 2008 Backup utility. You have to determine which type of backup you would like to perform nightly. Due to the small amount of data, you would like to back up all the data every night. What type of backup should you use?

    A. Full backup

    B. Copy backup

    C. Daily backup

    D. Incremental backup

10. You are the administrator for a small company that has only one Windows Server 2008 operating system machine. You decide that you want to back up the server every night. You purchase an external tape drive and multiple tapes. You decide to use the Windows Server 2008 Backup utility. You have to decide which type of backup you would like to perform nightly. Due to the large amount of data, you would like to back up only the files that have changed every day. What type of backup should you use?

    A. Full backup

    B. Copy backup

    C. Daily backup

    D. Incremental backup

11. You are the administrator for a large organization with ten Windows Server 2008 machines. You have decided to back up your servers using a third-party utility. You need to have the fastest recovery time without doing a full backup every night. What type of backup would you choose?

    A. Full backup

    B. Copy backup

    C. Differential backup

    D. Incremental backup

12. You are the administrator for a large organization with ten Windows Server 2008 machines. You need to install Microsoft Exchange on one of the servers. You want to back up the server before installing Exchange Server. What type of backup should you choose?

    A. Full backup

    B. Copy backup

    C. Differential backup

    D. Incremental backup

13. You are the administrator for a large organization with three Active Directory domain controllers. One of your IT members deletes an OU that is necessary. You need to recover the OU so that it is back in Active Directory. What type of restore do you need to do?

   A. Incremental restore

   B. Nonauthoritative restore

   C. Authoritative restore

   D. Differential restore

14. You are the administrator for a mid-sized tennis shoe company with two Active Directory domain controllers. One of your servers crashes and you need to rebuild it. What type of restore do you need to do?

   A. Incremental restore

   B. Nonauthoritative restore

   C. Authoritative restore

   D. Differential restore

15. You are the network administrator for a large organization that uses Windows Server 2008 and Hyper-V. You need to set up a backup strategy for your Hyper-V server. All of your virtual machines run Windows Server 2008 as the guest operating system. You want to back up the Hyper-V virtual machines without shutting them down. Which Microsoft application can you use?

   A. Windows Server 2008 Backup utility

   B. System Center Data Protection Manager

   C. Reliability and Performance Monitor

   D. None of the above

16. You are the network administrator for a small company that has decided to use the Microsoft Windows Server 2008 Backup utility. Which of the following backup types are supported in Windows Server 2008? (Choose all that apply.)

   A. Full backups

   B. Incremental backups

   C. Differential backups

   D. Copy backups

17. You are the network administrator for a small organization that has started using the Windows Server 2008 Backup utility. You do a full backup on Monday and incremental backups Tuesday through Friday. You have a server crash on Friday morning; which tapes do you have to restore?

   A. Monday's full backup and only Thursday's incremental backup tapes

   B. Monday's full backup tape only

   C. Thursday's incremental tape backup only

   D. Monday's full backup and Tuesday's through Thursday's incremental backup tapes

18. You are the network administrator for a small organization that has started using the Windows Server 2008 Backup utility. You do a full backup on Monday and differential backups Tuesday through Friday. You have a server crash on Friday morning; which tapes do you have to restore?

    A. Monday's full backup and only Thursday's differential

    B. Monday's full backup only

    C. Thursday's differential tape backup only

    D. Monday's full backup and Tuesday's through Thursday's differential backup tapes

19. You are the network administrator for a small organization. You need to restore an OU to just one domain controller. What type of restore would you perform?

    A. Authoritative restore

    B. Nonauthoritative restore

    C. Full restore

    D. ADSI restore

20. You are the network administrator for a mid-sized organization. You need to restore an OU to a domain controller in a multiple domain controller environment. You want to make sure the backup is the Active Directory copy that is used for all domain controllers. What type of restore would you perform?

    A. Authoritative restore

    B. Nonauthoritative restore

    C. Full restore

    D. ADSI restore

Answers to Review Questions

1. B. When you decide to start monitoring your servers, the first thing that you should do is create a baseline. This gives you something to compare against down the road. Your baseline allows you to see how your server is running at peak performance.

2. A,B,C,D. All four of these answers are correct. By monitoring these four main components, you can see if you are having any performance issues.

3. A,B,D. The three things that you can monitor using the Reliability and Reliability and Performance Monitor are counters, objects, and instances. OUs are organizational units, and they are storage containers within Active Directory.

4. C. The Report view is a numerical output that shows you the exact numbers of the counters, objects, and instances that you are monitoring.

5. B. The Histogram view represents the percentage of usage by using colored bar graphs. Histogram views are a good way to grab a point-in-time value of a counter. This view offers you an average measurement or a minimum and maximum value of a counter.

6. A. This is the default view when you start the Windows Server 2008 Reliability and Performance Monitor. This chart represents the percentage of usage by using colored lines for the different counters. These lines will represent the values by vertical and horizontal movements. Graph views are useful when capturing data over a long period of time.

7. B. The Reliability and Performance Monitor is an MMC snap-in that includes multiple tools that you can use to help monitor your servers.

8. A. The Windows Server 2008 Backup utility allows you to save your data in the event of a system failure or accidental deletion.

9. A. In a full backup, also referred to as a normal backup, you back up the machine's hard disks and files. At the same time you set up your full backup type you specify which files, folders, and hard disks you want to back up.

10. D. Incremental backups are backups of any files that have changed since the last full or incremental backup. The incremental backup finds all files that have an archive bit set to 1 and then proceeds to back up those files. After the backup is complete, all archive bits are reset to 0. Incremental backups are available using the Windows Server 2008 Backup utility.

11. C. Differential backups are backups of any files that have changed since the last full backup. Differential backups find all archive bits that are set to ones and then perform a backup of all those files. The advantage of using differential backups is faster recovery times. Since differentials are backing up from the last full backup, to recover you need to just load the last full tape and then the last differential tape and your data is recovered.

12. B. Copy backups are the same as full backups except for the archive bit. Copy backups do not reset the archive bits. You normally use copy backups to do a backup in the middle of the day and you do not want to affect your nightly backups by changing the archive bit.

13. C. An authoritative restore specifies a setting on the domain controller that states that no matter what the time stamp is on the OU, this domain controller has the accurate copy of the Active Directory database.

14. B. In this situation you would do a nonauthoritative restore. You would not want to make this domain controller authoritative because you would lose all the data that has changed since the backup. After the machine is rebuilt, you want it to grab the current data from the other domain controller.

15. B. Data Protection Manager is an excellent way to back up Hyper-V virtual machines because if the virtual machines have Microsoft Server software as the guest operating system, you do not have to shut down the virtual machines before doing the backup.

16. A,B. Full backups and incremental backups are available in Windows Server 2008, but Microsoft has removed Differential and Copy backups. Many third-party utilities still use all four types.

17. D. Incremental backs up since the last full or incremental backup. Tuesday's incremental backs up since Monday's full. Wednesday's incremental backs up since Tuesday's incremental, and so forth. So when there is a crash, all tapes up to the crash have to be loaded in order.

18. A. Differential backs up since the last full backup. Tuesday's differential backs up since Monday's full. Wednesday's differential backs up since Monday's Full , and so on. So when there is a crash, only the full and the latest differential tapes have to be loaded.

19. B. A nonauthoritative restore is when you bring anything back from your tape backup. Since there is only one domain controller, only a nonauthoritative is required.

20. A. Authoritative restores are needed when you have multiple domain controllers and you want to replicate a restore among the domain controllers. The authoritative backup sets a flag that states that even though the Active Directory object is from last night's backup, it is the correct Active Directory to use for replication.

Appendix

A

Extra Labs and Exam Questions

In this appendix we will walk through exercises and extra questions to help you prepare for the Microsoft 70-652 exam. The exercises will demonstrate the process of setting up a virtual network from start to finish.

We will install Hyper-V, virtual machines, and operating systems on those virtual machines; connect clients to the virtual machine domains; add DNS to the virtual machines; and even add Microsoft Exchange 2007.

Some of these exercises will resemble the exercises that we did in the course the book, but they will be a good refresher. If you follow these exercises from start to finish, you will set up your entire virtual network.

At the end of this appendix, we will cover new questions that will help you prepare for exam 70-652.

Setting Up a Virtual Network

Before we start with the exercises, I want to explain the current infrastructure setup that you will need to duplicate to follow along. I have a server that has been loaded with Windows Server 2008 Enterprise Edition and nothing else. There are no domain controllers or other computers currently on this virtual network. This virtual environment will be built from scratch.

We will start by loading Hyper-V and then Windows Server 2008 Enterprise Edition onto the virtual machines. I also have Windows Vista and Windows XP machines already prepared so that we can connect them to the virtual network. If you do not have Windows XP and Windows Vista loaded onto a test machine, you can load them into two virtual machines and use them as test boxes. We will be creating two virtual machines on our server.

The first virtual machine will have DNS, DHCP, and Active Directory. The second virtual machine, named MailServer, will have Microsoft Exchange Server 2007.

So before we begin installing virtual machines, we must install the Hyper-V role onto our Windows Server 2008 Enterprise Edition operating system (see Exercise A1).

EXERCISE A1

Installing Hyper-V

1. Start the Server Manager MMC by clicking Start ➢ Administrative Tools ➢ Server Manager.

2. In the left window click Roles; then in the right window click the Add Roles link.

EXERCISE A1 *(continued)*

3. On the Before You Begin screen, click Next.

4. Click the Hyper-V check box and click Next.

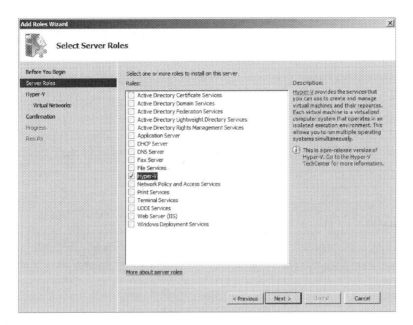

5. On the Introduction To Hyper-V screen, click Next.

6. The Create Virtual Networks screen appears. Click the Local Area Connection check box and click Next.

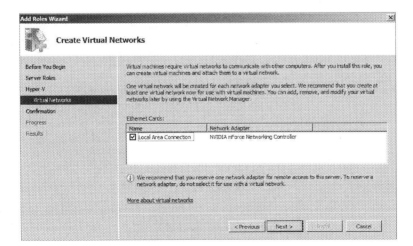

EXERCISE A1 *(continued)*

7. At the Confirm Installation screen, click Install.

8. At the Installation Results screen, click Close.

9. A dialog box appears asking if you want to reboot. Click Yes.

10. After the machine reboots, an Installations Results screen appears. Click Close.

11. Install any Hyper-V updates that may be released.

In Exercise A2 we will create a new virtual machine and install Windows Server 2008 Enterprise Edition onto a virtual machine.

EXERCISE A2

Creating a Virtual Machine

1. On the host operating system, start the Hyper-V Manager by clicking Start ➤ Administrative Tools ➤ Hyper-V Manager.

2. In the right window under Actions, click the Virtual Network Manager link.

3. When the Virtual Network Manager opens, click the Add button.

4. In the Name field, type **NIC Adapter**. Make sure that the External radio button is selected and that your network adapter is listed. Click OK.

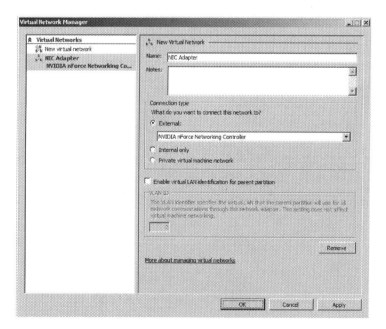

5. The Apply Networking Changes dialog box appears. Click Yes.

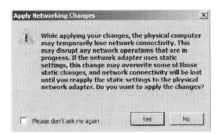

6. In the right window under Actions, click New ➢ Virtual Machine.

7. The New Virtual Machine Wizard appears. On the Before You Begin screen, click Next.

8. On the Specify Name And Location screen, type **Infrastructure** in the Name field. Accept the default location for the virtual machine and click Next.

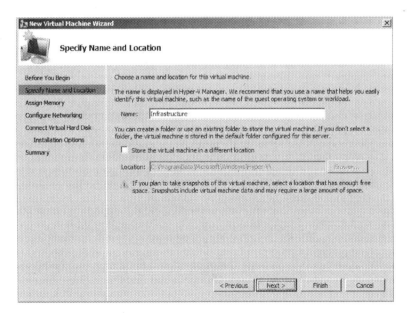

9. On the Assign Memory screen, type **512** (MB) and click Next. (You can enter a higher number if desired.)

EXERCISE A2 *(continued)*

10. On the Configure Networking screen, choose NIC Adapter from the drop-down list. Click Next.

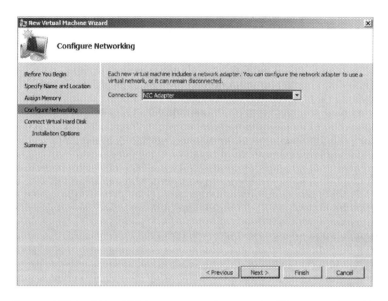

11. On the Connect Virtual Hard Disk screen, make sure the "Create a virtual hard disk" radio button is selected. Accept the defaults but in the Size field type **15** (GB). Click Next.

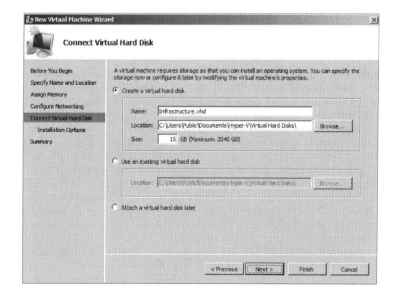

12. On the Installation Options screen, click "Install an operating system from a boot CD/DVD-ROM." Click Physical CD/DVD Drive and make sure your CD/DVD drive is selected. Click Next.

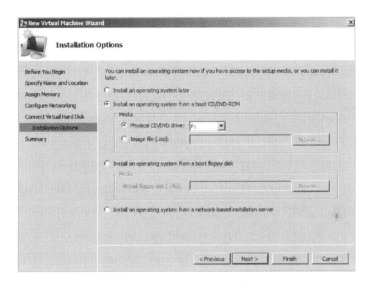

13. On the Summary screen, make sure the Windows Server 2008 Enterprise Edition DVD is inserted into your DVD drive. Check "Start the virtual machine after it is created" and click Finish.

14. The installation of Windows Server 2008 will begin. Install the Windows Server 2008 Full edition to the Infrastructure virtual machine.

15. After the Windows Server 2008 operating system is installed, you will need to change the password. Make the password **P@ssw0rd**. Click OK after the password has been reset.

16. Install any NIC drivers or video drivers needed on the virtual machine. After all drivers are loaded, reboot the system.

In Exercise A3 we will start by installing the Domain Name System (DNS) service in the virtual machine. We will then configure some of the DNS options. Before we can install DNS, we need to assign a static TCP/IP address to the virtual machine. We will then install Active Directory and then the Dynamic Host Configuration Protocol (DHCP).

All of the following exercises except for the installation of the Exchange Server 2007 virtual machine are done on either the Infrastructure or MailServer virtual machine and not on the host machine.

Installing DNS

1. Log into the Infrastructure virtual machine by pressing Ctrl+Alt+End (this is equivalent to Ctrl+Alt+Del).

2. Click the Start button and then right-click the Network link and choose Properties.

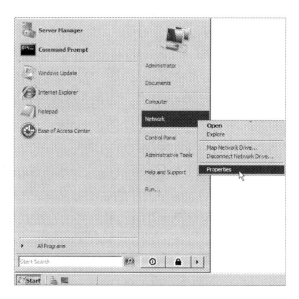

3. Under the Network (Public Network) section, click the View Status link.

4. In the Local Area Connection Status dialog box, click Properties.

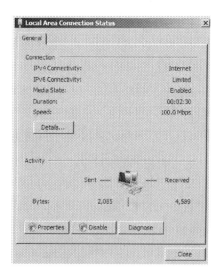

5. Click on Internet Protocol Version 4 (TCP/IPv4) and then choose Properties.

6. Click the "Use the following IP address" radio button and fill in the following properties. Then click OK.

Field	Value
IP Address	192.168.1.10 (You can enter a valid IP address for your network.)
Subnet Mask	255.255.255.0 (You can enter a valid subnet mask for your network.)
Default Gateway	192.168.1.1 (You can put in your router's IP address here,)
Preferred DNS Server	192.168.1.10 1 (You can put in your primary DNS server IP address here.)
Alternate DNS Server	Enter the DNS server for your Internet hosting company.

7. Close the Local Area Connection properties box and then close the Local Area Connection Status dialog box.

8. Close the Network and Sharing Center.

9. Continuing with the Infrastructure virtual machine, start the Server Manager MMC by clicking Start ➤ Administrative Tools ➤ Server Manager.

10. In the left window click Roles and then in the right window click the Add Roles link.

11. On the Before You Begin screen, click Next.

12. Click the DNS check box and click Next.

13. On the Introduction To DNS Server screen, click Next.

14. On the Confirm Installation Selections screen, click Install.

15. On the Installation Results screen, click Close.

DNS is a prerequisite of Active Directory, and you can install it beforehand (as we did) or during the Active Directory install. In Exercise A4 we will install Active Directory using the DCPromo.exe command.

EXERCISE A4

Installing Active Directory

1. On the Infrastructure virtual machine, start the Active Directory Installation Wizard by clicking Start ➤ Run and then typing **DCPromo**. Press Enter.

2. On the Welcome to Active Directory screen, click the Next button.

3. On the Operating System Compatibility screen, click Next.

4. On the Choose a Deployment Configuration screen, choose the "Create a new domain in a new forest" radio button. Click Next.

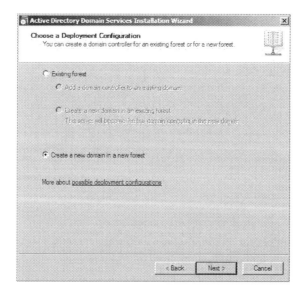

5. On the Name the Forest Root Domain screen, type *yourdomainname*.com and click Next. You can make the domain any name that you like for these exercises. We named ours Stellacon.com.

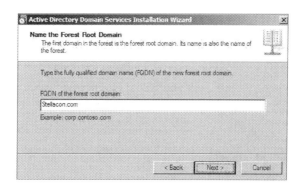

6. On the Set Forest Functional Level screen, choose Windows Server 2008 from the pull-down box and click Next.

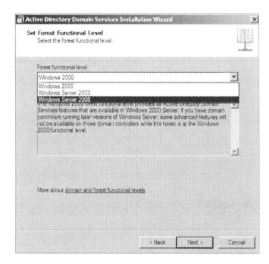

7. On the Additional Domain Controller Options screen, click Next.

8. If you are prompted to use a static IP assignment, choose Yes; the computer will use a dynamically assigned IP address box.

9. If you are prompted to use a delegation for DNS, click Yes.

10. On the Location For Database, Log Files, And SYSVOL screen, accept the defaults and click Next.

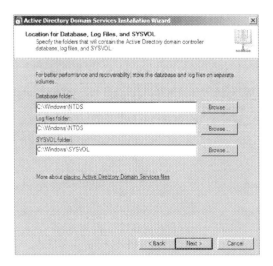

EXERCISE A4 *(continued)*

11. On the Directory Services Restore Mode Administrator Password screen, type **P@ssw0rd** and then confirm it. Click Next.

12. On the Summary screen, verify your settings and click Next.

13. When the Active Directory installation completes, click the Finish button.

14. A dialog box appears asking if you want to restart the machine. Click the Restart button.

15. Log back into the Infrastructure virtual machine as the administrator. To log in, click the Actions menu item and choose Ctrl-Alt-Delete or press the Ctrl+Alt+End keys.

16. Open the Active Directory Users and Computers console by clicking Start ➢ Administrative Tools ➢ Active Directory Users and Computers.

17. In the left window, expand your domain by clicking the plus (+) sign next to your domain name. Click on the Users OU and choose New ➢ User.

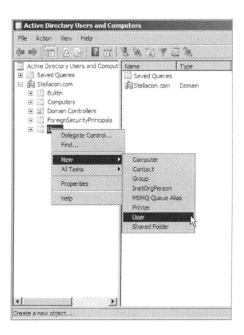

18. On the New Object - User screen, fill in the following fields and click Next:

Field	Value
First Name	John
Initials	N/A

EXERCISE A4 *(continued)*

Field	Value
Last Name	Smith
Full Name	John Smith
User Logon Name	Jsmith
User Logon Name (pre-Windows 2000)	Jsmith

19. On the Password screen, type **P@ssw0rd** and confirm it. Uncheck "User must change password at next logon" and click Next.

20. On the Summary screen, verify the settings and click Finish.

21. In the Users OU, right-click on John Smith and choose Properties.

22. Click the Member Of tab. Click the Add button.

23. On the Select Groups screen, in the Enter The Object name field, type **Administrators** and click the Check Names button. Click OK.

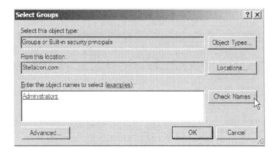

24. Click OK on the John Smith Properties screen.

25. Close Active Directory Users and Computers.

We now need to install the Dynamic Host Configuration Protocol (DHCP). In Exercise A5 we will use the Server Manager snap-in to install DHCP. DHCP automatically assigns TCP/IP information to your network hosts.

EXERCISE A5

Installing DHCP

1. Start the Server Manager MMC by clicking Start ➤ Administrative Tools ➤ Server Manager.

2. In the left windows click Roles, and then in the right window click the Add Roles link.

3. On the Before You Begin screen, click Next.

4. Click the DHCP Server check box and click Next.

5. On the Introduction To DHCP screen, click Next.

6. On the Select Network Connection Bindings screen, accept the default and click Next.

7. On the IPv4 DNS Server Settings screen, verify that the DNS server's IP address is in the Preferred DNS server box and click Validate. After the DNS server has been validated, click Next.

8. On the WINS screen, click the "WINS is not required" radio button and click Next.

9. On the Add or Edit Scope screen, click the Add button.

10. Fill in the following settings and click OK:

Field	Value
Scope Name	Scope1
Starting IP Address	192.168.1.100 (You can enter a valid IP address for your network.)
Ending IP Address	192.168.1.200 (You can enter a valid IP address for your network.)
Subnet Mask	255.255.255.0 (You can enter a valid IP address for your network.)
Default Gateway	192.168.1.1 (You can enter a valid IP address for your network.)
Subnet Type	Wired (Lease duration will be 6 days.)
Activate This Scope	Checked

11. Click Next.

12. On the Configure DHCPv6 screen, click the Disable DHCPv6 radio box and click Next.

EXERCISE A5 *(continued)*

13. On the DHCP Server Authorization screen, verify that the administrator account is listed and click Next.

14. On the Summary screen, verify your settings and click Install.

15. After the installation completes properly, click the Close button.

16. Close the Server Manager snap-in.

17. Shut down the Infrastructure virtual Windows Server 2008 operating system. We will restart the Infrastructure virtual machine after we install the new MailServer virtual machine.

In Exercise A6 we will walk through the steps of creating another new virtual machine and install the Windows Server 2008 Enterprise edition on the virtual machine. This virtual machine will have Exchange Server loaded onto it in the next exercise.

EXERCISE A6

Creating the Exchange Virtual Machine

1. Start the Hyper-V Manager by clicking Start ➢ Administrative Tools ➢ Hyper-V Manager.

2. In the right window under Actions, click New ➢ Virtual Machine.

3. The New Virtual Manager Wizard appears. On the Before You Begin screen, click Next.

4. On the Specify Name And Location screen, type **MailServer** in the Name field. Accept the default location for the virtual machine and click Next.

5. On the Assign Memory screen, type **512** (MB) (use the minimum) and click Next.

6. On the Configuring Networking screen, choose NIC Adapter from the pull-down list. Click Next.

7. At the Connect Virtual Hard Disk screen, make sure the "Create a virtual hard disk" radio button is selected. Accept the defaults but in the Size field type **15** (GB). Click Next.

8. On the Installation Options screen, click "Install an operating system from a boot CD/DVD-ROM." Click Physical CD/DVD Drive and make sure your CD/DVD drive is selected. Click Next.

9. On the Summary screen, make sure the Windows Server 2008 Enterprise DVD is inserted into your DVD drive. Check "Start the virtual machine after it is created" and click Finish.

10. The installation of Windows Server 2008 will begin. Install the Windows Server 2008 Full Enterprise 64-bit edition to the Infrastructure virtual machine.

EXERCISE A6 *(continued)*

11. After the Windows Server 2008 operating system is installed, you will need to change the password. Make the password **P@ssw0rd**. Click OK after the password has been reset.

12. Install any NIC drivers or video drivers needed in the virtual machine. After all drivers are loaded, reboot the system.

13. Start both virtual machines (Infrastructure and MailServer).

If you get a DVD-ROM error when trying to start both virtual machines, change the settings on the Infrastructure virtual machine to not use the DVD drive or change the DVD device.

In Exercise A7 we will join the Windows Server 2008 MailServer virtual machine to the domain we created in Exercise A4. We accomplish this in the same way as we join a Windows Vista machine to the domain. If you would like to join a Windows Vista machine to this domain, follow the steps of this exercise on a Vista machine. You would just need to change the IP address and machine name.

EXERCISE A7

Joining the MailServer VM to the Domain

1. Log into the MailServer virtual machine by pressing Ctrl+Alt+End (this is equivalent to Ctrl+Alt+Del). Log in as the domain administrator.

2. Click the Start button and then right-click the Network link and choose Properties.

3. Under the Network (Public Network) section, click the View Status link.

4. In the Local Area Connection Status dialog box, click Properties.

5. Click on Internet Protocol Version 4 (TCP/IPv4) and then choose Properties.

6. Click the "Use the following IP address" radio button and fill in the following properties. Then click OK.

Field	Value
IP Address	192.168.1.11 (You can enter a valid IP address for your network.)
Subnet Mask	255.255.255.0

Field	Value
Default Gateway	192.168.1.1 (You can put in your router's IP address here.)
Preferred DNS Server	192.168.1.10
Alternate DNS Server	Enter the DNS server for your Internet hosting company.

7. Close the Local Area Connection properties box and then close the Local Area Connection Status box.

8. Close the Network and Sharing Center.

9. Click the Start button and then right-click the Computer link and choose Properties.

10. Under Computer Name, Domain, And Workgroup Settings, click the Change Setting link.

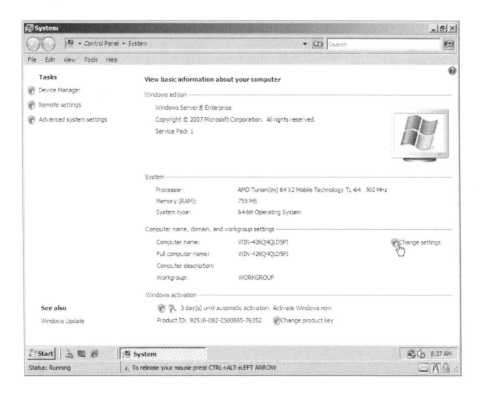

EXERCISE A7 *(continued)*

11. In the System Properties box, click the Change button.

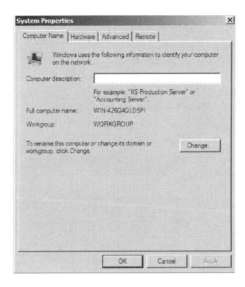

12. On the Computer Name/Domain Changes screen, type **Exchange** for the Computer Name. Click the Domain radio button and type the name of the domain you created in Exercise A4. Click OK.

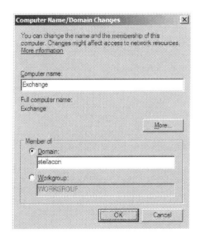

13. A Windows Security dialog box appears. Type **Administrator** for the username and **P@ssw0rd** for the password. Click OK.

14. A dialog box welcoming you to the domain appears. Click the OK button. If you did not join the domain, make sure the Infrastructure virtual machine is running.

EXERCISE A7 *(continued)*

15. A dialog box stating that you must restart the server appears next. Click OK.

16. Close the System Properties box by clicking the Close button.

17. When the dialog box asking you to reboot appears, click the Restart Now button.

18. Log into the MailServer virtual machine as the Administrator and using the password of P@ssw0rd.

Before we can install Microsoft Exchange Server 2007 onto your server, we must first install the Microsoft PowerShell feature and the IIS role. To do this we will use the Server Manager snap-in (see Exercise A8).

EXERCISE A8

Installing the PowerShell Feature and IIS Role

1. Start the Server Manager MMC by clicking Start ➤ Administrative Tools ➤ Server Manager.

2. In the left windows click Features and then in the right window click the Add Features link.

3. Scroll down the list and check the box for Windows PowerShell. Click Next.

4. On the Confirm Installation screen, verify the selection and click Install.

5. After the Windows PowerShell installs properly, click the Close button.

6. In the left windows click Roles and then in the right window click the Add Roles link.

7. On the Before You Begin screen, click Next.

8. Click the Web Server (IIS) check box.

9. The Add Features Required For Web Server (IIS) dialog box appears. Click the Add Required Features button. Click Next.

10. On the Introduction To Web Server screen, click Next.

11. Make sure the following check boxes are checked:

- Common HTTP Features
  - Static Content
  - Default Document
  - Directory Browsing
  - HTTP Errors
  - HTTP Redirection

EXERCISE A8 *(continued)*

- Health and Diagnostics
    - HTTP Logging
    - Request Monitor
- Security
    - Basic Authentication
    - Windows Authentication
    - Digest Authentication
    - URL Authorization
    - Request Filtering
- Performance
    - Static Content Compression
    - Dynamic Content Compression
- Management Tools
    - IIS Management Console
    - IIS 6 Management Compatibility (All below)

12. Click Next.

13. Verify all settings and click Install.

14. Close the Server Manager.

15. Reboot the server and then log back on as the domain administrator:

    Username: ***yourdomainname**\administrator*

    Password: **P@ssw0rd**

16. Click Start ➢ Run; then type **ServerManagerCMD -i RSAT-ADDS** and press Enter.

17. A command prompt window appears and starts to install services. Once the installation is complete, the window closes.

18. Reboot the server to complete the installation and then log back on as the domain administrator.

    Username: ***yourdomainname**\administrator*

    Password: **P@ssw0rd**

In Exercise A9 we will load Microsoft Exchange Server 2007 64-bit edition. If you do not have a copy of Exchange Server, you can download Exchange from Microsoft's website. You can load any application here if you do not want to use Exchange. The purpose of this exercise is to show how a server application will operate within a virtual machine.

After we install the Exchange Server 2007 application, we will create a new mailbox in the Exchange Management tool, which will create the user in Active Directory.

EXERCISE A9

Installing Microsoft Exchange Server 2007

1. Insert the Exchange Server 2007 DVD into your DVD drive.

2. On the MailServer virtual machine, the Exchange default.htm page will start. If it does not start automatically, click on the default.htm file on the DVD.

3. Click the Microsoft Exchange Server 2007 (English) link.

4. This should take you to the installation file. Execute the install file.

5. When the Choose Directory For Extracted Files dialog box opens, verify that the files are being extracted to the hard disk and not the DVD. Click OK.

6. After the files are extracted, open the folder where you extracted the files.

7. Double-click the Setup.exe file to start the installation of Exchange.

8. The Exchange Server 2007 installation screen appears. Under the Install section, the first three steps should automatically be completed. Click on Step 4: Install Microsoft Exchange Server 2007 SP1.

EXERCISE A9 *(continued)*

9. On the Exchange Introduction screen, click Next.

10. On the License Agreement screen, click the "I accept the terms in the license agreement" radio button and click Next.

11. The Error Reporting screen is next. This screen gives you the option to report errors back to Microsoft. Click the No radio button and click Next.

12. On the Installation Type screen, click on Custom Exchange Server Installation. Click Next.

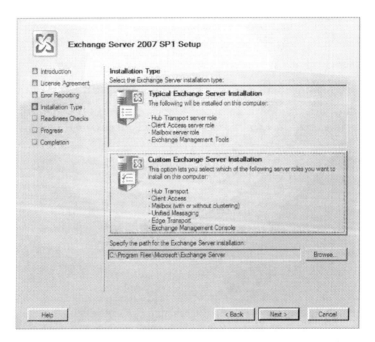

13. On the Server Role Selection screen, check the Mailbox Role, Client Access Role, and Hub Transport Role check boxes (the Management Tools check box will automatically become checked), and then click Next.

EXERCISE A9 *(continued)*

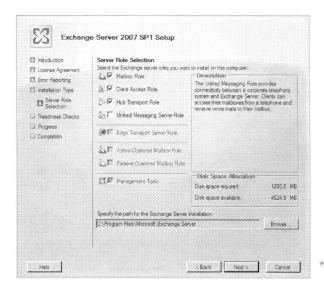

14. On the Exchange Organization screen, accept the default of First Organization and click Next.

15. On the Client Settings screen, click the Yes radio button and then click Next. Clicking Yes states that you will have clients using Outlook 2007 or earlier.

16. The Readiness Checks screen appears. Make sure that all checks pass and are completed. Click Install.

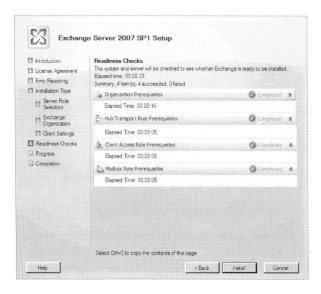

EXERCISE A9 *(continued)*

17. After the installation completes with no errors, click the Finish button.

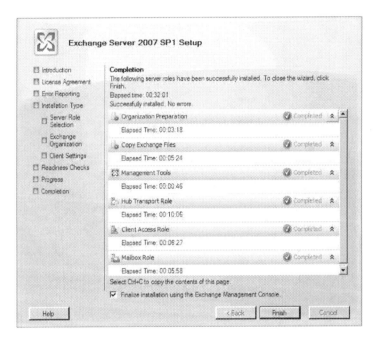

18. A dialog box stating that changes have been made and the system needs to rebooted. Click OK.

19. Reboot the server to complete the installation and then log back on as the domain administrator:

    Username: ***yourdomainname***\administrator

    Password: **P@ssw0rd**

20. Open the Exchange Management Console by clicking Start ➢ All Programs ➢ Microsoft Exchange Server 2007 ➢ Exchange Management Console.

21. In the left window expand Recipient Configuration and click the Mailbox link.

22. In the right window under Actions, click New Mailbox.

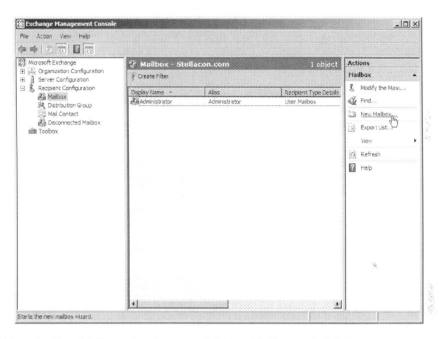

23. When the New Mailbox wizard starts, click User Mailbox and click Next.

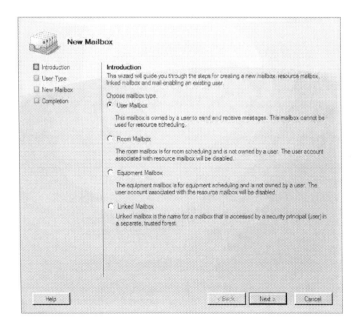

EXERCISE A9 *(continued)*

24. On the User Type screen, click New User and click Next.

25. Type in the following for all of the fields and then click Next:

Field	Value
First Name	John
Initials	W
Last Name	Potatohead
Name	John W. Potatohead
User Logon Name	JPotatohead
User Logon Name (pre-Windows 2000)	JPotatohead
Password	P@ssw0rd
User Must Change Password At Next Logon	Unchecked

26. At the Mailbox settings screen, accept the alias name. Click the Browse button next to Mailbox database and the First Storage Group. Click OK and then click Next.

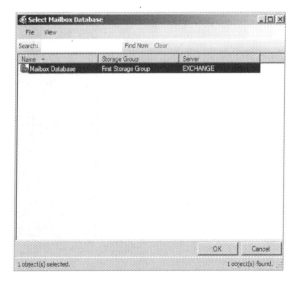

27. On the Summary screen, verify the settings and click New.

28. After Mr. Potatohead gets created, click the Finish button.

29. Close the Exchange Management Console.

30. Open Active Directory by clicking Start ➢ Administrative Tools ➢ Active Directory Users and Computers.

31. In the left window, expand your domain by clicking the plus (+) sign next to your domain name. Click on the Users OU. Verify that the user name John W. Potatohead has been created.

32. Close Active Directory Users and Computers.

Now that we've installed Exchange and created a new user, we need to add a workstation to the virtual network. In Exercise A10 we will join a Windows XP machine to the virtual network.

EXERCISE A10

Joining a Windows XP Machine to the Domain

1. Log onto the Windows XP machine with a local administrator account.

2. Click the Start button and then right-click My Computer and choose Properties.

3. Click the Computer Name tab.

4. Click the Change button next to "Rename this computer or join a domain."

5. In the Member Of section, click Domain and type the name of your domain.

6. A dialog box appears asking for the Administrator password. Type **P@ssw0rd**.

7. A Welcome To The Domain dialog box appears; click OK.

8. Click the Close button.

9. The machine will ask to be rebooted. Reboot the machine and log onto the domain.

In the previous exercises, we created services and applications on a network that allow your infrastructure to function properly. Many of these features require proper configuration, but the purpose of these exercises is to show how to install them on a virtual machine environment and to also show that all of these features can work together on one physical machine.

Many other tasks are required to make your network secure and complete, but these exercises helped show you how to configure a basic virtual network. Now let's take a look at some questions that will prepare you for the Microsoft exam.

Extra Review Questions

The following part of the appendix consists of additional exam 70-652 questions. Practice with these questions to help you prepare for the Microsoft 70-652 Virtualization exam.

1. You are the network administrator for a large organization that has decided to use Hyper-V. You want to load the Hyper-V role onto a server with the following components:

Component	Configuration
Memory (RAM)	4GB
CPU	Dual-core 32-bit
Hard Disk	2 SATA disks
Network Interface Card	1 single-port NIC adapter

    Which of the following components need to be upgraded or replaced before you can load Hyper-V onto this machine? (Choose all that apply.)

    A. Processor

    B. Network card

    C. Memory

    D. Hard disk

2. You are the network administrator for a large organization that has decided to use Hyper-V on the Windows Server 2008 Enterprise Server Core installation. You need to install Hyper-V onto the Server Core installation. What command should you use?

    A. `start /q servercore Microsoft-Hyper-V`

    B. `start /w ocsetup Microsoft-Hyper-V`

    C. `start /q scsetup Microsoft-Hyper-V`

    D. `start /w serverman Microsoft-Hyper-V`

3. You are the administrator for a large organization that has decided to implement Hyper-V. You install Hyper-V onto a server and create three virtual machines. You want to monitor the system. What components do all the virtual machines use that you should monitor? (Choose all that apply.)

    A. Memory (RAM)

    B. Processor

    C. Network

    D. Disk

4. You are the network administrator for a large organization. You have installed Hyper-V and you now want to install the System Center Virtual Machine Manager (SCVMM) 2008. Which of the following are prerequisites to install SCVMM 2008?

   A. Microsoft .NET Framework 3.0

   B. Windows PowerShell 1.0

   C. Windows Remote Management

   D. Windows Server 2008 x64-bit

5. You are the network administrator for a large organization. You have installed Hyper-V onto two servers and you create local virtual machines on each Hyper-V server. Both virtual machines have the Windows Server 2008 operating system loaded. Each of the virtual machines hosts the organization's internal website, and you want to provide redundancy in the event that one of the virtual machines fails. What can you configure to accomplish this task?

   A. Failover clustering on the two servers

   B. Network load balancing on the virtual machines

   C. Failover clustering on the virtual machines

   D. Network load balancing on the two Hyper-V servers

6. You are the network administrator for a large organization that has recently installed Hyper-V. On your Hyper-V server you would like to install the SCVMM 2008 utility. The Hyper-V machine is part of the IT department's workgroup. The machine has all preinstalled required software (IIS, PowerShell, etc.), but the SCVMM still fails to load properly. What do you need to do to install a proper installation?

   A. Add the Hyper-V server to the corporate workgroup.

   B. Join the Hyper-V server to the corporate domain.

   C. Reset the Hyper-V server's SID number.

   D. Remove the Hyper-V server SID number.

7. You are the IT administrator for your organization. You have installed Hyper-V on multiple servers and you want to create 15 virtual machines that will all host different operating systems, but the network configurations have to all be the same. What should you do to set this up?

   A. Create a hardware template.

   B. Create a hardware profile.

   C. Create a hardware share.

   D. Use the Add Hardware wizard.

8. You are the network administrator for a large organization that has implemented Hyper-V. You create a new virtual machine called VMserver. You want to create a second virtual machine and use the virtual disk from VMserver. When the new virtual machine starts, you want the mini-setup wizard to start. What command allows you to accomplish this?

    A. `setup /quiet/generalize/oobe/shutdown`

    B. `VMprep /quiet/generalize/oobe/shutdown`

    C. `sysprep /quiet/generalize/oobe/shutdown`

    D. `Winnt /quiet/generalize/oobe/shutdown`

9. You are the network administrator for a large organization that has installed Hyper-V on a new server. You install the SCVMM 2008 utility and configure two different virtual machines, both running Windows Server 2008 as the guest operating system. You need to allow a user named Will to remotely connect using the Hyper-V Manager. How should you configure Will to have the needed access to the Hyper-V server?

    A. Role assignment in the local group

    B. Role assignment in Active Directory

    C. Role assignment in Hyper-V group

    D. Role assignment in Authorization Manager

10. You are the administrator for an organization that has implemented the Hyper-V role on a new server. You just hired a junior administrator who will access the server by connecting to it from their Windows XP operating system. What do you need to configure on the Hyper-V server to allow the junior administrator to connect to the server remotely?

    A. Enable Remote Desktop on the server.

    B. Enable Remote Assistance on the server.

    C. Install the remote server toolkit.

    D. Install the `Servertools.msi` package.

Answers to Extra Review Questions

1. A. All the components except for the processor are valid for Hyper-V. Hyper-V requires that the processor be 64-bit.

2. B. The `ocsetup` command allows you to install many roles on the Windows Server 2008 Server Core installation.

3. A, B, C, D. The four main components that all virtual machines use and that should be monitored are the CPU (processor), memory (RAM), network, and disk.

4. A, B, C, D. To install the SCVMM 2008 utility, you also need to be a member of the domain and have the Windows Automated Installation Kit installed.

5. B. Network load balancing on the virtual machines is the best choice here since each Hyper-V server hosts its own local virtual machine.

6. B. A requirement of the SCVMM utility is to be a member of the Active Directory domain.

7. B. Hardware profiles allow you to preset the network configurations, and then virtual machines can all use that hardware profile.

8. C. The command `sysprep /quiet/generalize/oobe/shutdown` allows the virtual machine to run the mini-setup wizard when the virtual machines starts.

9. D. To assign a user a specific task for Hyper-V, you can set up role assignment in the Authorization Manager.

10. A. Enabling the Remote Desktop service on the server allows a user to connect to the machine remotely. Anyone who connects remotely to the server will still need a username and password to log on remotely.

Appendix

B

About the Companion CD

IN THIS APPENDIX:

✓ What you'll find on the CD

✓ System requirements

✓ Using the CD

✓ Troubleshooting

What You'll Find on the CD

The following sections are arranged by category and summarize the software and other goodies you'll find on the CD. If you need help with installing the items provided on the CD, refer to the installation instructions in the "Using the CD" section of this appendix.

Some programs on the CD might fall into one of these categories:

Shareware programs are fully functional, free, trial versions of copyrighted programs. If you like particular programs, register with their authors for a nominal fee and receive licenses, enhanced versions, and technical support.

Freeware programs are free, copyrighted games, applications, and utilities. You can copy them to as many computers as you like—for free—but they offer no technical support.

GNU software is governed by its own license, which is included inside the folder of the GNU software. There are no restrictions on distribution of GNU software. See the GNU license at the root of the CD for more details.

Trial, *demo*, or *evaluation* versions of software are usually limited either by time or by functionality (such as not letting you save a project after you create it).

Sybex Test Engine

For Windows

The CD contains the Sybex test engine, which includes two bonus exams located only on the CD.

PDF of Glossary of Terms

For Windows

We have included an electronic version of the Glossary in .pdf format. You can view the electronic version of the Glossary with Adobe Reader.

Adobe Reader

For Windows

We've also included a copy of Adobe Reader so you can view PDF files that accompany the book's content. For more information on Adobe Reader or to check for a newer version, visit Adobe's website at www.adobe.com/products/reader/.

Electronic Flashcards

For PC, Pocket PC, and Palm

These handy electronic flashcards are just what they sound like. One side contains a question or fill-in-the-blank question, and the other side shows the answer.

System Requirements

Make sure your computer meets the minimum system requirements shown in the following list. If your computer doesn't match up to most of these requirements, you may have problems using the software and files on the companion CD. For the latest and greatest information, please refer to the ReadMe file located at the root of the CD-ROM.

- A PC running Microsoft Windows 98, Windows 2000, Windows NT4 (with SP4 or later), Windows Me, Windows XP, or Windows Vista

- An Internet connection

- A CD-ROM drive

Using the CD

To install the items from the CD to your hard drive, follow these steps:

1. Insert the CD into your computer's CD-ROM drive. The license agreement appears.

> *Windows users*: The interface won't launch if you have autorun disabled. In that case, click Start ➤ Run (for Windows Vista, Start ➤ All Programs ➤ Accessories ➤ Run). In the dialog box that appears, type D:\Start.exe. (Replace *D* with the proper letter if your CD drive uses a different letter. If you don't know the letter, see how your CD drive is listed under My Computer.) Click OK.

2. Read the license agreement, and then click the Accept button if you want to use the CD.

The CD interface appears. The interface allows you to access the content with just one or two clicks.

Troubleshooting

Wiley has attempted to provide programs that work on most computers with the minimum system requirements. Alas, your computer may differ, and some programs may not work properly for some reason.

The two likeliest problems are that you don't have enough memory (RAM) for the programs you want to use or you have other programs running that are affecting installation or running of a program. If you get an error message such as "Not enough memory" or "Setup cannot continue," try one or more of the following suggestions and then try using the software again:

Turn off any antivirus software running on your computer. Installation programs sometimes mimic virus activity and may make your computer incorrectly believe that it's being infected by a virus.

Close all running programs. The more programs you have running, the less memory is available to other programs. Installation programs typically update files and programs, so if you keep other programs running, installation may not work properly.

Have your local computer store add more RAM to your computer. This is, admittedly, a drastic and somewhat expensive step. However, adding more memory can really help the speed of your computer and allow more programs to run at the same time.

Customer Care

If you have trouble with the book's companion CD-ROM, please call the Wiley Product Technical Support phone number at (800) 762-2974. Outside the United States, call +1(317) 572-3994. You can also contact Wiley Product Technical Support at http://sybex .custhelp.com. John Wiley & Sons will provide technical support only for installation and other general quality-control items. For technical support on the applications themselves, consult the program's vendor or author.

To place additional orders or to request information about other Wiley products, please call (877) 762-2974.

Glossary

A

Active Directory   A directory service available with the Windows Server 2008 platform. Active Directory stores information in a central database and allows users to have a single user account (called a *domain user account* or Active Directory user account) for the network.

Authorization Manager   Allows administrators to assign user-integrated role-based access control to applications.

B

baseline   Starting point for monitoring. Baselines give you a point in time that you can compare to later.

C

checkpoints   This point-in-time virtual machine backup gives you the ability to save the state of each virtual hard disk that is associated with a virtual machine.

copy backups   Same as a full backup without resetting the archive bit. See *full backup*.

counters   Specific data that is being measured within the Reliability and Performance Monitor tool.

D

daily backups   Backs up only files that have changed during that day. Uses the time stamp to operate properly.

Data Protection Manager (DPM)   Utility that allows you to back up certain Microsoft applications.

differencing VHD   A differencing disk is configured in a parent-child relationship with another disk that stays left intact and where it doesn't affect the parent disk.

differential backups   Backs up data since the last full backup. Differentials are not supported in Windows Server 2008.

Domain Name System (DNS)   The TCP/IP network service that translates textual Internet network addresses into numerical Internet network addresses.

domains   In Microsoft networks, an arrangement of client and server computers referenced by a specific name that shares a single security permissions database. On the Internet, a domain is a named collection of hosts and subdomains, registered with a unique name by the InterNIC.

Dynamic Host Configuration Protocol (DHCP)   Server on the network that assigns TCP/IP information to your computers dynamically.

dynamic VHD   Dynamic VHDs only use the amount of space that is currently being used for the VHD.

F

failover cluster   Failover clusters were formerly known as server clusters. They provide high availability to servers that run mission-critical applications or services.

fixed-size VHD   Fixed-size VHDs have a set amount of hard disk space and that amount does not change.

full backups   Backs up all files, folders, and hard disks specified in the system.

G

Global Catalog   Database of all Active Directory objects without all of the attributes. The Global Catalog is a partial representation of the Active Directory objects.

Guest   These are the containers (virtual machines) that are running the guest operating system. They are also referred to as child partitions.

H

hardware profiles   Preset hardware specifications that can be applied to a new virtual machine or a virtual machine template.

Hyper-V   The next generation hypervisor-based virtualization technology. Hyper-V is a role-based feature that allows an organization to have multiple virtual machines on a Windows Server 2008 machine.

HyperCall adapter   This thin software layer allows Microsoft's Hyper-V to work with the Xen. Created as a collaboration of engineers from Microsoft and Novell.

I

image libraries   A secure, centrally located location where all of your virtual machines can reside.

incremental backups   Backs up data since the last full or incremental backup. Incremental backups reset the archive bit and are supported in Windows Server 2008.

Integration Services   Services that you want to offer to the Hyper-V virtual machine.

L

logical unit number (LUN)   A unique identifier used on a Small System Computer Interface (SCSI) bus to differentiate up to eight separate devices.

N

nodes   Machines that are part of a cluster.

P

performance object   Represents data on specific component of the system that you can monitor in the Reliability and Performance Monitor.

physical-to-virtual (P2V)   A utility that converts physical machines to virtual machines.

Pre-Boot Execution (PXE)   PXE devices are network interface cards (NICs) that can talk to a network without the need for an operating system. PXE NIC adapters are network adapters that have a set of pre-boot commands within the boot firmware.

Q

quick migration   Allows a virtual machine to easily migrate from one host server to another to help prevent downtime.

quorum   The number of votes that must remain online for the cluster to continue to operate properly.

R

read-only domain controller (RODC)   A domain controller that has a noneditable copy of Active Directory.

Redundant Array of Inexpensive (Independent) Disks (RAID)   Allows you to have redundancy through the use of multiple disks. Redundancy is the ability to recover data from a single failed disk.

Reliability and Performance Monitor   Microsoft monitoring utility that is included in Windows Server 2008.

S

security identifier (SID)   A unique number issued to an Active Directory security principle. The primary security principals are Users, Groups, and Computers.

Server Core   The Server Core installation is a minimal Windows Server 2008 environment for running specific server roles.

Server Manager   A Microsoft Management Console (MMC) snap-in, included with Windows Server 2008, that allows an administrator to view information about server configuration, status of roles that are installed, and links for adding and removing features and roles.

System Center Virtual Machine Manager   Application for administrators who are responsible for managing virtual networks.

System Preparation (Sysprep)   A Microsoft utility that allows you to get an image ready for transfer by third-party software.

T

template   Preconfigured virtual machine that allows you to mass-produce virtual machines with the same hardware and software settings.

trust   A relationship between domains that allows for the sharing of resources.

V

virtual hard disk (VHD)   The hard disk that Hyper-V uses to install the operating system on.

virtual machine (VM)   Implementation of an operating system that runs in its own virtualization window.

Virtual Machine Additions   Enhancements to a virtual environment to allow operations within that virtualization environment to function properly.

virtual machine snapshots   Copies of your virtual machine; these copies are placed in a specified location for restores and recoverability.

Virtual Network Manager   Application that allows you to add, remove, modify, and manage virtual networks from one location.

virtual PC   A client-based virtualization system.

Virtual Server   Microsoft's first server-based virtualization server environment.

virtual-to-virtual machine conversion (V2V)　A utility that converts third-party virtual machines to a Hyper-V virtual machine.

VMM Self-Service Portal　A web-based utility that gives you the ability to allow a select set of users the right to create, manage, and operate virtual machines.

VMware　A virtualization company that produces products similar to Microsoft Hyper-V.

W

Windows Deployment Services (WDS)　A new version of RIS that allows you to deploy the operating system through a network installation.

Windows hypervisor　A thin layer of software that sits between the hardware and the Windows Server 2008 operating system. This thin layer allows one physical machine to run multiple operating systems in different Hyper-V virtual machines at the same time.

Windows PowerShell　A command-line shell and scripting language utility.

Windows Server 2008 Backup utility　A Microsoft utility that is included in Windows Server 2008 and is used for backup and recovery of the server operating system.

Index

Note to the Reader: Throughout this index **boldfaced** page numbers indicate primary discussions of a topic. *Italicized* page numbers indicate illustrations.

A

Accept License Agreement screen, 52
Access Point for Administering the Cluster screen, 268, *268*
accounts
    Active Directory, 7
    for failover clusters, 262
    MAP, 39–40
    peer-to-peer networks, 6
    SCVMM hosts, 143
Action When Physical Server Starts setting, 220
    P2V conversion, 169
    SCVMM, 147
Action When Physical Server Stops setting, 217, 220
    P2V conversion, 169
    SCVMM, 147
Actions window
    SCVMM, 146
    virtual machines, **216–218**, *217*, 220
Activate This Scope field, 340
activating Windows Server 2008, **16–20**, *17–20*
Active Directory
    AD RMS, 11
    DNS requirements, 10
    Global Catalog, 10
    installing, **336–339**, *336–339*
    MAP options, 32
    overview, **7–9**, *8*
    RODC, 12
Active Directory Installation Wizard, 336–337, *336–337*
Active Directory Users and Computers, 353
    editing users, 13
    new users, 8, 338–339, *338*
AD Rights Management Services (AD RMS), **11**
adapters
    HyperCall, **227**
    network, 99, 212, *212*, 236
    NIC, 43
    SCSI, 211
Add Features Required For Web Server (IIS) dialog box, 345
Add Features Wizard
    failover clusters, 264, *264*
    .NET framework, 90–91, *90–91*

Add Host action, 142
Add image to the Windows Deployment Server option, 136
Add Library Server action, 142
Add Library Server dialog box, 232, *232*
Add Library Share window, 233, *233*
Add Library Shares option, 172
Add or Edit Scope screen, DHCP, 340
Add Required Features option, 345
Add Role Wizard, 314
Add Roles Wizard
    IIS, 149
    WDS, 133
Add VMware VirtualCenter Server action, 142, *142*, 148
Additional Domain Controller Options screen, 337
Additional Properties screen
    hardware profiles, 237
    master templates, 230
    P2V conversion, 169, *169*
    SCVMM, 147
    VMware machine conversions, 175, *175*
Adjust The RAM option, 189
Admin Password setting, 229
Administrator Console installation, **138–142**, *138–142*
administrator passwords, 20, 353
Agent Version item, 222
Allocation Unit Size field, 259
Alternate DNS Server field
    DNS, 335
    virtual machines, 343
Always Automatically Turn On The Virtual Machine option, 175, 217
Answer File setting, 229
Appearance tab, 294, 296
Application Development option, 149
Application group, 84
Apply Networking Changes dialog box, 331, *331*
Assign Drive Letter or Path screen, 258, *258*
Assign Memory screen
    virtual machines, 123, 125, 331, 341
    Virtual Server migration, 191
/audit switch for Sysprep, 130
authoritative restores, **303**

Authorization Manager, **82**
   configuring, **87–89**, *87–88*
   installing, **84–87**, *85–86*
   setting up, **83–84**
authorization rules, 82
Automatic Start Action screen, 80, *81*
Automatic Stop Action setting, 81
Automatically Check For Device Compatibility
   option, 34
Automatically Turn On the Virtual Machine if
   It Was Running When the Physical Server
   Stopped option, 217
availability. *See* high availability
Availability settings for virtual machines, **213**
Average setting, 294

B

backup domain controllers (BDCs), 9
Backup Once Wizard, **304–308**, *304–308*
Backup Options screen, 304, *304*
Backup Progress screen, 307, *307–308*
Backup (Volume Snapshot) service, 80
backups and recoverability, **286**, **296–297**
   checkpoints for, **214**
   DPM, **312–317**, *315–317*
   exam essentials, **319**
   Hyper-V benefits for, 3
   importance, **296**
   review questions, **320–326**
   software, 302
   summary, 318
   types, **297–299**, *297–298*
   Windows Backup feature
      backups, **301–303**, *301*
      full backups, **303–308**, *304–308*
      installing, **299–301**, *300*
      recovery, **308–312**, *309–311*
baselines in monitoring, 287
Basic Application groups, 84, 88
basic disks, **251–252**
bcdedit command, 54
BDCs (backup domain controllers), 9
Before You Begin screen
   DHCP, 340
   DNS, 335
   DPM, 314
   failover clusters, 265, 267
   high availability, 274
   Hyper-V, 46, 329
   Powershell feature, 345

   quorums, 271
   virtual disks, 118, 120–121
   virtual machines, 123–124, 331, 341
   WDS, 133
BIOS setting and requirements
   hardware profiles, 235
   Hyper-V, 43, 76, *76*
   P2V conversions, 163
   startup order, 209
   virtual machines, 209, 219
   virtualization support, 42
Block All Incoming Connections option, 104
Browse for Shared Folders dialog box, 272, *272*
Bus field for virtual machines, 184
Business Rule Application group, 84

C

centralized management, **83**
Channel field, 167
Check For The Latest Virtual Machine Manager
   Updates option, 97, 140
checkpoints
   for recoverability, **214**
   virtual machines, **213–215**, *214*, 219
Checkpoints tab, **213–215**, *214*, 219
child domains, 7
child partitions, 68–69
Choose a Deployment Configuration screen,
   336, *336*
Choose Action screen, 121, *121*
Choose Computer Discovery Methods screen,
   38, *38*
Choose Directory For Extracted Files dialog box,
   347, *347*
Choose Disk Type screen, 69, *70*, 117, *117*,
   119, 122
Client Access Role option, 348
client machines
   defined, 9
   firewalls, 105
   networks, 98
   WDS, 132
Client Settings screen, 349
cloning virtual machines, 207
Cluster Quorum Wizard, 270, *270*
clusters, 2
   failover. *See* failover clusters and Failover
      Cluster Management
   Hyper-V, 69
   SCVMM support, 89

COM ports settings
  Hyper-V, 78
  virtual machines, 211
Common HTTP Features option, 149
Completing The New Mirrored Volume Wizard
  screen, 259, *259*
Completing the New Virtual Machine
  Wizard screen
  Virtual PC tool, 189, *189*
  Virtual Server migration, 192, *192*
Computer Configuration roles, 83
Computer Management utility, 254–256,
  255–256, 260, *260*
Computer Name/Domain Changes screen,
  344, *344*
Computer Name or IP Address field, 164
Computer Name settings
  SCVMM, 144
  Windows XP machines, 353
Configuration Complete screen, 136
Configuration Components screen, 181–182,
  181–182
Configuration Settings screen, 138, 145
Configure Cluster Quorum Settings option, 271
Configure Cluster Quorum Settings screen, 273
Configure DHCPv6 screen, 340
Configure Disk screen, 70, *70*, 119, *119*, 122
Configure File Share Witness screen, 272, *272*
Configure Hardware screen
  hardware profiles, 236, *236*
  SCVMM, 146, *146*
  templates, 229–231
Configure Networking screen
  virtual machines, 123, 125, 332, 341
  Virtual Server migration, 191
Configure the Administration Website to Always
  Run As The Authenticated User option, 181
Confirm Installation screen
  Hyper-V, 330
  Powershell feature, 345
Confirm Installation Selections screen
  DNS, 335
  DPM, 314
  failover clusters, 264
  Hyper-V, 48, *48*
  Windows backup, 301
Confirmation screen
  backups, 307, *307*
  failover clusters, 268, *268*
  high availability, 275
  IIS, 149
  .NET Framework, 91

  quorums, 273
  restores, 311
  WDS, 134
Connect To Server settings
  SCVMM hosts, 143
  Virtual Server, 183, *183*
Connect To Virtual Machine option
  P2V conversion, 170
  virtual machines, 206
Connect Virtual Hard Disk screen
  virtual machines, 123, 125–126, *125*, 332,
  332, 341
  Virtual Server migration, 192
Connection Requirements section, **212**
Connection Status item, 222
Conversion Information screen, 169
Conversion Options field, 167
conversions
  exam essentials, **194–195**
  fixed disks to dynamic disks, **120–121**, *120–*
  121, 255, *255*
  P2V, 140, **162–171**, *165–170*
  review questions, **196–202**
  summary, **194**
  V2V, **171–177**, *172–177*
  from Virtual Server and Virtual PC, **177–193**,
  179–186, *188–192*
Convert Physical Server action, 140
Convert To Dynamic Disk dialog box, 255, *255*
Convert Virtual Hard Disk screen, 121
Convert Virtual Machine action, 142
copy backups, **298–299**
Cost Center setting, 209, 218
counters in monitoring
  adding, 288, **291–293**, *291–292*
  description, 287
CPU Percentage resource, 224
CPU processor requirements and settings
  DPM, 313
  hardware profiles, 235
  Hyper-V, 43, 77–78, *77*
  MAP, 33
  virtual machines, 209, *210*, 219
  Virtual PC tool, 187
  Windows Server 2008, 15
CPU window in monitoring, 287
Create a new domain in a new forest option, 336
Create A New Library Share option, 96
Create a shortcut to the VMM Administrator
  Console option, 140
Create a virtual hard disk option, 332, 341
Create A Virtual Machine option, 188

Create An Inventory Database screen, 37
Create Cluster wizard, 265, 268–269, *268–269*
Create Or Select A Database screen, 37
Create the new virtual machine with a blank
   virtual hard disk option, 146, 236
Create Virtual Networks screen, 47, *47*,
   329, *329*
credentials
   failover clusters, 262
   SCVMM, 232
Current setting in monitoring, 294
Custom tab for virtual servers, **227**
Custom Properties tab for virtual
   machines, **215**, *215*, 220
Customer Experience Improvement
   Program screen
   DPM, 317
   SCVMM, 93, *93*, 138
Customer Information screen, 180, *180*

D

daily backups, **298–299**
Data Execution Prevention (DEP), 43
Data Protection Manager (DPM), **312**
   feature installation, **314–315**
   installing, **315–317**, *315–317*
   requirements, **312–313**
Data tab in monitoring, 294, *295*
DCPromo command, *54*, 336
Default Gateway field
   DHCP, 340
   DNS, 335
   virtual machines, 343
defaults
   monitoring, 294
   snapshot locations, **75**
   VHD storage locations, 72, *72*
Delay Start (Sec) field
   P2V conversion, 169
   virtual machines, 220
Delete option for virtual machines, 129, 207
Delete Virtual Machine dialog box, 129
DEP (Data Execution Prevention), 43
deployment software, 131
description settings
   P2V conversion, 166
   virtual machines, 209, 218
   virtual servers, 221
development, Hyper-V benefits for, 4

DHCP (Dynamic Host Configuration
   Protocol) servers
   defined, **10**
   installing, **340–341**
   WDS, 135, *135*
DHCP Option 60 screen, 135, *135*
DHCP Server Authorization screen, 341
DHCP Server option, 340
differencing disks
   creating, **121–122**, *122*
   description, 117
   overview, 69–70
Different Options option, 304
differential backups, **298–299**, *298*
Directory Services Restore Mode Administrator
   Password screen, 338
Disable DHCPv6 option, 340
Disable Undo Disks option, 206–207
Discard Saved State option, 206
Disk/LUN, 42
Disk Management utility, **253–260**, *254–260*
Disk Space (in MB) resource, 224
disk striping, **250**
Disk windows in monitoring, 288
Diskette Drive setting, 79
disks and disk settings
   DPM, 313
   Hyper-V, 78
   pass-through, **72–73**, *73*, 117
   RAID, **250–251**
      Disk Management utility, **253–260**,
         254–260
      disk storage types, **251–253**
      mirroring configuration, **256–260**,
         257–260
   storage types, **251–253**
   virtual. *See* virtual hard disks (VHDs)
   virtual machines, 184
   Virtual PC tool, 187
   Windows Server 2008, 16
domain controllers, 9, **12–13**, 41
Domain Name System (DNS)
   failover clusters, 262
   installing, **334–335**, *334*
Domain Name System (DNS) servers, **9–10**
Domain or Computer Name field, 165
Domain/Workgroup setting, 229
domains
   Active Directory, 7
   failover cluster roles, 262
   guest systems, 229
   joining virtual machines to, **342–345**, *343–344*
   joining Windows XP machines to, **353**

security, 7
virtual machines, 165
downloading
    MAP, **33–36**, *34–36*
    SCVMM, **92**, *92*
    Virtual PC tool, **188**, *188*
    Virtual Server, **179**
downtime, Hyper-V benefits for, 3
DPM (Data Protection Manager), 312
    feature installation, **314–315**
    installing, **315–317**, *315–317*
    requirements, **312–313**
drives. *See* disks and disk settings
dual-booting, 252
Dynamic Datacenter, 4
dynamic disks, **252**
    benefits, **253**
    configuring, **254–256**, *255–256*
    converting fixed disks to, **120–121**, *120–121*
Dynamic Host Configuration Protocol (DHCP)
    servers
    defined, **10**
    installing, **340–341**
    WDS, 135, *135*
dynamic virtual disks, 69, 116

E

EIDE disks, 118
Enable File And Folder Compression field, 259
Enable System Recovery option, 305
Enable Virtual LAN Identification field, 212
Enable Virtual Server Exceptions in Windows
    Firewall option, 182
Ending IP Address field, 340
Enter Credentials screen, 232, *232*
Enter The Object Names To Select option, 88
Enter WMI Credentials screen, **39–40**, *39*
Entering Computer Names And Credentials
    Manually option, 32
Error Reporting screen, 348
Ethernet (MAC) Address section, **213**
Exchange Introduction screen, 348
Exchange Organization screen, 349
Exchange server
    and domain controllers, 124
    installation, **347–353**, *347–352*
Exchange Server 2007 installation screen, 347, *347*
Export Virtual Machine dialog box, **128**, *128*
exporting virtual machines, **128**, *128*
External settings for network adapters, 99

F

failover clusters and Failover Cluster
    Management
    configuring, **260–261**
    creating, **265–269**, *265–269*
    high availability, 274–275
    installing, **263–264**, *264*
    managing, **261–263**, *261*
    quorums, **269–273**, *270–273*
Failover Share folder, 272
fault tolerance, **250–251**
File System field, 259
firewalls
    configuring, **103–105**, *103–104*
    Virtual Server, 182
First Name field
    Active Directory, 338
    Microsoft Exchange Server 2007, 352
fixed disks, 116
    converting to dynamic disks, **120–121**, *120–121*
    description, 69
Floppy Disk settings, 211
Format This Volume With The Following Settings
    field, 259
Format Volume screen, **258–259**, *259*
forward lookups, 10
full backups
    completing, **303–308**, *304–308*
    description, 297, 299
Full Name field for Active Directory, 339

G

General tab
    hardware profiles, 235, *235*
    in monitoring, **293–294**, *293*
    virtual machines, **208–209**, *208*, 218
/generalize switch in Sysprep, 130
geographically dispersed clusters, 263
Getting started screen, 309, *309*
Global Catalogs, **10**
Graph view in monitoring, 289, *289*, 292, *292*, 294, *295*
Guest Operating System screen, **229**, 231
guests in Hyper-V, 68
GUIRunOnce setting, 229

H

Hard Disk Size field, 184
hard disks. *See* disks and disk settings
Hard Drive setting, 78
Hardware Configuration tab, 209–213, *210,
     212,* 219
Hardware Profile Test option, 236
hardware profiles, 234–237, *235–236*
hardware RAID, 250
hardware requirements
     DPM, 312–313
     Hyper-V, 42–43
     MAP, 33
     virtual machines, 184
     Virtual PC tool, 187
Hardware tab, 225, *225*
Hardware Settings tab, 235–236, *235*
Heartbeat service, 80
high availability, 248
     configuring for, 248–250
     exam essentials, 277
     failover clusters. *See* failover clusters and
          Failover Cluster Management
     importance, 249
     quick migration, 273–276, *274*
     RAID, 250–251
          Disk Management utility, 253–260,
               254–260
          disk storage types, 251–253
          mirroring configuration, 256–260, *257–260*
     review questions, 278–284
     summary, 276
     virtual machines, 274–275, *274*
Histogram view in monitoring, 290, *290*
home folders, 253
Host Properties screen, SCVMM, 145
hosts
     Hyper-V, 68, 102
     SCVMM, 143–146, *143–145*
Hub Transport Role option, 348
Hyper-V, 2–3
     Active Directory, 7–9, *8*
     benefits, 3–4
     configuration, 68
          Authorization Manager, 82–89, *85–88*
          exam essentials, 106–107
          pass-through disk access, 72–73, *73*
          remote administration, 102–104, *102–104*
          review questions, 108–114
          SCVMM, 89–98, *90–97*
          settings, 76–82, *76–81*
          summary, 105–106

     tools and techniques, 68–69
     virtual hard disks, 69–72, *70–71*
     virtual machine snapshots, 73–75, *74*
     virtual networking, 98–101, *99–101*
exam essentials, 21–22
features, 4–5
high availability. *See* high availability
installation, 30
     exam essentials, 58
     hardware requirements, 42–43
     MAP tool. *See* Microsoft Assessment and
          Planning (MAP) tool
     network evaluation, 30–31
     overview, 41
     process, 328–330, *329*
     review questions, 59–65
     summary, 57
     with Virtual Machine Manager, 56–57
     on Windows Server 2008 full installation,
          43–49, *45–49*
     on Windows Server 2008 Server Core,
          49–56, *51–52, 55–56*
review questions, 23–28
summary, 21
Windows peer-to-peer networks, 5–6, *6*
Windows Server 2008. *See* Windows
     Server 2008
Hyper-V License Agreement, 48
Hyper-V Manager
     overview, 102, *102*
     virtual disks, 118, 120
     virtual machines, 124
Hyper-V Settings dialog box
     snapshot locations, 75
     VHD storage locations, 71–72, *71*
HyperCall adapters, 227
hypervisors
     architecture, 123, *123*
     counter, 288
     description, 3
     Hyper-V installation, 55
     overview, 41
     VMBus, 69
     Xen, 227

I

IDE Controller setting, 78
IDE devices
     pass-through, 72–73
     virtual machines, 211

IDE Devices - DVD field
   hardware profiles, 235
   virtual machines, 219
IDE Devices - VHD field, 219
Identity Information setting, 229
IIS component installation, **149–150**, 182
image libraries, **231–234**, *232–234*
Import Virtual Machine screen, 129, *129*
importing
   computer names from files, 32
   virtual machines, **129**, *129*
Importing Computer Names From A file option, 32
incremental backups, **297–299**, *297*
Initials field
   Active Directory, 338
   Microsoft Exchange Server 2007, 352
Install From Previous Downloaded Installation
   Files option, 35
Install Microsoft Virtual Server 2005 R2 SP1
   option, 180
Install Now screen, 51
Install Virtual Guest Services option, 207
Install Windows screen, 17–20, *17–20*
Installation Complete screen, 140, *140*
Installation Folder screen, 34
Installation Location screen, 150
Installation Options screen, 124, 333, *333*, 341
Installation Results screen
   DNS, 335
   failover clusters, 264, *264*
   Hyper-V, 330
   IIS, 150
   .NET Framework, 91, *91*
   WDS, 134
   Windows Backup, 301
Installation Settings screen
   DPM, 316, *317*
   SCVMM, 94, 138
Installation Successful screen, 36
Installation Type screen, 348, *348*
installing
   Active Directory, **336–339**, *336–339*
   Authorization Manager, **84–87**, *85–86*
   DHCP, **340–341**
   DNS, **334–335**, *334*
   DPM, **315–317**, *315–317*
   DPM required features, **314–315**
   failover clusters, **263–264**, *264*
   Hyper-V. *See* Hyper-V
   IIS components, **149–150**
   MAP, **33–36**, *34–36*
   Microsoft Exchange Server 2007, **347–353**,
    347–352
   .NET Framework, **90–91**, *90–91*

operating systems into virtual machines,
   185–186, *185–186*
Powershell feature, **345–346**
SCVMM, **92–98**, *92–97*
SCVMM Administrator Console, **138–142**,
   138–142
Server Core, **13**
Virtual Server, **180–183**, *180–183*
WDS, **133–134**
Windows Backup feature, **299–301**, *300*
Windows Server 2008, **16–20**, *17–20*
Installing The Microsoft Assessment And
   Planning Solution Accelerator screen, 36, *36*
Installing Windows screen, 20, *20*
instances in monitoring, 288
Integrated Services settings for virtual machines,
   213, 219
Integration Services
   options, 79–80, *80*
   overview, **178–186**, *179–186*
Integration Services screen, 79–80, *80*
Internal settings for network adapters, 99
Introduction To DHCP screen, 340
Introduction To DNS Server screen, 335
Introduction to Hyper-V screen, 47, 329
Introduction To Web Server screen, 345
Introduction to Web Server (IIS) screen, 90
Inventory Account screen, 40
IP Address field
   DNS, 335
   virtual machines, **342–345**, *343–344*
IPv4 DNS Server Settings screen, 340
Issues Reported By The Wizard message, 169

J

Jobs dialog box
   hardware profiles, 237
   master templates, 230–231
   P2V conversion, 170, *170*
   SCVMM, 145, *145*, 148
   V2V conversion, 172
   VMware machine conversions, 176–177, *176*

L

Last Name field
   Active Directory, 339
   Microsoft Exchange Server 2007, 352
LDAP (Lightweight Directory Access Protocol)
   queries, 84

LDAP Query group, 84
libraries
    image, **231–234**, *232–234*
    SCVMM, 96
library servers, **232**, *232*
Library Share Settings screen, 96, *96*
License Agreement screen
    MAP, 34
    Microsoft Exchange Server 2007, 348
    Virtual Server, 180, *180*
License Terms screen
    SCVMM, 138
    VMM Self-Service Portal, 150
licenses
    DPM, 316
    Hyper-V, 48, 52
    image libraries, 231
    MAP, 34
    Microsoft Exchange Server 2007, 348
    SCVMM, 93, 138
    Virtual Server, 180, *180*
    VMM Self-Service Portal, 150
    Windows Server 2008, 16, 19, *19*
Lightweight Directory Access Protocol (LDAP)
    queries, 84
live migration, 275
Local Area Connection option, 329
Local Area Connection Status dialog box
    DNS, 334–335, *334*
    virtual machines, 342
local two-node clusters, 263
Locate Virtual Hard Disk screen, 120
Location For Database, Log Files, And SYSVOL
    screen, 337, *337*
logical unit numbers (LUNs)
    DPM, 313
    Hyper-V, 42–43

M

MAC addresses, **213**
Mailbox Role option, 348
Mailbox settings screen, 352
Mailserver virtual machines, 342
Make this server my default option, 143
Manage Checkpoints option, 206
Management Tool option, 149
MAP. *See* Microsoft Assessment and Planning
    (MAP) tool
master templates, **230–231**, *230*
Maximum Disk I/O per Second (IOPS)
    resource, 224

Maximum setting in monitoring, 294
Member Of tab, 339
member servers, 9
Members tab, 88, *88*
Memory (in MB) resource, 224
Memory (RAM) section, 288
Memory screen, 189, *189*
memory settings and requirements
    DPM, 313
    hardware profiles, 235
    Hyper-V, 43, 76
    in monitoring, 288
    virtual machines, 211, 219
    Virtual PC tool, 187, 189, *189*
    virtual servers, 224
    Windows Server 2008, 15
Microsoft Assessment and Planning (MAP) tool,
    31–32
    configuring, **36–37**, *36–37*
    downloading and installing, **33–36**, *34–36*
    inventory reports, **193–194**
    requirements, **33**
    roles and services migration, **37–40**, *37–40*
Microsoft Assessment and Planning Solution
    Accelerator Setup wizard, 34–35, *34–35*
Microsoft Exchange Server
    and domain controllers, 124
    installation, **347–353**, *347–352*
Microsoft Installer Package (MSI) support, 13
Microsoft License Terms screen, 93
Microsoft Software License Terms screen, 316
Microsoft Virtual Server 2005 R2 SP1 Setup
    dialog box, 180, *180*
Migrate option, 206
Migrate Specific Roles And Services To Windows
    Server 2008 option, 37
migration
    quick, **273–276**, *274*
    roles and services to Windows Server 2008,
        37–40, *37–40*
    virtual machines, 206
    Virtual Server, **190–193**, *191–192*
/mini switch in Sysprep, 130
Minimum setting in monitoring, 294
mirroring
    configuring, **256–260**, *257–260*
    description, **250**
monitoring and optimizing virtual machines,
    286–290, *287, 289–290*
    counters, **291–293**, *291–292*
    properties, **293–295**, *293–296*
Move This Service or Application to Another
    Node option, 275

MSI (Microsoft Installer Package) support, 13
multisite clusters, 263
multivendor virtualization support, 89

N

Name screen, 79
Name the Forest Root Domain screen, 336, *336*
names
    importing from files, 32
    Microsoft Exchange Server 2007, 352
    servers, 79, *79*
    virtual machines, 208–209
NAP (Network Access Protection), **11–12**
.NET Framework installation, **90–91**, *90–91*
net localgroup command, 54
net start command, 54
net user command, 54
netdom join command, 53
netdom remove command, 53
NetSh command, 54
Network Access Protection (NAP), **11–12**
Network Adapter screen, 236
network adapters
    hardware profiles, 236
    requirements, 43
    setting up, 225, *226*
    virtual machines, 212, *212*
Network Capacity Percentage resource, 224
network load balancing (NLB), 4
Network Location field, 212
Network Tag field, 212
Network window in monitoring, 288
Networking tab, **225**, *226*
networks
    Active Directory, 7–9, *8*
    evaluating, **30–31**
    failover cluster settings, 262
    monitoring, 288
    peer-to-peer networks, **5–6**, *6*
    planning, **31**
    terms and roles, **9–10**
    virtual, **98–101**, *99–101*
    virtual machines, 212
Never Automatically Turn On the Virtual
    Machine option, 217
New Application Group dialog box, 88, *88*
New Authorization Store dialog box, 87, *87*
New Checkpoint dialog box, 219, *219*
New Checkpoint option, 206
New Hardware Profile dialog box, 234–235, *235*
New Mailbox wizard, 351, *351*

New Mirrored Volume option, 257
New Mirrored Volume wizard, 258–259, *258–259*
New Object - User screen, 338
New Template option, 207
New Virtual Hard Disk wizard
    disk configuration, 70, *70*
    disk types, 69, *70*
    storage locations, 71, *71*
    working with, 117–120, *117*, *119*
New Virtual Machine dialog box, 236, *236*
New Virtual Machine Wizard
    master templates, 230
    SCVMM, 140, *141*
    virtual machines, 124
    virtual networks, 331–333, *331–333*
    Virtual PC, 188–189, *188–189*
    Virtual Server migration, 191–192, *191–192*
New Virtual Manager Wizard, 341
New Virtual Network option, 168
New Virtual Network screen, 101, *101*
New Windows From Here option, 86
NIC (Network Interface Card) adapter
    requirements, 43
NLB (network load balancing), 4
No Issues Detected message, 169
No Majority: Disk Only Quorum mode, 270
Node and Disk Majority Quorum mode, 270
Node and File Share Majority Quorum mode,
    270–271
Node Majority Quorum mode, 270
nodes, cluster, 260
nonauthoritative restores, **303**
normal backups, 297
/nosidgen switch in Sysprep, 130
NTDSUTIL.exe utility, 303
NTLM Authentication, 186

O

oclist command, 54–56
offline P2V conversions, 163
/oobe switch in Sysprep, 130
Open File dialog box, 179
Operating System Compatibility screen, 336
Operating System settings
    guest system, 229
    virtual machines, 219
    Virtual PC tool, 189
Operating System Shutdown service, 79
operating systems
    Hyper-V support, 4
    MAP, 33

partitioning, 69
virtual machines, **185–186**, *185–186*, 209
Options screen, 188
Overall Status item, 221
Overview screen, 134, *134*
Overwrite existing files with recovered files
option, 311
Owner field
P2V conversion, 166
virtual machines, 209, 218

P

P2V (physical-to-virtual) conversion
overview, **162–163**
SCVMM for, 140, *141*, **163–171**, *165–170*
parent partitions, 68–69
partitions, 251–252
Hyper-V, 68–69
vs. volume, 252
pass-through disks, **72–73**, *73*, 117
Password Has Been Changed screen, 20
Password screen field, 339
passwords
Active Directory, 339
library servers, 232
Microsoft Exchange Server 2007, 352
P2V conversion, 165
peer-to-peer networks, 6
servers, 39–40
virtual machines, 186, 333, 342
Windows Server 2008, 20
Pause option, 205
PDCs (primary domain controller), 9
peer-to-peer networks, **5–6**, *6*
Pending state, 275
Perform A Quick Format field, 259
Performance and Resource Optimization (PRO)
utility, 89
performance monitoring, **286–290**, *287*, *289–290*
counters, **291–293**, *291–292*
properties, **293–295**, *293–296*
permissions in Authorization Manager, 82
physical security
guidelines, **44**
Server Core for, 51
physical-to-virtual (P2V) conversion
overview, **162–163**
SCVMM for, 140, *141*, **163–171**, *165–170*
Placement tab, **225**

planning networks, **31**
/pnp switch in Sysprep, 130
Port Assignment screen, 96
ports
firewalls, 104
SCVMM, 96, 138, *139*
virtual machines, 211
Powershell utility
conversion scripts, 163
installing, **345–346**
P2V conversion, 170
Pre-Boot Execution (PXE) environment
network devices, 136
support, 99–100
Preferred DNS Server settings
DHCP, 340
DNS, 335
virtual machines, 343
Prerequisites Check screen, 94, *94*
DPM, 316
SCVMM, 138, *138*
VMM Self-Service Portal, 150
primary domain controller (PDCs), 9
primary partitions, 251
Priority settings
hardware profiles, 235
virtual machines, **213**
Private settings for network adapters, 99
PRO (Performance and Resource Optimization)
utility, 89
Processor Functionality option, 78
processor requirements and settings
DPM, 313
hardware profiles, 235
Hyper-V, 43, 77–78, *77*
MAP, 33
virtual machines, 209, *210*, 219
Virtual PC tool, 187
Windows Server 2008, 15
product keys
guest system, 229
Windows Server 2008, 16
product registration screen, 93
profiles, hardware, **234–237**, *235–236*
Progress screen for Hyper-V
installation, 48
Properties option for virtual machines, 207
PXE (Pre-Boot Execution) environment
network devices, 136
support, 99–100
PXE Server Initial Settings screen, 136, *136*

Q

quarantines, 100
quick migration, **273–276**, *274*
/quiet switch in Sysprep, 130
quorums for clusters, **269–273**, *270–273*
Quota Point field, 216

R

RAID (Redundant Array of Inexpensive Disks),
    250–251
    Disk Management utility, **253–260**, *254–260*
    disk storage types, **251–253**
    mirroring configuration, **256–260**, *257–260*
RDP (Remote Desktop Protocol), 102–103
read-only domain controllers (RODCs), **12–13**
Readiness Checks screen, 349, *349*
Ready To Install screen
    Hyper-V, 35, *35*
    Virtual Server, 182, *182*
/reboot switch in Sysprep, 130
Recover Data option, 308
recoverability. *See* backups and recoverability
Recovery Progress screen, 311, *311*
Recovery Wizard, **308–312**, *309–311*
Redundant Array of Inexpensive Disks (RAID),
    250–251
    Disk Management utility, **253–260**, *254–260*
    disk storage types, **251–253**
    mirroring configuration, **256–260**, *257–260*
Registration screen, 316
Relative Weight setting, 77
Release keys setting, 81–82
Reliability and Performance Monitor, **286–290**,
    287, 289–290
    counters, **291–293**, *291–292*
    properties, **293–295**, *293–296*
remote administration configuration, **102–104**,
    102–104
Remote Desktop option, 104
Remote Desktop Protocol (RDP), 102–103
Remote Installation Folder Location
    screen, 135
Remote Installation Services (RIS) utility, 132
Remote Shared Folder option, 305
Remote tab for virtual servers, 226, *226*
Rename this computer or join a domain
    option, 353
Repair option, 207
Report view in monitoring, 290, *290*

requirements
    DPM, **312–313**
    failover clustering, 262
    Hyper-V, **42–43**
    MAP, **33**
    virtual machines, 184
    Virtual PC tool, 187
    Windows Server 2008, **15–16**
Reserves tab, **223–224**, *224*
Restore Security Settings option, 311
restores, **286**, **303**. *See also* backups and
    recoverability
Results screen, 48
reverse lookup, 10
Review Settings screen, 40, *40*
RIS (Remote Installation Services) utility, 132
RODCs (read-only domain controllers), **12–13**
roles
    migrating to Windows Server 2008, **37–40**,
        37–40
    servers, **42**
Run All Tests option, 267

S

Save State option
    V2V conversion, 175
    virtual machines, 205, 217
Save The Virtual Machine State option, 81
sc config command, 54
sc query command, 54
sc start command, 54
scalability
    Active Directory, 7
    Hyper-V for, 4
Scan An IP Address Range screen, 32, **38–39**, *39*
schemas, changing, 8
Scope Name field, 340
SCSI disks
    adapters, 211
    pass-through, 72–73
    virtual, 118
SCVMM. *See* System Center Virtual Machine
    Manager (SCVMM)
Search Results window, 144, *144*
security
    DPM, 317
    guidelines, **44**
    HyperCall adapters, 227
    IIS, 149
    Server Core for, 51
    Virtual Server, 186

Security Identification (SID) numbers, 131

Security Settings screen, 317

Security Warning dialog box, 186

Select A Database option, 36

Select Additional Members From setting, 88

Select backup configuration screen, 304, *304*

Select Backup Date screen, 309, *309*

Select Backup Items screen, 305, *305*

Select Destination screen
    hardware profiles, 236
    master templates, 230
    SCVMM, 147

Select Disks screen, 258, *258*

Select Features screen
    .NET framework, 90, *90*
    Windows Backup, 300, *300*

Select Folder screen, 128

Select Groups screen, 339, *339*

Select Host screen
    hardware profiles, 236
    master templates, 230
    P2V conversion, 168, *168*
    SCVMM, 147, *147*
    VMware machine conversions, 174, *174*

Select Host Location screen, 143, *143*

Select Host Servers screen, 144–145, *144*

Select Items to Recover screen, 310, *310*

Select Library Server screen, 229, 231–232

Select Network Connection Bindings screen, 340

Select Networks screen
    master templates, 230
    P2V conversion, 168
    SCVMM, 147
    VMware machine conversions, 174, *175*

Select Path screen
    hardware profiles, 236
    P2V conversion, 168
    SCVMM, 147
    templates, 229–231
    VMware machine conversions, 174

Select Quorum Configuration screen, 271

Select Recovery Type screen, 310, *310*

Select Reports And Proposals screen, 38, *38*

Select Role Services screen
    .NET framework, 90
    WDS, 134

Select Server Roles screen
    DPM, 314
    Hyper-V, 47, *47*

Select Servers screen, 266, *266*

Select Source screen
    master templates, 230
    P2V conversion, 164, *165*
    VMware machine conversions, 173

Select The Operating System You Want To Install screen, 52, *52*

Select Virtual Machine screen, 274, *274*

Select Virtual Machine Source screen, 173, *173*

Select Volume option, 167

Selected Snap-ins window, 85, *85*

Self-Service Portal setting, 149, *149*

Server Core
    commands, **53–54**
    Hyper-V installation on, **49–56**, *51–52, 55–56*
    installation, **13**

Server Manager
    description, **11**, *12*
    failover clusters, 263
    Hyper-V installation, 46, *46*
    roles managed by, **44–46**, *45*
    Windows Backup features, 300–301, *300*

Server Role Selection screen, 348, *349*

servers
    configuration changes, **75**
    consolidation benefits, 3
    converting, **164**
    defined, 9
    roles, **42**
    virtual. *See* virtual servers

service migration, **37–40**, *37–40*

Set Forest Functional Level screen, 337, *337*

Settings tab for virtual machines, **215–216**, *216*, 220

Setup Complete screen, 183, *183*

Setup Type screen, 181, *181*

Shadow Copy feature, 74

shared storage for failover clusters, 262–263

shares for libraries, **233–234**, *233–234*

sharing VMware files, **172**, *172*

Show Shared Folders option, 272

Shut Down option, 206

Shut Down Guest OS option, 217

Shut Down The Guest Operating System option, 81

shutdown command, 53

SID (Security Identification) numbers, 131

Single Instance Storage (SIS), 315

single-node clusters, 263

SMP (Symmetric Multiprocessor) support, 4

snapshots with virtual machine, **73–75**, *74*

SoftGrid client, 32

software RAID, 250

software requirements for failover clustering, 262
Source tab in monitoring, 294, *294*
Specify Advanced Options screen, 306, *306*
Specify Backup Time dialog box, 303
Specify Destination Type screen, 305, *305*
Specify Name And Location screen
    virtual disks, 119, *119*
    virtual machines, 123–124, *125*, 331, *331*, 341
    Virtual Server migration, 191, *191*
Specify Recovery Options screen, 311, *311*
Specify Remote Folder screen, 306, *306*
Specify The Operating System You Will Install In
    The Virtual Machine setting, 147
SQL Server 2005 Express screen, 35, *35*
SQL Server 2005 Express License Agreement
    screen, 35
SQL Server Settings screen, 95, *95*
stager clusters, 263
stand-alone servers, 9
start ocsetup command, 53
Start option, 205
Start the virtual machine after it is created option,
    126, 192, 333
Starting IP Address field, 340
Startup Order setting, 76
status
    hard disks, 254
    role and service migration, 40
    virtual servers, **221–223**, *222*
Status tab, **221–223**, *222*
Status window, 40
storage locations for VHDs, 72, *72*
Store In Library option, 207
Subnet Mask field
    DHCP, 340
    DNS, 335
    virtual machines, 342
Subnet Type field, 340
Summary screen
    Active Directory, 338–339
    DHCP, 341
    DPM, 317
    failover clusters, 269, *269*
    hardware profiles, 237
    library servers, 232
    library shares, 234, *234*
    Microsoft Exchange Server 2007, 353
    P2V conversion, 170
    quorums, 273
    SCVMM, 145, *145*, 148
    templates, 229–231
    virtual disks, 120–121

virtual machines, 124, 126, 333
virtual servers, **221**, *221*
VMM Self-Service Portal, 151
VMware machine conversions, 176, *176*
Summary Of Settings screen, 97, 139, *139*
Symmetric Multiprocessor (SMP) support, 4
synthetic devices, 118
Sysprep (System Preparation) tool, **129–132**, *131*
System Center Data Protection screen, 315, *315*
System Center Virtual Machine Manager
    (SCVMM), **89**, *137*, 138
    downloading and installing, **92–98**, *92–97*
    hardware profiles, 234
    Hyper-V installation with, **56–57**
    master templates, 230, *230*
    .NET Framework, **90–91**, *90–91*
    for P2V conversion, **163–171**, *165–170*
    virtual machines
        adding, **146–148**, *146–148*
        Administrator Console, **138–142**, *138–142*
        configuring, **136–137**, *137*, **205–207**,
            205–207
        hosts, **143–146**, *143–145*
        IIS components, **149–150**
        VMM Self-Service Portal, **150–151**, *150*
        VMware VirtualCenter server,
            148–149, *149*
    virtual servers, **220–221**
System Center Virtual Machine Manager 2008
    Setup screen, 92, *92*
System Information screen, 166
System Preparation (Sysprep) tool, **129–132**, *131*
System Properties dialog box, 344–345, *344*
System Volume Warning dialog box, 135

T

tags
    virtual machines, 209, 212, 219
    VLAN, 99
TCP/IP addresses for failover clusters, 262
Template Identity screen, 228, 230
templates, **228–231**, *230*
TestGroup Properties screen, 88, *88*
testing
    failover clusters, 267, *267*
    Hyper-V benefits for, 4
Testing Options screen, 267, *267*
This Host Is Available For Placement option, 223
Time Synchronization service, 79
Time Zone setting, 229

trust relationships, 7
Turn Off Source Computer After Conversion
    field, 167
Turn Off Virtual Machine option, 81, 217
two-node clusters, 263

U

/uninstall command, 54
Use an existing virtual hard disk option,
    125, 192
Use the dedicated instance of SQL Server
    option, 316
Use the following IP address setting, 335, 342
User Authorization roles, 83
User Logon Name field
    Active Directory, 339
    Microsoft Exchange Server 2007, 352
User Logon Name (pre-Windows 2000) field
    Active Directory, 339
    Microsoft Exchange Server 2007, 352
User Mailbox option, 351
User Must Change Password At Next Logon
    option, 352
User Name field, 165
User Type screen, 352
usernames
    library servers, 232
    P2V conversion, 165
    peer-to-peer networks, 6
    servers, 39–40
    virtual machines, 186
Using Active Directory Domain Services
    option, 32
Using The Windows Networking Protocols
    option, 32

V

V2V (virtual-to-virtual) conversion, 171–177,
    172–177
Validate a Configuration Wizard, 267, 267
Validating screen, 267, 267
Validation Summary screen, 268
Validation Warning screen, 266, 266, 268
verifying Hyper-V installation, 48–49, 49
.vhd files, 178
VHD Size field, 167
VHD Type field, 167
VHDMount utility, 75

VHDs (virtual hard disks)
    converting fixed to dynamic, **120–121**, *120–121*
    creating, **116–120**, *119*
    differencing disks, **121–122**, *122*
    Hyper-V, **69–72**, *70–71*
View Networking option, 207, *207*
View Saved Reports And Proposals option, 40
Viridian, 3
Virtual CD/DVD Drive settings, 211
Virtual Hard Disk screen, 189
Virtual Hard Disk Name and Location screen, 189
Virtual Hard Disk settings for virtual machines,
    184, 211
virtual hard disks (VHDs)
    converting fixed to dynamic, **120–121**,
        120–121
    creating, **116–120**, *119*
    differencing disks, **121–122**, *122*
    Hyper-V, **69–72**, *70–71*
virtual local area networks (VLANs), 98–99
Virtual Machine Additions enhancements, 178
Virtual Machine Configuration screen
    P2V conversion, 168
    VMware machine conversions, 174
Virtual Machine Connection utility, 102
Virtual Machine Identity screen
    hardware profiles, 236
    master templates, 230
    P2V conversion, 165, *166*
    SCVMM, 146
    VMware machine conversions, 173, *173*
Virtual Machine Limit (Percentage) setting, 77
Virtual Machine Manager. *See* System Center
    Virtual Machine Manager (SCVMM)
Virtual Machine Manager (VMM)
    Self-Service Portal
    installing, 150–151, *150*
    for policies, 149, *149*
Virtual Machine Memory field, 184
Virtual Machine Name And Location screen, 189
Virtual Machine Name field
    P2V conversion, 166
    virtual machines, 184
Virtual Machine Remote Control (VMRC) Server
    Properties screen, 186
Virtual Machine Reserve (Percentage) setting, 77
virtual machines (VMs), 2, **116**
    backing up. *See* backups and recoverability
    conversions
        P2V, **162–171**, *165–170*
        V2V, **171–177**, *172–177*
        virtual server and virtual PC, **177–193**,
            179–186, 188–192

creating, **122–128**, *123*, *125–127*, **330–333**, *330–333*, 341
exam essentials, **152, 238**
exporting, **128**, *128*
highly available, **274–275**, *274*
image libraries, **231–234**, *232–234*
importing, **129**, *129*
installing operating systems into, **185–186**, *185–186*
joining to domains, **342–345**, *343–344*
migrating, 4, **275–276**
monitoring and optimizing, **286–290**, *287*, *289–290*
  counters, **291–293**, *291–292*
  properties, **293–295**, *293–296*
properties
  Actions tab, **216–218**, *217*, 220
  Checkpoints tab, **213–215**, *214*, 219
  configuring, **218–220**, *218–219*
  Custom Properties tab, **215**, *215*, 220
  General tab, **208–209**, *208*
  Hardware Configuration tab, **209–213**, *210*, *212*, 219
  Settings tab, **215–216**, *216*
quarantines, 100
review questions, **153–159**, **239–245**
SCVMM for, **136–137**
  adding, **146–148**, *146–148*
  Administrator Console, **138–142**, *138–142*
  configuring, **136–137**, *137*, **205–207**, *205–207*
  hosts, **143–146**, *143–145*
  IIS components, **149–150**
  VMM Self-Service Portal, **150–151**, *150*
  VMware VirtualCenter server, **148–149**, *149*
settings, 204
snapshots, **73–75**, *74*
summary, **151, 237**
System Preparation tool, **129–132**, *131*
templates, **227–231**, *230*
virtual disks, **116–122**, *117*, *119–122*
Virtual Server for, **183–185**, *183–184*
WDS, **132–136**, *133–136*
Virtual Network Adapter field, 184
Virtual Network Manager, **98–100**, *99–100*, 330, *330*
virtual networks
  configuring, **98–101**, *99–101*
  connections, **100–101**, *100–101*
  setting up, **328–330**, *329*
Virtual PC Console screen, 190

Virtual PC tool, **187**
  configuring, **188–190**, *188–190*
  downloading, **188**, *188*
Virtual PCs, converting virtual machines from, **177–193**, *179–186*, *188–192*
Virtual Server
  installing, **180–183**, *180–183*
  migrating, **190–193**, *191–192*
  for virtual machines, **183–185**, *183–184*
Virtual Server 2005 Migration Toolkit (VSMT), 163
Virtual Server 2005 R2 Administrative website, 184, *184*
virtual servers, **220–221**
  converting virtual machines from, **177–193**, *179–186*, *188–192*
  Custom tab, **227**
  Hardware tab, **225**, *225*
  Networking tab, **225**, *226*
  Placement tab, **225**
  Remote tab, 226, *226*
  Reserves tab, **223–224**, *224*
  Status tab, **221–223**, *222*
  Summary tab, **221**, *221*
  VMs tab, **223**, *223*
virtual switches, 98
virtual-to-virtual (V2V) conversion, **171–177**, *172–177*
virtualization
  overview, **2–3**
  SCVMM support, 89
Virtualization Service Status item, 222
Virtualization Service Version item, 222
Virtualization WMI tool, 103
VLANs (virtual local area networks), **98–99**
VMBus, 69
VMM Self-Service Portal Setup screen, 151
VMM (Virtual Machine Manager) Self-Service Portal
  installing, **150–151**, *150*
  for policies, 149, *149*
VMs tab, **223**, *223*
VMware
  file sharing, **172**, *172*
  Hyper-V conversions, **173–177**, *173–177*
  PRO with, 89
  SCVMM for, **142**, *142*
VMware VirtualCenters, 142, *142*, **148–149**, *149*
Volume Configuration screen, 166, *167*
Volume Label field, 259
Volume Shadow Copy Service, 306

volumes vs. partitions, 252
VSMT (Virtual Server 2005 Migration
    Toolkit), 163
VSS Full Backup option, 306

W

WDS (Windows Deployment Service),
    132–133, *133*
    configuring, **134–136**, *135–136*
    installing, **133–134**
Web Server (IIS) option, 345
Web Server Settings screen, 150, *150*
Welcome screen
    DPM, 316, *316*
    mirroring, 258
    WDS, 135, *135*
Welcome to Active Directory screen, 336
Welcome To The Domain dialog box, 353
What Type Of Virtual Network Do You Want To
    Create? option, 100
Where Do You Want To Install Windows? screen
    Hyper-V installation, 53
    Windows Server 2008, 19, *19*
Which Type Of Installation Do You Want?
    screen, 19
.wim (Windows image) files, 136
Windows And Active Directory option, 88
Windows Backup feature
    backups, **301–303**, *301*
    full backups, **303–308**, *304–308*
    installing, **299–301**, *300*
    recovery, **308–312**, *309–311*
Windows Deployment Service (WDS),
    132–133, *133*
    configuring, **134–136**, *135–136*
    installing, **133–134**
Windows Firewall
    configuring, **103–105**, *103–104*
    Virtual Server, 182

Windows hypervisor. *See* hypervisors
Windows image (.wim) files, 136
Windows Management Instrumentation (WMI)
    tool, 103
Windows peer-to-peer networks, **5–6**, *6*
Windows PowerShell utility
    conversion scripts, 163
    installing, **345–346**
    P2V conversion, 170
Windows Remote Management (WinRM)
    utility, 103
Windows Remote Shell (WinRS) utility, 103
Windows Security dialog box, 344
Windows Server 2008, **11**
    activating and installing, **16–20**, *17–20*
    migrating roles and services to, **37–40**, *37–40*
    new features, **11–15**, *12*
    requirements, **15–16**
    SCVMM support, 89
Windows Server 2008 Readiness And Role
    Migration option, 38
Windows Server Virtualization, 3
Windows Users and Groups group, 83
Windows Vista Hardware Assessment Solution
    Accelerator, 31
Windows XP machines, joining to domains, **353**
WinRM command, 54
WinRM (Windows Remote Management)
    utility, 103
WinRS (Windows Remote Shell) utility, 103
WINS is not required option, 340
WINS screen, 340
WMI (Windows Management Instrumentation)
    tool, 103

X

x64 Vista Update tool, 102
x86 Vista Update tool, 102
Xen hypervisor, 227

MCTS: Windows Server Virtualization Configuration Study Guide

Exam 70-652

OBJECTIVE	CHAPTER
INSTALLING HYPER-V	
Select and configure hardware to meet Hyper-V prerequisites. This objective may include but is not limited to: evaluate the existing environment, disk/logical unit number (LUN), memory requirements, correct CPU/BIOS, networking/Network Interface Card (NIC)	2
Configure Windows Server 2008 for Hyper-V. This objective may include but is not limited to: identify requirements, deploy Hyper-V with Virtual Machine Manager (VMM), Microsoft Assessment and Planning tool, install on Full, install on Core	2
Configure Hyper-V to be highly available. This objective may include but is not limited to: failover clustering, disk structure (RAID, quorum, shared storage), network	7
CONFIGURING AND OPTIMIZING HYPER-V	
Manage and optimize the Hyper-V server. This objective may include but is not limited to: VHD (virtual hard disk) location, snapshot location, Systems Center, Virtual Machine Manager (SCVMM), Authorization Manager, release key, performance monitoring of 2k8	3, 8
Configure virtual networking. This objective may include but is not limited to: Virtual Network Manager tool, SCVMM, virtual switches, VLAN tagging, external/private/ internal switches	3
Configure remote administration. This objective may include but is not limited to: install Hyper-V manager on Windows Server 2008 and Windows Vista; WMI, WinRM, firewall settings, RDP	3
DEPLOYING VIRTUAL MACHINES	
Migrate a computer to Hyper-V. This objective may include but is not limited to: from Virtual Server 2005, from third-party (Acronis), from VPC (virtual PC), from Hyper-V (import/export), Intel to AMD virtual machine state, by using SCVMM vNext (P2V and V2V), Integration Services/Virtual Machine additions, Assessment and Planning tool	5
Create or clone a virtual machine. This objective may include but is not limited to: prepare guest operating system for duplication (sysprep), differencing disks, copying Virtual Hard Drive (VHD), SCVMM vNext, PXE Boot (legacy network adapter), manage the Self Service portal, Windows Deployment Services (WDS)	4

Sybex®
An Imprint of
WILEY

OBJECTIVE	CHAPTER
Create a virtual disk. This objective may include but is not limited to: pass-through disks, fixed versus dynamic, differencing disks, IDE versus SCSI, Virtual Hard Disk Wizard	4
Manage templates, profiles, and the image library by using SCVMM vNext. This objective may include but is not limited to: ISOs, VHDs, deployment from library	6

MANAGING AND MONITORING VIRTUAL MACHINES

Monitor and optimize virtual machines. This objective may include but is not limited to: Tool: Reliability and performance monitor, Tool: SCVMM, processor, optimize memory, network, disks	8
Manage virtual machine settings. This objective may include but is not limited to: DVD/ISO, NIC, Integration Services, state of virtual machines, Hypercall adapter availability requirements, reboot/start options, BIOS, memory, Processor (Windows NT 4.0)	6
Manage snapshots and backups. This objective may include but is not limited to: live backups of a VM by using VSS Data Protection Manager (DPM), backup within a virtual machine, snapshots	8
Configure a virtual machine for high availability. This objective may include but is not limited to: quick migration, storage redundancy, perform a manual failover, live migration if available, networking redundancy	7

Exam objectives are subject to change at any time without prior notice and at Microsoft's sole discretion. Please visit Microsoft's website (www.microsoft.com/learning) for the most current listing of exam objectives.

Sybex®
An imprint of
WILEY

Wiley Publishing, Inc.
End-User License Agreement

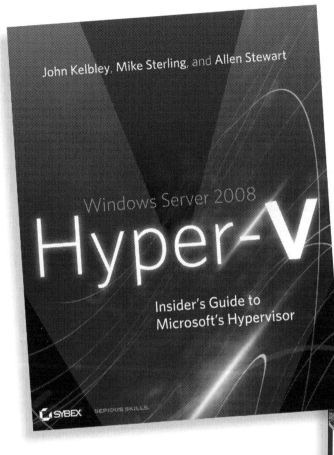

The Best MCTS: Windows Server Virtualization, Configuration Book/CD Package on the Market!

Get ready for your Microsoft Certified Technology Specialist: Windows Server Virtualization, Configuration certification with the most comprehensive and challenging sample tests anywhere!

The Sybex Test Engine features:

- All the review questions, as covered in each chapter of the book

- Challenging questions representative of those you'll find on the real exam

- Two full-length bonus exams available only on the CD

- An Assessment Test to narrow your focus to certain objective groups.

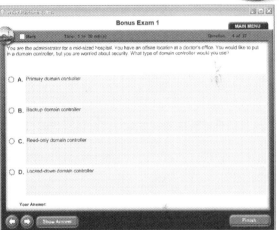

Search through the complete book in PDF!

- Access the entire *MCTS: Windows Server Virtualization Configuration Study Guide* complete with figures and tables, in electronic format.

- Search the *MCTS: Windows Server Virtualization Configuration Study Guide* chapters to find information on any topic in seconds.

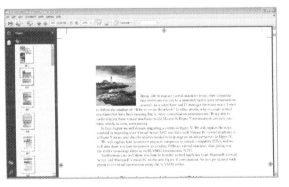

Use the Electronic Flashcards to jog your memory and prep last-minute for the exam!

- Reinforce your understanding of key concepts with these hardcore flashcard-style questions.

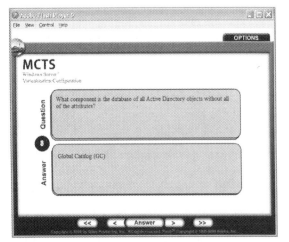